STUDIES IN
JEWISH THEOLOGY

DR. ARTHUR MARMORSTEIN
1882–1946

THE ARTHUR MARMORSTEIN
MEMORIAL VOLUME

STUDIES IN
JEWISH THEOLOGY

BY
ARTHUR MARMORSTEIN

EDITED BY
J. RABBINOWITZ
AND
M. S. LEW

Essay Index Reprint Series

BOOKS FOR LIBRARIES PRESS
FREEPORT, NEW YORK

Library of Congress Cataloging in Publication Data

Marmorstein, Arthur, 1882-1946.
    Studies in Jewish theology.

    (Essay index reprint series)
    English and Hebrew.
    Bibliography: p.
    CONTENTS: The master, an appreciation, by the
editors.--My father, a memoir, by E. Marmorstein.
--Bibliography of the works of Arthur Marmorstein (p.
[   ]-   ). [etc.]
    1. Talmud--Theology. 2. Aggada. I. Title.
[BM177.M37 1972]   296.3   76-39174
ISBN 0-8369-2702-8

PRINTED IN THE UNITED STATES OF AMERICA
BY
NEW WORLD BOOK MANUFACTURING CO., INC.
HALLANDALE, FLORIDA 33009

TABLE OF CONTENTS

PREFACE

THIS volume is published in memory of Dr. Arthur Marmorstein, Professor at Jews' College, London, for over thirty years.

Dr. Marmorstein was a voluminous writer who, in addition to his larger works and monographs, published studies, essays, and reviews in many learned periodicals. Much of his literary work is thus dispersed over a number of journals which are not easily accessible. The essays and studies selected for this book represent but a small part of his original contributions in the fields of Jewish theology and history. While their appeal will be primarily to the student, the general reader, too, will be able to obtain a view of Dr. Marmorstein's wide interests and gain an insight into his illuminating interpretations of the religious beliefs and spiritual ideals of Israel.

Dr. Marmorstein's enthusiasm for the literary revival of Hebrew is illustrated by his many contributions to Hebrew journals and periodicals throughout his career. His output in Hebrew is represented in this volume by three essays which comprise the Hebrew part. Two of the studies in the English section ('The Imitation of God' and 'The Holy Spirit in Rabbinic Legend') have been translated from the German and one ('Participation in Eternal Life in Rabbinic Theology and in Legend') from the French. As the articles contained in this book appeared over a long series of years and in different languages we have endeavoured to introduce a measure of uniformity through some slight changes of phrase and diction, always paying regard to the author's own style.

Our thanks are due to Mr. Maurice Simon, M.A., for his valuable help and advice in the preparation of the volume for publication; and to Mr. C. Moss, B.A., of the Oriental Department, British Museum, for assistance in reading the proofs and for verifying a number of references.

We have also to express our deep appreciation of the financial support we have received which made the production of this volume possible. We are especially grateful to Rabbis H. F. Reinhart and M. Spira and the Revs. A. Barnett, M. Berman, M.B.E., Dr. E. Grunpeter, I. Levy, I. Livingstone, and Dr. A. Tobias for obtaining financial help from friends; and to the Council of Jews' College for voting a grant towards the cost of publication.

Lastly we thank the Readers and Staff of the Oxford University Press for the care with which they have seen the book through the Press.

In undertaking the editorship of this volume we have been prompted by the desire to make our Master's words live again in the minds of a large circle of students and scholars. 'Great men need no monuments, their own words are their best memorial' (J. Sheḳalim, 47a).

J. RABBINOWITZ
M. S. LEW

LONDON
July 1950

ACKNOWLEDGEMENTS

THE articles printed in this volume appeared originally in the following publications.

Hebrew Union College Annual.
The Unity of God in Rabbinic Literature (vol. i, 1924).
The Background of the Haggadah (vol. vi, 1929).
Judaism and Christianity in the Middle of the Third Century (vol. x, 1935).

Jeschurun.
The Imitation of God (*Imitatio Dei*) in the Haggadah (vol. xiv, 1927).

Archiv für Religionswissenschaft.
The Holy Spirit in Rabbinic Legend (vol. xiv, 1930).

The American Journal of Theology (The University of Chicago Press).
The Doctrine of the Resurrection of the Dead in Rabbinic Theology (vol. xix, No. 4, Oct. 1915).

Revue des Études Juives.
Participation in Eternal Life in Rabbinic Theology and Legend (vol. lxxxix, 1930).

Sinai (Jerusalem).
האמונה בנצח ישראל בדרשות התנאים והאמוראים (vol. ix, 1945).
רעיון הגאולה באגדת התנאים והאמוראים (vols. v, vii, viii, 1942–3–4).

Essays in honour of Professor Samuel Krauss (published by Rubin Mass, Jerusalem, 1936) מאמר על ערכה ההיסטורי של האגדה.

To the editors and proprietors who have kindly given permission to reprint articles from their respective publications we tender our warmest thanks. We should like to add that owing to circumstances beyond our control we have not succeeded in all cases in contacting the editors of publications. We have, however, assumed that in those cases, having regard to the personality whose memory the volume is designed to honour, such permission would be forthcoming.

J. R.
M. S. L.

THE MASTER—AN APPRECIATION

By the Editors

TO give a full appreciation of a master at whose feet one has sat and from whose learning and wisdom one has benefited is no easy task. To do justice to him it is not enough to tell of his deep erudition and vast learning, of his work and achievement, but one has also to assess the influence he wielded on his disciples, the vital contribution he made to knowledge, and the path he has trodden out for others to traverse. The true master is not only a great teacher but also a navigator in the uncharted seas of knowledge, guiding his disciples carefully and saving them from foundering on the rocks of error and illusion. He is also the creator of character, a spiritual force, and an intellectual stimulus. It is the combination of these qualities which make him an outstanding figure in his generation.

In attempting a brief appreciation of our beloved and revered master it is not our object to give a full biographical account of him. That has admirably been done by his son in his Memoir appearing in this volume. Our aim is to portray in outline, from our intimate knowledge of him both as friends and disciples, his character as a man, his work as a teacher, and his place as a scholar.

Born and reared in an environment of piety, learning, and culture, Arthur Marmorstein remained loyal throughout his life to his early upbringing. Possessed of a deep faith in God, he communicated this faith to others by his teaching and life. An untiring seeker of truth, he never spared himself in search of it. An ardent lover of culture, he never ceased from pursuing it. With his deep learning he combined a saintliness and a refinement of soul which added elevation and spiritual grace to his character. Though continuously engrossed in his studies and researches he yet was at all times accessible and was ever ready to give a sympathetic hearing to anyone who sought his guidance and help. His was a nature incapable of meanness or malice and no pettiness or egotism marred his innate nobility. He hated all sham and make-belief. Truth alone was to him the one standard by which he measured all things. By nature a lover of freedom and humanism, he was early in life drawn to England, the motherland of liberty, and here he found the fullest scope for the expression of his genius and for his original researches, which yielded so rich a harvest, as is evidenced by the Bibliography published for the first time in this volume.

As a teacher Dr. Marmorstein was gifted with fine powers of exposition and presentation. He never overawed his students by his vast erudition, but used the stores of his knowledge to keep them enthralled by his striking interpretations and by the fresh material which he unearthed for them from ancient manuscripts and old literary documents. He cherished a high sense of duty from which nothing could deflect him. Neither failing health nor impaired eyesight—a legacy from his painstaking study of manuscripts—ever kept him away from the lecture-hall. Even the grief he suffered at the loss of his youngest son, Michael Cecil, killed in action in Italy in 1943 whilst leading his men into battle, did not make him withdraw from the Seminary or desert his study. He was beloved and revered by his students, upon whom he exerted a very deep influence based largely on a genuine personal interest in their welfare and concern for their future. Possessed himself of a passion for research, he succeeded in communicating to his students the spirit of literary adventure. To those who were willing and eager to work he gave freely of his time and of his vast store of learning, guiding them tenderly and lovingly through the thorny paths of research, encouraging them to battle with the initial difficulties, and saving them from the many pitfalls that so often beset the literary beginner. Nothing gave him greater satisfaction than when one of his students produced a creditable doctorate thesis. These theses, whether published or in manuscript, he treasured dearly on the crowded shelves of his study as his own 'literary children'. It was wholly due to his encouragement and help that many of his students were attracted to research and produced works which form a valuable addition to the treasury of Jewish knowledge.

To the world at large he will best remain known as a profound scholar and voluminous author. Commencing literary work at the early age of twenty-two he continued year after year to the very end of his life to produce books, scientific articles, and reviews of learned publications. There was hardly a Jewish scientific journal to which he did not contribute original studies. But whilst he wrote mainly for the student and scholar he also felt impelled on occasion to cater for the general reader. He firmly believed that knowledge was never meant to remain the monopoly of a caste or class but was to be disseminated far and wide amongst the masses and to be made readily accessible to all. Yet these articles also never descended to superficiality but were based on solid scholarship, humanized, and made attractive.

His scholarship was wide in range and uniformly of a high quality. Rabbinics, Jewish history and theology, Jewish folk-lore and Hebrew bibliography, all these came within the purview of his studies and all these subjects he enriched with his researches. But whilst he touched nothing which he did not illumine, it is in the field of Jewish theology in particular that his most valuable and permanent contributions are to be found. A master of Haggadah, he penetrated deeply into the meaning of Midrash and Talmud and revealed to the world the moral and ethical teachings and the religious poetry underlying the utterances of the ancient rabbis. To him these rabbis were not only great teachers of Judaism but also the embodiment of the Jewish spirit through whose teachings and dicta the Jewish genius proclaimed its divine message to humanity. 'If religion has a purpose in life and the world', he writes, 'it must bring God near to man, and man must become like unto God' (*The Old Rabbinic Doctrine of God*, p. 217).

To a prodigious memory he added a fine critical acumen which enabled him to contribute to the elucidation of many problems in the field of Jewish Science. His style was vivid and forceful and was free from the ponderousness which often encumbers the writings of specialists. He felt that he had a message to deliver and preferred to convey that message in language which he who runs may read. In all his works there is ever discernible the man of deep faith in God and the great lover of his fellow men.

In this brief appreciation of our master we have made no attempt at a critical estimation of his works. We have humbly endeavoured to depict his character and to pay homage to the memory of a man endowed with a high aim and clearness of vision. His nobility and sincerity, his quiet enthusiasm and modest righteousness have influenced generations of students who, in proud and grateful recollection of his life, will ever cherish his name and memory.

MY FATHER

A Memoir

by EMILE MARMORSTEIN

I

THIS picture of my father's life, character, and achievements is intended to be rather more than a task dictated by filial piety. I have three main aims. I would like to keep his memory fresh in the minds of those who loved him. I want those of his descendants who did not know him to form an impression of the nature of their ancestor. Finally, in view of the utilitarian attitude to Jewish studies which prevails at the present time, I consider it a duty to draw a moral from the life of one of the last survivors of the tradition of Scientific Jewish Learning, who followed its paths with devotion. It is difficult for a son to write objectively about his father, but I feel that he would like me to make the attempt. He loathed hypocrisy, flattery, and sycophancy. Efforts to whitewash ancestral failings were sure to make him give a contemptuous chuckle. Again, I had the advantage of spending many happy hours with my paternal grandfather in Szenicz and hearing reminiscences of my father's childhood and youth. I have drawn freely upon biographical details contained in my father's writings, but, above all, I must rely upon my own memory of his own words. We were together a great deal and enjoyed each other's company. Summer after summer we travelled together over a large part of Europe, and on our journeys we listened not only to exhaustive accounts of the regions through which we passed but also to entertaining anecdotes about places and people of significance in my father's life.

2

My father, who was always particularly fascinated by genealogical trees and family histories, loved to talk about his ancestors and their times, their polemics, their witticisms, and their writings. Whenever I returned from my travels I was catechized about the most distant of relatives, some of whom he had never met. I often used to read to him the works of his great-uncle, Solomon Hirsch Schück, the Rabbi of Karezag, or the introduction to the *Responsa* of his great-grandfather, Abraham Zwebner, the Rabbi of Kobersdorf, which contained a considerable amount of biographical material. My father was named after Abraham Zwebner, who was generally called Abraham Schag, after the place from which he originated. He was an uncompromising religious leader. At the Congress of Orthodox Rabbis in Budapest in 1866 he opposed the majority decision to form a separate orthodox community. In his view the traditionalists should have fought the reformers with all the means in their power within an undivided community. On his defeat, he set off for the Holy Land, accompanied by two sons, a son-in-law, and a number of pupils and grandchildren. He spent his last years in Jerusalem, urging everyone to conduct himself as if the Messiah were expected at any moment.

My paternal great-grandfathers were two very different kinds of men. Bernat Marmorstein fought in Kossuth's ranks in 1848, was wounded at the battle of Segesvar, wore Hungarian national dress at a time when these clothes were proscribed, and divided his time between chanting psalms and making patriotic speeches. Mayer Rosenfeld, the Rabbi of Miscolcz, was an eloquent preacher, an inspiring leader, a humanist who believed in the appreciation of beautiful things, a scholar well versed in the Hungarian and German classics, and, first and foremost, a confirmed Jew, whose guides throughout life were the Scriptures and their Rabbinic interpreters. His daughter, Regina, who was my grandmother, died a few months after my birth. According to all accounts she was very calm and reserved, spoke very little, and gained the devotion of all who knew her. My grandfather, Leopold Marmorstein, the Rabbi of Szenicz, I knew very well. He was a quiet, scholarly Rabbi, who, like his father-in-law, sometimes allowed Goethe to trespass on the time allotted to Talmudic study. He took an interest in practically every form of human activity and particularly enjoyed social intercourse. He made friends easily and kept them.

3

My father, their first-born, came into the world on 20th September 1882 in Miscolcz, where my grandparents then lived. Hungarian was his mother tongue and throughout life he enjoyed speaking it. Hungarians in London have told me that they found it difficult to believe that he had been away from Hungary for so long. After his early schooling in Szenicz he was sent, at the age of nine, to Tapolcan to study under Rabbi Isaac Schweiger and Rabbi Mandel Deutsch. He quickly gained a reputation as an infant prodigy. Rabbi Schweiger begged my grandfather to promise him that my father should devote himself to the Talmud without the distractions of secular education. My grandfather, who had just heard Rabbi Schweiger boasting of his own son's feat in reading the whole of Graetz in German at an equally tender age, indignantly refused this request. At the age of thirteen my father was sent to the Yeshivah in Pressburg, where most of his companions were much older than he was. During his two years in Pressburg the foundations of his vast Talmudic learning were laid. When he arrived in Miscolcz at his grandfather's house at the age of fifteen, his views were treated with respect in learned Jewish discussions.

The atmosphere of Miscolcz was particularly favourable for the development of my father's personality, tastes, and interests. The Calvinist Gymnasium introduced him to Latin and Greek. His school reports reveal his interest in these subjects. He appears to have excelled in Hungarian

b

and German literature and in History. My uncles and aunts have confessed to me that they used his essays with advantage throughout their own school careers. Grandfather and grandson were inseparable companions throughout this period, and their studies were not entirely confined to Talmud and Codes. They read Deak and Kossuth together in Hungarian. The early hours of the morning before the time of prayer were considered most suitable for Biblical studies and it is to these dawn sessions that my father attributed his knowledge of the Book of Job, which he could recite from memory. He was present on all the numerous occasions when the Rabbi of Miscolcz was called upon to decide questions of ritual law or to adjudicate between the members of his community on their personal or commercial disputes. It was, therefore, with high rabbinical qualifications as well as an immense appetite for knowledge that my father left his grandfather's house for the University of Budapest.

During his academic career at Budapest, Berlin, and Heidelberg, where he graduated, Semitic languages occupied much of my father's time. He specialized in Assyriology and even in later life, in spite of lack of practice, he could read cuneiform texts with apparent ease. Syriac he knew well and the marginal notes in his copy of the Koran, which he presented to me when I began studying Arabic, show that he made his way through the text from cover to cover. One would have thought that this was sufficient for any ordinary man's busy life. Yet my father seems to have found time to lecture, preach, teach, write, attend political meetings, and to listen to the lectures of the foremost intellectual figures of the day. Throughout his life he loved the theatre, read thousands of novels, and kept in touch with contemporary literature. After graduating he received a research-grant from James Simon, the well known patron of learning, and spent a year wandering from library to library in this country, France, and Italy. He returned with notebooks filled with transcriptions of manuscripts and a working knowledge of English, French, and German.

This survey of my father's career as a student is not intended as a biography, but as an indication of the cultural background and equipment with which he took up his first rabbinical post at Jamnitz at the age of twenty-four. The Bibliography contained in this volume shows the use he made of his studies during six years as an officiating Rabbi and especially after his arrival in London in 1912 to take up a position of Lecturer at Jews' College, a post which he held until his passing in October 1946. As a teacher of Ministers and Rabbis he inspired many of his students to pursue research in various fields of Jewish learning. Here, too, he devoted himself to his passion for research, untrammelled by the demands of social functions, which he regarded as an irksome and soul-destroying part of the life of a modern Rabbi.

My father regarded the critical study of the Jewish heritage as the outstanding achievement of the Emancipation. It would seem from a foreword to an article published in a volume of essays in honour of Professor Blau that his passion for this form of research was aroused already in his Yeshivah days.

'His [Blau's] articles in the periodical *Magyar Zsidó Szemle* made a profound impression upon us, the students of the Yeshivot, who had studied nothing beyond Talmud, Commentaries and Codes. These essays brought a new light into the rooms of the *Bahurim* and showed us that there was yet another way of studying Bible and Talmud. He also opened up for us the treasures of the Midrashim, which had been laid aside and used only for sermons . . . and I will always remember the writings of this great scholar on the order and sources of the liturgy, which made an impression on me which will never be wiped out from my mind.'

My father's enthusiasm for research can be attributed largely to his desire that the legacy of Judaism should be revealed in all its glory, to his profound historical sense, to his interest and pride in our spiritual ancestry, and to his feeling that justice should be done to the learned men of the past. He once wrote that if the rediscovery of forgotten Jewish writers were the only achievement of modern Jewish learning, it would have been sufficient to justify its existence.

His published works covered most aspects of Jewish studies. His monographs on Rabbinic doctrines are, perhaps, his main contribution to Jewish learning. In them he collected all the available material on the religious beliefs of our sages. He took a delight in proving that there was a system in the arrangement of their writings. He edited a number of texts of which, perhaps, the most important is his critical edition of the *Midrash Haserot Weyetherot*, which he published for the first time. He edited texts of Gaonic *responsa*, liturgical poems, and manuscript variants. He was keenly interested in folk-lore and completed a number of interesting studies on the motives of primitive life. The 'Medieval moralists' was another subject to which he made contributions. In his student days he published an account of early Christian Hebraists in Hungary. He edited a number of manuscripts which threw light on the obscure history of the Hungarian Sabbatarians. He was inspired by his teacher, Steinschneider, to take an interest in bibliography. Jewish history always attracted him, and his studies ranged from Oriental Jewish Viziers to the discovery of scholars in Angevin England. A large part of his work dealt with the relations between Judaism and Christianity in the early centuries of the current era. A principle which he always maintained was that there was never a time in which Judaism was isolated from the outside world, and he enjoyed tracing the interplay of Jewish and Gentile influences upon one another. His 'Background to the Haggadah' proves that some of the Midrashic homilies consisted of polemics against doctrines preached by contemporary pagan and heretical philosophers.

The effect upon my father of his research work was two-fold. In the first place he tended to judge events of our time by the lessons of Jewish history, and he was usually right in his judgements and prophecies, however surprising and improbable they seemed at the time. We find him writing, for example, in 1933 in the *London Quarterly Review*, that Germany was destined to suffer a fate far worse than that of Versailles. He regretted that this calamity had to come upon a nation which had rendered such valuable services to European culture, but saw that there was no alternative. Reading that article now, one cannot help being reminded of the visions of the prophets of the destruction of the great cities of the East. Again, he usually foresaw the future in a rather pessimistic light. His exceptional prophecies of good tidings were, therefore, all the more encouraging. His faith in the final victory of the Allied cause, for example, gave us all confidence. In this belief he never wavered for a moment, even in the darkest times. Secondly, connected with this historical sense was a trust and faith in the workings of the divine will. He tended to be critical and could even be described as a rationalist in his attitude towards religious origins, but his knowledge and learning never appeared to conflict with his faith. He insisted upon academic freedom of discussion and research. He felt that the field of Jewish learning was one in which Jews and non-Jews of all shades of belief and unbelief could co-operate on an equal footing and, although accepting and defending the dogmas of Judaism with much firmness, resented any attempt to restrain research within sectarian boundaries.

In his youth my father wrote mainly in Hungarian and German. After 1912 he began to publish articles in English and in French. Between 1918 and 1933 the bulk of his writings appeared in English, French, and German with a certain number of contributions to Hebrew periodicals, and after 1933 he wrote mainly in Hebrew and English. This choice of language was not determined by his prejudices, but rather by the wish to see his work published in a medium which could be understood by those interested in the subject. He therefore chose the language according to the theme of the article. I know of only one case in which my father's ideological motives resulted in the refusal of his co-operation. For many years prior to the accession of Hitler to power, my father had collaborated with Professor Gerhard Kittel of Tübingen in the production of a number of editions of Rabbinic texts with translation, notes, and commentaries. In 1933 Professor Kittel, fearful no doubt of the consequences of his sympathetic attitude towards Judaism and Jewish studies under the new régime, thought it prudent to write a brochure under the title of *Die Judenfrage*, in which he appeared to have changed this attitude to one of hostility. I remember how my father ordered a copy of this brochure, confident that the Gerhard Kittel whom he knew so well would make a stand in defence of Judaism and the Jewish people. My father read this work with bitter disappointment and then sat down to write to the publisher to ask him to delete his name as joint-editor of the series. Kittel then wrote to him two long letters, pleading with him to reconsider his decision, pointing out the difficulties which surrounded him, and urging as an excuse that he had been misunderstood, that he had not proclaimed the inferiority of Israel, but had merely attempted to show the differences between the nature of Israel and that of Christian Germany. My father replied with a bitter and angry refusal.

My father's bias in favour of research influenced his teaching, although he enjoyed teaching even where it did not lead to original work. In fact he derived considerable satisfaction from expounding Rabbinic teachings to laymen who had some background of Jewish knowledge. He had a certain prejudice against dilettantes and popularizers, but that was due to his resentment of their pretensions and the imperfections of their work. But it was when he was stimu-

lating research by his teaching that he derived most satisfaction. The dissertations of his pupils made him happy to
feel that he had inspired them to throw some light on
obscure problems and he deplored any tendency to lower
the standards of original work required by learned institutions.

In polemics with other scholars my father was sometimes
vigorous in the expressions which he used. An instance
which comes to my mind is his review of Aptowitzer's
Parteipolitik in der Hasmonäerzeit, which provoked a rather
angry reply from the author and a cold but indignant re-
joinder from the reviewer. But there was no malice in it.
Father considered Jewish learning as a sacred undertaking,
as a fight for the truth in which compromise was treason.
Nor was he offended by those who opposed his theories.
He was by nature and training critically minded and he
expected a learned work to be exposed to the most search-
ing criticism. His prodigious memory, his absorption and
assimilation of everything he read, aided by his system of
indexing references, made him a formidable adversary in
disputations. He set a very high standard, both for himself
and for others.

My father's life and teaching were influenced mainly by
his conviction of the truth of Judaism. He accepted without
reservation the doctrine of the Divine Revelation of the
Written and Oral Law from Mount Sinai and therefore
found it simple and logical to practise Judaism as a way of
life. As he wrote in his essay on 'The Religion of the Jew', to
him Judaism was 'a signpost on the cross roads to guide all
pilgrims here in the valley of the shadow of death'. It was
because of the firmness of his belief, combined with a
positive enthusiasm for the teachers of Midrashic and
Talmudic times, that he found no inconsistency between
his critical examination of the sources of Judaism and
comprehensive study of comparative religion and his life
as an observant Jew. Although he resented obscurantism,

the religious hypothesis which he had accepted was never shaken. Let me quote his own words:

'Healthy and harmless assimilation never ceased throughout Jewish history. Any assimilation in whatever form it appears, which undermines the real religious foundation and the historical basis of Judaism, regardless of whether it is propagated in nationalistic forms or in religious garb, is dangerous.

'The Jew looks upon all advances in science and medicine, mechanics and physics, chemistry and astronomy as part and parcel of a Divine plan and economy. Yet as soon as innovations approach the sacred precincts of religion, the Jew stands on his guard and scrutinises the value of their achievements. As a matter of course, teachers of Judaism in the past opposed and some sections of modern Jewry still oppose, the study of secular wisdom lest it disturb the spiritual equilibrium of the Jew. Such a conception of Judaism may be disregarded.'

Arguments to the effect that the Commandments were valuable merely to keep Israel united in exile made him particularly scornful.

'If our laws are made by men, why should they be more binding in the dispersion than in Palestine, and if they are divine and not merely artificial measures to keep Judaism alive in exile, then their authority is binding everywhere.'

The originality of Judaism seemed to him to lie in the importance attached to study, of which he was passionately fond. But study was not the whole of his religion. He enjoyed fulfilling rabbinical functions even when he did not occupy rabbinical office. Preaching God's word was to him a sacred duty. Whether it was at the Synagogue or at the house of mourning, or at a domestic celebration, whenever he was asked to speak he responded readily. He was a powerful preacher and his sermons were rich in parables from the Midrashim. He never shouted, never touched on political themes, but devoted himself to the duties of man towards his Creator and towards his fellow men. He rebuked materialism, apathy, hypocrisy, and lack of charity, but gave comfort and sympathy to those who needed it. He always spoke without notes and his sentences may have lacked the polish of a written or memorized address, but they were obviously sincere, marked by a fullness of knowledge and they made the audience feel that he had their spiritual welfare very much at heart. For many years he preached regularly at the Cricklewood Synagogue, before large congregations, and his spiritual influence contributed much towards creating a warm Jewish atmosphere in that place of worship. My father often used to receive letters from people who had heard him preach. I remember particularly some very moving ones from a Jew of German origin who attended divine service (in 1933) for the first time for many years and happened to hear my father preach. It was as a result of my father's encouragement and continued contact with him that he became a devout Jew once again.

The month of Ellul always marked a great change in him. He used to spend long hours in meditation and study, and when he came to bless us on the eve of Yom Kippur, before we left home for the Synagogue, tears flowed from his eyes. On the New Year, he read aloud in the Synagogue the notes for the Shofar with a depth of feeling. On the Eve of the Day of Atonement, his white-clad figure as he held up the sacred scroll by the side of the Cantor was extraordinarily impressive. There were tears in his eyes when he preached, and there were soon tears in the eyes of his audience.

He was born on the Day of Atonement and departed this life on the Holy Day suddenly without warning. Only a few hours before, he had spoken with prophetic force and fervour on the need for separation from sin before the Day of Judgement. His end was characteristic of the man. His health had been poor for some time. My mother begged him to take care of himself and to hold services at home, but he refused to absent himself from the Synagogue. His father, his grandfather, and most of his ancestors, he said, to the end of their days, had preached God's word on

the Holy Day, and he would follow their example. He died
as he had lived, walking in the footsteps of his forebears.

4

The picture which should emerge from these pages is
not one of a meek unworldly scholar, absorbed in his
studies, but of a man of spirit, hasty and impetuous at
times, occasionally hard and unrelenting in his judgement
of people, sometimes bitter in his resentment of injustices,
intolerant of the less dignified of human failings but kindly,
helpful, and generous to the obscure and unpretentious,
passionate in his devotion to his faith and his mission as a
Jewish scholar. He will be remembered working in his
study late at night, struggling against sickness to fulfil his
self-imposed tasks, speaking from the pulpit in his quiet,
fervent way, praying wrapped in his *Talit* among the
Hassidim, presiding over his family circle, answering the
questions of those who came to him for guidance. Future
generations will know him by his works, as long as men are
interested in the spiritual legacy of Israel. It is for them that
I have tried to depict the figure of a man of learning and a
man of God.

BIBLIOGRAPHY OF THE WORKS OF ARTHUR MARMORSTEIN

ABBREVIATIONS

ARW = Archiv für Religionswissenschaft.
EJ = Encyclopaedia Judaica.
EPK = Egyetemes Philologiai Közlöny.
HUCA = Hebrew Union College Annual.
JQR = Jewish Quarterly Review.
JRAS = Journal of the Royal Asiatic Society.
MGWJ = Monatsschrift für Geschichte und Wissenschaft des Judentums.
MJV = Mitteilungen zur jüdischen Volkskunde.
MR = Magyar Rabbik.
MZS = Magyar Zsidó Szemle.
OLZ = Orientalistische Literaturzeitung.
OW = Dr. Bloch's Oesterreichische Wochenschrift.
OY = Ozar Yisrael.
PEF = Quarterly Statement, Palestine Exploration Fund.
REJ = Revue des Études Juives.
SU = Szombati Ujság (Miskolcz).
ZAW = Zeitschrift für Alttestamentliche Wissenschaft.
ZDMG = Zeitschrift der Deutschen Morgenländischen Gesellschaft.
ZNW = Zeitschrift für Neutestamentliche Wissenschaft.
ZfHB = Zeitschrift für Hebräische Bibliographie.

1904

ZfHB, vol. viii, No. 2. Christliche Hebraisten in Ungarn, I: pp. 48–50.

—— vol. viii, No. 3. Christliche Hebraisten in Ungarn, II: pp. 80–4.

—— vol. viii, No. 5. Christliche Hebraisten in Ungarn, III: pp. 141–3.

EPK, vol. xxviii, No. 1. Temesvári pelbárt egy példágának eredetéhez: pp. 50–4.

Keleti Szemle, vol. v. Az ékiratok 'Kumani' népéröl (1905): pp. 288–90.

Pozsony. *Studien zum Pseudo-Jonathan Targum*, I. Das Targum und die Apokryphen Literatur. 40 pp. (Dissertation.)

ZfHB, vol. ix, No. 4. Christliche Hebraisten in Ungarn, IV: pp. 111–13.

—— vol. ix, No. 5. Review of Stein's *Magyar Rabbik*: pp. 129–31.

ZAW, vol. xxv, No. 1. Die Namen der Schwestern Kain's und Abel's in der midraschischen und in der Apokryphen Literatur: pp. 141–4.

—— vol. xxv, No. 2. Zu den traditionellen Namenserklärungen: pp. 368–74.

Israelitische Monatsschrift, 14 July. Raschi, Vortrag gehalten bei der Gedenkfeier des Rabbiner Seminars (Berlin): pp. 25–7.

—— 18 Aug. Raschi (concluded): pp. 30–1.

MR, vol. i, No. 6. Raschi, I: pp. 73–6.

—— vol. ii, No. 1–2. Raschi, II: pp. 7–10.

—— vol. ii, No. 3. Raschi, III: pp. 25–8.

MZS, Buda varosa egy XVI. századbeli responsumban: pp. 37–40.

1906

ZAW, vol. xxvii. Midrasch der vollen und defektiven Schreibungen: pp. 33–48.

MGWJ, vol. l. Beiträge zur Geschichte und Literatur der gaonaischen Periode, I: pp. 589–603.

REJ, vol. lii. Les Signes du Messie: pp. 176–86.

EPK, vol. xxx. A Magyar Ádám-Legenda Keleti Elemei: pp. 362–6.

—— vol. xxx. Az újszövetség héber fordítói: p. 715.

ZfHB, vol. x, Nos. 1–2. Genesis Rabba Fragmente I: pp. 58–60.

—— vol. x, No. 4. Zwei Midrasch-Tehillim Fragmente, I: pp. 120–2.

—— vol. x, No. 6. Review of Bondi's *Zur Geschichte der Juden in Böhmen, Mähren und Schlesien*: pp. 163–5.

—— vol. x, No. 6. Zwei Midrasch-Tehillim Fragmente, II: pp. 182–4.

MR, vol. ii, No. 4. Review of Friedländer's commentary on Seder Nashim of the Jerusalem Talmud: pp. 40–3.

—— vol. ii, No. 6. Magyar zsidó községek és tudósok egy XV századbeli gyüjteményben: pp. 81–2.

—— vol. iii, No. 2. Notes on Guttmann's *Clavis Talmudi*, vol. i: pp. 15–19.

SU, 19 Jan. 'Leszek' Küldött hozzátok: pp. 4–5.

—— 26 Jan. Modena Leo (1571–1648): pp. 4–5.

—— 2 Feb. Egy elmaradt beszéd a missió ünnepélyéról: pp. 6–7.

—— 16 Feb. A Jesivák rendezése: pp. 1–2.

—— 11 May. Az angyalok a héber varaszlatban: pp. 4–5.

1907

ZAW, vol. xxvii. Zu den Hebräischen Finalbuchstaben: pp. 283–4.

ZNW, vol. x. Jüdische Parallelen zur Petrusapokalypse: pp. 297–300.

MGWJ, vol. li, Nos. 11–12. Beiträge zur Geschichte und Literatur der gaonäischen Periode, II: pp. 733–46.

REJ, vol. liv. Les 'Epicuriens' dans la littérature talmudique: pp. 181–93.

EPK, vol. xxxi. Parabolae Vulpium.

—— vol. xxxi. Steinschneider Mór (Nekrolog): pp. 262–3.

—— vol. xxxi. Pontius Pilatus: pp. 890–1.

ZfHB, vol. xi, No. 5. Die Superkommentare zu Raschi's Pentateuchkommentar, I: pp. 156–7.

—— vol. xi, No. 6. Die Superkommentare zu Raschi's Pentateuchkommentar, II: pp. 188–91.

Jüdisches Literaturblatt, vol. xiii, No. 5. Leopold Dukes und sein Lehrer Chajim J. Pollak, I: pp. 52–4.

—— vol. xiii, No. 8. Leopold Dukes und sein Lehrer Chajim J. Pollak, II: pp. 91–2.

OW, 5 Apr. Review of Ziegler's Der Kampf zwischen Judentum und Christentum in den ersten drei christlichen Jahrhunderten: pp. 241–3.

—— 7 June. Review of Guttmann's Clavis Talmudi: pp. 385–7.

—— 4 July. A comment on the 'Nikolsburger Geist': p. 15.

—— 30 Aug. Review of Aicher's Das alte Testament in der Mischna: pp. 581–2.

Monatsschrift der Oesterreichisch-Israelitischen Union, vol. ix, No. 9. Pastor Kalthoff über die Judenfrage: pp. 1–6.

MR, vol. iii, No. 4. A budai számüzöttek történetéhez: pp. 54–5.

—— vol. iii, No. 6. Notes on Guttmann's Clavis Talmudi, vol. ii: pp. 87–90.

—— vol. iii, Nos. 7–8. Notes on Guttmann's Clavis Talmudi, vol. ii (continued): pp. 108–11.

—— vol. iii, No. 9. Review of Baruch Toledano's edition of Rabbenu Abraham ben Nathan Hayarhi's commentary on Tractate Kallah Rabathi: pp. 126–8.

—— vol. iv, Nos. 1–2. Review of Fischer's Daniel und seine drei Gefährten im Talmud und Midrasch: pp. 14–16.

1908

Talmud und neues Testament. 54 pp. Vinkovci.

EPK, vol. xxxii, No. 10. Egy Oxyrhynchusi töredék: pp. 750–5.

ZfHB, vol. xii. Die Superkommentare zu Raschi's Pentateuchkommentar, III: pp. 26–8.

Jüdisches Literaturblatt, vol. xiv. Review of Fuchs's *Textkritische Untersuchungen zum hebr. Ekklesiastikus*: p. 46.

MJV, vol. xi. Eine hebräische Anekdotensammlung aus dem 18ten Jahrhundert: pp. 120–22.

OW, 2 Oct. Review of Jawitz's *Geschichte Israels*: p. 710.

1909

Kunszentmiklós זכר צדיק *Főtisztelendő Rosenfeld Mayer Miskolczi főrabbi emlékezete*: 60 pp.

ZAW, vol. xxix. Jesus Sirach: pp. 287–93.

MJV, Eisik Tyrnau: pp. 119–21.

—— Review of *Ethnographia*, a Hungarian folkloristic journal: p. 128.

OW, 5 Feb. Review of Strack's *Einleitung in den Talmud*: p. 106.

—— 6 Aug. Hat das Judentum Dogmen oder nicht?: p. 544.

Židovska, 31 July. Zionistische Bestrebungen im Mittelalter: pp. 238–40. Smotra.

Allgemeine Zeitung des Judentums. Review of Unger's *Gesammelte Aufsätze*: p. 444.

OY, vol. iii. ביתוסים: pp. 74–5.

—— vol. iii. במדבר רבה: p. 94.

1910

Religionsgeschichtliche Studien, I. Heft: *Die Bezeichnungen für Christen und Gnostiker im Talmud und Midrasch*: 83 pp. Skotschau.

Magyar Könyvszemle, vol. xviii, No. 3. Egy ismeretlen magyar hebraista: p. 283.

EPK, vol. xxxiv. A γενέσια ünnepély.

—— vol. xxxiv. Review of Blaufuss's *Römische Feste und Feiertage nach dem Traktaten über fremden Dienst*: pp. 417–18.

—— vol. xxxiv. Review of Blau's *Bacher Vilmos élete és működése*: pp. 587–8.

—— vol. xxxiv. Review of Krauss's *Antoninus und Rabbi*: pp. 731–2.

REJ, vol. lx. L'Épitre de Barnabe et la polémique juive: pp. 213–20.

ARW, vol. xiii. Genesis oder Parentalia?: pp. 630–2.

OLZ, vol. xiii, No. 10. Einige hebräische Redensarten, I: pp. 434–5.

Zur Geschichte der Juden in Jamnitz. 12 pp. (Reprinted from *MJV*.) Skotschau.

MJV. Notes on Beilin's *Sprichwörter und Redensarten aus Russland*: pp. 39 and 90.

OY, vol. iv. הגדות ומסורות: p. 106.

—— vol. iv. הושענא רבא: pp. 132–3.

—— vol. iv. ויכוחים: pp. 198–200.

1911

REJ, vol. lxi. La Dignité de Guérousiarque de la Synagogue: pp. 288–92.

OLZ, vol. xiv, No. 3. Einige hebräische Redensarten, II: pp. 108–10.

EPK, vol. xxxv. Review of Hans Blaufuss's *Götter Bilder und Symbole nach den Traktaten über fremden Dienst* (*Aboda Zara*) *in Mischna, Tosefta, Jerusalemer und Babylonischer Talmud*: pp. 500–1.

—— vol. xxxv. Review of Gerhard Loeschke's *Jüdisches und Heidnisches im Christlichen Kult*: pp. 834–5.

ZfHB. Bemerkungen über Natanel oder Abu'l Barakat Hibbat allah: p. 159.

MJV, vol. xiv, No. 1. Notes on Sal. Goldschmidt's German Translation of the Zeena Ureena, I: pp. 37–47.

—— vol. xiv, No. 2. Notes on Sal. Goldschmidt's German Translation of the Zeena Ureena, II: pp. 49–63.

—— vol. xiv, No. 2. Die Wiener Exulanten in Hotzenplotz: p. 81.

—— vol. xiv, No. 3. Notes on Sal. Goldschmidt's German Translation of the Zeena Ureena, III: pp. 130–5.

OW. Die Deutungen der hebräischen Buchstaben: pp. 412–13.

OY, vol. v. יום הלדת: p. 112.

—— vol. v. יעקב איש כפר נבוריא: pp. 173–4.

—— vol. v. כתות: pp. 306–7.

—— vol. vi. לשון נקייה: pp. 65–6.

—— vol. vi. מינות: pp. 186–7.

—— vol. vi. משל: pp. 314–16.

1912

Religionsgeschichtliche Studien, II. Heft: *Die Schriftgelehrten*: 118 pp. Skotschau.

REĴ, vol. lxiv. L'Opposition contre le Patriarche R. Juda II: pp. 59–66.

OLZ, vol. xv, No. 7. Kranz und Krone in den Oden Salomos: pp. 306–8.

—— vol. xv, No. 10. Zu OLZ Sp. 254: p. 449.

ARW, vol. xv. (*a*) Der Ritus des Küssens bei den Juden, (*b*) Die Leberschau in Talmudischer Zeit, (*c*) Die Zahl der Frommen: pp. 306–8.

MĴV, vol. xv, No. 2. Notes on Sal. Goldschmidt's German Translation of the Zeena Ureena, IV: pp. 49–71.

—— vol. xv, No. 3. Über eine Toledot Jeschu (Leben Jesu) Handschrift: pp. 95–7.

EPK, vol. xxxvi. A világirodalom legrégibb irott mesekönyve: pp. 581–3.

OW, 30 Aug. Die neuentdeckten Oden Salomos: pp. 581–3.

Monatsschrift der Oesterreichisch-Israelitischen Union, May. Erinnerungen aus den Jahren 1815–17.

OY, vol. vii. סופרים: pp. 160–1.

—— vol. viii. פרושים: pp. 302–3.

—— vol. viii. פושע ישראל: pp. 317–18.

1913

REĴ, vol. lxv. Deux observations: pp. 310–11.

—— vol. lxvi. La Réorganization du doctorat en Palestine au IIIᵉ siècle: pp. 44–53.

—— vol. lxvi. David Kimḥi Apologiste. Un fragment perdu dans son commentaire des Psaumes, pp. 246–51.

OLZ, vol. xvi, No. 10. Einige hebräische Redensarten: pp. 437–8.

ZDMG, vol. lxvii. Über das Gaonat in Palästina (980–1160 C.E.): pp. 635–44.

ARW, vol. xvi. Legendenmotive in der Rabbinischen Literatur, I: pp. 160–75.

EPK, vol. xxxvii. Az onolatria a zsidóknál és az őskereszténységben: pp. 141–2.

—— vol. xxxvii. Review of Guenter's *Die christliche Legende des Abendlandes*: pp. 196–8.

EPK, vol. xxxvii. Még egy szó a zsidó-keresztény onolatriaról: p. 288.

—— vol. xxxvii. Bagáthı Fazekas Mihály és Nagyernyei Magyári Péter: p. 790.

Magyar Könyvszemle, vol. xxi, No. 2. Szombatos Kodexek: pp. 113–22.

Preface to *Tam Ha-Kesseph*, consisting of eight treatises by R. Joseph Ibn Kaspi, edited and published by Isaac Last, London.

OW, 25 Apr. Review of *Tam Ha-Kesseph*: pp. 84–91.

—— 19 Dec. Isaac Last. (Obituary.)

ZfHB. Die Memoiren Beer Bolechovs: pp. 84–91.

—— Einige vorläufige Bemerkungen über Genizafragmente: pp. 91–3.

Jewish Review, vol. iv, No. 21. Review of Schweitzer's *Paul and his Interpreters*: pp. 276–8.

OY, vol. x. תלמיד חכם: pp. 286–9.

MJV, vol. xvi, No. 1. Notes on Sal. Goldschmidt's German Translation of the Zeena Ureena, V: pp. 21–5.

—— vol. xvi, No. 4. Notes on Sal. Goldschmidt's German Translation of the Zeena Ureena, VI: pp. 14–31.

1914

Volume in honour of David Hoffman's 70th birthday. Über die Mechilta des R. Ismael zum Buche Vajikra: pp. 362–8.

REJ, vol. lxviii. Les Gueonim en Palestine aux XIe et XIIe siècles: pp. 37–48.

—— vol. lxviii. Quelques problèmes de l'ancienne apologétique juive: pp. 161–73.

—— vol. lxviii. Additions et rectifications: pp. 317–18.

ZNW, vol. xv. Einige Bemerkungen zum Evangelienfragment in Oxyrhynchus Papyri: pp. 336–8.

EPK, vol xxxviii. Új adatok a kazárok történetéhez: pp. 148–52.

JQR, vol. iv, No. 4. Joseph ben Abraham Hakohen: pp. 621–34.

MJV, vol. xvii, No. 1. Notes on Sal. Goldschmidt's translation of the Zeena Ureena, VII: pp. 9–10.

Jewish Review, vol. iv, No. 23. Review of *Studies in Jewish Literature* issued in honour of Professor Kaufmann Kohler's 70th birthday.

—— vol. v, No. 25. The Apologetics of the Rabbis: pp. 62–74.

1915

JQR, vol. vi, No. 1. To *JQR*, vol. v, pp. 443–52 (A reply to Davidson): pp. 157–62.

American Journal of Theology, vol. xix, No. 4. The Doctrine of the Resurrection of the Dead in Rabbinical Theology: pp. 577–91.

Theologisch Tijdschrift, vol. xxxix. Juden und Judentum in der Altercatio Simonis Judaei et Theophili Christiani: pp. 360–83.

1916

Studies in Honour of the 70th Birthday of Professor Adolf Schwarz. Spuren Karäischen Einflusses in der Gaonäischen Halacha, pp. 455–70.

Journal Asiatique. Fragments du Commentaire de Daniel al-Kumissi sur les Psaumes: pp. 177–240.

London Quarterly Review, Oct. Synagogue Sermons in the First Three Centuries: pp. 227–40.

1917

מדרש חסירות ויתירות, 96 pp.

JQR, vol. viii, No. 1. Solomon ben Judah and some of his Contemporaries: pp. 1–29.

1918

JQR, vol. viii, No. 3. A Fragment of the Visions of Ezekiel: pp. 367–78.

1919

Expositor, vol. xlv, Jan. Jews and Judaism in the earliest Christian Apologies I: pp. 73–80.

—— vol. xlv, Feb. Jews and Judaism in the earliest Christian Apologies (concluded): pp. 100–16.

Haivri, vol ix, No. 32. עליית רגלים אחר חרבן ביתר: pp. 6–8.

—— vol. ix, No. 41. בן־מאיר: pp. 9–10.

London Quarterly Review, Oct. The Treasures in Heaven and upon Earth: pp. 216–28.

1920

The Doctrine of Merits in Old Rabbinic Literature: 199 pp. London.

JQR, vol. ix, No. 1. The Takkanot of Ezra: pp. 367–9.

REJ, vol. lxx. Review of Poznański's *Babylonische Geonim im nachgaonäischen Zeitalter:* pp. 97–111.

—— vol. lxx. Deux renseignements d'Origène concernant les Juifs: pp. 190–1.

Jeschurun, vol. vii. Die Gotteslehre in der jüdischen Apologetik, I: pp. 92–105.

—— vol. vii. Die Gotteslehre in der jüdischen Apologetik, II: pp. 168–76.

Expositor, vol. xlvi, September. Ecclesiastes xii. 6: pp. 203–7.

PEF, vol. lii, July. The Jewish Inscription from 'Ain Duk: pp. 139–41.

Haivri, vol. x, No. 44. מחשבי קצים: pp. 11–13.

Jewish Guardian, 27 Feb. Review of *The Pavement of Sapphire*, by David Ben Judah the Pious, edited with a preface by Rabbi S. A. Wertheimer: p. 7.

—— 25 May. Review of Bergmann's *Die Legenden der Juden*: p. 9.

—— 31 Dec. Review of Zuri's *Rab, sein Leben und seine Anschaungen* and *Rabbi Jochanan, der erste Amoräer Galiläas.*

1921

REJ, vol. lxxiii. Notes et Mélanges: (1) Ancienneté de la poésie synagogale, (2) Meschoullam b. Moïse et les Gueonim palestiniens, (3) Nouveaux renseignements sur Tobiya b. Eliézer, (4) Hai Gaon et les usages des deux écoles: pp. 82–100.

Hazofeh, vol. v, No. 4. קדוש ירחים דרבי פנחם: pp. 225–55.

PEF, vol. liii, No. 1. The Inscription of Theodotus: pp. 23–8.

—— vol. liii, No. 4. Review of Samuel Klein's *Jud. Pal. Corpus Inscriptionum*: pp. 187–90.

Haolam, 13 June. רשימות ביבליוגרפיות (גזרת ווינה): pp. 11–12.

Jewish Chronicle (Supplement), 25 March. Review of Tschernowitz's *Kizzur ha-Talmud*: pp. iv and v.

1922

ARW, vol. xxi. Zu Archiv 19, p. 547. Das Sieb im Volksglauben: pp. 235–8.

—— vol. xxi. Eine Parodie: pp. 502–4.

Hazofeh, vol. vi, No. 1. נספחים למאמרי קדוש ירחים דרבי פנחם: pp. 46–59.

MGWJ, vol. lxvi. Die Einleitung zu David ben Merwan's Religionsphilosophie wiedergefunden: pp. 48–64.

Ginze Kedem, vol. i. מס״ המפתח לרבינו נסים על מסכת נדרים: pp. 81–3.

Zeitschrift für Assyriologie, vol. xxxiv. Zu ZA xxxii, 212: p. 94.

Jewish Chronicle, 18 Sept. A Chapel dedicated to the Maccabees.

1923

REJ, vol. lxxvi. Review of Lewin's *Ginze Kedem*: pp. 99–104.

—— vol. lxxvi. Sur un auteur français inconnu du treizième siècle: pp. 113–31.

—— vol. lxxvii. Les Persécutions religieuses à l'époque de R. Johanan b. Nappaḥa: pp. 166–76.

Expositor, vol. xlix. The Attitude of the Jews towards Early Christianity: pp. 383–9.

MGWJ, vol. lxvii. Mitteilungen zur Geschichte und Literatur aus der Geniza, I: pp. 59–62.

—— vol. lxvii. Mitteilungen zur Geschichte und Literatur aus der Geniza, II: pp. 132–7.

—— vol. lxvii. Mitteilungen zur Geschichte und Literatur aus der Geniza, III: pp. 257–61.

Jahrbuch für Jüdische Volkskunde. Beiträge zur Religionsgeschichte und Volkskunde, I: pp. 280–319.

Devir, vol. i. מדרש אבכיר: pp. 113–44.

ZNW. Die Nachrichten über Nekyomanteia in der altrabbinischen Literatur: pp. 299–304.

MZS. Tanulmányok a Midras Haggádól első könyvéhez: pp. 138–40.

—— A Kanon (κανών) szó történetéhez: pp. 144–5.

MZS. A Notarikon és méz néhány műszó a középkosi szintirás-magyarázatban.

Jewish Chronicle, 8 June. A Short Shulchan Aruch.

—— 21 Sept. Kol Nidre.

1924

MGWJ, vol. lxviii. Mitteilungen zur Geschichte und Literatur aus der Geniza, IV: pp. 150–60.

Jeschurun, vol. xi. Eine angebliche Verordnung Hadrian's: pp. 149–56.

—— vol. xi. Einige Messianologische Vorstellungen des dritten Jahrhunderts neu beleuchtet: pp. 323–42.

Hazofeh, vol. viii, No. 1. I. שרידים מפתרוני הקראי דניאל אלקומסי: pp. 44–60.

—— vol. viii, No. 4. II. שרידים מפתרוני הקראי דניאל אלקומסי: pp. 321–37.

Devir, vol. ii. חכם ופוסק איטלקי: pp. 213–43.

HUCA, vol. i. The Unity of God in Rabbinic Literature: pp. 467–99.

Hator, 25 Jan. קדיש עתיק בימי הגאונים: pp. 9–11.

—— 30 May. פרק חדש בדברי ימי א׳: pp. 6–7.

Jewish Chronicle, 26 Sept. Some Unknown English Rabbis: pp. 16–18.

Jewish Forum, 25 Jan. The Existence of God: pp. 16–26.

1925

MGWJ, vol. lxix. Mitteilungen zur Geschichte und Literatur aus der Geniza, V and VI: pp. 30–40.

—— vol. lxix. Review of Vischnitzer's *Memoirs of Ber of Bolechow*: pp. 121–2.

—— vol. lxix. Mitteilungen zur Geschichte und Literatur aus der Geniza, VII: pp. 361–4.

REJ, vol. lxxxi. Les Enseignements d'Akabia ben Mahalalel: pp. 181–7.

JQR, vol. xv, No. 3. The Amidah of the Public Fast Days: pp. 409–18.

ZAW. 1 Samuel, 25–9: pp. 119–24.

Jeschurun, vol. xii. Ein Fragment einer neuen Piska zum Wochenfest und der Kampf gegen das mündliche Gesetz: pp. 34–53.

—— vol. xii. Eine alte liturgische Schwierigkeit: pp. 198–211.

Jahrbuch für Jüdische Volkskunde. Beiträge zur Relig onsgeschichte und Volkskunde, II: pp. 344–83.

Hazofeh, vol. ix, No. 2, III. ‏שרידים מפתרוני הקראי דניאל אלקומסי‏: pp. 192–5.

London Quarterly Review, Apr. Learning and Work: pp. 217–25.

1926

REJ, vol. lxxxii. ‏מאמר על איזה תנועות רוחניות בדורו של ר׳ יהושע בן לוי‏ (In honour of Israel Lévi's 70th birthday): pp. 1–16.

A Volume dedicated to Professor L. Blau. ‏שבלים‏: pp. 209–15.

MGWJ, vol. lxx. Mitteilungen zur Geschichte und Literatur aus der Geniza, VIII: pp. 24–32.

MGWJ, vol. lxx. Review of Scheftelowitz's *Altpalästinensischer Bauern-glaube in vergleichender Beleuchtung*: pp. 209–15.

—— vol. lxx. Eine apologetische Mischna: pp. 376–85.

ZAW, vol. iii. Zur Erklärung von Jesajas 53: pp. 260–5.

ZNW, vol. xxv. Miscellen: pp. 249–58.

Jeschurun, vol. xii. Eine messianische Bewegung im dritten Jahrhundert, I: pp. 369–83.

—— vol. xiii. Eine messianische Bewegung im dritten Jahrhundert, II: pp. 16–28.

—— vol. xiii. Eine messianische Bewegung im dritten Jahrhundert, III: pp. 171–86.

Quest, vol. xii, No. 12. Some Remarks on the Slavonic Josephus: pp. 145–57.

Haolam, 19 Feb. ‏פריסת הסודר‏: pp. 159–60.

—— 20 Aug. ‏כרעי המטה‏: pp. 670–1.

—— 12 Dec. ‏כותבי הערות‏: pp. 1010–1011.

Zion, vol. i. ‏קברי אבות‏: pp. 3–11.

Near East and India, 30 June. Review of *Enzyklopädie des Judentums*: p. 750.

—— 19 Aug. Review of *The Jews at the Close of the Bible Age*: pp. 187–8.

—— 16 Sept. Review of Browne's *Story of the Jews from the Earliest Times to the Present Day*: p. 304.

Jewish Chronicle, Supplement, 29 Jan. Some Greek and Rabbinic Ideas of God: pp. v to vii.

Jewish Graphic, 6 Aug. The Jewish Problem: My Solution: p. 10.

1927

The Old Rabbinic Doctrine of God, I. *The Names and Attributes of God*: 217 pp. London.

Poznański Memorial Volume. לתולדות ר' סעדיה גאון: pp. 136–44.

MGWJ, vol. lxxi. David ben Jehuda Hasid: pp. 39–48.

ZNW, vol. xxvi. Iranische und jüdische Religion: pp. 231–42.

REJ, vol. lxxxiv. Anges et hommes dans l'Aggada: pp. 37–50.

—— vol. lxxxiv. Note complémentaire à Anges et hommes dans l'Aggada: pp. 138–41.

Jeschurun, vol. xiv. Rabbi David Kohen und das Rabbinerwesen in der ersten Hälfte des 16ten Jahrhunderts: pp. 174–89.

—— vol. xiv. Die Nachahmung Gottes in der Agada (Imitatio Dei): pp. 617–32. (In honour of Prof. Wohlgemuth's 60th birthday.)

MJV. Beiträge zur Religionsgeschichte und Volkskunde, III: pp. 31–48.

Quest, vol. xxii, No. 4. Rabbinic Religion: pp. 381–95.

Hazofeh, vol. xi, No. 1. שבלים (continued): pp. 33–5.

PEF. About the Inscription of Judan ben Ishmael: p. 101.

Hator, 25 Feb. תלמוד מסכת כלים: pp. 7–8.

Haolam, 20 May. שמנה בעשרה: p. 399.

Near East and India, 2 June. Review of *Apella or the Future of the Jews*: p. 658.

EJ, vol. i. Aaron (im Talmud und Midrasch): cols. 13–16.

—— vol. i. Ab Bet-Din: cols. 104–9.

—— vol. i. Abba aus Akko: cols. 141–3.

—— vol. i. Abba bar Kahana: col. 149.

—— vol. i. Abba bar Memel: cols. 154–5.

—— vol. i. Abba bar Pappa: cols. 155–6.

—— vol. i. Ablat: cols. 334–5.

—— vol. i. Aboda Sara: cols. 352–9.

—— vol. i. Aboth de-Rabbi Nathan: cols. 368–70.

—— vol. i. Adda der Feldmesser: col. 806.

—— vol. i. Agada und Kirchenväter: cols. 972–9.

1928

תשובות הגאונים 76 pp. Reprinted from different issues of אוצר החיים, a periodical edited by Rabbi Ehrenreich, *Deva* (Rumania).

Luncz Memorial Volume. לקורות היהודים בארץ ישראל במאה החמישית למספרם: pp. 41–50.

Zion, vol. ii. מנהגים קדמונים בארץ ישראל: pp. 17–27.

ZNW, vol. xxvii. Die Quellen des neuen Jeremia-Apokryphons: pp. 327–37.

MGWJ, vol. lxxii. Eine angeblich korrupte Borajta: pp. 391–5.

MJV, vol. xxxi/xxxii. Eine Geisteraustreibung aus neuerer Zeit: pp. 11–19.

JQR, vol. xix, No. 1. Some Hitherto Unknown Jewish Scholars of Angevin England: pp. 17–36.

Jeschurun, vol. xv. Vier Probleme des Rabbi Jose ben Chanina: pp. 387–400.

REJ, vol. lxxxv. L'Acte de se couvrir la tête chez les Juifs: pp. 66–9.

—— vol. lxxxv. Review of Gottheil and Worrell's *Fragments from the Cairo Genizah in the Freer Collection*: pp. 101–6.

—— vol. lxxxvi. Conceptions théocentriques et anthropocentriques de l'Agada: pp. 36–46.

PEF, Jan. Coins of Alexander Jannaeus and the History of the Pronunciation of the Divine Name: pp. 48–50.

Iyyim, vol. i. Review of Tschernowitz's *Kizzur Ha-Talmud*: pp. 11–23.

Hator, 3 Feb. שמירת השבת בגולה בסוף תקופת האמוראים: p. 7.

—— 3 Apr. שלש מצות: p. 19.

Near East and India, 5 July. Review of Margolis and Marx's *History of the Jewish People*: p. 11.

EJ, vol. ii. Alphabet des R. Akibas: cols. 451–3.

—— vol. ii. Antoninus im Talmud: cols. 1116–19.

1929

HUCA, vol. vi. The Background of the Haggadah: pp. 141–204.

MGWJ, vol. lxxiii. Review of Aptowitzer's *Parteipolitik der Hasmonäerzeit im rabbinischen und pseudo-epigraphischen Schrifttum*: pp. 244–50.

MGWJ, vol. lxxiii. Der Midrasch von den Widersprüchen in der Bibel: pp. 281–93.

—— vol. lxxiii. Zu Aptowitzer's Parteipolitik in der Hasmonäerzeit: pp. 478–87.

REJ, vol. lxxxvii. R. Josué ben Hanania et la sagesse grecque: pp. 200–8.

London Quarterly Review, Jan. Primitive and Higher Ideals in Religion: pp. 59–71.

JRAS. Review of Gaster's *Texts and Studies*: pp. 587–90.

Archiv für Orientforschung, vol. v, Nos. 5/6. Review of Chanoch Albeck's *Untersuchungen über die halachischen Midraschim*: pp. 242–3.

Zion, vol. iii. דרשות דניאל אלקומסי: pp. 26–42.

Jewish Guardian, 5 Apr. Review of Louis Untermeyer's *Moses*: p. 9.

—— 19 Apr. Review of R. Lowe Thompson's *History of the Devil*: p. 15.

—— 24 May. Review of Dalman's *Arbeit und Sitte* and Obermeyer's *Die Landschaft Babyloniens*: p. 12.

—— 9 Aug. The Minister Saʿdu 'd-Dawla: pp. 7, 8.

—— 23 Aug. Review of Ulrich von Wilamowitz-Moellendorff's *Erinnerungen 1848–1914*: p. 9.

—— 20 Dec. Review of *Iggeroth Sopherim*: p. 8.

Near East and India, 4 July. Review of Melvin Grove Kyle's *Explorations at Sodom*: p. 12.

EJ, vol. iii. Arachin: cols. 93–6.

—— vol. iii. Armut im Talmud: cols. 370–4.

—— vol. iii. Baba Kamma, Mezia, Bathra: cols. 843–8.

—— vol. iii. Be Rab: cols. 1195–6.

—— vol. iii. Bechorot: cols. 1205–8.

—— vol. iv. Bene Bathyra: cols. 85–6.

—— vol. iv. Berachot: cols. 167–71.

—— vol. iv. Beschneidung (Agadische Begründungen): cols. 352–6.

—— vol. iv. Bet Schammai und Bet Hillel: cols. 419–21.

—— vol. iv. Beza: cols. 455–7.

—— vol. iv. Bikkurim: cols. 787–9.

1930

ARW, vol. xxviii. Der heilige Geist in der rabbinischen Legende: pp. 286–303.

REJ, vol. lxxxix. La Participation à la vie éternelle dans la théologie rabbinique et dans la légende: pp. 305–20.

MGWJ, vol. lxxiv. Zur Erforschung des Jelamdenu-Problems: pp. 266–84.

MGWJ, vol. lxxiv. Review of Hirschberg's und Murmelstein's יחס האגדה להלכה: pp. 469–71.

JQR, vol. xx, No. 4. A Misunderstood Question in the Yerushalmi: pp. 313–20.

Tarbiz, vol. ii, No. 1. רעיונות האגדה וקורות הזמן: pp. 134–47.

Hazofeh, vol. xiv, No. 1. שבלים (continued): pp. 24–33.

PEF, July. Some Notes on Recent Works on Palestinian Epigraphy: pp. 154–57.

Hator, 17 Jan. לתולדות היהודים בארצות המזרח: pp. 9–10.

Jewish Guardian, 31 Jan. Review of Fiebig's *Der Talmud: seine Entstehung, sein Wesen, sein Inhalt unter besonderer Berücksichtigung seiner Bedeutung für die Neutestamentliche Wissenschaft*: pp. 7, 8.

—— 11 Apr. Review of Bischoff's *Das Blut in jüdischen Schrift und Brauch*: pp. 16–17.

—— 25 July. Review of the Dziubas edition of Iggereth R. Jochanan ben Zakkai: p. 10.

—— 28 Sept. Review of Festschrift in honour of the 60th birthday of Chief Rabbi Dr. Brody of Prague: p. 4.

EJ, vol. v. Chagiga: cols. 150–3.

—— vol. v. Chullin: cols. 569–72.

—— vol. v. Daniel im Talmud und Midrasch: cols. 771–3.

—— vol. v. Datan und Abiram im Talmud und Midrasch: col. 814.

—— vol. v. Demai: cols. 926–8.

—— vol. v. Derech Erez: cols. 939–42.

—— vol. v. Dina in der Agada: col. 1120.

—— vol. v. Doeg im Talmud und Midrasch: cols. 1166–7.

—— vol. vi. Dualismus im Talmud und Midrasch: cols. 93–5.

—— vol. vi. Ebel Rabbati: cols. 147–9.

—— vol. vi. Eduyyot: cols. 185–6.

—— vol. vi. Engel im Talmud und Midrasch: cols. 639–44.

—— vol. vi. Erubin: cols. 741–2.

—— vol. vi. Exil im Talmud und Midrasch: cols. 868–70.

1931

ZAW, vol. viii. Einige vorläufige Bemerkungen zu den neuentdeckten Fragmente des jerusalemischen (palästinensischen) Targums: pp. 231–42.

Tarbiz, vol. iii, No. 3. דורו של ר' יוחנן ואותיות המשיח: pp. 161–80.

ZNW, vol. xxx. Paulus und die Rabbinen: pp. 271–85.

Transactions of the Jewish Historical Society, vol. xii. New Material for the Literary History of the English Jews before the Expulsion: pp. 103–15.

MGWJ, vol. lxxv. Die Gottesbezeichnung Elohim im Jelamdenu: pp. 377–9.

JRAS. Review of S. Assaf's *Book of Shetaroth (formulary) of R. Hai Gaon*: pp. 729–31.

Zeitschrift für Volkskunde, vol. xi, No. 3. Der Nikolsburger Geist: pp. 275–82.

EJ, vol. vii. Gott im Talmud und Midrasch: cols. 561–71.

—— vol. viii. Jelamdenu: cols. 1069–71.

Jewish Guardian, 1 May. Review of Herford's *Pirke Aboth*: pp. 7–8.

—— 26 June. Jewish Moralists: Zbi Hirsch Keidanower: pp. 8–9.

—— 7 Aug. Review of Lidzbarski's *Auf rauhem Wege*: p. 7.

1932

JQR, vol. xxii, No. 3. Philo and the Names of God: pp. 295–306.

REJ, vol. xcii. Les Rabbins et les Évangiles: pp. 31–54.

Studi e Materiali di Storia delle Religioni, vol. viii. The 'Mirror' in Jewish Religious Life: pp. 37–41.

Qiriath Sepher, vol. ix, No. 1. הוספות ומלואים לאוצר השירה והפיוט׳ של י. דודזון: pp. 1–9.

London Quarterly and Holborn Review, Apr. Measure for Measure: pp. 224–36.

Tekuphatenu, vol. i, No. 2. הרעיון הלאומי בספרי בעלי מוסר הקדומים: pp. 276–83.

Views, vol. i, No. 1. A Story of the Devil: pp. 70–5.

—— vol. i, No. 2. German Jewish Moralists, I: pp. 140–6.

—— vol. i, No. 3. German Jewish Moralists, II: pp. 233–8.

—— vol. i, No. 4. A Remarkable Centenary. Leopold Zunz's *Gottesdienstliche Vorträge*: pp. 251–5.

Near East and India, 27 Oct. Review of Lods's *Israel from its Beginnings to the Middle of the Eighth Century*.

EJ, vol. ix. Jews College: cols. 101–2.

1933

Rabbinische Texte (14 volumes) edited in conjunction with Professor Gerhard Kittel (published between 1933 and 1936).

MGWJ, vol. lxxvii. Review of Gollancz's *Biographical Sketches*: p. 236.

Studi e Materiali di Storia delle Religioni, vol. ix. The Contest between Elijah and the Prophets of Baal: pp. 29–37.

ZNW, vol. xxxii. Jüdische Archäologie und Theologie: pp. 32–41.

PEF, vol. lxv. The Inscription of Er-Rame: pp. 100, 101.

Search, vol. iii, No. 2. The Jews and Jesus: pp. 129–47.

—— vol. iii, No 3. Gnosis and Qabbala: pp. 388–94.

London Quarterly and Holborn Review. Antisemitism: Past and Present: pp. 393–5.

Near East and India, 9 Feb. Review of Newman's *Agricultural Life of the Jews in Babylonia between the Years 200 C.E. and 500 C.E.*: p. 109.

—— 9 Feb., 7 Sept. Review of Kennett's *Ancient Hebrew Social Life and Custom as indicated by Law, Narrative and Metaphor*: p. 971.

1934

Jubilee Volume in Honour of Chief Rabbi Dr. S. Hevesi. ארבעה מחקרים בתלמוד ובמדרש: pp. 51–67.

MGWJ, vol. lxxviii. Das Motiv vom veruntreuten Depositum in der jüdischen Volkskunde: pp. 183–95.

REJ, vol. xcvii. L'Âge de la Kedoucha de l'Amida: pp. 35–49.

—— vol. xcviii. Dioclétien à la lumière de la littérature rabbinique: pp. 19–43.

Studi e Materiali di Storia delle Religioni, vol. x. Rites of Mourning in Judaism: pp. 80–94.

Qiriath Sepher, vol. xi. Review of Klausner's ישו הנוצרי: pp. 22–8.

—— vol. xi. Review of Danby's Translation of the Mishnah: pp. 315–16.

Near East and India, 1 Mar. Review of Danby's Translation of the Mishnah: p. 169.

Dos Freie Wort, 5 Jan. דאס שטרעבען צו אסימילאציע אמאל און היינט: pp. 8–11.

—— 23 Feb. דאס שטרעבען צו אסימילאציע אמאל און היינט: pp. 4–5.

—— 4 May. דאס שטרעבען צו אסימילאציע אמאל און היינט: pp. 8–11.

Jewish Times. Greetings on the Paper's 21st Anniversary.

Jewish Chronicle, 2 Sept. German Jews in Spain: p. 17.

1935

Festschrift für Aron Freimann. Zum Wortlaut der Keduschah: pp. 162–6.

HUCA, vol. x. Judaism and Christianity in the Middle of the 3rd Century: pp. 223–63.

Maimonides. Anglo-Jewish Papers in connection with the Eighth Centenary of his birth. The place of Maimonides's *Mishne Torah* in the history and development of the Halacha: pp. 157–74.

Tarbiz, vol. vi, No. 3. Maimonides Number. ספר דיני תפלה ומועדים של ר' מימון אבי הרמב"ם: pp. 182–4.

London Quarterly and Holborn Review, July. Judaism and Gentile Christianity in the 3rd Century: pp. 363–71.

JRAS. Review of Davidson's *Book of the Wars of the Lord*: pp. 767–70.

Alim, vol. ii, No. 2. דברים אחדים על המוכיחים במאה הי'ד למספרם: pp. 37–41.

Near East and India. Review of Kaplan's *Redaction of the Babylonian Talmud*: pp. 106–7.

1936

Studies in Honour of Haham Dr. Gaster's 80th birthday. Comparisons between Greek and Jewish Religious Customs and Popular Usages: pp. 409–23.

Studies in Honour of Chief Rabbi Dr. Landau. מלחמתה של הכנסיה הנוצרית נגד היהדות ע'פ אגדה אחת: pp. 44–50.

Essays in Honour of Professor Samuel Krauss. מאמר על ערכה ההיסטורי של האגדה: pp. 55–68.

Hasoqer, vol. iv. מחקרים באגדה, pp. 131–45. (Reprinted in the Blau memorial volume.)

1937

The Old Rabbinic Doctrine of God, II. *Essays in Anthropomorphism.* Essays: 163 pp. London.

Studies in Honour of Professor Edward Mahler's 80th Birthday. Egyptian Mythology and Babylonian Magic in Bible and Talmud: pp. 469–87.

Volume in Honour of Professor Freimann's 70th Birthday. המצב הכלכלי של היהודים בגליל בדורו של רבי יוחנן בר נפחא ובדור שלאחריו: pp. 72–80.

JQR, vol. xxvii, No. 4. The Synagogue of Claudius Tiberius Poly-
charmus in Stobi: pp. 373–84.

MGWJ, vol. lxxxii. Review of Grünwald's *Vienna*: pp. 511–14.

1940

Studies in Honour of Dr. B. M. Lewin's 60th Birthday. מעלת תלמוד
תורה: pp. 140–60.

1942

Essays presented to J. H. Hertz. The Confession of Sins for the Day of
Atonement: pp. 293–305.

Sinai, vol. v, May. I. רעיון הגאולה באגדת התנאים והאמוראים: pp. 298–
311.

1943

*Saadyah Studies: in commemoration of the Thousandth Anniversary of
the death of R. Saadya Gaon.* The Doctrine of Redemption in
Saadya's Theological System: pp. 103–18.

JQR, vol. xxxvii, No. 2. The oldest form of the Eighteen Benedictions:
pp. 137–59.

Sinai, vol. vii, Aug.–Sept. II. רעיון הגאולה באגדת התנאים והאמוראים:
pp. 156–74.

Mezudah, vol. i, Feb. בעלי מוסר בישראל: pp. 87–96.

—— vol. ii, Dec. מרעיונות הגאולה באגדת האמוראים: pp. 94–105.

1944

Melilah, vol. i. הקיסר יוליאנוס באגדת רב אחא: pp. 93–120.

Sinai, vol. viii, June–Sept. III. רעיון הגאולה באגדת התנאים והאמוראים:
pp. 43–53.

1945

Sinai, vol. ix, June–Sept. האמונה בנצח ישראל בדרשות התנאים והאמוראים:
pp. 314–24.

Studies in Honour of Professor Louis Ginzberg's 70th Birthday. The
Introduction of R. Hoshaya to the first chapter of Genesis Rabba:
pp. 247–52.

Mezudah, vol. iii, June. תורת „בריה חדשה" באגדת ישראל ובאגרות השליחים:
pp. 134–51.

The Religion of the Jew: pp. 13–23. London.

1946

JQR, vol. xxxvii, No. 2. A Greek Lyric and a Hebrew Prophet: pp. 169–74.

Edoth, vol. i, No. 2. I. מקום האגדה בקורות הדתות: pp. 75–89.

—— vol. i, No. 3. II. מקום האגדה בקורות הדתות: pp. 169–74.

POSTHUMOUS
1948

Journal of Jewish Studies, vol. i, No. 1. The Jewish 'Blessing of Virginity': pp. 33–4.

Mezudah, vol. iv. מלחמת התנאים והאמוראים בהתבוללות: pp. 207–15.

Compiled by EMILE MARMORSTEIN

PART I (ENGLISH)

THE BACKGROUND OF THE HAGGADAH

PART I

Marcion and the Jewish Religion

I

IT was up till recently impossible to ascertain Marcion's place in, and influence on, the history of the Jewish religion. That we must make room on the pages of our history for Marcion was rightly recognized by H. Graetz,[1] who, however, in spite of his diligent researches into Jewish history and his keen sense for Gnostic movements and their influence on Judaism, devotes only about half a dozen lines to this truly extraordinary personality. He is surely not to be blamed for being brief on this occasion, and merits praise for even mentioning him in his description of Jewish conditions, spiritual and intellectual, in the second century C.E. Marcion with his adherents and followers did in fact contribute a great deal towards shaping Rabbinic theology and Jewish religion. Although his name is never mentioned in Jewish sources, nor is there any reason for supposing him to have been of Jewish origin, he is the ultimate source of many criticisms and attacks made on the Jewish doctrine of God, the Scriptures, and Israel. The real importance of Marcion was often surmised by scholars but was first truly established only a few years ago by Adolf von Harnack in his work on Marcion.[2] The wealth of material collected and the far-reaching conclusions arrived at by the great German theologian in this publication concern students of Jewish theology in no lesser measure than they interest the student of Christian origins and cognate problems.

---

[1] *Geschichte*, iv. 4 (Leipzig, 1908), pp. 87, 90 ff.
[2] *Marcion, das Evangelium vom Fremden Gott* (Leipzig, 1921 f.).

B

It is idle to speculate nowadays what the history of the
world would have looked like, how the course of humanity
would have shaped itself, if the Gospel of Marcion had
triumphed over the teaching of early Christianity. His
horror of bloodshed, of war, of cruelty of all kinds, on the
one side, might have been the greatest blessing to a world
steeped in blood and murder during the last 1,800 years.
His condemnation of marriage, his loathing of the propaga-
tion of children, on the other, might have out-balanced this
and led to the extermination of the human race. Who can
dare to say what, under these conditions and circumstances,
might have been the course of Jewish history? It is better
to eschew such dreams and visions and remain on the firm
ground of the actual life and work of the heresiarch, about
which we have plenty of information.

The city of Sinope, in the Pontus, on the south coast of
the Black Sea, produced a number of great men. The cynic
Diogenes, the Jewish Bible-translator Aquila, and the
greatest critic of the Bible, Marcion, first saw the light of
day there. The two latter, the great admirer and the great
enemy of the Bible, were contemporaries. It would be of
the greatest interest to know whether these two men ever
met, ever saw each other, ever aired their views one before
the other. No record is available to answer these queries.
Jews and Jewish communities were scattered over all the
towns and cities of the Pontus. Old-Rabbinic literature preserved the name of Pontus.[1] There is a possibility that
another translator of the Bible, namely Theodotion, also
hailed from the Pontus,[2] if reliance can be placed on a
somewhat obscure report. Marcion's personal relations with
Jews and Judaism are not recorded; even his contacts with
Christianity are not very clear. Altogether the heresiarch
did not provide his admirers and opponents with biographical material, as lesser men in his and all times have

---

[1] Krauss, *Gr. L. W.* ii. 429.
[2] *v.* Harnack, op. cit., p. 21, n. 1.

done. Many saints are prone to self-advertisement, sometimes under the cloak of humility. His date, and this is of primary importance for our investigation, can be fixed, with some certainty, between 85 and 165 C.E. His personal influence was at one time so great and his intellectual power so predominant that the whole edifice of the Christian Church was in great danger of collapsing in face of the churches founded by him. In the West a host of clergy and Church Fathers, like Justin, Irenaeus, Tertullian, Origen, and others, fought against Marcion and his followers, and prevailed. The crisis passed in the West. Not so in the East. There Marcion's teaching had a longer life. There it flourished till the fifth century, or longer, till it grew old, and was supplanted by new sects, e.g. the Manichees.

We Jews, naturally, can only look as outsiders on the struggle between Marcion and the Church Fathers. It concerns us, however, that Marcion was followed in Syria, Mesopotamia, and Palestine during a part of the Tannaitic period and the whole of the age of the Amoraim. Yet, it may be asked, how does that affect Jews and Judaism? The answer is that, since Marcion's thoughts centred around the Hebrew Bible and the Jewish Doctrine of God, his activity, his influence, could not remain limited to Christians, but left very remarkable traces on Jews and Jewish communities. It must have provoked a response among Jews, just as among Christians. Jewish teachers were forced to protest against Marcion's doctrine or to defend their own, just as was done by the Church Fathers. However great the gulf was between the latter and the former, practical considerations taught both that with the loss of the Bible, Church and Synagogue, Christianity as well as Judaism, are doomed for ever. One has only to look at the *Antitheses* of Marcion—that is to say, at the fragments of it preserved in the works of the Church Fathers, to find clear proofs for these statements. Marcion's teachings contained just as great a danger for the Church as for the Synagogue.

However that may be, Jews who came into contact—and how could they avoid it?—with Marcion's pupils and followers in Rome or Antioch, in Tiberias or Caesarea, were very deeply impressed by the questions raised or the contradictions pointed out by agitators and fanatics. The Bible, the only treasure which escaped the fire of Jerusalem, was in the greatest possible danger. The doctrine of God, as taught and believed in the synagogues and the houses of the Jews, was at stake. The very existence of the Jewish people, weakened as it was by so many political disasters and sectarian quarrels, seemed threatened.

The difficulties felt by readers of the Bible are older than Marcion and his age. When readers of the Scriptures asked their questions and expressed their surprise at this or that law or story, Jewish circles as well as Jewish Christians applied to them the allegorical method of interpretation by which troublesome passages could be smoothed out. Old Alexandrian doctrines and Philonic ideas were brought forward from antiquated storehouses of learning and dusty corners of religious or philosophic thought to defend the Bible. Marcion contended that the letter of the text must be adhered to. There were others who eliminated inconvenient passages as forgeries. Marcion was more consistent than these. Either the whole, or nothing. Is it at all likely that such a gigantic fight, for and against the Bible, should have left the Jews cold? Or could it remain unknown to them; a secret to those who visited the synagogues, and their spiritual leaders? Our object here is to consult the Rabbinic sources on these questions. By such an investigation we can only gain. First of all we may be enabled by it to pierce through the darkness covering those ages, and secondly to comprehend better the background of the teachings of the Haggadah.

II

The chief feature of Marcion's teaching was the doctrine of the two gods—the Demiurgos, the god of the Jews, the god of this world, the known god, on one side, and the highest god, the great unknown god, on the other side. We shall have to say something about the nature of these two gods later on. Here it may be sufficient to point out that this dualistic conception of the Godhead is common to all teachers and sects who sail under the flag of Gnosticism. They differ from one another in many details, both important and petty, but in the principle of dualism they concur. Marcion's dualism is, however, at variance with the dualism of the other Gnostics. He speaks of an unknown God, who is none else but Jesus, the Christian God. ʾ ʾnolars are still arguing and inquiring whence this dualistic theory originated; whether it came from Iran or Greece;[1] whether it purposed to answer the old query: *Unde malum?* or syncretize Polytheism and Monotheism, or bridge over the unbridgeable. Who knows? One fact is clear, that these theories made considerable inroads among Jews as well as among Christians and pagans. Otherwise their frequent occurrence in earlier and later sources of the Midrashic literature cannot be properly accounted for.

Let us consider first statements bearing on this point, on the dualistic theories of the Gnostics. We begin with the Unbeliever,[2] or according to another source the Emperor, who essayed to prove to R. Gamaliel II from the Scriptures that the God who created the mountains did not create the wind. This interlocutor was a dualist, but by no means a Marcionite, for the latter would never have raised such a difficulty. Surely, the one Demiurgos created both. We can

---

[1] *v.* Zeller, *Philosophie der Griechen*, 3rd ed., vol. ii a. 591 ff.

[2] B. Sanh. 39a א"ל האי כופר cf. Yalḳuṭ Makhiri, *Amos*, ed. Greenup (London, 1910), p. 69 קיסר inst. of כופר. cf. also Yalḳuṭ Makhiri, *Psalms*, ed. Buber, 94.11.

hardly suppose Marcionite teaching to have been current
so early as in the time of R. Gamaliel. Marcion never tried
to prove, nor did he assert that the Bible teaches the existence of more than one God, one Creator. What he said was
that he is not the Supreme Being, he is inferior to the Unknown God. Next to R. Gamaliel II, his contemporary R.
Akiba has to be mentioned. His polemic is directed against
dualists who believe in two gods, e.g. Heaven and Earth.[1]
Expounding according to his own exegetical methods
Gen. i. 1, he says that some people might infer from this
verse that Heaven and Earth are two gods but the particles
את nullify such a construction. Marcion knew better than to
teach such doctrines. The dualists of R. Akiba could not,
therefore, have been followers of Marcion. A late Talmudic
tradition makes Elisha ben Abuyah, a contemporary of R.
Akiba, a believer in dualistic theories. No dicta of his are
preserved which would enable us to form a correct opinion
of his attitude towards Gnostic doctrines. There is a report
in Aramaic,[2] according to which Aḥer saw Metatron sitting
and writing the merits of Israel. This vision gave rise to
doubts and scepticism in the heart of Aḥer. There was
namely a tradition that there is neither sitting, nor strife,
nor weariness above. Aḥer, therefore, concluded that there
must be two powers, God and Metatron.[3] Too much weight

---

[1] Tanḥ. (ed. Buber) i. 5 f. R. Ishmael and R. Akiba, אלו נאמר שמים
וארץ היינו אומר'/ שתי אלהות הן Gen. R. 1. 14. v. also Midrash Abkhir,
ed. Marmorstein, Dvir, i (1923), 126–7; v. also Aptowitzer, MGWJ lxxiii
(1929), 114, who sees in this discussion between R. Ishmael and R. Akiba an
allusion to the Christian doctrine of the Trinity, because the idea of Heaven
and Earth being regarded as deities must appear stupid (unsinnig). It is still
to be proved that R. Akiba had the faintest idea of the Trinity, furthermore
whether R. Akiba paid any attention at all to Christian beliefs and teachings.
R. Akiba must have known more about the Greek conception of divinity
and about the mythological meaning of Ge and Uranos among his contemporaries than we give him credit for.

[2] B. Ḥag. 15a.

[3] Metatron has been the subject of many ill-founded speculations. One
identifies him with Mithra, v. ZfWTh xxvii. 357, Graetz, Gnosticismus und
Judenthum, p. 44 with the Demiurgos; also MGWJ viii. 105; v. also Dukes,
Zur Kenntnis der Poesie, p. 108; Joel, Blicke, i. 127, n. 1; Kerem Ḥemed, iii. 51,

should not be attached to this statement in any attempt to establish Aḥer's peculiar heresy. As a Jewish Gnostic, he might have taught and believed in the existence of the Highest and Metatron. The next teacher who is to be mentioned here is a contemporary of Marcion, R. Simon ben Yoḥai. He combats dualism by means of a parable about citizens criticizing a palace built by their king. The original form is preserved in the Tannaitic Midrash on Deuteronomy, the Sifre; the later sources have an altered and adapted version. This can be clearly seen by comparing the text of the different sources. These are: (a) Sifre,[1] (b) Midrash Tannaim,[2] (c) Gen. R.,[3] and (d) Eccl. R.[4] In Gen. R. and Eccl. R. Simon ben Yoḥai's parable appears in a series, the order of which is somewhat puzzling. Both have R. Huna (two sayings), R. Ḥona, R. Naḥman (two parables), R. Simon ben Yoḥai, R. Levi ben Ḥayta, and R. Isaac ben Meryon. The Haggadah concludes with a saying of R. Levi in the name of R. Phinehas. The order cannot be justified and appears strange. Yet the name of R. Simon ben Yoḥai cannot be a mistake for a later teacher, for instance R. Simeon ben Laḳish, since the saying agrees, with variants, with a saying ascribed to R. Simon ben Yoḥai in the older sources.

suggested to read מטטרון. v. also H.B. ix. 38, xx. 36. We find the term in Sifre Deut. § 338 באצבעו היה מראה מטטרון למשה, Gen. R. 5.3 (Ben Azzai) יושב ומלמד תורה לתינוקות, B. AZ. 3b נעשה קולו של הקב"ה מטטרון למשה של בית רבן, B. Sanh. 38b. R. Idi זה מטטרון ששמו כשם רבו, Jellinek, BhM iii. 16 and 33, Tractate Aṣilut 76b. הנהפך מבו"ד לאיש לוהט, Ps. El. Zutta, ch. 26, ed. Friedmann, p. 31 קורא למטטרון וא"ל קראתי שמך בשמי A.B. of R. Akiba, ed. Wertheimer, p. 10. He is identified with the prophet Elijah, v. קבוצת חכמים 31, Geiger's Jüd. Zeitsch. vi. 166 v. 66. Goldziher, Kobak's Jeschurun, viii. 103 Schorr החלוץ viii. 4, Roth, ZDMG vi. 69; Windischmann, Mithra, p. 36; Weinstein, Zur Genesis der Agada, ii, p. 57.

[1] Sifre Deut. § 307, ed. Friedmann, 132b f.
[2] ed. Hoffmann, p. 187.
[3] Gen. R. ch. 12, ed. Theodor, p. 98 f.
[4] Eccl. R. to 2. 12.

Sifre	Midr. Tannaim	Eccl. Rabba	Gen. Rabba
הצור תמים פעלו הצייר שהוא צר העולם תחלה וצר בו את האדם תמים פעלו פעולתו שלימה על כל באי העולם ואין להרהר אחר מדותיו אפי׳ עוולה של כלום ואין אחד מהם שיסתכל ויאמר אלו היה לי ג׳ עינים, אלו היה לי ג׳ ידים, אלו היו לי ג׳ רגלים, אלו הייתי מהלך על ראשי, אלו היו פני הפוכים לאחורי כמה היה נאה, ת״ל כי כל דרכיו.	תמים פעלו פעולתו שלימה עם כל באי העולם¹ אין אדם בעולם שיאמר² אלו היו לי שלש עינים, אלו היו לי שלש רגלים אלו היו לי שלש ידים, אלו היו פני הפוכות לאחור אלו הייתי מהלך על ראשי הייתי נאה³ למה? כי כל דרכיו משפט.	ארשב״י מלה״ד למלך בו״ד שבנה פלטין וכלהעוברים ושבים נכנסים לתוכה ואמרואילו היו עמודיה גבוהים היתה נאה, אילו היו כותליה גבוהים היתה נאה, אילו היתה תקרתה גבוהי היתה נאה⁴ שמא יבוא איש ויאמר אילו היו לי ג׳ ידים או ג׳ עינים או ג׳ אזנים או ג׳ רגלים הייתי נאה ת״ל את אשר כבר עשוהו אכ״ב עשהו אלא עשוהו כביכול הקב״ה ובד״עשוהו, נמנים על כל אבר ואבר משלך ומעמידך על תוכנך וא״ת שתי רשויות הן והלא כבר נאמר והוא עשך ויכוננך.	אמר רשב״י משל למלך בו״ד שבנה פלטין והביריות נכנסין בתוכה ואומרים אילו היו העמודים גבוהים היתה נאה, אילו היוהכתלים גביהים היתה נאה, אילו היתה תיקרה גבוהה היתה נאה, שמא יבוא אדם ויאמר אילו היו לי ג׳ עינים או ג׳ רגלים אתמהא! ואתאשר כבר עשהו אין כתיב כאן אלא את אשר כבר עשוהו, כביכול מלך מלכי המלכים ברוך הוא ובית דינו ממנין על כל אבר ואבר משלך ומעמידך על תוכנך הוא עשך ויכוננך.

¹ S. reads על, MT. עם.

² This version is shorter and simpler than that of Sifre.

³ Notice the difference in the order between S. and MT. Sifre has (a) eyes, (b) hands, (c) feet; MT. (a), (c), (b). Further S. has first מהלך על ראשי and then פני הפוכים MT. vice versa. The omission in the Sifre and MT. of the reference to God and His heavenly court, and its insertion in the younger Midrashim, is very instructive. It corroborates an assumption made by the present writer in another place, that the whole conception of God with His heavenly court, or academy, is not older than the third century, and was apparently unknown to the Haggadists of the Tannaitic age. See Marmorstein, 'Anges et hommes dans l'Agada', REJ lxxxiv (1927), 37–51, and ibid. 138–41.

⁴ The parable of the king and his palace is not in S. and MT. The agreement begins with שמא יבוא. Attention may be called to the fact that in the

A comparison of these passages leaves no doubt about the origin of the saying. Just as there can be no question as to the mutual relation of these four sources to one another, so there can be no doubt as to the origin of these criticisms. What necessity was there on R. Simon ben Yohai's part to bring such questions to the pulpit? He obviously wants to ridicule the Marcionite talk about the *pusillitates* of the Creator, the Demiurgos. Tertullian inveighs against the 'impudent' Marcionites in the Church just in the same way as, at the same time, R. Simon ben Yohai in the Synagogue. Tertullian says about the Marcionites: 'contravertuntur ad destructionem operum creatoris; nimirum, inquiunt, grande opus et dignum deo mundus'.[1] The creation of the world and man are bad, an abominable failure. R. Simon ben Yohai retorts: Nobody can complain about not having three hands, eyes, ears, legs, &c.

III

This Piska, which is ascribed to R. Simon ben Yohai, will amply repay closer examination. Bearing in mind the *pusillitates* of the Demiurgos, ascribed to him by Marcion, we may find in the four homilies preserved in our Piska four sermons dealing with Marcion's objections to the Bible. We have observed that one of these homilies is older than the third century; and the same date may be given to the other homilies. All of them expound Deut. 32. 4. Each sentence brings out with great force the perfectness of God's work, the justice of His ways, and His truth and uprightness, all of which were partly misjudged, partly denied by Marcionite theologians; for though they recognized His justice they declared it to be faulty.[2]

---

parable people are allowed to visit the palace. The parable exaggerates in assuming that the palaces might have been open to sightseers and passers-by. The visits, surely, were limited to guests and distinguished visitors.

[1] *Adv. haeres.* i. 13.

[2] Each of the first three homilies is closely connected with the text, the fourth is rather fragmentary, yet can be completed by means of the Ps.-

The first homily, undoubtedly, rejects one of Marcion's criticisms of the work of the Creator. The creation of man must not be considered as a gross failure. God trusted the world. Man was not created to be wicked, but to become just. He deals rightly with man. Each of these concluding sentences of this first homily is a retort against Marcionite calumnies, that God is envious of the world, inspired by evil desires to make man wicked, and is treating him badly. The second homily refutes another of Marcion's much emphasized *pusillitates*. The subject of the homily is the same as that of the first one. The Creator's deeds are perfect with all his creatures. Evil intentions, unworthy aims, which the Creator is alleged to have harboured in his innermost heart, must not be mentioned or thought of. 'None can or may say: Why was the generation of the Flood drowned, why was the generation of the Tower dispersed from one end of the earth to the other, why were the inhabitants of Sodom burnt by fire and brimstone, Korah and his set swallowed up by the earth, Aaron distinguished by the dignity of the priesthood, or why was David crowned? Why? Because God grants to each individual what he rightly deserves.' What had the preacher in mind in referring to the punishment of the generations of the Flood and the Dispersion, Sodomites and Korah on one side, and about the priesthood of Aaron and the Kingdom of David on the other side? Without Marcion we cannot fathom the purpose of this homily. We have only to compare this homily with Marcion to discuss clearly the undoubted background of this Haggadah. Marcion proves the Creator to be *conditor malorum* by relating and elaborating the story of the Flood, the destruction of Sodom, the plagues of Egypt, the hardening

Jonathan Targum on Deut. 32. 4. The arrangement of the different homilies illustrates types of sermons as preached in the second century. Put in their proper light they reflect the anxieties and worries felt by preacher and audience alike. The proper understanding of the external form is as much needed as the history of the thoughts which agitated the minds of the authors of these homilies; however, that must be left for discussion in a later chapter.

of Pharaoh's heart, the visiting of the fathers' sin on their children, and the favouring of the wicked, and giving honour to and exalting bad men. Among the latter, naturally, one would not miss David, Solomon, Lot and his daughters, Moses, and Joshua.[1] Does our homily not read exactly like a refutation of Marcion's theories? Can it be an accident that the Jewish preacher mentions in the first part the Flood, Sodom, Korah, &c., and in the second part Aaron and David, almost the same people whom Marcion selects for the opposite view? That cannot be a mere accident. There must have been channels which led from the Marcionites to the synagogues and back. We shall soon be able to show that this homilist was by no means the only one who felt himself forced to stand in the breach. There were a number of Jewish sages who repelled Marcionite attacks. Our preacher concludes with describing God as a faithful treasurer, who rewards and punishes according to man's deeds.

The third homily[2] is also of the same age, and pursues the same aim as the previous two. God pays the reward of the righteous, and punishes the wicked, but the good deeds of the latter and the sins of the former are not lost sight of. Everything will right itself at the future judgement. These doctrines are pointed out very sharply in order to combat heretical opinions on these subjects. Marcion believed in and stated very precisely God's justice, just like the Rabbis, but even this virtue was marred by being faulty. This seems to me to be the subject of the fourth homily, which is preserved only in a fragmentary form.

IV

Was there any need on the part of Jewish teachers and

---

[1] For fuller details about Marcion, v. von Harnack, op. cit., p. 95.

[2] The first two homilies have as their subject: פעולתו שלימה על (עם) כל. The third one is headed: פעולתם של באי העולם שלימה לפניו‏:
the deeds of creatures are perfect before Him.

preachers to pay such attention to these heretical views?
Is it not something of an exaggeration to suppose that these
few resemblances and refutations reveal new spiritual and
intellectual influences, of which the commentators of these
Rabbinic documents never dreamt? What evidence have
we of such close social and commercial relations between
Jews and Gentiles as would justify us in assuming such a
far-reaching influence of Marcionite propaganda among
Jews? The reply is that such a long and dry catalogue of
God's sins and shortcomings, as was preached and proclaimed in the assemblies and schools of Marcion's followers,
could not have remained a secret to Jews who dwelt among
them. The Rabbis, just like the Church Fathers, and perhaps even more so, had to take up the cudgels for their
God and Bible. It is well established that the list of God's
sins in the Clementine Homilies (ii. 48 f.) faithfully reproduces the attitude of Marcion and his followers to the
Hebrew Bible. Here it is in brief. 'God lies, makes experiments as in ignorance, deliberates and changes his purpose,
envies, hardens hearts, makes blind and deaf, commits
pilfering, mocks, is weak, unjust, makes evil things, does
evil, desires the fruitful hill, is false, dwells in a tabernacle,
is fond of fat, sacrifices, offerings, &c., is pleased with
candles and candlesticks, dwells in shadow, darkness,
storms and smoke, comes with trumpets, shoutings, darts
and arrows, loves war, is without affection, is not faithful
to his promises, loves the wicked and adulterers and murderers, changes his mind, chooses evil men.' Twenty-four
charges—the number is a favourite in Rabbinic writings—
all of them based on narratives in the Scriptures! Such
voices could not have been silenced at any time merely
by ignoring them. These assertions must have made an
immense impression on Jews of the most varied types of
upbringing and sentiment. They must have turned with
their troubles and difficulties to their spiritual guides and
leaders. Are there any traces of these attempts to refute

these slanders and damaging attacks against the religion of the Jews? I propose to treat them individually.

1. God lies! The Rabbis assert in many places that God's name or seal is truth. R. Isaac, in the third century, seems to have had this heresy in mind when preaching on God and Truth. His sermon is based on Ps. 119. 160 ('The beginning of thy word is truth'), cf. Jer. 10. 10 ('and the Lord God is truth'). Since He is truth and His word is truth, all His decrees are just, and no creature could plead that *two powers* gave the Law, two powers created the world.[1] No student of Marcion's religion can miss the significant points in this preacher's homily, while on the other hand no pilpulistic Midrash exegesis could ever guess them. Analysing the preacher's words, we see first of all that God's truthfulness or His identification with truth is deduced from Scriptural evidence. God does not lie, but He is truth. Secondly, whence do people get the notion of God's untruth or lack of truth? By finding fault with God's justice. This, however, is no ground, for His deeds and decrees are just. Thirdly, this being the case, that God is truthful and just, the whole theory of the two gods falls to the ground. R. Isaac, whose teachings are full of the defence of Judaism and polemics against heathendom, Gnostics, and probably Christians as well, may have known or heard of Marcion's teachings.[2] R. Abin,[3] another teacher of the same type and predilections as R. Isaac, explains the same passage in Jeremiah by emphasizing the doctrine of God's Eternity and single Rulership of the world. An often repeated saying has it that truth is the seal of God.[4] In later

[1] Gen. R. ch. 1, ed. Theodor, p. 4.

[2] *v.* Marmorstein, *Religionsgeschichtliche Studien*, i, p. 17, p. 42; ii, p. 62, p. 69.

[3] J. Ber. i. 5.

[4] R. Ḥanina b. Ḥama, B. Sabb. 55a חותמו של הקב״ה אמת, B. Yoma 69b, J. Sanh. 18a. R. Bibi in the name of R. Reuben, חותמו של הקב״ה אמת. Deut. R. 1. 7, Cant. R. 1. 45, Gen. R. 81.

sources truth becomes one of the Divine names.[1] On what
basis the actual charge of God's untruthfulness might have
been made is not recorded.

2. The accusation that God makes experiments, and is
not omniscient, is based on God's testing Abraham (Gen.
22. 1). The difficulty in the text stands, whether one
translates 'God did test Abraham' or 'God tempted Abraham'. The Haggadah shows traces of discussions on this
point, which prove that the generations before Marcion
must have paid close attention to this problem. At least no
direct influence of Marcion can be established. R. Yose the
Galilean must have had a very cogent reason for stating
that נסה means neither 'tested' nor 'tempted', but that
God exalted Abraham as the flag of a boat is hoisted.
R. Akiba is inclined to take the verb literally. God really
tested Abraham; he was free to obey or disobey. Why did
God test him and leave him free choice? In order that the
nations should not argue: 'He was confused, bewildered,
and he was not conscious of his actions!'[2]

Another difficulty of the same sort was provided by
Exod. 15. 25, and was felt strongly before Marcion launched
his destructive criticism of the Bible. This case is noteworthy from more than one point of view, showing as it
does the persistence of the attack as well as of the defence.
R. Joshua ben Ḥananya disposes of the difficulty of ושם
נסהו in the same manner as R. Yose the Galilean did later on
with והאלהים נסה.[3] R. Eleazar of Modi'im agrees with R.

---

[1] v. Marmorstein, *The Old Rabbinic Doctrine of God*, i (London, 1927),
p. 73.

[2] Gen. R. 55, ed. Theodor 589, Tanḥ. (ed. Buber) וירא, old ed. fol. 26,
Agadat Bereshit 31. 2. Pes. R. 170a. It is difficult to establish with any degree
of certainty whom R. Akiba had in mind when quoting this real or possible
assertion of the nations. All the same, the argument must actually have taken
place. The same diatribe is used by the Syrian Church Father Ephraem,
v. *MGWJ*. xliii. 530, yet it is doubtful whether he copied R. Akiba; or did
he quote a saying current in his days? It is not impossible that both Akiba
and Ephraem disputed with representatives of the same schools.

[3] Mekh. 46a, MRSbY, p. 73 שם נשא לו גדולה or שם נעשה נסאון לישראל
based on II Kings 25. 27.

Akiba.[1] The two latter do not object to the literal meaning
of the text, the former explain the difficulty away. A later
teacher, disregarding the text, makes of the sentence:
'Our fathers tested God'.[2] Surely only under great pressure
of Gnostic attacks could such a forced explanation have been
given!

Exod. 20. 20 לבעבור נסות אתכם offered Gnostics and Bible
critics of various schools a good opportunity to assert that
God makes experiments and is ignorant, otherwise why
should He say: 'In order to test you?' Here, the Mekhilta,
disregarding the view of R. Eleazar of Modi'im and R.
Akiba, records merely the alternative opinion. The verb
לנסות does not mean 'to test', but 'to exalt', 'magnify'.[3]
Nevertheless, the view and teaching of R. Akiba was
adopted and expanded in the following centuries. R. Isaac,
R. Yose b. Ḥanina, and R. Eleazar b. Pedat exemplified by
parables the conception that God actually tested Abraham.
A potter knocks harder on the sound pots than on the weak
ones. A flax maker tries the strong flax, the farmer places
the heavier burden on the strong animal; so God tests the
righteous people, and not the wicked; the former can stand
trials, not so the latter.[4] But could these Tannaim and

---

[1] Ibid. שם נסה המקום את ישראל.

[2] MRSbY, p. 73 ד"א ושם נסהו שם ניסו אבותינו את המקום.

[3] Mekh. 72a, MRSbY, p. 114 בשביל לגדל אתכם בא האלקים Ps.-
Jonathan, Gen. 22. 1, Exod. 15. 25 (ותמן נסייה בנסיונא עשיריתא) and 20. 17
(מן בגלל לנסיותכון) follows R. Akiba's school and methods.

[4] Gen. R. ch. 55. 1, ed. Th. 585, ch. 32, ed. Th. 290, where, however,
R. Isaac's parable is cited in the name of R. Jonathan b. Eli'ezer, ch. 34,
ed. Th., p. 314, likewise Tanḥ. (ed. Buber) שמות 10, וירא 43, Cant. R.
21. 6. M. Ps. 11. 4 with variants, pointed out in Theodor's commentary.

One may take the opportunity here to call attention to the affinity between
Stoic teaching and Haggadah, another large subject which illuminates the
background of the Haggadah from a different point of view. The idea and the
aim of this teaching, as represented by the teachers mentioned in the text,
fully agrees with maxims to be found in the writings of the Stoa. Seneca,
de Prov. i, says: 'God does not keep a *good man* in prosperity, *He tries*, He
strengthens him, He preserves him for Himself.' Or, ibid. iv: 'Those whom
God approves of, whom He loves, He *burdens*, *He proves*, *He exercises*, but
those whom He seems to indulge and spare, He prepares for future ills.'

Amoraim not see the danger of broadcasting the idea that
God tests people? Did they not confirm the antagonists in
their view that God makes experiments and acts in ignorance? No! The tests were real, but not as experiments and
marks of God's ignorance, but to serve as proofs to the world
that God's chosen ones were pious, righteous, and worthy
of God's favour. Now, this latter point, as we saw already
above, and will have frequent occasion to mention again,
was harped on most religiously and continuously by Marcion
and his followers. The allegation of God's ignorance was
not so dangerous as the teaching that God chooses unworthy,
and punishes good people.[1] It was therefore emphasized
that the pious and worthies of the Bible were not evildoers
and culprits, they only proved their worth. A feeble but
very interesting solution of our difficulty is offered by R.
Abin. He makes Israel point out contradictions between
Scriptural passages. They are like pupils, we are told, who
find discrepancies between their master's word on the one
side and his doings on the other side. The questioners are
here Jews. Lev. 19. 18 prohibits the taking of vengeance.
Nahum 1. 2 states clearly that God takes vengeance.
Similarly, Deut. 6. 16 says 'Ye shall not test God', yet Gen.
22. 1 says 'And God tested Abraham'. The preacher explains by drawing a line between Israel and the Gentiles.[2]
However unsatisfactory the reply seems to be, one fact is
certain, that Marcion's *antitheses* penetrated into Jewish
circles, just as they found their way into Christian homes,
and stirred up feelings of contempt for the Bible. For these
questions are neither Christian nor pagan, but Marcion's, to
prove the great contrast between doctrine and practice in
the Bible.[3]

It must not be thought that the view of the opponents of

---

[1] v. above p. 11 and later on pp. 45 f.
[2] Gen. R. ch. 55, ed. Th. 586; Eccl. R. 8. 4, R. Levi.
[3] On this subject v. Marmorstein, 'Learning and Work', in *London Quarterly Review*, April 1925, 217–25.

R. Akiba, R. Joshua, and R. Yose the Galilean found no
followers, though curiously enough—and it must not be
accounted a mere accident, but may have a deeper reason,
which cannot be discussed here—it is found only in the
anonymous Haggadah. There the verb נסה is taken and
expounded in the sense ascribed to it by these teachers. God
did not test, but exalted Abraham. The anonymous teachers
of the Amoraic age preached under the dark shadow of
Marcionite influence. Why (was Abraham found righteous,
was he exalted)?—was the impatient and impertinent
question raised by the opponents. The answer is: In order
that the attribute of Justice should be justified![1] The
fragments of Marcionite teaching make it quite clear that
Marcion's chief objection was to the מדת הדין, the attribute
of strict justice. The known God, the God of the Jews,
shows no traces of affection, no signs of love, no vestige of
kindness. Strictest justice is observed, so that God becomes
cruel in Marcion's eyes. All the same, God is found guilty of
injustice in choosing wrong and unworthy people. There,
said the Rabbis, is one of Marcion's greatest blunders, one
that a schoolboy might commit. Such was this otherwise
great man's blindness. 'If a man tells thee: God makes rich,
poor, a king, in an arbitrary way! Abraham became rich,
a king! Reply to him: Canst thou do what Abraham did?'[2]
These two terms שלא יתן פתחון פה ל and ... אם יאמר לך אדם
are just as characteristic in the Jewish Haggadah as they
are significant for the Cynic-Stoic diatribe, as will be shown
in the second part of this essay. In the Haggadah as well as
in the Cynic-Stoic sermon the preacher or philosopher
introduces ideas, sayings, or arguments of real or imaginary
questioners. In order to refute their views, which the preacher
dislikes or deems harmful, they are put in this manner

---

[1] שתתקשט מדת הדין בעולם.

[2] Gen. R. ch. 55, ed. Theodor, 584 f. Tanḥ. (ed. Buber) וירא 43 concludes
כדי שלא ליתן פתחון פה לאומות לומר הוא מגדלן והוא לא נסה אותן ועמדו
בנסיון v. also Tanḥ. where the instances of Daniel and his friends are cited.

C

hypothetically. In our case we are not without proofs that such questions were actually raised, such objections aired by people who belonged to Marcion's way of thinking. It will suffice to refer the reader to the Matrona, who worried R. Yose b. Ḥalafta with about a score of Bible questions[1] and must have been imbued with Marcionite doctrines, as will be shown further on. She obviously was echoing her master's point of view when she said: 'Your God chooses whomsoever He likes! He is arbitrary in His choice.' The Scribe has no difficulty in demonstrating to her that God is capable of selecting the right people and rejecting the wrong ones.[2]

3. These tests and experiments of God are signs of His ignorance. So are the questions asked of Adam[3] and of Cain;[4] so, too, are His descents to various places, especially Sodom and Gomorrah.[5] He must descend, in order to see for himself what happens in Sodom, otherwise He would not be aware of the events below. These are some of His *pusillitates et infirmitates et incongruentes*. The first of these allegations was dealt with by one of the earliest Apologists of the Church, by Theophilus in his work addressed to Autolycus. This writer has many ideas and teachings in common with those found in the literary productions of the Scribes, before and after his day.[6] We cannot be wrong in assuming that Theophilus knew of Marcion and of his views. Theophilus surely had in mind teachings emanating from that quarter when he said: God did not ask this question (namely, 'Where art thou, Adam?' Gen. 3. 9) out of ignorance, but in his long-suffering. God wanted to give Adam a fair opportunity for *repentance* and *confession*.[7] I

---

[1] *v.* the list in my Midrash Abkhir, *Dvir*, i, p. 125.
[2] Num. R. 3. 2.
[3] *Ignorans ubi esset Adam*, Tert. iv. 20, *v.* Harnack, op. cit., p. 93.
[4] *De Cain sciscitatur ubinam frater ejus?* ibid.
[5] Tert. i. 11; Origen, *Hom.* viii. 8.
[6] *v.* A. Marmorstein, 'Jews and Judaism in the Earliest Christian Apologies, *Expositor* 1919, pp. 104 ff.
[7] ii. 21.

italicize these two words for a reason. The very same defence is preserved in a late Midrash, which surely used older material, the date of which must go back as far as the third century. I mean the Midrash Haggadah,[1] where we read: 'And God said to Adam: "Where art thou?" Did not God know where Adam was? Surely, He did, but He wanted to open a way for him, perhaps he might repent.' The very same point must have figured as one of the many attacks against the Bible collected and published in the period of the Geonim by Ḥiwi of Balkh, who is related spiritually to Marcion, and who inherited his views.[2] Dark corners of the East may have preserved Marcionite doctrines and writings, especially in Ḥiwi's native place or country, and he may have perused some of them. Of course, the possibility of Ḥiwi's acquaintance with Midrashic literature must not be lost sight of. The old heretical writings perished, yet their poisonous queries lived on in the literature of the Rabbis as well as in that of the Church Fathers. From wherever derived, they are eloquent witnesses to Marcion's influence in the Synagogue. The alteration of the word אַיֶּכָּה (Where art thou?) into אֵיכָה (How?) must be considered as an endeavour on the part of the Scribes to avoid our very troublesome query.[3]

Theophilus[4] secondly mentions God's question to Cain, Where is thy brother Abel? He says: 'But God, being pitiful, and willing to afford to Cain, *as to Adam*, an opportunity of repentance and confession, said: "Where is Abel thy brother?" ' Striking parallels can be quoted from the Midrash Haggadah,[5] Pseudo-Jonathan Targum,[6] the Chap-

---

[1] ed. Buber (Vienna, 1894), p. 8. A similar question may have been put by some heretical group also as to Num. 22. 9, and answered in a similar manner.

[2] v. Poznanski, *Hagoren*, vii. 118. Ibn Ezra's longer commentary on Genesis, ed. M. Friedländer, p. 39.

[3] Gen. R. 19. 9, ed. Theodor, p. 178 f. R. Yose b. Ḥanina, R. Abbahu in his name וקוננתי עליו איכה Pes. (ed. Buber) 119a, Lam. R. Intr. 4.

[4] ii. 29; v. Marmorstein, *Expositor*, l.c.

[5] Op. cit., p. 11.

[6] Gen. 3. 9.

ters of R. Eli'ezer,[1] the *Vita Adami*,[2] and the Gaon Saadia,[3] proving the antiquity and wide dissemination of this question. God is not ignorant, but He likes to open the door of repentance and confession to sinners, who are His creatures. The negation is just as important as the affirmation, considering the attitude of Marcion.

We turn from this later Haggadah to the earlier one, in which R. Abba b. Kahana refutes the third proof of this charge. Marcion, as far as our evidence goes, based his theory of the ignorance of the Demiurgos on Gen. 18. 21. An omniscient God need not go down and see! The Amora explains this phrase in the sense of giving the people of Sodom a fair chance of repentance.[4] Again the same argument as we met with in Theophilus and Rabbinic sources. The idea, however, is older. A preacher, whose name is not preserved, affirms that the generations of the Flood, of the Tower, the people of Sodom, and the Egyptians were granted an opportunity of repentance, but they did not avail themselves of God's offer.[5] Now, it cannot be a pure accident that these tannaitic homilists should have catalogued the very same people whom Marcion pointed out as examples of the gross cruelties committed by the Demiurgos. The last-mentioned preacher is not concerned about the ignorance of the Demiurgos, only about his justice. R. Abba b. Kahana, however, combined in his refutation both the charges of his opponents, namely, God's ignorance and His cruelty.

We have evidence of the great antiquity of the argument that God dces not, or did not, condemn the generations or the wicked without just cause and without giving them ample opportunity to repent. The Mekhilta offers a striking parallel to the passage of the Sifre Deut. already analysed.[6]

---

[1] Ch. xxi.
[2] Kautzsch, *Pseudepigraphen*, p. 522.
[3] *v. Saadia's Polemic against Ḥiwi al-Balkhi* (New York, 1915), p. 40.
[4] Gen. R. ch. 21, Theodor, p. 201, p. 359; and ch. 49, p. 504.
[5] Mekh. 38b, MRSbY, p. 62 f., but shortened.
[6] *v.* above, pp. 10–11.

In both Haggadahs God's action against the generations of
the Flood, the Tower, Sodom, and Egypt is defended or
excused, which shows, of course, that His actions had been
criticized. One has to bear in mind Marcion's and his followers' attitude towards these Bible narratives to grasp what
induced the older and younger teachers to recur so often to
this subject of the generations of the wicked. There is no
other explanation except the need to combat Marcionite
influence. Otherwise, one would like to know what need
is, or was, there to justify God's judgement? He is not
responsible to anyone! Who can call Him to account for
His deeds? There are many more passages in the Midrash
grouping these and other people of the same type together.
One preacher proves that just as God punished by the
East Wind the generations of the Flood, the Tower, Sodom,
Egypt, the Ten Tribes, Judah and Benjamin, Tyre, so will
He treat the wicked in the future.[1] The generations of the
Flood, of the Tower, and the Sodomites were punished
according to their deeds.[2] R. Abba b. Kahana, who lived in
the latter part of the third century and was more or less
acquainted with contemporary culture and knew some of the
manifestations of what was then considered modern thought,
found it necessary to refute heretical teachings. The older
way of thinking, as represented by Tannaim, saw no cause
for deviating from the accepted literal interpretation of these
passages. They enumerated the descents of God from
heaven[3] just as they did not mind enumerating the ten
trials of Abraham,[4] in spite of the great difficulties involved
in their teaching, as shown above, and in spite of the fact
that so early a writer as Aristobulus taught that these

---

[1] Mekh. 30b, אלא . . . וכן אתה מוצא שלא נפרע המקום מאנשי דור המבול
ברוח קדים עזה.

[2] Sifre Deut. § 310; v. also Gen. R. 9. 8; 5. 1; 12. 5, M. Ps. 13d, 16d.

[3] Mekh. 64a, MRSbY, 101, omitted; Sifre Num. § 93, Gen. R. ch. 38, ed.
Theodor, p. 358; R. Simon ben Yoḥai as author, ch. 49, p. 504, Abot R.
Nathan i, ch. 34, ii. 37. Pirḳe R. Eli'ezer, ch. 14 ff. (incomplete), Tanḥ.
§ 13a.

[4] Abot V. 3, Abot R. N. ch. 33, 34; Pirḳe R. E. ch. 26 ff.

descents must not be understood literally.[1] Furthermore, one of the Tannaim himself proclaimed that the passages speaking of God's descent and ascent must not be taken literally. It is not surprising to learn that this statement was made in one of his many discussions on religious problems with a lady who was rather inclined to the Gnostic way of thought.[2] Marcion's questions, as we see, produced many Dead-Sea fruits of apologetics. Yet there was also some practical result. The doctrine of God's omniscience was closely defined and concisely formulated in Rabbinic theology. God's omniscience is without limit and knows no boundary either in time or in space.

4. The Demiurgos suffers from ignorance, therefore he tests people, but he also deliberates and changes his purpose. The Church Fathers furnish several instances of this charge, and combine with it the *contrarietates preceptorum*. He regrets having created man, because he turned evil.[3] Marcion thought of Gen. 6. 6. R. Judah b. Ilai' and R. Nehemiah, teachers of the second century, pondered on the word וינחם (and he repented), and they try to soften the rather harsh meaning of the verb.[4] R. Joshua b. Ḳorḥa, also of the same period, had a discussion with a man who may have been a Marcionite, although he is styled גוי in our sources,[5] on this subject. God does not know the future. Consequently, He cannot be omniscient. A number of preachers of the third century, like R. Aibu, R. Levi, and many others, dealt with our problem. No wonder that in contemporary literary documents the wicked are made to say: 'God does not know what we are meditating, or doing in secret.'[6] Here again, one can only guess whether Ḥiwi of Balkh copied this heresy

---

[1] Eus. *Pr. Ev.* viii. 10, *Quest. Phil.* ii. 45.

[2] Mekh. 65b, MRSbY 101 the saying is omitted; *v.*, however, B. Sukkah 8a, B.Shabb. 89a, Marmorstein, *Doctrine of God*, i. 149.

[3] Harnack, op. cit., p. 93.

[4] Gen. R. ch. 27, ed. Th., p. 258, Tanḥ. (ed. Buber) נח 4.

[5] Gen. R. ch. 27, ed. Th., pp. 258-9.

[6] *v.* Agadat Ber., p. 4. Midrash on Job, Yalḳuṭ Makhiri Ps. 146. 5 אוי להם לרשעים שהם אומרים אין הקב״ה רואה ויודע. *v.* also B. Sanh. 98b. B. Ned.

from the Gentile's question in the Midrash, or drew from some remnant of Marcion's antitheses. Our material about Ḥiwi's life and age is so scanty that in our present state of knowledge the solution of such a question cannot be even attempted. Daniel al-Kumīssi[1] and Saadia[2] tried to smooth over this difficulty as in a previous instance.

Gen. 6. 6 was certainly not the only passage which could be used by trouble-makers like Marcion. He also could, and surely did, make use of other passages of the Bible, for instance, I Sam. 15. 11 נחמתי כי המלכתי את שאול in contrast with I Sam. 15. 29 ולא ינחם כי לא אדם הוא להנחם. Marcion, for reasons known to him but unknown to us, did not press this contradiction.[3] He saw, however, in Saul's history an instance of God's changeability. First God selected Saul, then He rejected him. The same happened with Solomon. These are some of God's contradictions. An omniscient God should not commit such errors of judgement, and ought to be above such *contrarietates*. Work on the Sabbath was prohibited, yet Joshua was commanded to carry the Ark around Jericho for seven days, during which he was bound to disregard the Law of the Sabbath. This is a Marcionite thesis which recurs very often in the works of the Church Fathers and Christian apologists to justify the change of the Law, especially of Sabbath, wrought through the advent of Jesus.[4] Under these conditions we cannot be surprised to find this argument among a number of heretical objections to God and Bible discussed in Rabbinic sources.[5]

38a, further, Marmorstein, 'Eine apologetische Mischna', *MGWJ* lxx (1926), pp. 381 f.

[1] *v.* Marmorstein, שרידים מפתרוני הקראי דניאל (Budapest), p. 14 f.

[2] *v.* ed. Davidson, op. cit., p. 48.

[3] *v.* Tertullian ii. 21–4.

[4] *v.* Marmorstein, *Religionsgeschichtliche Studien*, i. 39 ff., ii. 102, and 'Juden und Judentum in der Altercatio Simonis Judaei et Theophili Christiani', *Theol. Tijdschrift* xlix (1915), 379.

[5] Tanḥ. (ed. Buber) iv. 42, Num. R. 14. 1. אם יאמר לך אדם למה חילל יהושע את השבת ביריחו א״ל על פי הגבורה עשה. Similar answers are given in other instances as well, which will be discussed more fully in the second part of this essay.

All the questions involved are introduced by the rhetorical catchword אם יאמר לך אדם common to the diatribe and favoured by orators of old. The answer given does not at all meet the objection of the questioner. This was that God contradicts Himself by forbidding work on the Sabbath on one side, and commanding the breaking of the Sabbath on the other side. The reply was not addressed to outsiders, but only to Jews, who were worried by Marcionite teachings, yet still attended the Synagogue and did not give up entirely their loyalty to their people. Other contradictions pointed out are: the prohibition of images on the one hand, and the erection of the brazen serpent on the other hand; or the pleasure and displeasure with sacrifices. There are traces of polemics against the brazen serpent in sources which are certainly older than Marcion, e.g. the Wisdom of Solomon and the Mishnah.[1] One of the interlocutors of Justin alleges that he tried in vain to elicit a reasonable explanation of this incident from the Scribes.[2] The Matrona, mentioned above,[3] seemed to have been a serpent worshipper, a member of the sect of the Ophites who were closely connected with the Marcionites.[4] In one of her dialogues with R. Yose ben Ḥalafta we read the assertion: 'My God is greater than yours!'[5] The opposition to the sacrifices is also older than Marcion, and the contradiction was most likely felt by earlier generations. The whole question of sacrifices will be discussed in a further paragraph.

5. Next to God's ignorance and changeability the Demiurgos's envy and jealousy were a stumbling-block to Bible-readers. A philosopher asked R. Gamaliel II: Why should

---

[1] Sap. Sol. 16. 7. M. RH. 3. 8 Freudenthal, *Alexander Polyhistor*, p. 75; Weinstein, *Genesis der Agada*, p. 20; Marmorstein, 'Eine apologetische Mischna', *MGWJ* lxx (1926), 376–85.

[2] *v.* Harnack, *Juden und Judentum im Dialoge Justins mit Trypho*, p. 56.

[3] *v.* p. 18.

[4] *v.* Harnack, *Marcion*, p. 206.

[5] Exod. R. 3. 16, אלהי גדול מאלהיך, scil. the serpent.

God be jealous of idols, since there is nothing at all in idols?
R. Gamaliel compares idolatry with a man calling his dog by
his father's name, and whenever he took an oath he exclaimed, 'By the life of this dog, my father!' Of whom will
the father be jealous? Of the dog or the son? Thereby the
philosopher tries to prove the futility of the idols.[1] Similar
discussions are preserved between philosophers and the
Elders in Rome,[2] Tinaeus Rufus and R. Akiba,[3] and a
general called Agrippa and Rabbi.[4] All these dialogues
reflect the attitude of the pagan world. Pagans were greatly
surprised at reading in the Jewish Scriptures of God's
envy and jealousy, and ridiculed the claims of Jewish
propagandists who preached the superiority of the Jewish
doctrine of God. Marcion, with his strong anti-Jewish bias,
must have been greatly swayed by older anti-biblical and
Jew-baiting sentiments. The later Haggadah modified the
older view.[5] God is not jealous. He is the Lord of jealousy,
but this passion does not master Him. Or, God is merciful
in all circumstances, but punishes idolatry with vengeance.
The dividing line between the older and the later Tannaitic
Haggadah is here clearly marked; we have previously noted
a similar division on the question whether God tests or
tempts people.

The spreading of this idea that the Demiurgos is full of
petty jealousy became a most characteristic dogma of the
Gnostics. By it the Minim were recognized. To combat
them R. Nehemiah, a teacher of the second century, makes
up a dialogue, in the familiar style of the old diatribe,
between God and Moses. When Israel made the calf,
Moses tried to avert God's wrath, by saying: 'Lord of all

---

[1] Mekh. 68a, B. AZ. 54b.
[2] B. AZ. 54 a, f.
[3] B. BB. 9a.
[4] B. AZ. 55a, v. *Geonic Responsa*, ed. Cassel, 40a; MRSbY, p. 105, cf. S.
Krauss, *MGWJ* xlix (1905), 667 f.
[5] Mekh. 68a בקנאה אני נפרע, v. ibid. אני שולט בקנאה ואין קנאה שולטת בי
מן ע״ז אבל רחום וחנון אני בדברים אחרים.

worlds! They (Israel) provided you with an helper, and you are angry for that? The Calf will assist you! You will bring forth the sun, your helper will busy himself with the moon; you with the stars, he with the planets; you will give dew, he will cause the wind to blow; you will give rain, he will hasten the growth of the plants!' God replies: 'Moses, hast thou become a Min? There is no reality in the calf!' 'Then', says Moses, 'if so, why art thou angry, O God!'[1] Moses in this dialogue actually repeats the argument of the Gnostics. One can well imagine the impression made by such a sermon in the synagogue. Other sources reproduce the same dialogue in the name of R. Isaac, a teacher of the Amoraic period, and also anonymously.[2] The problem was as actual in the third and fourth centuries as in the second century.

6. God hardens the heart! For this shortcoming of the God of the Jews Marcion could find many proofs in the Bible. One can easily imagine the rhetors in the squares and the philosophers in the streets of Tiberias and Caesarea denouncing and blaspheming the God of the Jews for hardening the tender heart of kind old Pharaoh. The sound of the speeches delivered by gesticulating and mocking Greeks and pseudo-Jews must have penetrated into the quiet study of R. Yohanan b. Nappaha in Tiberias, and greatly upset his equilibrium. So much so that he exclaimed when reading Exod. 10. 1: 'Thence the Minim have found a support for their argument that God prevented him (Pharaoh) from repenting of his evil doings!' Considering some of the Gnostic arguments we referred to above, and their refutation by the Rabbis, we can fully appreciate this teacher's perplexity. God does not punish without giving the evildoer a chance of repentance. Here the wicked was prevented from reforming his ways and deeds! But if R. Yohanan could find no way out of his perplexity, his

[1] Exod. R. 43. 7.
[2] Deut. R. 1. 2, Num. R. 2. 15, Pes. R. 46a.

colleague, R. Simon ben Laḳish, was less perturbed. He
says: 'Let the mouth of the Minim be closed for ever! God
warns a man once, twice, thrice, and he does not repent.
Then He prevents him from repenting, hardens his heart,
in order to punish him for all his sins! This is what
happened with Pharaoh! God sent to him His prophets five
times, and he did not take to heart God's words. Thereupon
God said: "Thou hast stiffened thy neck and hardened thy
heart, behold I will add to that defilement." '[1] Our teacher
found a Scriptural support for this theory in Prov. 3. 34
('Surely he scorneth the scorners'); a later Haggadist, R.
Phinehas ha-Kohen, deduced it from Job 36. 13 ('But they
that are godless in heart lay up anger; they cry not for help
when he bindeth them').[2] God waits, with great patience,
for the return of the wicked! They, however, do not repent.
At the end God *takes their heart*,[3] so that ultimately they
cannot repent. Rab, a Babylonian sage, who was perhaps
less troubled by Gnostic cavillings and criticisms, repeats
the older, somewhat harsher doctrine.[4] God leads the nations
astray, entices them to worship idols, in order to punish them
in the end. This teaching can be traced to the older Haggadah.[5] It is a surprising doctrine, which can be found also
in older Greek theological conceptions.[6] The difference
between these two trains of thought, as outlined here, is
most remarkable. It is surely due to Gnostic agitation and
Marcionite activities in the third century. According to the
later doctrine, God is not cruel, not jealous so as to mislead
people, but in His long-suffering He waits for their change
of heart. Failing this, He punishes them as severely as they
deserve.

---

[1] Exod. R. 13. 4, *v.* also B. Sabb. 104a, B. Yoma 28b, B. Men. 29b.
[2] Exod. R. 11. 2, מעין גנים (ed. Buber), p. 114.
[3] הכבד לבם=נוטל את לבם.
[4] B. AZ. 55a.   [5] Mekh. 13b, 26a.
[6] *v.* for a further discussion of this point, Marmorstein, 'Some Greek and
Rabbinic Ideas of God', in the *Jewish Chronicle Literary Supplement*, 29 Jan.
1926, p. vi f.

7. God makes blind and deaf. It is not quite clear what the heresiarch meant by this. Did he think of his favourite protégés of Sodom (Gen. 19. 11)? or similar occurrences? We have no means for deciding this question.

8. God commits pilfering! The interlocutor, who figures under the name of Caesar and discussed religious problems with R. Gamaliel II[1] and the already twice-mentioned Matrona of R. Yose b. Halafta,[2] repeated this Marcionite allegation. Both of them bluntly assert: *Your God is a thief!* Here again we find a proof of our suggestion that Gnostic, or Marcionite, objections were drawn from earlier anti-Jewish polemics. Many of the Church Fathers taught that Marcion's calumnies against the Demiurgos in his antitheses included the assertion that the God of the Jews induced his people to spoil the Egyptians.[3] The anti-Semites of Alexandria never wearied of repeating this statement in order to defame the Jews as thieves and robbers. The authors of such works as the Book of Jubilees[4] and the Wisdom of Solomon[5] felt themselves forced to defend the Jews against it. The Talmud[6] copied from an old source a discussion, or a claim put forward by the people of Egypt and a defence of the Jews in the presence of Alexander the Great. The former asked for the restitution of the spoil taken by the Israelites from the Egyptians at the Exodus. A man called Gebiha ben Pesisa defended, and put forward a counter-claim for wages due to the slave builders in Egypt. This defence agrees with the view of the writers of the books in the Apocrypha and later in the patristic literature.[7] All these various writers and apologists agree that the spoil was

---

[1] B. Sanh. 39a, *The Exempla of the Rabbis*, ed. Gaster, p. 34; Midrash Abkhir, ed. Marmorstein, *Dvir*, i. 132.

[2] Gen. R. ch. 17, ed. Theodor, p. 158; Midrash Abkhir, op. cit., p. 133.

[3] *v.* Harnack, op. cit., p. 104.

[4] ch. 48.

[5] ch. 10. 20 and ch. 12 f.

[6] B. Sanh. 91a, *v.* also Gen. R. 61. 6.

[7] *v. Clem. of Alex. Strom.* i. 23, a com. on the Psalms of the 6th cent. *WZKM* ix. 183, *Iren. haer.* iv. 30.

in lieu of wages for the services and the work performed by
the Israelites in Egypt. The Egyptians were still the debtors,
and the Israelites were not to be blamed for their action.
The reproach must have been felt very keenly by the Jews,
seeing that many Scribes refer to this subject.[1]

9. God mocks! Marcion might have used Prov. 3. 34 for
his argument, a passage which was by R. Simon ben
Laḳish quite appropriately applied to Gnostics and the
like.[2] There must have been other passages, too, in the Bible
used by Marcion to substantiate his blasphemies against
God. R. Aḥa reports in the name of R. Samuel b. Naḥmani[3]
that the verb ישחק (mock; laugh at) occurs four times with
reference to God in the books of Psalms and Proverbs.[4]
Now as far as we know this great Haggadist was neither a
lexicographer nor the compiler of a concordance; what then
was his purpose in registering these four passages? He
certainly did not mean to supply heretics with weapons
against the Jewish doctrine of God. On the contrary, he
defended it and refuted or minimized the force of their
apparently strong proofs of God's mocking at people. He
explains that the verb does not mean *God mocks*, but God
says that the wicked are laughing at one another. Another
teacher, R. Isaac b. Ḥama,[5] denies altogether the possibility
of such an action on God's part. All his deeds and manifestations are in holiness. God's holiness excludes the
shadow of such an action, of mocking at his creatures.
There must have been teachers to whom the fact that God

---

[1] R. Akiba, Mekh. 14b, MRSbY 109, Gen. R. 28. 7, R. Yose ha-Gelili,
Exod. R. 3. 14, 14. 13, 19. 7, Tanḥ. f. 73a. R. Abun ha-Levi b. Rabbi,
Esther R. ch. 7, Midrash in Yalḳuṭ 18. 16 (R. Eleazar b. Pedat, R. Samuel
b. Isaac, B. Ber. 9ab), *v.* also *REJ* lxiii, 211–15, ibid. lxv. 310, Bermann,
Jüd. Apologetik, p. 149.

[2] *v.* above, p. 27.

[3] M. Ps. 2. 6, ed. Buber, p. 26; Yalḳuṭ Makhiri Ps. 2. 18: אמר הקב״ה
שוחקין אלו באלו.

[4] e.g. Pss. 2. 4, 37. 13, 59. 9; Prov. 1. 26.

[5] J. Ber. 13a, Tanḥ. (ed. Buber) קדושים 73. M. Ps. l.c., Marmorstein,
The Old Rabbinic Doctrine of God, i, p. 214.

mocks, or makes fools of sinners, was not repugnant at all. God helped the people of the generation of the Tower. They succeed by God's help in order that He may laugh at them at the end. This is in a new garb the old idea known to us from many mythologies, that the gods lead people to their destruction! Why does God do such a thing? In order that the wicked should not be enabled to say: 'Had we built the tower, we would have ascended to heaven, and dethroned Him. Well, you built the Tower, and what was the result?'[1] A similar thought recurs in a sermon speaking of the suspected woman. God says to her: 'You can mock, laugh at your husband, but not at me! I am sitting on high and am laughing at my creatures!'[2] A Babylonian teacher modified this rather crude conception of God by saying that God laughs with, and not at, His creatures, except on the day when idolatry will be judged and condemned.[3]

10–11. God is weak! and unjust! Jews and Christians alike were taunted both by heathens and Gnostics with this argument. It is treated at some length in the present writer's *The Old Rabbinic Doctrine of God*, i, pp. 170–6, which can be briefly summarized here. Marcion's Church shared to some extent in the persecutions and martyrdom of the Christians and Jews, and the new aspect in his theology is that the God of the Jews is the cause of all these evils and He directs the hearts of the powers of this world against the pious. The charge against God of injustice, of making evil things and doing evil, requires some further elaboration. Marcion never denied the justice of God. The known God is the δίκαιος θεός in contradistinction to the foreign, unknown God, the ἄγνωστος θεός.[4] Simon Magus says to Peter that neither man nor God can be just and good at the same time.[5] Peter replies in real Haggadic style:

---

[1] Tanḥ. (ed. Buber) נח 28, Ps. 2. 4.
[2] Tanḥ. (ed. Buber) נשא 9, Ps. 2. 4.
[3] B. AZ. 3a: עם בריותיו משחק על בריותיו אינו משחק אלא אותו היום בלבד. The first version gives the sentence in the name of R. Isaac.
[4] v. Harnack, op. cit., pp. 86 ff.   [5] Clem. Hom. xviii. 2.

'For He is good, in that He is now long-suffering with the
penitent, and welcomes them; but just when acting as a
judge. He will give to everyone according to his deserts!'
These sentences are repeated, almost literally, scores of
times, in the folios of Rabbinic writings.[1] It is not unlikely
that these dangerous denials of God's justice and pernicious
teachings of God's injustice impressed the Jewish mind
much more and with greater force than that of the Christians,
who were not reared in this fundamental belief of Judaism.
Moreover, Christians themselves found fault with this
teaching, the Jewish conception of reward and punishment.

The crisis engendered by Marcion and others like him
threatened the whole edifice of Judaism not less than that
of the Church, and led to a spiritual fight between Gnosis
and Judaism. R. Ishmael teaches[2] that the reward of the
righteous and the retribution of the wicked are alike im-
measurable. The former ascend as high as the mountains of
God, the latter sink as low as the abyss. R. Akiba[3] taught
that God is very particular with both, the righteous as well
as the wicked. He punishes the righteous for their small
shortcomings in this world and rewards their virtue in the
world to come. Just the reverse with the wicked. The same
teaching is given in the sermon quoted above[4] from the
Sifre.[5] There it is anonymous, here the name of the teacher
is mentioned. This view is often repeated and was adopted

[1] Torat Kohanim (Sifra) 82b. דיין ליפרע ונאמן לשלם שכר v. also 71a,
75a, R. Eleazar b. Azarya says: אני דיין אני מלא רחמים v. 74a, and several
other passages, v. also Sifre Zuṭṭa, MGWJ, 1900, 220.

[2] Lev. R. 271. הצדיקים שעושין את התורה שניתנה מהררי אל הקב"ה עושה
עמהן צדקה כהררי אל, אבל רשעים שאין עושין את התורה שניתנה מהררי אל
תהום רבה v. also Pesiḳta. הקב"ה מדקדק עמהם עד

[3] Ibid. ר' עקיבא אומר אלו ואלו מדקדק עמהן הקב"ה הצדיקים גובה מהן מיעוט.
מעשים רעים שעשו בעוה"ז בשביל ליתן להם שכר טוב לעתיד לבא ומשפיע שלום
לרשעים ומשלם להם מיעוט מעשים טובים שעשו בעוה"ז כדי להפרע מהם לע"ל.

[4] v. p. 11.

[5] Deut. § 307. כשם שמשלם שכר צדיק גמור שכר בעולם הזה לעולם הבא כך
משלם לרשע גמור שכר מצוה קלה שעשה בעוה"ז, וכשם שנפרע מרשע גמור
מעבירה שעשה בעוה"ז לעוה"ב כך נפרע מצדיק גמור על עבירה שעשה בעה"ז.

by many Haggadists.[1] The teachers essay to reconcile God's
justice with His goodness. Both are shown to just and wicked
alike; both share, according to R. Akiba and his followers,
reward and punishment. A teaching was current that God
does not withhold from any creature his reward.[2] Yet we
learn that God measures, or is particular with, the deeds of
the righteous to a hair's breadth.[3] It was not easy to balance
between two extreme views. One insisted on God's un-
swerving and, as it were, pedantic justice, the other extended
His goodness to the utmost limits. Neither view actually
agrees with daily experience, with the brighter and darker
colours of human existence! There must be a middle
course, but to find it is almost impossible. Yet a healthy way
of thinking was to be found here, as well as in other exas-
perating perplexities!

12–13. How can God be good, since He made evil things?
Moreover, He himself does evil! He, the creator of the
world, made bad things and made the bad things badly.
Gnostics never stopped finding fault with the Demiurgos.
We have already seen the Rabbis at work dealing with
their opponents' questions; nor did they neglect this
one. The physical man is not a failure, his creation is
perfect.[4] Tertullian and others mention among other *pusillitates* of the Creator ridiculed by Marcion the creation of
small, stupid insects. It must be in view of these Gnostics
and other enemies of the Bible that some preachers enun-

---

[1] *v.* J. Ta'anit 65, Pes. (ed. Buber), p. 161b, M. Ps. ed. Buber, p. 436. R.
Samuel b. Naḥmani מאריך רוחו עם הרשעים ונותן להם מיעוט מעשים טובים
שעשו בעוה״ז, ומאריך רוחו עם הצדיקים וגובה מהם מיעוט מעשים רעים שעשו
בעוה״ז, וחוזר ונותן להם שלוה. *v.* also ibid. p. 374. Some texts ascribe the
authorship of this saying to R. Jonathan b. Eliezer, further B. Sanh. 96a, and
Marmorstein, *The Doctrine of Merits*, s.v. 'Gentiles, merits of'.
[2] *v.* B. BK. 38b, B. Nazir 23a, B. Hor. 16a, Deut. R. (ed. Buber), p. 23,
Mid. Agada (ed. Buber), p. 123.
[3] *v.* Tanḥ. (ed. Buber), Introduction, p. 132. Pes. R. p. 115, Seder El. R. p.
3, B. Yebamot 121b, B. BK. 50a, J. Shek. 48d, J. Beṣah 62b, Lam. R. p. 65.
v. also Ginzberg, *Geonica*, ii. 50.
[4] *v.* above, pp. 9 ff.

ciated an often repeated saying: 'Even those things which
seem to you superfluous in the creation (world), e.g. flies,
&c., are part of the creation, and act as God's messengers.'[1]
The Prophet Elijah asked R. Nehorai, who was contemporary with the originator of this apologia, about the
purpose served by their creation. R. Nehorai says: 'When
people sin, God looks at these insects, and says: "They are
useless things, yet do I preserve them! Men might become
righteous; how much more then should they not, as they
deserve, be utterly destroyed!" '[2] The same interlocutor
asked of the same Scribe about the origin of and the reason
for earthquakes. It seems that Elijah acted in both dialogues
as the mouthpiece of Gnostic arguments and heresies.[3] The
two cases are, naturally, different from each other. The
first, the creation of insects, illustrates the *making* of bad
or evil things, the second, the earthquake, shows God as
doing evil. Since Marcion's theology was so bitter against
the *conditor malorum*,[4] it is no wonder that the Scribes had
to pay close attention to such views and opinions, most
harmful to the believer.

The whole Bible was ransacked by Marcion to establish
the evildoings of the Demiurgos. It cannot be a mere accident that Marcion as well as the preachers of the Synagogue
group together the generations of the Flood, of the Tower
of Babel, Sodom and Gomorrah, Pharaoh, Sisera, Nebuchadnezzar, Sennacherib, and others. We have already seen
once or twice the inner connexion between Gnosis and

---

[1] Gen. R. ch. 19, ed. Theodor, p. 80 אפילו דברים שאתה רואה כולן יתירים
לבריתו של עולם כגון פרעושים יתושים זבובין אף הן בכלל בריתו של עולם ובכל
הקב״ה עושה שליחותו. Lev. R. 22. 1, Eccl. R. 5. 8, M. Eccl. Zutta 104, Exod.
R. 10, Tanḥ. חקת, Num. R. 18. 22, B. Sabb. 77b. The saying is quoted in the
name of the Rabbanan; coming as it does next to those of R. Judah b. Ilai‘
and R. Nehemiah, the date cannot be later than the second half of the 2nd
cent., the critical period of Marcionite influence.

[2] J. Ber. 13c, M. Ps. 18. 12 (ed. Buber), p. 142, Seder El. R., ch. 1, ed.
Friedmann, p. 51.

[3] J. Ber. ibid., M. Ps., pp. 141, 447.

[4] v. Harnack, op. cit., p. 95.

Haggadah on this point.[1] We will now consider further two homilies, one ascribed to R. Eliezer, the son of R. Yose the Galilean,[2] and the other to one of the latest Palestinian Haggadists, R. Tanḥuma.[3] The first is based on Deut. 32. 34. The word כמוס there used means that the cup of chastisement is kept in store by God for those who despise, ridicule, and laugh at the words of the Torah. One drop is missing. This is because the aforenamed wicked people have drunk some of it, while some part of it is left for all the generations till the resurrection. There is no healing for the nations, but there will be for Israel. This is very obscure, and, though the Midrash Tannaim furnishes some variants and supplements the shorter version of the Sifre, we cannot reconstruct the text in such a way as to clear up all the difficulties surrounding this ancient homily. The long list of peoples who cruelly suffered at the hand of the *conditor malorum* suggests that we should look here for some defence against calumnies levelled at Biblical doctrines. Those sufferers tasted merely a part of their well-deserved punishment. It was a mere drop, and not the full measure of their deserts due to their wickedness. God is good, even in the hour of punishment. The problem is again the incompatibility between justice and goodness, coupled with the doctrine of the evildoing of the Creator.

The relation of these two attributes crops up again and again in the Haggadah. R. Eliezer ben R. Yose the Galilean, who must have felt very strongly the harmful influence exercised by Marcion's well-aimed criticism of the Bible, was a very prominent teacher after the Bar Kokhba war, a time when agitators and writers did not appeal in vain to the cruelly defeated victims of Rome in their darkest hour of disappointment and despair. The combined effects of political helplessness and spiritual agitation made

[1] *v.* above, pp. 10, 20 f.
[2] Sifre Deut. § 324, Mid. Tannaim, p. 200, M. Ps. 75. 4.
[3] Mid. Ps. ch. 18, ed. Prag, 16d.

themselves most strongly felt among the Galilean Jews.
Bearing these facts in mind, we can see our teacher's
homilies in their proper perspective. Once he said: 'One
may utter a part of God's praise in addressing Him directly,
and His whole praise in speaking of Him indirectly.' The
proof for the first half of the sentence is adduced from
Ps. 66. 3: 'Say unto God: How terrible are Thy works!'
That implies God's justice. This is only a part of His praise.
The second proof, Ps. 136. 1, comprises the whole of God's
praise, namely, His goodness, His mercy that endureth for
ever. The terrible works of justice are in complete harmony
with God's everlasting mercy.[1]

The same teacher has preserved also in another place a
nice piece of Gnostic dogmatics and exegesis which must be
discussed here. God in dispensing blessing and curse treats
alike the doers of good and evil, sinner and righteous.[2]
In other words, considering God's justice divorced from
the conception of goodness, we can find no difference
between good and evil, curse and blessing, righteousness
and sin. Marcion was thus the forerunner of Nietzsche in
preaching the gospel of the *Umwertung der Werte*. Let us
analyse now the homily of our Scribe, based on Gen. 4. 7
('If thou doest well, shalt thou not be accepted? and if thou
doest not well, sin croucheth at the door'), Prov. 18. 21
('Death and life are in the power of the tongue, and they
that love it shall eat the fruit thereof'), and Prov. 11. 31
('The righteous shall be recompensed in the earth, how
much more the wicked and the sinner'). The actual arguments of the heretics are not repeated, but are only alluded
to in the way of the Haggadic diatribe by the words אם לחשך

---

[1] Sifre Num. § 10. מצינו שאומרים מקצת שבחו של מי שאמר והיה העולם
שנ' אמרו לאלהים כי נורא מעשיך אם אומרים מקצת שבחו של מי שאמר והיה
העולם ק'ו לבו"ד. The text has to be completed by means of Gen. R. 32. 3
אבל שלא בפניו אומר הודו as above in the text. Religious scruples induced
the writer to omit אבל שלא בפניו.

[2] Sifre Deut. § 54, Midr. Tannaim, p. 46, Yalk. Makh. Ps. 24. 19 and
18. 21.

which corresponds to the later אם יאמר לך אדם.¹ These three
passages, apparently, have been selected and combined
to demonstrate that under the rule of the Creator, and
under his peculiar sense of justice, there is in practice a
world of difference between good and evil, virtue and sin,
piety and wickedness. All are treated as they deserve. The
theories advanced and developed by R. Ishmael and R.
Akiba are of no practical value. R. Eliezer proves from
Deut. 11. 26, Prov. 14. 14, and Prov. 16. 4 that those who
do well will partake of blessing, while the doers of evil will
be cursed; both depend on man's relation to God, on his
obedience or disobedience to the word of God; lovers of
good and evil will eat the fruits of *their* lips; and, finally, the
Lord has made all things for Himself, yea, even the wicked
for the day of evil. Yes, there is a difference between good
and evil. God in His justice combines mercy with Law.

We have yet a third homily of R. Eliezer b. R. Yose the
Galilean which has a bearing on Marcion's antitheses.
Marcion, as we have seen, liked to contrast the unworthi-
ness of God's friends with the worthiness of God's enemies.
Our Tanna reverses the process. He adduces a list of
Biblical personages who show humility; their humility
increases the more they are exalted, e.g. Abraham, Moses,
Aaron, and David,² not so Nimrod, Pharaoh, Sennacherib,
Nebuchadnezzar, and Hiram. God invested them with
greatness, magnified them, and finally they rebelled.³ What
did our Tanna mean by this antithesis?⁴ His purpose can
be understood and illustrated from contemporary heretical
doctrines. These sayings of R. Eliezer b. R. Yose the
Galilean are really masterpieces of Haggadic lore. No
wonder that R. Yoḥanan b. Nappaḥa, a special connoisseur

---

¹ The full phrase is still to be found in B. Ber. 7b, 8a, B. Meg. 6b, אם
לחשך אדם לומר בני אל תתחר וכו׳ Num. R. 6. 2, M. Ps. 57a.
² v. Gen. 18. 27, Exod. 16. 7, Ps. 22. 7.
³ Gen. 11. 4, Exod. 5. 2, II Kings 18. 25, Isa. 14. 14, Ezek. 28. 2.
⁴ B. Ḥullin 89a, R. Yoḥanan in his name.

of literary documents, drew his hearers' attention to the words of this master of religious thought.

We skip over the centuries between this teacher and one of the latest great Haggadic teachers of Palestine, R. Tanḥuma. The centuries which elapsed between the former and the latter brought many changes in thoughts and feelings. The chief idea expressed by R. Tanḥuma is at once remarkable and surprising. All the wars, we are told, which Israel fought in the past will be renewed in the future, all the proud ones will be severely punished, by fire. Then the whole list from the generations of the Flood till Edom is repeated. God is not the *conditor malorum*, but the wicked have to thank themselves for their fate.

14. We arrive at the second group of arguments against the divine attributes. Some repetitions and obscurities must be overlooked. It is difficult to guess what Marcion meant by God 'desiring the fruitful hill'. The unseemliness of God's dwelling in a tabernacle, his fondness for fat and sacrifices, and his delight in candles and candlesticks, is often pointed out. These criticisms are by no means new, nor have the Scribes allowed them to pass without some defence of their own. The LXX altered the words and expounded the text of 2 Chron. 6. 2, saying: 'I built a house for thy name, which is ready for thy veneration during all generations to come.'[1] The sanctuary is erected not for God, but for humanity's sake. The philosopher Zeno spoke with the greatest contempt of those who build sacred edifices for the Godhead. For how can a building be sacred which is erected by builders and human labourers?[2] Scepticism penetrated into Jewish circles in Palestine, and was by no means limited to the Greek-speaking Jews of the Diaspora. Such views found ready listeners among Jews as well as non-Jews, in antiquity as to-day.

[1] v. Dähne, *Gesch. Darstellung*, ii. 46; v. also I Kings 8. 43, v. also Jos. Ant. 8. 4.
[2] Plutarch, *De Stoicorum repugnantiis*, vi. 1; Diog. Laertius, *Lives of Eminent Philosophers*, vii. 33.

A number of Tannaim and Amoraim turned their attention to this question. Thus R. Ṭarfon taught that the
presence of the Shekhinah in the tabernacle was a reward
for the pious work done by the workmen, a blessing for the
work accomplished for heaven's sake.[1] The Temple was not
built to supply God with an abode, a dwelling-place, but
to make Israel worthy of receiving the Shekhinah. Like
his teacher in Lydda, so R. Judah b. Ilai' in Usha devoted
thought to this problem, teaching in close agreement with
Alexandrian theology that the Tabernacle was erected for
Israel's honour, and not for God's need.[2] R. Simon ben
Yohai was also swayed by apologetic tendencies when he
preached that the building of the tent of meeting was
the completion of the creation of the world. Up till then
the whole existence of the world was doubtful. It became
firm and well established by the erection of the tabernacle.
He surely wanted to convey the idea that the tabernacle
was for the sake of the whole world but not for God.[3]

The attacks must have grown stronger and stronger during
the succeeding centuries, since Haggadists more frequently
recur to this subject. R. Yohanan b. Nappaḥa rather dramati-
cally depicts the surprise and astonishment of Moses when
he heard the commandments respecting the building of the
tabernacle, the sacrifices, and the Half Shekel.[4] How can
God desire an earthly abode, when the heavens and all the
heights cannot contain Him? They put here in the mouth of

---

[1] Abot R.N., ed. Schechter, p. 45 אף הקב״ה לא השרה שכינתו על ישראל עד
שעשו מלאכה.

[2] Pes. (ed. Buber) 2a, Cant. R. 3. 9, Num. R. 13. The Tanna refers in
his parable to a custom (Jewish or pagan?) that a father does not talk to his
own daughter in public, in a square or a thoroughfare, after she is grown up,
but he makes a *pupilio* (פפליון) for her.

[3] R. Joshua ben Levi in his name, Pes. (ed. Buber) 6a, v. also 7a. להקים את
המשכן לא נאמר אלא הוקם המשכן, מה הוקם עמו עולם הוקם עמו שעד שלא הוקם
המשכן היה העולם רותת משהוקם המשכן נתבסס העולם.

[4] Pes. (ed. Buber) 20a, Pes. R. 84b, Tanh. נשא. Num. R. M. Ps. 91, Pes. R.
19a, v. sub R. Levi further on p. 41, Exod. R. 34. 1, and Midrash of R.
Shemaya of Soissons, MGWJ xiii. 226.

Moses the question which was raised by Marcion and his successors. R. Levi likens the building of the Tabernacle and the dwelling of the Shekhinah therein to a cave by the shore of the sea. The cave is filled with water, yet the sea does not lack a drop of its contents. God's glory is not diminished by His dwelling in the Temple.[1] The Haggadah served, perhaps, in the first instance, the purpose of reconciling the doctrine of God's omnipresence with His dwelling in a certain sacred place. Yet it also refuted the conception that God needed a dwelling-place. These instances, which can easily be multiplied, will suffice to show the extent of heretical influence on the Jews in the third century, and how it was met on the part of the teachers with more or less valid refutations.

15. It can cause us no surprise that the problem of sacrifices was coupled in R. Yoḥanan's sermon or legend, cited above with that of the Tabernacle. Both are catalogued next to each other in the long list of God's sins. The conception and the laws of sacrifices were a difficult problem for the Rabbinic apologists and theologians from more than one point of view. Contemporary philosophy abhorred sacrifices, mocked at their cruel uselessness, and saw in them a strange and abominable survival of a primitive religious aberration. The masses never ceased to adhere to this practice; leaders of thought performed it in spite of their better knowledge, and prominent men of affairs, notwithstanding their disbelief in sacrifices, attended worship and stood in solemn silence or prayer at these ceremonies. Among the Jews there must have been large numbers who were disquieted by this type of religious worship. Yet the vast majority of the people felt the cessation of sacrifices after the destruction of the Temple much more deeply than one would be inclined to believe. Prominent Scribes had to comfort pious souls, who, without sacrifices, thought themselves lost in their sins, and defiled by impurity. Charity is much greater than

[1] Pes. (ed. Buber) 2b; R. Joshua of Sikhnin in R. Levi's name.

sacrifices! Do you cleanse yourselves before God, your Father in Heaven! He grants your atonement. Study, prayer, good deeds, fasts, &c., are worthy substitutes for them. These theories were repeatedly advanced with several variations and developments, in answer to questions raised, both in good faith and in a spirit of mockery, which deeply stirred Jews, and shook the foundations of the whole fabric of Jewish piety. Christians went even a step farther. The abolition of sacrifices, and the doctrine that piety was independent of priests and Temple, sacrifices and cults, encouraged them to claim the abolition of Sabbath, circumcision, dietary laws, &c. The Law can be respected and observed without them. These theories and problems, and their handling and refutation, occupy a considerable space in the Haggadah. They are the background of many teachings and sayings which can here merely be hinted at. The present study is chiefly concerned with the Gnostic attitude towards sacrifices, and the stand against it taken by the Scribes.

The offering of sacrifices ceased with the destruction of the Temple. Whether some sects or over-zealous Jews still practised this mode of religious worship afterwards, or renewed it in later centuries, cannot be established with our present scanty knowledge of the subject. We have no records of such a thing as far as the third century is concerned. Yet many of the teachers living at that time essayed to defend this institution. R. Yoḥanan used a legend for this purpose.[1] His friend, R. Simon ben Laḳish, must have met or heard of people who argued from the commandments about the sacrifices that God needs food and drink. That is the reason for sacrifices and libations. His reply must have been somewhat like this:[2] 'Look at Moses, who

----

[1] v. above, p. 39.

[2] Pes. R. 194a, כי בהר סיני קרבו קרבנות? אלא אמר הקב״ה אם באת להרהר שמא יש אכילה לפני, הרי משה שעלה להר סיני ועשה אצלי מ׳ יום ומ׳ לילה יבא משה ויעידני אם יש לפני אכילה.

stayed with God for 40 days and 40 nights, let him testify whether God needs food!' According to a second version, R. Simon ben Laḳish answered: 'Look at Moses, who is a human being; when he is among you he requires food and drink, yet when he spent those days and nights with me he neither ate nor drank; how could one assert of God that He is in need of food?'[1] There are several other refutations in the same strain based on Ps. 50. 12, denying the same erroneous conception.[2] Another somewhat younger teacher, R. Judah b. Pazzi, develops and applies an earlier defence to our case.[3] God does not require offerings, candles, sanctuaries, food, and drink. They were not ordered for His own sake, but for the benefit of humanity, to purify them, to give them opportunities to acquire merits, make them fit for the Shekhinah to rest on them, and to draw them near to their Father in Heaven.[4] Most interesting is the position taken by R. Levi, a great Haggadist of this age. On the one hand, he cannot find strong enough words for emphasizing the importance of sacrifices. God loves Israel's sacrifices very much indeed;[5] they are Israel's benefactors and defenders.[6] Yet, on the other hand, he is as well aware as the author of the Pseudo-Clementine works,[7] as in later centuries Maimonides,[8] or nowadays any student of the history of religions, that sacrifices were a temporary measure adapted to the needs of Moses' pupils.[9] Moses allowed sacrifices as a concession to people who were steeped in idolatry and blinded by the example of that form of religious worship in their surroundings. He centralized

[1] Ibid. 184a.
[2] Ibid.
[3] v. above, p. 38.
[4] Lev. R. 30. 12.
[5] Pes. (ed. Buber) 192b.
[6] Pes. R. 201b.
[7] Rec. of Clem. i. 36, Hom. ii. 46, 'Diestel, Das AT in der Kirche, p. 52, Schliemann, Die Clementinen, p. 222.
[8] Moreh iii. 32; J. Oppenheim, האסיף vi, 1894, 102.
[9] Lev. R. 22. 5.

sacrificial worship in order to alienate Israel from the idols. From our scanty references it is difficult to establish whether the former or the latter view expresses the final thought of our great teacher. The latter, surely, sheds greater lustre on his name and memory, according to our way of thinking. One fact, a very important one, it seems to me, can be adduced with certainty from R. Levi's attitude as well as from the sayings of the other teachers, of those who are named here as well as of those not mentioned here by name, that all of them must have been cognizant of voices raised against the sacrifices. More than two hundred years had elapsed since the whole question had ceased to be actual, yet the origin, the meaning, and the religious influence of these sacrifices were still matters of lively dispute and controversy.[1] Why? Because the doctrine of God and the place of the Bible in both religions, in that of the Catholic Church as well as in the Jewish Synagogue, were going through one of their most dangerous crises. The agreement between R. Levi and the Clementines is more than a chance coincidence. R. Levi, on his part, may be more or less indebted to Alexandrian wisdom—his Haggadah as a whole favours such an opinion. The Clementines, on their part again, may not be immune from Palestinian teachings—there is evidence for this idea also. The agreement is, all the same, most striking. The same is the case with R. Judah b. Simon ben Pazzi and the Clementines. Both group together the alleged needs of God by pointing to tabernacles, sacrifices, and light. Can that be accidental, or is there not more in such a coincidence? The Amora must have faced the same people against whom the Church Fathers were arrayed on the common battle-ground. Naturally, they fight with different tactics and in a different style and language.

16. While Marcion placed tabernacles, sacrifices, and lights on a par, the question of the lights played a more

---

[1] v. Marmorstein, 'The Existence of God', *Jewish Forum*, Jan. 1924, pp. 16–26, and *Jeschurun*, vii, 1920, Nos. 1–4; *Expositor*, Jan. 1919, pp. 104 f.

prominent part in the Rabbinic sources than the other two.
It will be necessary to discuss here the views and conten-
tions more fully than on the earlier occasions. R. Judah bar
Ilai' demonstrates the absurdity of the belief that God needs
light. He points to the impossibility of man looking into
the sun—a favourite argument in Rabbinic theology; can
man then assert that God requires light?[1] The lights were
ordered for man's sake, that he might acquire a share in
future life. R. Simon ben Yohai saw in the candlesticks, the
dietary laws (clean and unclean beasts), and the sanctification of the New Moon three difficulties which greatly perturbed Moses.[2] If we turn to the Amoraic Haggadah, we
have first of all R. Yohanan b. Nappaha, who rejects the
allegation that God needs light. The candles ordained by the
Law cannot be explained, just as the faculty of man or his
use of his eyes cannot be fathomed.[3] R. Aha[4] compares the
commandment of the light (Num. 8. 2) with Ps. 139. 12
(darkness and light are both alike to Thee). 'God, Thou art
light, Thy garments are light, Thy servants are beings of
light, the whole world enjoys light from Thy glory, and
Thou commandest us to kindle light? What is our light
before Thee?' 'Nevertheless I do not', says God, 'want any

---

[1] Tanh. (ed. Buber) ii. 98 השמש הזה נתון בחיקו (צ״ל בנרתיקו) ובתקופת
תמוז הוא יוצא מנרתיקו לבשל את הפירות. ואין העולם יכול לעמוד בו, למה
שהוא קשה באורו אמר הקב״ה בבריה שלי אי אתה יכול להסתכל ואני צריך לאורה
לעה״ב משלך אלא למה אמרתי לך לעה״ב. v. also Tanh. ibid. in an anonymous
homily.
[2] Pes. (ed. Buber) 54b, Tanh. (ed. Buber) iv. 46, B. Men. 29a, Mekh.,
Tanh. iii, Pes. R.
[3] Tanh. (ed. Buber), Ex. p. 97, העין הזה לבנה, והשחור באמצע, מהיכן הוא
צריך לראות, לא מן הלבנה, ואינו כן, אינו רואה אלא מתוך השחור, ועל אור
עינים אין אתה יכול לעמוד, ואתה מבקש לעמוד על דרכי, שלא יטעה אותך יצרך
לומר שמא צריך הוא אורה. For a similar way of argument v. R. Huna, Gen.
R. 12. 1 הרעם הזה בשעה שהוא יוצא כתקונו אין כל בריה יכולה לעמוד עליו, וכו'
אם על סדורו של רעם אין אתה יכול לעמוד על סדורו של עולם אבכו״ב. v. also
R. Hanina, Tanh. iv. 48.
[4] Tanh. (ed. Buber) iv. 49, Num. R. 15. 8 without the name of the Haggadist, who is mentioned in the Midrash ha-Gadol, MS. Adler.

but yours.' The light is a sign of God's love of them. A similar idea is expressed by R. Berekhyah[1] and many anonymous preachers.[2] In an anonymous homily, Dan. 2. 22 and Ps. 139. 12 are quoted to show that God does not need light. The reason for this law is, therefore, to be looked for somewhere else, e.g. Isa. 42. 21. God gave this as well as other laws as an opportunity for Israel to acquire merit.[3] Another theory saw the secret of this law in God's endeavour to distinguish Israel before the whole world. The people of Israel are so exalted that they were chosen to serve as light-bearers before God.[4] R. Abin ha-Levi, in his mystic way of thinking, saw in the sanctuary the source supplying light to the whole world. Light comes from God's House, how can one assert that God needs light? Light is needed by humanity, not by Him, who is Himself light.[5] These sermons and sayings centre around the false allegation, 'God needs light!' That God is, or ought to be, free from want and need was well known to philosophers and theologians before the Christian Era; therefore we can well imagine how Marcion used these passages and laws for his theories, and what impression the shafts of his ridicule made on Jews and Christians alike. For this very reason Scribes and teachers in the second and third centuries had to discuss this topic in the pulpit.

17–18. The statements that God dwells in shadow, dark-

---

[1] Tanḥ. (ed. Buber) iv. 48, אמר הקב״ה איני צריך לאור שלכם, ולמה אמרתי לכם אלא כדי להעלותך.

[2] Tanḥ. (ed. Buber) iv. 49 ואני צריך לאור שלכם? אלא בשביל לעלותך. להודיעך שאינו צריך אורה, למה אמר לך, בשביל לזכותך Tanḥ. (ed. Buber) ii. 98 שלא יטעך יצרך לומר צריך הוא אורה introduced by למאור.

[3] Tanḥ. (ed. Buber) iv. 48 להודיעך שכולו אור ואינו צריך לאורה משלך ולמה צויתי אתכם בשביל לזכותכם.

[4] Tanḥ. (ed. Buber) iv. 49 א״ל הקב״ה לא שאני צריך לאורכם אלא שתאירו לי כמו שהארתי לכם כדי לעלות אתכם בפני כל האומות.

[5] Tanḥ. ii. 97 האור יוצא מתוך ביתי, ואני צריך לאורה? וא״ת למה צריך לנר? להאיר לנו.

ness, storms, and smoke, and comes with trumpets, &c., are inspired by Biblical passages which were understood in their literal sense by Marcion and his followers. Their proper place is in a treatise on the anthropomorphism and anthropopathism in the Haggadah, and they will be treated fully in another connexion.

19. Owing to Marcion's pacifism and hatred of war, Exod. 15. 3 and other passages in which God plays the role of a war-god are severely criticized and strongly repudiated. R. Judah bar Ilai' remarks: 'The chief idea of this verse recurs very frequently in the Scriptures.' He quotes six proofs from Psalms, Isaiah, and Habakkuk.[1] Yet God does not want all these weapons and darts, He carries out His decrees with His Name.[2] The Mekhilta preserved a number of homilies on this subject, all of which seem to be directed against heretical arguments. In one of them there is an unmistakable reference to Gnostics who speak of two powers, i.e. the God of war and the other God who revealed the Decalogue. Both are, however, really the same. Preachers took the opportunity to emphasize God's might, unchangeability, love, and providence.[3] Special attention should be called to the form of these theological doctrines, which could be called Tannaitic Antitheses.

20. Finally we turn to Marcion's twice-repeated thesis that God loves the wicked, adulterers, and murderers, and chooses evil men. A commentary on these words is offered by the writer of the Clementine Homilies and by Marcion himself. Peter[4] denies that Adam was a transgressor, Noah drunken, that Abraham lived with three wives at once, and Jacob associated with four, that Moses was a murderer. There can be no doubt that these 'sins of the saints', which

---

[1] Ps. 18. 11, Isa. 59. 17, Ps. 45. 4, Hab. 3. 9, Ps. 35. 2, Hab. 3. 11 (so MRSbY), Mekh. has in addition II Sam. 22, Ps. 91.

[2] Mekh. 37b, MRSbY 61 without the name of the Tanna.

[3] MRSbY, p. 66, has a fuller list of these antitheses than Mekh. 37b, some of them also MRSbY, p. 61. Both are derived from an older collection, which was probably still known to the preachers of the Amoraic period.

[4] Clementine Homilies, ii. 52.

go back to the letter of the Bible, re-echo the antitheses of
Marcion and the syllogisms of Apelles in thirty-eight books,
all lost. From such a company the robber Joshua, the im-
pious Lot and his daughters, the adulterers David and
Solomon, could not be left out. A certain anonymous teacher,
whose date I am unable to fix, seems to me to have known
of both: the sharp attack against the Scriptures, and the
clumsy denial of Peter. He makes God say:[1] 'Adam is a
thief, Noah a drunkard, Abraham a stranger, Isaac loved
God's enemies, Jacob is the right man.' The sins of Abraham and Jacob, their polygamy, play a considerable part in
Jewish apologetics of the first three centuries. R. Judah b.
Ilai' and R. Nehemiah, who, as our previous observations
will confirm, must have had a more intimate knowledge of
Bible criticism than they are generally credited with, both
take great pains to identify Keturah with Hagar.[2] The fact
that Jacob married two sisters and lived with four wives
was also mitigated or explained away. Moses did not murder
the Egyptian with ordinary weapons, but by pronouncing
the Divine Name.[3] Even the action of Lot and his daughters
found apologists in the Synagogue as well as in the Church.[4]
David as well as Solomon have had to bear the brunt of
attack and blame for their sins and iniquities, which fill
many pages of Haggadic literature. The biographies of the
saints and the wicked of the Bible, as depicted and illumi-
nated by the teachers of the Haggadah, must be investigated
from this point of view. This can be done under the light

---

[1] Tanḥ. (ed. Buber) iii. 72 f., v. Marmorstein, *The Old Rabbinic Doctrine
of God*, p. 214.

[2] Gen. R. 61. 4.

[3] v. Ps.-Jonathan Targum on Exod. 2. 13.

[4] v. Gen. R. 41. 7; 51. 9, M. Ps. 75. 4, Pirḳe, ch. 25, Yalḳ. Deut. § 808,
AB of Ben Sirach 6b, 2 Peter ii. 7–8, Clem. ch. xi, Qoran, Sura 6. Further B.
Nazir 23a in the name of רבא or R. Isaac, Gen. R. has the same by R.
Tanḥuma b. Ḥiyya in the name of R. Hoshaya. Further Ag. Ber. ch. 25, reads
בכל שנה ושנה instead of כל שבת ושבת, v. Bet Talmud, iii. 335; *MEDZ*, ed.
Buber, p. 3; Wisdom of Solom. 10. 6; Grünbaum, *Neue Beiträge zur sem.
Sagenkunde*, p. 175; *Magazin*, 1893, 253 f.

thrown on them by Gnostics on one side, and Church Fathers on the other side. We are here concerned with the background furnished by the former. Such investigations would reveal clearly the religious and intellectual conditions in the period in which our material first took shape.

V

Our material leaves no doubt that the great teachers of the second and third centuries faced people who, more or less, were under the spell of the Marcionite way of thinking. These were the Minim, who, either entirely or in part, severed their connexions with the Synagogue. Socially or economically, they could not be separated from members of the community or from their own family. Teachers and preachers used to have disputes or discussions with them. Some of these took rather an unfriendly shape, e.g. in the case of R. Meir or in that of R. Joshua ben Levi. Considering the nature of their questions and their attitude towards Jews, one cannot, in the Minim of the early times (up to the third century) and especially in places where Christians were not to be found at all, see Christians, whether Jewish or Gentile. Jews who were imbued with Gnostic doctrines are known by the name of Minim. Most if not all of the teachers mentioned in the previous pages came into contact with people who inclined to the way of the Minim. About thirty Tannaim and Amoraim named in the previous chapters supply a part of the problems which agitated the minds of Minim and Scribes. Their list could be greatly enlarged. Our purpose, however, which is to throw light on Marcionite influence and to make clear a part of the Haggadic background, can be better served by investigating the anonymous Haggadah and the teachings of the Haggadists whose names have become familiar to us in our present investigation. This leads us to point out a second aspect of the Haggadah, which has, as far as I know, not yet been fully investigated.

PART II

Diatribe and Haggadah

1. The Greek word διατριβή has many meanings. In rhetoric it signifies an 'occasion for dwelling on a subject' (Arist. *Rhet.* 3. 17). The addresses and speeches of Cynics and Stoics developed the diatribe into an art. The best representatives of those schools used it in both the spoken and written word. In reading E. Norden's *Die Antike Kunstprosa* (2 vols., Leipzig, 1895) I was struck by the new light which the investigations of that scholar can throw on the style of the Haggadah. This impression became even stronger in studying Rudolf Bultmann's *Der Stil der paulinischen Briefe und die Kynisch-Stoische Diatribe* (Göttingen, 1910). It is almost a platitude that the inner content of a literary work cannot be properly understood without understanding its external form. Yet, in our studies and researches up till now, the latter has been more or less neglected. It is customary to ignore or to deny style, form, and beauty in the literary productions of the Scribes, in their homilies and sermons, their parables and similes, their thoughts and teachings. The inner meaning is the chief thing, the external form is of no consequence. The history and the state of preservation of our literature, which is partly fragmentary and partly sketchy, apparently confirms such a belief. This, however, is an erroneous view. The Haggadah has a style of its own, worth studying. The preachers and teachers, whose immortal names are enshrined in the Haggadah of the two Talmuds and the Midrashim, developed a homiletical style which is not much behind that of the masters of oratory in Latin and Greek. We are told frequently that educated and intellectual circles among the heathen of the first centuries looked somewhat pityingly on the barbarism of the Gospels. Learned and wise pagans treated rather with contumely the sacred writings of early Christianity. This

is not surprising at all. The Gospels in Greek must have struck them, as far as style and language go, as strange or foreign to their literary taste. I am not aware, however, of having read anything similar of the Hebrew Bible. The Haggadah, properly investigated and studied, reveals many similarities between the style of the diatribe and the homilies of the Scribe.

It is impossible in the present stage of our knowledge to decide the question whether or how far the Rabbinic preachers actually were indebted to the diatribe of Stoics and Cynics. This question will have to be answered sooner or later. Really, it is part and parcel of a much larger and more important problem, which has to be tackled and answered either in the affirmative or in the negative. I mean the traces of external, secular knowledge possessed by the Scribes, their relation to Greek wisdom and science. Apart from the comparative method, the study of the Haggadic style reveals many new aspects of the inner meaning of obscure sayings and sentences, forms and ways of our homilies. These enable us to listen to the living voice of the ages, to objections raised to teachings and legends, to criticisms made against exegesis and theology expounded from the pulpit, to abuse and ridicule heaped on the religion and history of the Jews by heathen and Christians, by believers and unbelievers, by masters and pupils. By understanding the form in which a discourse was cast, we are enabled to revive many a long-forgotten historical fact, and reconstruct some intellectual movements, which are otherwise lost in the deep sea of the ages past. Scientific research into the ancient documents of our literature cannot dispense with the investigation of the external forms of the material at our disposal.

2. One of the most usual forms of the diatribe is that of dialogues between two parties. The speaker, or writer, steps into the background, he develops his *own* ideas by constructing a dialogue between two or more different

persons. The dialogue in the Haggadah has not so far been
studied from this point of view. Its part and importance in
Jewish theology and apologetics has not yet been made clear,
as has been done in Christian theology and apologetics,
where learned works are at the students' disposal. It cannot
be done in this short essay. Yet two or three facts should
here be pointed out. First of all the dialogues between God
and the Kenesset Israel (כנסת ישראל). Some instances will
suffice. Thus, R. Yoḥanan b. Nappaḥa depicts in a parable
a king who had in his service two ill-famed quaestors.
These were made use of by him if he wanted to chastise a
rebellious province. Once a province became restless. The
king dispatched one of them to this place. When the people
heard this, they entreated him: 'Whatsoever you want to
do in order to punish us, do, but save us from the presence
of this man!' Israel says similarly before God: 'Lord of the
Universe! Rebuke me not in thine anger neither chasten
me in thy wrath' (Ps. 6. 2). God replies: 'What is mine
anger and my wrath for?' Israel says: 'Pour out thy wrath
upon the heathen' (ibid. 79. 6). God accepts their words,
and acts accordingly, saying: 'And I will act in anger and
fury against the heathen (Mic. 5. 14), but not against Israel'
(cf. Hos. 11. 9).[1]

This instance, by the way, shows another characteristic
feature of the diatribe: It was customary to put in the mouth
of the arguing parties quotations from Homer or other well-
known authors, poets, or philosophers. The Jewish or
Christian preacher borrowed from the Bible. Our second
instance will show this even more clearly. It is a dialogue
between Israel and God, or the Holy Spirit.[2] The dialogue
consists of six[3] parts. Israel quotes one passage, the Holy

---

[1] M. Ps. (ed. Buber) 6. 3; Yalḳuṭ Makhiri Ps. (ed. Buber) 6. 6.
[2] Midr. Tanḥ. reads המקום instead of רוח הקודש. In the Sifre, Holy Spirit
means in several places God; v. Marmorstein, *The Old Rabbinic Doctrine of
God*, London, 1927.
[3] M. Tan. has eight: vii, Cant. 5. 10 and 7. 2; viii, Deut. 4. 7.

Spirit replies with another from the Scriptures. The dialogue reads as follows:

I. Israel says: There is none like God.
   Holy Spirit: Jeshurun is like God (Deut. 33. 26).
II. Israel: Who is like thee among the gods, O Lord? (Exod. 15. 11).
   Holy Spirit: Happy art thou, Israel, who is like thee (Deut. 33. 29).
III. Israel: Hear O Israel, the Lord is our God, the Lord is one (Deut. 6. 4).
   Holy Spirit: Who is like thy people Israel, a unique nation on the earth? (I Chron. 17. 21).
IV. Israel: Like the apple tree among the trees of the forest, so is my beloved among the sons (Cant. 2. 3).
   Holy Spirit: Like the lily among the thorns, is my beloved among the daughters (ibid. 2. 2).
V. Israel: This is my God, I will exalt him (Exod. 15. 2).
   Holy Spirit: This people I have created unto me (Isa. 43. 21).
VI. Israel: For thou art the glory of his might (Ps. 89. 18).
   Holy Spirit: Israel, through thee I am glorified (Isa. 49. 3).[1]

One can faintly imagine or reconstruct after so many centuries the exact purpose and impression of a sermon of this type. At present the quotations look to the reader like a mere string of gems from Pentateuch, Prophets, and Psalms, which lack the key to the secret of their inner connexion. No doubt the most sublime theological doctrines of the preacher's age were derived from or put into these words, and were surely expounded at length by the orator on that occasion. The Unity, the Incomparability, the Uniqueness both of God and Israel, the relation between God and Israel, the mutual choice of both, were the themes expounded, as pointed out in another place.[2] The introduction and the peroration are unfortunately missing, or perhaps

---

[1] Sifre Deut. § 355, p. 148a, b; Midr. Tannaim, p. 221; Mekh. 16b; Midr. Zutta, ed. Buber, p. 16.
[2] v. Marmorstein, 'Die Nachahmung Gottes' (Imitatio Dei), *Jeschurun*, xiv, 1928 (*infra*, pp. 106–21).

misplaced; therefore the actual theme cannot with certainty be established, but merely guessed. For our purpose it is enough to recognize that the preachers knew and used this method of the diatribe.

In some cases the speech, prayer, or request of the Kenesset Israel is preserved, the reply of God either originally omitted or lost through the copyists of our ancient Midrashim. R. Yose b. Ḥanina, one of the most eloquent preachers of the third century in Tiberias, whose life and teaching deserve a full monograph, dealt with Ps. 140. 6 in one of his homilies. The Kenesset Israel says before God: 'Lord of the Universe! The nations of the world spread out a net before me in order to catch me! They say: "Worship idols!" If I listen to them, I am condemned by Thy law, if I do not obey, then they slay me. I am like a thirsty wolf, who stands before the well with a snare, saying: "If I descend to drink, I shall be caught by the snare, if not, I shall die of thirst." '[1] There we have the address of Israel; the answer of God is not reported. The preacher was satisfied with describing the feeling of his hearers, who had undergone some persecution. The same preacher offers another instance,[2] which for style and contents deserves more attention than it has so far received. He delivered a sermon in which we are told that Moses decreed four decrees which have been abolished by four prophets. The sayings of Moses are: (1) Deut. 33. 28; (2) Deut. 28. 65; (3) Exod. 34. 7; and (4) Lev. 26. 38. They were annulled by Amos 7. 5–6, Jer. 31. 1, Ezek. 18. 4, and Isa. 27. 13. This preacher did not fear to declare that the prophets objected to or even abolished the words of the father of the prophets. The homily, which may have been delivered on a New Year's Day (cf. the passages from Jeremiah and from Isaiah), reveals the problems agitating the minds of Galilean

[1] Esther R. ch. 7, Yalḳ. Makhiri Ps. 140. 1.
[2] v. B. Makkot 24a, variants in En Ya'aḳob, Yalḳuṭ Shim'oni ii. 313 and Pirḳe de Rabbenu ha-Ḳadosh, ed. Schönblum (Lemberg, 1877), 24b.

Jews in that period, viz. the question of assimilation, the relation of Jews to the outside world, the sins of the fathers being visited on their children, and Israel's very existence. These questions, which trouble us, children of the twentieth century, so greatly in all countries of our dispersion, were alive and pressing in Tiberias in the third century. In order to develop this theme or these themes, the preacher put his arguments into the mouth of Moses and the prophets. The attitude of the preacher is not clearly and distinctly stated. We do not gather from his words on this occasion whether he favoured the point of view of Moses and condemned the others or vice versa. Other homilies of his throw some light on his views.[1]

3. Another type of the diatribe is presented in *Haggadot* which comprise dialogues between Biblical personages, heroes of antiquity, saints and sages on one side, and God on the other side. Just as in the Cynic-Stoic diatribe heroes of poetry and mythology, e.g. Odysseus or Heracles, are introduced as defenders or propagators of philosophical ideas and ethical norms,[2] so in their dialogues the 'Fathers of the World',[3] prophets and kings, teach or admonish, defend or accuse, rebuke or praise their contemporaries before God. Here also a few instances will convey an idea of the similarity between the Haggadists and ancient rhetors in their application of the diatribe. The first instance is taken from the Haggadah of R. Jonathan ben Eleazar, reported in his name by R. Samuel b. Naḥmani. He depicts Moses as writing the story of the creation in the Torah. When he arrived at Gen. 1. 26 (let us make man), Moses exclaimed: 'Lord of the Universe! Wherefore dost Thou

---

[1] *v.* Marmorstein, 'Eine messianische Bewegung im dritten Jahrhundert', *Jeschurun*, xiii, 1926, 16–18.

[2] *v.* Bultmann, op. cit., pp. 12 f.

[3] As to the term אבות העולם *v.* Tanḥ. (ed. Buber) i. 196, Deut. R. 11. 1, Gen. R. 12. 14, 58. 4, Lev. R. 36. 1, Pirḳe R. ha-Ḳadosh iii. 115, Midr. Abba Gorion, p. 33, J. R. H. 56d, M. Eduyyot 1. 4, Ozar Midrashim, ed. Wertheimer, p. 80.

give an opening of the mouth (occasion) to the Minim?'
i.e. to assert that there were two powers assisting at the
creation of man. God replies: 'Write, and he who likes
to err, let him err.'[1] God said: 'What about the man,
whom I created? Does he not produce big and small ones?
Now, if the former should ask permission of the latter, will
they not say: Why should people standing socially higher
ask permission of lower ones? Well, let him learn from his
Creator, who created the upper and lower ones, and yet at
the creation of man, he consulted his ministering angels.'[2]
Gen. 1. 26 gave rise to one of the thorniest questions of
ancient Jewish apologetics, and was characteristically mis-
used, first by Gnostics, afterwards by Christians, to prove
the truth of their respective theories from the Bible of the
Jews.[3]

Sometimes the dialogue represents a free, dramatized
elaboration of the Bible narrative. R. Levi has a homily on
Gen. 18. 25. Abraham said: 'If thou desirest the world,
there is no strict judgement, if judgement, there is no world.
Thou holdest the rope by both ends,[4] thou desirest both,
world and judgement. The world cannot exist with the
strict measure of judgement, without forgiveness.' God
replies: 'Abraham: thou lovest righteousness, hatest wickedness, therefore has thy God anointed thee (Ps. 45. 8).
From Noah till thy time ten generations perished, and to
none of them did I speak, except to thee.'[5]

4. Among the manifold subjects dealt with by preachers,

---

[1] One would be inclined to read א״ל הקב״ה, כתוב, אמר משה, הרוצה לטעות
יטעה, instead of א״ל כתוב, והרוצה לטעות יטעה. Moses asks this question,
which fits in with the next א״ל הקב״ה, משה וכו׳.

[2] Gen. R. ch. 8, ed. Theodor, p. 62.

[3] v. Marmorstein, 'Juden und Judentum in der Altercatio Simonis
Judaei et Theophili Christiani', in *Theol Tijdschrift*, xlix (1915), p. 379.

[4] A proverb אתה תופס את החבל בב׳ ראשין often used by the teachers,
e.g. R. Simlai, Tanh. (ed. Buber) 6 ואתחנן. Samuel b. Naḥmani Deut. R.
1. 10 in Aramaic and in Hebrew.

[5] Gen. R. ch. 39, ed. Theodor, p. 369, ch. 49, ed. Theodor, p. 500, Pes.
(ed. Buber) 139a.

the most popular and best calculated to impress public opinion was the national catastrophe and the religious consequences of the destruction of the Temple. The choice of homiletical subjects was as difficult then as it is now. Even the best preachers experienced some disappointments. Special days were set apart for the commemoration of that sad historic event, which marked such a great change in the course of Jewish history. R. Samuel b. Naḥmani depicted in a rather lengthy homily the scene of the destruction of the Temple. The homily belongs to the form of diatribe described in the previous paragraph. There are, however, two features which specially distinguish it. This Haggadah shows that sometimes more than two persons take part in the discussion. Abraham appears tearing his beard, plucking his hair, smiting his face, rending his garments, with ashes on his head, lamenting and crying amidst the ruins of the destroyed Temple. He says, or rather asks God: 'Why am I different from all other languages and nations? Why has this shame and disgrace fallen to my lot?' There intervene the angels, who endorse his lament by *binding laments lines by lines*,[1] and expounding Isa. 33. 8. The paths and roads leading to Jerusalem, established for pious pilgrims, are desolate. The pilgrimages have ceased; the covenant of Abraham is abolished, Jerusalem and Zion are despised, Israel is treated worse than the idolators, the generation of Enosh.[2] Thereupon God appears asking for the reason for all these lamentations. The angels take it upon themselves to reply: 'Abraham, Thy friend, came to the ruins of Thy house, and Thou payest him no regard whatsoever!' God replies: 'Since he departed unto the House of Eternity (בית עולמו, i.e. grave, or cemetery), he did not appear in

---

[1] The term קשר הספד occurs also J. Yoma 1. 1, J. Soṭah 1. 10, J. Yeb. 16. 4, Tos. Yeb. ed. Zuckermandel, p. 259. Yelam. Yalḳ. i. 787, Nahmanides תורת האדם 78a. v. Zunz, *Literaturgeschichte*, 15 n. 3; Perles, *MGWJ* x. 387; Brüll, *Jahrb.* i. 239; *Zion*, 1841, 164; *Hamagid*, viii. 29; Marmorstein, *Jahrb. für jüd. Volkskunde*, i. 291 ff.

[2] v. R. Yoḥanan, B. Sabb. 118b, M. Ps. 2. 2, Pirḳe R. E., ch. 18.

My house, and now, what has My friend to do in My house?'
(Jer. 11. 15). Abraham lifts up his voice, and says: 'Lord
of the Universe! Why hast Thou exiled my children? Why
hast Thou delivered them to the nations who have slain
them with cruel deaths? Why hast Thou destroyed Thy
sanctuary, where I brought my son Isaac, the father of the
nation, as a burnt offering.'[1] God says: 'Because they have
transgressed the Torah, and the twenty-two letters in her!'
So far the first part.[2]

The second part of this homily illustrates another form
of the diatribe, I mean the method which is known as
Personification.[3] Abstract conceptions and qualities, like
truth, virtue, loving-kindness, charity, or the reverse, are
introduced into the speech as arguing, defending, contradicting, or confirming the speaker's statement. Here, as so
often in the Haggadah, the Torah steps forward to plead
against Israel. Abraham addresses the Torah, calling to her:
'*My daughter*! Thou comest to testify against Israel, that
they are guilty of transgressing the Law? Dost thou not
feel ashamed before me? Remember the day, when God
offered His Torah to all the nations, and they refused to
receive His Law. No nation wanted to accept thee except
Israel before Mt. Sinai!'[4] Thereupon the Torah departs.
Then appear one by one the twenty-two letters of the
Hebrew alphabet as witnesses, and are put to shame by
Abraham. Our text has only the first three letters, each
standing for one abstract idea, offended by Israel. Originally
all the twenty-two letters were represented. Later the text
was shortened for obvious reasons. The rest of the homily,
which has nearly the character of a legend, contains several
speeches delivered by Isaac, Jacob, and Moses, the last
quoting elegies in Aramaic, and a dialogue between Moses

---

[1] *v.* Gen. R. 55. 9.
[2] Midr. Lam. (ed. Buber), p. 26.
[3] *v.* Bultmann, op. cit., p. 12.
[4] This Haggadah is often repeated, *v.* Mekh. 67a, ולפיכך נתבעו אומ״ה כדי
שלא ליתן פתחון פה להם כלפי שכינה. Sifre Deut. § 343; B. AZ. 3b.

and the sun, concluding with an address by Rachel to God, who responds.

5. The Haggadah preserved furthermore another significant feature of the diatribe, shorter than the dialogues mentioned in the previous paragraphs, but manifesting certain characteristics of the dialogue. The homilists interrupt their discourse, or begin it with an alleged or a real objection to their theme or the Bible by some opponent. The first class of these objections can be grouped together under the heading אם יאמר לך אדם. The preacher develops an idea, and in the course of his sermon he interjects: 'but, if someone tells you, so reply to him'. Many times the homilist begins his exposition: כל מי שאומר 'whosoever says so and so'. Thirdly, the audience is reminded of a fact שלא יאמרו 'in order that people should not say', &c. A fourth group has תשובה למי שאומר 'a reply to those, who say', &c. The name or character of the objector is omitted, though in many cases either the מינים, פושעי ישראל, or אומות העולם are mentioned as actual or possible critics. Here belong further the sayings introduced by שלא ליתן פתחון פה in order not to give an opening of the mouth, i.e. occasion, or opportunity to the nations of the world, Minim (Gnostics) or Christians to say, &c. Finally, one comes across the phrase אל תתמה 'do not wonder', especially after legends and stories which tax the credulity even of the simplest mind. I will give a few instances of each of these diatribic forms, especially bearing in mind the relation between Minim and Scribes.

The first, אם יאמר לך אדם, is to be found as early as the middle of the second century in the Haggadah of the Tannaim, R. Judah b. Ilai' and R. Nehemiah. Both of these, as shown in the first part of this study, must have taken a prominent part in the fight against Gnostic speculations and Bible criticism.[1] Here[2] we are concerned with their exposi-

---

[1] v. above, pp. 22, 25, 46.
[2] Lev. R. 27. 4, Pes. RK. 76a fuller than Lev. R. Tanḥ. iii (ed. Buber), 90. Eccl. R. 3. 15, where the sayings are interchanged, Eccl. Zuṭṭa 98, Yalḳ. Eccl. 967.

tions of Eccles. 3. 15. Ecclesiastes teaches that that which has been is now, and that which is to be has already been. Some sceptic objected to the first as well as to the second clause saying: אם יאמר לך אדם שאלו לא חטא אדם הראשון ואכל מאותו העץ היה חי וקיים לעולם: 'if Adam had not sinned and tasted of that tree, he could have lived for ever'. Koheleth says: 'What has been is now. Supposing Adam had not sinned, would he be alive?' Further, אם יאמר לך אדם שהקב״ה עתיד להחיות לנו מתים: 'God will in future revive the dead', consequently, there will be something new, which has not been in the past? The reply is: 'Tell him (אמור לו), the first question can be met by Elijah, who is still alive, the second by the deeds of Elijah, Elisha and Ezekiel.' R. Nehemiah raises other questions of a similar type: אם יאמר לך אדם אפשר שהיה העולם כולו מים במים? אמור לו כבר הוא אוקיינוס כולו מים במים; ואם יאמר לך אדם שהקב״ה עתיד לעשות את הים יבשה אמור לו כבר היה כך לא עשה על ידי משה. The first part of the verse is attacked by one who doubts the teaching that the world was 'water in water', the second by one who asks: Will there be a time when the sea will become dry land? Otherwise how could Koheleth assert: 'that which is to be, has already been?' The teacher reminds one first of the ocean, then of the crossing of the Red Sea. It is quite probable that the objections affected Rabbinic lore more than Ecclesiastes' wisdom. Could Adam have lived for ever if he had not sinned? Does Koheleth not deny the belief in resurrection? How can Rabbinic cosmology and eschatology be reconciled with the teachings of Koheleth? The objectors thought of must have been Gnostics, who took the greatest pleasure in finding faults in the Bible. The teachers are contemporaries of Marcion, whose influence reached those who visited the synagogues. As a consequence of Gnostic agitation, we hear from this period onwards the teaching: *Whatsoever God will create in the future has its counterpart in the past.*[1] Yet there is another possibility. It may be that

---

[1] The doctrine is ascribed to R. Ḥalafta (Lev. R.), R. Eleazar b. Ḥalafta (Pes.), Simon ben Ḥalafta (Cant. R.).

pious souls could not yet acquiesce in the canonicity of Ecclesiastes. There might have been a set of Jews who, in order to combat the Gnostic movements, repeated old or invented new objections to Ecclesiastes, and agitated for the removal of this book from the Canon. Some traces of such an agitation are still to be discerned in our sources. But even this was due to Gnostic cross-currents, as we see Minim tackling the same questions in the third century.[1]

R. Simon ben Laḳish delivered a sermon on Ps. 60. 9, 'Gilead is mine, and Manasseh is mine; Ephraim is also the defence of my head, Judah is my law-giver.' God says: (1) If a man tells you God will not revive the dead, point to the case of Elijah, who came from *Gilead*, and revived the dead son of the woman of Zarephath. (2) If a man tells you that God does not receive those who repent, point to *Manasseh*, who was a king of Judah. (3) If a man tells you that God does not help the barren woman, point to the wife of Elkanah, who came from *Ephraim*. (4) If a man tells you that God does not save from fire (or, according to a second version, from wild beasts), point to the three young men, or Daniel, who came from *Judah*. (5) If a man tells you that God does not heal lepers, refer him to the instance of *Moab* (or, according to another version, that God does not save from water, point to Moses, who was drawn from the water). (6) If a man tells you that God cannot redeem the weak from the hand of the strong without sword and spear, let David come and testify against him.[2]

---

[1] Num. R. 14. 4, סימא בר כתפה in the name of R. Simon ben Laḳish, introduced by אם יאמרו לך המינים, shortened Tanḥ. (ed. Buber) iv. 41. Agadat Bereshit, ch. 52, in the name of R. Berekhyah, 4th cent., in a slightly different order.

[2] Tabulating these six different objections, according to the names of the teachers cited, we learn first of all that there are themes common to all of them; secondly, we may be able to establish the connexion existing between them, and finally learn the development of these heresies. The first rubric represents the questions mentioned by R. Judah ben Ilai' (RJ), the second, the third, and the fourth by R. Nehemiah (RN), R. Samuel b. Naḥmani

The Minim against whom these Rabbis argued could not
have been Christians of any sort, but were Jewish Gnostics,
who doubted or denied the belief in the resurrection, the
possibility of repentance, and God's ability to help, or assist
the ailing and those in danger of life. They opposed doctrines accepted and believed by the average Jew in the third
century. Even Christians and pagans concurred in such
beliefs.

On the whole, the term אם יאמר לך אדם–אמור לו, while not
rare in the Tannaitic Haggadah, is quite frequent in the
Amoraic teachings. It is the term used in the anonymous
Haggadah quoted above about God testing human beings,[1]
whereas in another version another form of the diatribe is
substituted, namely, שלא ליתן פתחון פה.[2]

Interesting is another homily, based on Ps. 60. 9,[3] which
answers criticisms of Elijah, Gideon, David, and Joshua,
for committing some act or other in breach of the commandments of the Law. *Elijah* built an altar on Mt. Carmel, and
brought sacrifices thereon, in spite of the fact that there was
a Sanctuary at that time. Such an action was against Lev.
17. 3–4. *Gideon* did a similar thing, offering sacrifices on
the high places, whilst the Temple in Shiloh was in exist-

(RSbN), and R. Simon b. Laḳish (RSbL) respectively. The underlined words
recur in all or in some of the rubrics.

RJ	RN	RSbN	RSbL
אדם הר׳ חי וקיים	מים במים	<u>ים יבשה</u>	תחיית המתים 1
לעולם	<u>ים יבשה</u>	פוקח עורים	מקבל שבים 2
<u>מחיה מתים</u>		פוקד עקרות	פוקד עקרות 3
		מלכים משתחוים	מציל מן האש 4
			מציל מן חיות 4a
			מרפה צרעת 5
			מציל מן המים 5a
			מציל מן העץ 5b
			מציל חלש 6

[1] *v.* above, p. 17. Gen. R. ch. 55. 1, ed. Theodor, 584–5.
[2] Tanḥ. (ed. Buber) i. 58a.
[3] Num. R. 14. 5, Tanḥ. (ed. Buber) iv. 41.

ence. *David* sinned against the Law, and *Joshua* broke the Sabbath before Jericho. All of them, was the reply, acted on God's command (על פי הגבורה), and for His sake. David's case is interpreted as a special example to sinners to repent, since the gates of repentance are always open. It thus forms a connecting link between No. 2 in R. Simon ben Laḳish's list and this present diatribe. Here we can avail ourselves of material outside our own literature to identify the objectors whom the preacher had in mind. Early writings of the Church refer to Joshua as a proof for the mutability of the Law,[1] and I have shown that Marcion and his followers raised the same questions from their own point of view.

The diatribe form is more usual in the Amoraic Haggadah. This, however, does not in itself prove that it is a sign of the later Haggadah. Such a question cannot be finally settled in the course of a brief essay, such as the present one, since it requires a review of the whole material, for which there is no room here. We find this term in the Haggadah of the following Amoraim: R. Joshua ben Levi, R. Yose ben Zimra, R. Ḥanina b. Ḥama, R. Isaac, R. Levi, R. Abbahu, R. Ḥiyya b. Abba, R. Huna, R. Yose b. Abin, R. Abba Serungaya, besides those mentioned previously. Three instances taken from the anonymous Haggadah shall, for the present, conclude this part of our investigation. They relate to three different subjects, and may be used to illustrate different aspects of the intellectual, political, and religious conditions of the first centuries. The canonicity of some portions of the Hebrew Bible, the relation of the Torah to worldly wisdom, or the Torah to Early Christianity, and finally the shattered hopes of the Jews in the period after the Emperor Julian's death, are the subjects concerned.

(A) 'God made his covenant with Israel for the sake of the Torah.' One should not say (שלא יאמר אדם): 'The Psalms are not Torah.' No, they are Torah, as are also the

---

[1] *v.* above, p. 23.

Books of the Prophets, and not only the Psalms but also the Riddles and Parables.[1] The text is unfortunately in a bad condition. This is the more to be regretted, since a very grave question of far-reaching importance is here touched on. The homily presupposes opposition from some unknown quarter to a part of the established Canon of the Bible. The date is also of great importance. If we could trust the Yalḳut,[2] we might ascribe the homily to R. Samuel b. Naḥmani, which is not impossible. Another source[3] states the same principle in the form of a dialogue between Israel and the singer Asaph. Israel says: 'Is there another Torah?' Asaph: 'The פושעי ישראל assert that the Prophets and Hagiographa are not included in the Torah, and they do not believe in them.' A similar assertion is repeated in a Pisḳa for Pentecost, discovered and published by the present writer, where we read: 'In order that ye shall not say: God gave Israel the Torah (but not Nebi'im and Ketubim).'[4] Who are these enemies of the two latter sections of the Bible? Christians are *a priori* excluded, since Prophets and Hagiographa were as sacred to them as to the majority of the Jews. Samaritans and Sadducees are reputed to have rejected both Prophets and Hagiographa, yet it is unlikely that after so many centuries of separation from the people of Nablus, and after the Sadducees had lost all their influence and power, this should be the subject of homilies, though some Sadducees may have survived in some corners of Galilee, or may have amalgamated with Minim of different sorts; and it is against them that the homily is directed.

(B) A homily on Lam. 2. 9b (Her king and her princes are among the Gentiles, there is no Torah)[5] begins: 'If one

---

[1] M. Ps. (ed. Buber), p. 344.   [2] Ps. § 819.

[3] Tanḥ. (ed. Buber) v. 19; v. Marmorstein, *Religionsgesch. Studien*, i. 33, and in the essay given in the next footnote.

[4] v. Marmorstein, 'Ein Fragment einer neuen Piska zum Wochenfest und der Kampf gegen das mündliche Gesetz', in *Jeschurun*, xii (1925), 24–53.

[5] Midr. Lam. (ed. Buber), p. 114.

tells you there is wisdom among the nations, believe him
(cf. Obad. 1. 8), but if he tells you, there is Torah among
them, do not believe him.' A fuller version[1] of this homily
is to be found in a Midrash on Deuteronomy. 'It is not
hidden from thee (Deut. 30. 11), but it is hidden from the
nations of the world. If one tells thee that there are heroes
and wealthy people among the nations of the world, believe
him, but if that there is Torah among them, do not believe
him.' This homily is directed against Christian views.
Christians claimed the Scriptures as their inheritance, and
accused the Jews of forgeries. The preachers of the synagogues declared that in spite of Tertullian, Clement of
Alexandria, Origen, and others there is no Torah among
the Gentiles.

(C) (a) This is a reply to those, who say: 'It is true that
God said: "I build a sanctuary!", and He built one, but ye
sinned, and He destroyed it, and will rebuild it no more!'
The refutation is based on the future in the verbs ישכון and
ויתלונן (Job 39. 28).[2] The taunting voice must have come
from Christian circles, who ridiculed the hopes of the Jews
or put obstacles in the way of their attempts at rebuilding
the Sanctuary in Jerusalem. The passage would fit many
historical situations from 68 C.E. till the time of the Emperor
Julian. It is not unlikely that this Haggadah voices the views
of Julian's enemies, their joy at the failure of the hopes
of the Jews, and the bitter disappointment of the latter.
Julian's relations with the Jews are shown in his letters to
them, in which the promise to rebuild the Temple is
plainly expressed.[3] Our homily reflects the feeling among
Jews after the death of the Emperor.

(b) A second group is that of sayings and sentences introduced by כל האומר, 'anyone who says', or כל מי שאומר, 'whosoever says'. There is, e.g., a long catalogue of persons,

---

[1] Midr. Deut. (ed. Buber), p. 28.
[2] Pes. R. 10b, Yalḳuṭ Job.
[3] v. Graetz, *Geschichte*, iv. 338, and note 34.

such as the sons of Eli, Samuel, David, Josiah, and Solomon, who are supposed to have erred and committed sins. All who say that these persons, or one of them, transgressed the Law are mistaken.[1] Similar statements are made about the Queen of Sheba,[2] and Manasseh, King of Judah.[3] The first group is by R. Jonathan ben Eleazar, whom we know to have been greatly concerned with heretical views. He defended also Reuben's action, though this apology is much older. R. Eliezer ben Hyrcanus, R. Joshua ben Ḥananyah, R. Eleazar of Modi'im, R. Simon ben Eleazar, and R. Simon ben Gamaliel, preachers of the Tannaitic age, found it necessary as early as their time to deal with this point from the pulpit.[4] Bearing in mind Marcion's antithesis about God's favouring the wicked and condemning the good, we know where to look for an explanation of Jonathan's endeavours to justify or to defend the errors of these persons. The same preacher attacks those who think that the Queen of Sheba was a woman. The queen is not meant at all, but the Kingdom of Sheba. The defence of Manasseh is ascribed in our texts to R. Yoḥanan. Since the names of these two teachers are very often confused, is it too bold to assume that here also R. Jonathan is the original reading, instead of R. Yoḥanan? 'Whosoever asserts that Manasseh has no share in the future life, weakens the hands (מרפה ידיהן) of those who desire to repent!' We saw a few pages earlier that preachers had to combat a false doctrine of the Minim, that there is no repentance, and that God does not receive those who repent. In combating this highly pernicious conception, the Scribes went to the other extreme, and taught that there is no transgression or iniquity, not even excepting the cardinal sins of idolatry, bloodshed, and immorality, which, where

[1] B. Sabb. 55a.
[2] B. BB. 15b.
[3] B. Sanh. 103a.
[4] v. Sifre Deut. §§ 347, 355, Gen. R. 87. 8, B. Soṭah 7b, J. Soṭah 1. 4, Tanḥ. 58b.

forgiveness is proper, is not forgiven.[1] Only one of the
Scribes, R. Ḥanina b. Ḥama, thought it necessary to warn
against the idea of such leniency as misleading.[2] God's
forgiveness and goodness must not be misinterpreted.
'Whosoever proclaims that God is too forgiving, let his
inside be pierced. God is merciful, but He exacts His due.'
Both teachers must have been prompted to teach thus by
the views of Marcion who denied God's mercy and love.
The teaching can be traced back to Sirach, who wrote
against a similar attitude towards sin many centuries before
our period.[3] Then, as now, people denied God's goodness,
or the possibility of repentance, on one side, and on the
other side thought that God's forgiveness had no limits.
The contemporaries of Sirach expressed exactly the same
views as the Jews in the third century C.E. against whom
R. Ḥanina b. Ḥama protested. God is full of forgiveness,
consequently we may sin as much as we like. We trust
in His goodness, and may therefore heap iniquity upon
iniquity. His mercy is unlimited. Sirach tells them: 'Do
not say so! His mercy and anger go together!' The Mishnah
Yoma[4] may have thought of Sirach's contemporaries, who
said, 'I will sin, and repent!' or 'I will sin, and the Day of
Atonement will bring forgiveness!' In the third century the

---

[1] Tanḥ. f. 26a, Lev. R. 23. 9, R. Joshua ben Levi in the name of Bar
Kappara הזנות מן חיין מותר הקב״ה הכל על, M. Ps. 24d. R. Abba b. Kahana,
על הקב״ה שויתר מצינו השם חילול על ויתר ולא וש״ד ג״ע ע״ז, על הקב״ה ויתר
וש״ד ג״ע ,ע״ז. Lam. R. 1. 2, השם חילול על ויתר ולא וש״ד ג״ע ,ע״ז. Lam. R.
1. 2, תורה של מאסה על ויתר ולא וש״ד ג״ע ,ע״ז על הקב״ה שויתר מצינו. Cf. M.
Ps. 14b.
[2] Gen. R. 67. 4, ed. Theodor, 75f, J. Sheḳ. 48b, J. Beṣah 62b, J. Ta'anit
65b, B. BK. 50a, Pes. (ed. Buber) 161a. Tanḥ. תשא כי 26, M. Esther, 3,
16, 41. (ed. Buber), s.v. הרעים, Agadat Esther, s.v. יצא ומרדכי M. Ps. 10. 3,
Num. R. 14. 6 מעיו יתוותרון הוא וותרן הק״בה האומר כל.
[3] Hebr. 5. 4 ff. הוא! על כי יהוה ארך אפים הוא! אל תאמר: חטאתי ומה יעשה לי, כי יהוה ארך אפים הוא! על
סליחה תבטח אל להוסיף עון על עון ואמרת רחמיו רבים לרוב עונותי יסלח כי
רחמים ואף עמו ועל רשעים ינוח רגזו.
[4] Ch. 8. 9.

Meturgeman of R. Simon b. Laḳish, R. Judah b. Naḥmani, preached, 'If the Yeẓer ha-Ra' tells thee: "Sin, and God will forgive thee!" do not believe him!'[1]

(c) Thirdly, preachers were fond of introducing ideas which they rejected in a negative form, e.g. שלא יאמר לך אדם. One instance has been mentioned above.[2] These sayings give us a deeper insight into the thoughts and feelings of both parties. A homily on Job 41. 4 teaches: 'God said: In order that the children of man should not say (שלא יאמרו בני אדם): "We may also speak to God, as Abraham spoke, and He kept silent!", God replies: "I will not keep silent, although I kept silent unto Abraham." '[3] The same homilist makes Abraham say before God: 'Lord of the Universe! Far be it from Thee, &c., in order that people should not say (שלא יאמרו באי עולם): "That is His way, He destroys the generations in cruelty. He destroyed the generations of Enosh, of the Flood, of the Dispersion, He cannot abandon His way!" ' We now know the background of this saying of the באי עולם. It was made clear above that this argument is actually copied from Marcion's storehouse of arguments against the 'cruel' God.[4] It is most unlikely that the preachers themselves invented such words about a defeated or cruel God. They introduced them from speeches delivered, or writings compiled by Gnostics. Rhetoricians in the squares of the cities, or in assemblies, argued and were listened to by Christians and Jews, Gnostics and pagans. The orators of the synagogues were bound to pay the closest attention to these opinions of the market philosophers, and counteract their mischievous influence. Another example will illustrate this: R. Judah b. Simon, a well-known Haggadist of the fourth century, asserts that besides Moses and Aaron, God Himself took an active part in the numbering of Israel in the wilderness. Why did God join with Moses and Aaron in counting them? God said:

---

[1] B. Hag. 16a.
[2] v. p. 61.
[3] Tanḥ. (ed. Buber) i. 91.
[4] v. above, p. 20 f.

'In order that one should not say, "How could Moses and Aaron correctly count the multitudes of Israel?" ' Therefore, he who doubts the numberings of Moses and Aaron is to be considered as if he criticized God Almighty![1] We have other and earlier evidence that the correctness of the numbers in the Scriptures was often questioned.[2] Another preacher compares the virtue of work with the merit of the fathers. Jacob was saved owing to his own work, and not through the merit of the fathers, in his contest with Laban. We derive hence the teaching that a man should not say: 'I will eat and drink, and see good, but I will not toil, for Heaven will provide for me!'[3] This saying can be paralleled with another by Ulla, in the name of R. Ḥiyya b. Ammi, who teaches: 'Greater is he who earns his own living than he who fears Heaven.'[4] In sharp contrast with these views is the preaching of R. Eleazar of Modi'im: 'He who says, "what shall I eat tomorrow?" is one of those who have little faith in Heaven.'[5] The difference in attitude towards this problem between the teacher of Modi'im and the preachers of the third century seems to me most remarkable.

(d) A fourth diatribic form in the Haggadah uses the term למי שאומר תשובה or למי שאומרים connecting the reply with the alleged interruption of the interlocutor. We quoted above an instance[6] which perhaps throws new light on the history of the Jews after the age of the Emperor Julian. An earlier passage uses this form to refute the views of heretics who deny the existence of the heavenly kingdom, who allege the existence of two powers, and who teach that neither can

---

[1] Num. R. 7. 2.

[2] e.g. the interlocutor of R. Yoḥanan b. Zakkai.

[3] Tanḥ. f. 39b, Num. R. 22. 9 למד שלא יאמר אדם אכל ואשתה ואראה בטוב ולא אטריח עצמי ומן השמים ירחמו.

[4] B. Ber. 8a גדול הנהנה מיגיעו יותר מירא שמים.

[5] Mekh. 26a, B. Soṭah 48a, Exod. R. 25. 14, Tanḥ. f. 88b, Matt. 6. 30ff., Epictetus, Dis. I. 9. 19. Bergmann in Cohen's Judaica, p. 158.

[6] v. pp. 63–64.

God revive nor is death in His power, He can perform neither good nor evil.[1] Atheists, Dualists, and Epicureans stand in the background of this Haggadah. We come across the same term in a refutation of the Christian dogma, proclaiming the idea of God's son.[2] This apology or polemic utterance is not earlier than the fourth century.

(e) We turn now to arguments, allegations, accusations, and libels, which are repeated in Rabbinic homilies in the name of a whole set or group of people. Up till now we have considered anonymous interlocutors, whose words or views were quoted by homilists, without disclosing the names, characters, origins, or positions of the persons concerned. Some sayings, however, clearly indicate the source whence they came. Here we consider, first of all, sayings ascribed to the *nations of the world*, introduced by או''ה מונים או''ה or אומרים or שלא יאמרו או''ה. These sayings cover the whole ground of anti-Jewish polemics of the first four centuries, and reveal the darkest forces in the background of Rabbinic apologetics. The polemical interlocutions touch Israel's relation to God, Israel's past, present, and future, Israel's Bible and faith, Israel's character and achievements. Some of these calumnies dragged on, as it were, a miserable existence for more than a millennium in word and script, and are heard up to this hour in the literature and press of the gutter. No wonder! They originated in the alehouses of Alexandria, in the dens of vainglorious demagogues, in the perverted hearts of philosophic charlatans, who successfully imposed on their stupid contemporaries with empty catchwords and battle-cries. Pious Church Fathers were infected and used those hateful words in the misguided campaign against the sanctity of the Synagogue. Other attacks were illegitimately born under the shadow of narrow-minded and petty pulpits of the Ancient Church. Some are the wild fruits of the bitter struggle between Early Christian-

---

[1] Sifre Deut. § 329, Midr. Tann. p. 202.
[2] M. Ps. (ed. Buber), p. 28, *v.* also ed. Prague 4b.

ity and Judaism, written with the poisonous quills of prejudice by men whose professed task it was to spread love
and benevolence. It would have been less than human if
some of the Scribes had not paid back their arch-enemies
with the very same coin. The anti-Jewish polemical literature
produced such tissues of falsehood, such a network of the
most abominable and humiliating accusations, that one
could not be surprised at the prevalence of that most dis-
graceful historical phenomenon, called, for want of a
better name, anti-Semitism.

The limited space at our disposal here does not permit
a full description of this terrible conflict, which may be
regarded as one of the most tragic chapters of the history of
human intellect. We can merely point out the brief items
which are grouped together under the diatribic form או"ה
אומרים. *God*, or the God of Israel, was depicted as cruel and
weak. Actually the pagan mind was not greatly concerned
about God, whom they somehow could tolerate or ignore,
although the Scribes assert that the nations of the world
hate God. But this very fact was supposed to be the hidden
secret of the great enmity against Israel, God's people,
representing the King of Heaven on earth. God's relation
to Israel, and Israel's loyal adherence to God, was a thorn
in their side. Where is your God? How is He superior to
all other Gods? Did He not perish when His House was
destroyed? Is there a God, whose believers are defeated,
and whose people are exiled? Could an almighty God suffer
His city, His temple to become a prey of flames, His adherents the victims of a foreign sword, and the survivors
of that catastrophe the exhibits of the slave-markets all over
the world? Christians adapted and developed these pagan
taunts by asserting that they are the true Israel, God has
forsaken Israel, moreover, they never have been God's
people, by the *deed of the calf* they broke the divine covenant.
To the heathen mind the national misfortune was a proof of
God's weakness, to the Christian a weapon in their propa-

ganda that Israel is rejected by God, and His love and grace
transferred to the New People. The Apostles of Love found
out that God hates Israel. They will never be redeemed.
God loves the nations of the world, and finds no pleasure
in Israel. Israel has to assimilate either with pagan or with
Christian Rome. Both stretched out their loving arms to
embrace the Jews. Many succumbed, yet the old remnant
kept to God. Thus the blackening of the Jews goes on for
many centuries, with greater or lesser force, to this very day.
We hear: 'The Jews are idolaters, immoral, guilty of bloodshed, robbers, they are the descendants of Egyptians, lepers,
despised and low people, never of any use to the world,
enemies of law and society, an obstinate, stiff-necked race?'
This catalogue of misdoings and faults on the part of the
Jews is much longer than could be reproduced here. It
is significant of the inner relation of Judaism to Christianity that the latter is styled in these diatribes by the same
title as is used for the pagans by early writers of the Church
as well as by Jews. Both appeared to the Jews as the nations
of the world. Christians were no longer in the eyes of the
Jews the small group of Nosrim, or Posh'e Israel, they
became estranged altogether. Further, it is to be noticed
that neither pagans nor Christians attacked the Bible as
such; the former, with very few earlier exceptions, out of
indifferentism, the latter out of veneration for the sacred
texts. This was left to the Minim, whose interlocutions
engaged our attention in the first chapter.

(f) In conclusion, a few instances of the diatribic form of
אל תתמה, 'do not wonder', may be given. It is used when the
preacher gives rein to his fancy in depicting miracles or
repeating legends from the pulpit. There must have been
critics among the audience who by shaking their heads, or
faint smiles, showed their disapproval. For instance, when
describing Moses' endeavour to find Joseph's coffin. He
was directed by Serah, the daughter of Asher. Moses took
a pebble (צרור), cast it into the Nile, and the coffin came

floating to the surface. There may have been a stir among the
hearers, and the preacher uses אל תתמה and moderates their
surprise and amazement by repeating the story of II Kings
6. 6.[1] R. Levi teaches in the name of R. Simon b. Menasya
that the heel of Adam darkened the sun;[2] and adds אל תתמה,
a man who makes two bedchambers (קיטונים, κοιτών), one
for himself, the other for his household, which will be more
beautiful? the latter or the former? Surely the former!
Adam was created for the service of God, the sun for the
use of man. R. Berekhyah expounded the fanciful doctrine
that Solomon's temple was not built by human hands but
was ready-made. Even the stones came from great distances,
and placed themselves in the layer (דימוס, δόμος). This
strange teaching, naturally, provoked amazement. Thereupon Dan. 6. 18 is quoted. 'Are there stones in Babylon?
Certainly not, but a stone flew from Palestine and settled
itself on the mouth of the pit.'[3] These, and many more
instances which can be adduced,[4] prove clearly that the
statements of the preachers were not accepted on their face
value, but criticized.

[1] Mekh. 24a, b, Tosefta Soṭah 300; v. Marmorstein, 'Beiträge I' in Dr.
Grünwald *Jahrbuch*, i. 281–8 for parallels and explanation.
[2] Pes. (ed. Buber) 36b and parallels.
[3] Cant. R. 1. 5 and parallels.
[4] Gen. R. 4. 9 and parallels.

THE UNITY OF GOD IN RABBINIC LITERATURE

I

NO teaching of the Law and Prophets acquired such a prominent place in the liturgy and the homilies of the Jews as the doctrine proclaimed in Deut. 6. 4: 'Hear, O Israel, The Lord is our God, the Lord is One.' These words and their continuation formed an integral part of the daily service morning and evening as early as the period of the second Temple.[1]

Josephus tells us also: 'Let every one commemorate before God the benefits which He bestowed upon them at their deliverance out of the land of Egypt, and this twice daily, both when the day begins and when the hour of sleep comes on.'[2] We find the *Shema'* in four other places in the prayer-book. First of all, it is recited when the Scrolls are taken from the Ark for the reading of the Law on Sabbaths and Festivals.[3] Secondly, in the *Trisagion* (קדושה) of the *Mussaf* service for Sabbath and Festivals.[4] Thirdly, in the daily prayers before ברוך שאמר;[5] and finally, on the Day of Atonement after the *Neilah*.[6] Each of these insertions of the *Shema'* in the liturgy has its own more or less authentic history. Their conspicuousness in the service testifies to the zeal and devotion with which the teachers of Judaism propagated and guarded the chief religious doctrine the Jews taught mankind. For Jews could not have become the teachers of monotheism, unless they themselves had been deeply conscious of the greatness and loftiness of this doctrine.

---

[1] Mishnah Ber. i. 1; Tamid 5. 1.
[2] *Ant.* iv. 8. 13.
[3] Sôferîm 14. 8 שבלי הלקט Sec. 77, Eisak Tyrnau, ed. Munkács, i. 23.
[4] Seder R. Amram Gaon, Maḥzôr Vitry, p. 99, p. 108; Pardes 5d., Or Zarua ii. 11c; Ginzberg, *Geonica*, ii. 50–1.
[5] *v.* שבולי הלקט S. 6 Friedmann.
[6] *v.* Maḥzôr Vitry, p. 395.

In order that this thought should take deep root in the soul of Judaism, it had to be repeated again and again. It was expressed in the most solemn moments of the Jew's life, as well as on joyous occasions. The Deuteronomist's injunction and desire that these words should accompany the Jew when sitting in his house and walking by the way, when lying down and rising up, was realized in the fullest sense. On New Year's Day, when the Jewish soul trembles in the presence of its Judge, being aware of all its short-comings and feeling more than ever its disappointments and sorrows, the awe-inspiring declaration is heard in the assemblies, 'Holy art Thou, fearful is Thy name, there is no God beside Thee!'[1] It is reaffirmed in the impressive litany commencing 'Our Father! Our King! we have no God beside Thee',[2] in the *Nishmat* prayer,[3] and, again, in the '*Amîdah* for Sabbath afternoon: 'Thou art one and Thy name is one.'[4] With special reference to Christian doctrines emphasis was laid on the thought: 'We have no forgiving and atoning Lord beside Thee.'[5] We could adduce proofs for the importance of this doctrine in the service and worship from other parts of the liturgy as well, for the prayer book was and is, up to this day, a vast storehouse of Jewish 'theology and apologetics'. It was very necessary to emphasize this idea in the liturgy, for the doctrine of God's unity was more exposed to the opposition of the world outside the Synagogue, and to misrepresentation inside the Synagogue, than any other teaching of Judaism. Somehow, one could obtain tolerance for the teaching that there exists a God in heaven, but the idea that God is One and almighty, omniscient and omnipotent, the Creator of heaven and earth, infinite and everlasting, the giver and sustainer of life, was met with incredulity by some, with doubt by others.

[1] *v.* Maḥzôr Vitry, p. 383.
[2] Ibid. 389.
[3] *v.* Elbogen, *Der jüd. Gottesdienst*, 211 f.
[4] *v.* 'Orḥôt Ḥayyim, pp. 64c, 66a.
[5] *v.* Maḥzôr Vitry, p. 391.

The truth, in its most simple form, must be preached again and again till the masses are able to grasp it, at least approximately. He who proclaims it should not grow weary, for it is easier to move mountains than to eradicate falsehood and unbelief, especially when supported and maintained by the priests of selfishness and prophets of wickedness. The teachers of Israel did not grow weary. With great force and stirring eloquence they exhorted Israel, in spite of hundred-fold death, incredible martyrdom and cruel tortures, in face of strong foes and mighty empires, to adhere to God and declare twice daily His Unity with the same words which the Deuteronomist used in dispelling the darkness of idol-worship. With pride they point out that Israel enters daily the Houses of Prayer, and declares that there is only One God.[1] They see in this faithful observance Israel's greatest glory and hope for the future, which no temporary power can diminish or destroy.[2]

Next to the prayers and homilies, we have legends which kept alive in the homes and hearts of the Jews the teaching inculcated in the schools and synagogues. Legends were more powerful allies of the theologians and teachers, apologists and preachers, than is generally realized. The story of Abraham breaking the idols in his father's house, as well as the martyrdom of Hannah's seven children, brought the teaching home to the broad masses of the people. The Rabbis had to avail themselves of all possible means to strengthen the belief in the Unity of God against the different influences which endangered it.

Three forces were arrayed against this doctrine in fierce battle; it had to be defended against three spiritual armies, from three different points of view, and with many different weapons. There were first the heathen who believed in the

---

[1] v. Lam. R. 1. 44; Deut. R. 2. 23; Lam. R. 3. 19 and 22; M. Ps. ed. Frankft. 53a; Tanḥ. 40a, v. also the benediction quoted by Abudarham, 31a, JQR, x. 654 f.

[2] Gen. R. 98. 3; M. Ps. 17. 8; Gen. R. 65. 17 and 21; Cant. R. 8. 15; Deut. R. 4. 4.

existence and rule of various deities, gods, and goddesses, or who disbelieved, yet wished for various political or intellectual reasons to preserve the gods as safeguards of the existing world order. The second army was that of the Gnostics, who proclaimed and believed in two powers, degrading the God of Israel to a national Deity, to a source of evil in this world, to the imperfect Demi-god. The third force comprised Christians and Jewish heretics, who darkened the sky of Israel's pure monotheism by teaching their peculiar theory of Jesus, identifying him with God, and declaring him to be God's son by advancing the dogma of the Trinity on one side and false conceptions about angels and their relation to God on the other side.

II

1. The battle against heathendom and idol-worship in their various manifestations did not cease in Judaism with the birth of Christianity, nor with its growth into a world power. The notion that rabbinical Judaism, or as it is usually disparagingly called Pharisaic Judaism, lost its interest in the fight against idolatry with the entrance of Christianity on the scene, that Judaism as such moved, or was pushed, into the background altogether and looked upon the struggle between Monotheism and Polytheism as a neutral, without taking any, or only a slightly active part in it, is one of the numerous injustices which a biased and prejudiced study of history has inflicted on the memory of the Scribes. This verdict is not borne out by historical facts! As a matter of fact, we shall meet in the course of our study learned and unlearned men who up to the fifth century, either in the quiet halls of study, or in the busy marketplaces, were forging weapons against the unbearable chains by which idolatry enslaved the human mind and heart, destroying with their teaching the statues and temples of the idols, or lifting the heavy curtains of senseless cruelty

with which polytheism shrouded the eyes and the vision of the best representatives of antiquity.

In the dialogues of the Talmudists we come across the theatre-theologians, as one of the greatest teachers of the Church called them, as well as the idle salon-philosophers. The doctrine of God's Unity had to be defended against the attacks of the refined philosophers, just as the influence of the lowest fetishism which appeared in the guise of animal or planet worship had to be combated. The classification of various kinds of idolatry, which the apologists of the Church borrowed from Jewish Hellenistic writers, can be found also in Haggadic literature.

We begin the description of the struggle between polytheism and monotheism with R. Gamaliel II. The first problem he had to deal with was the general question of the helpfulness of the idols. The interlocutor, who addressed the Patriarch, asked: 'How can you assert that the idols do no good, or serve no purpose whatever? Have you never observed, when fire destroyed a city, that the flames never reached or destroyed the Temples or other sacred places belonging to the gods?' R. Gamaliel answered in a parable: 'A king declares war against a country—whom is he going to fight, the dead or the living? Certainly, the latter', i.e. the fire is not sent against the Temples, which do not count. 'But', argued the interlocutor, 'why does He not destroy them, being Almighty?' R. Gamaliel replied: 'You worship so many things, e.g., sun and moon, stars and planets, mountains and hills, valleys and rivers, yea, even human beings and animals—should God make all of these perish on account of some fools, who worship them?'[1] The same question recurs in a dialogue between the 'Elders' and the 'Philosophers',[2] with the additional objection on the part of the latter: 'Let Him destroy the useless things, which are worshipped!' The Elders reply: 'If that were so,

---

[1] Mekh. 68a; B. 'Ab. Zarah 54b.
[2] B. 'Ab. Zarah 54b; B. 'Ab. Zarah 44a; Tos. 469, l. 31.

then, of course, the idolaters who worship useful things would be the more confirmed in their folly and proclaim: "They are deities, for He did not destroy them!" ' In another version we read the last argument somewhat differently: 'What, do you suppose, if somebody has stolen a measure of wheat and sowed it in his field, the ground would become barren and produce nothing? No, that is impossible. Nature takes its own course.' The triumph of folly and wickedness cannot be regarded as a sign of the inferiority of wisdom and virtue.

These dialogues enable us to see more deeply into the intellectual status of the first century. These philosophers, who certainly were not the best representatives of their contemporary schools of thought, but those who shouted loudest in the markets, anyhow reflect the feelings of, we may say, some higher strata of society. We can reconstruct from their words the general opinion of their contemporaries. They thought that the God of the Jews cannot be almighty, if He tolerates other gods beside Him. Secondly, they pointed out that the might of their gods is confirmed by so many proofs and instances, which every sophist and charlatan could count many times on his fingers. These arguments are old, but by no means antiquated. They belong to the store of superstition which has persisted undiminished for nineteen hundred years down to our own day. Even the progress of natural science, the growth of knowledge, and the spread of culture could not withstand the victorious march of superstition. The sages could have given, and, as a matter of fact, did give different and stronger answers to the questions raised. Yet we have to bear in mind whom they were facing. Their replies were always suited to the class of people who entered into discussion with them. Therefore, they had to choose their words according to the intelligence of the interlocutors.

These dialogues enable us further to understand the proper meaning of many *Haggadot* which look, at first sight, strange and unintelligible. Thus, for instance, the homilies based on Exod. 14. 2, which take a great deal of trouble to explain why *Baal-zephon* was saved, why the first-born of the captives died in prison, and why the first-born of the cattle perished. *Baal-zephon* was saved in order to entice the heathen and confirm them in their folly, according to Job 12. 23. The first-born among the captives died, so that they should not be able to say: 'Our gods are mightier than those of Egypt.' The cattle perished, in order that the Egyptians who worshipped the cattle should not argue: 'Our deities visited us with these plagues and trials. Mighty are our gods, who chastised us! Mighty are our gods who escaped the plague which befell our country!'[1] These arguments are not free from contradictions. They might have originated in two different schools of thought. Yet both have a direct bearing on our problem. According to one school, the idols are preserved to confirm the nations in their mistaken idol-worship. The other train of thought argues that the idols and their worshippers are destroyed and punished in order to free mankind from the false belief that idolatry can be of any use.

Our problem also recurs in the dialogues of R. Akiba, whose first interlocutor is likewise styled a philosopher, by name Zenon, while the second is the often mentioned Tinaeus Rufus. Zenon gives himself the air of an enlightened person, who knows very well that the gods worshipped by the crowd are stone and wood, they are useless and helpless, they can *do neither good nor harm; yet*, experience teaches that people often turn to them in trouble and illness with great success. This perplexed our philosopher, and he asked R. Akiba, 'How do you account for it?' 'Well', said R. Akiba, 'I will illustrate your case by a parable! There was once in a certain place a highly trustworthy person. The people of the city deposited with him their treasures without witnesses. One citizen, however, made it a rule not to go to

[1] Mekh. 13b, 26a.

him without two reliable witnesses. Once he came without
them. The wife of the trustworthy person said: "Now, you
have an excellent opportunity to overreach him!" The man
replied: "Shall I lose my good name, because he did a
foolish thing?" The same is the case with the sick person,
who sought healing in the temple of the gods and found it.
We may put it in this way. "It was decreed concerning a
certain man that he should be sick and ailing, and that after
so and so many days, or hours, by the help of this or that
surgeon or physician, by means of this or that medicine,
he should recover. When this time arrives and the ailing
person goes to the temple for help, the illness says: 'I
really ought not to depart from this person, yet is it right to
fail in my duty because this man acted in a foolish way?'" [1]
It is irrelevant whether the questioner was a Jew or the
philosopher of the same name who wrote a treatise against
idolatry.[2] Important is the fact that then, as now, even
educated, enlightened people were at a loss to explain
alleged or true miracles. Minucius Felix dealt with the same
difficult problem. His reply sounds somewhat different:
'Where the oracles of heathendom', says the apologist of the
Church, 'the bird-seers and sacrifice-diviners foretold the
future, that was either a play of accident, or the treachery
of the demons was responsible for it!'[3] Here is a remarkable
difference between the Synagogue and the Church! Whilst
the latter held that the idols and images were the work of
the demons, Judaism of the first centuries taught practically
without dissenting voice that the idols are nothing at all.
There is no reality in them.[4] The teachers of the Syna-

---

[1] B. 'Ab. Zarah 55a.
[2] v. Wendland, Hell.-röm. Kultur, p. 17.
[3] v. Zöckler, Die Apologie des Christentums, p. 71, and Harnack, Diodor von Tarsus, p. 80.
[4] For the point of view of the Church, see Gibbon, Decline and Fall, ii. 280; Wendland, op. cit., p. 123; Michel, Gebet und Bild, p. 10; Rhein. Mus. li, 279; For the teaching of the Rabbis, v. Marmorstein, Midrash Ḥaserot we Yetherot, p. 59; v. also Mekh. 42b, Lam. R. 1. 24; Deut. R. 2. 19; and other passages.

gogue had, consequently, to face the question: 'Why are they
called in the Bible by the name of God?' אלהים. This confirms the idolaters in their conviction that the Scriptures
also acknowledged the divine character and the existence
of these deities.[1] There are many attempts to explain the
term אלהים אחרים. R. Yose ben Ḥalafta, for instance, follows
the argument of R. Gamaliel II.[2] R. Phineas ben Ḥama
says: 'They are called so in order to give a higher reward
to him who separates himself from idolatry.' God says
to Israel: 'Although there is really nothing in idol-worship,
still, if one separates himself from it, I reward him for acting
as if there were something in it, and yet he gave it up.'[3]

There are many other attempts[4] to explain this difficulty,
which gave rise to a much more serious problem. If idolatry
is nothing, why does the law deal so severely with idolators?
Why is God so jealous? The question was asked of R.
Gamaliel twice, once by the philosopher whose acquaintance
we have made already[5] when introducing his dialogue, and
once by a general called Agrippa.[6] Also by Tinaeus Rufus
in his dialogue with R. Akiba. Tinaeus Rufus asked R.
Akiba, 'Why does your God hate us? as it is said: "I hate
Esau." '[7] R. Akiba asked leave to postpone his answer.[8]
Next morning R. Akiba came, and the Roman dignitary
asked him: 'What have you dreamed, Akiba?' R. Akiba
replied, 'I dreamed of two dogs, one called Rufus, the other
Rufina'. That annoyed Tinaeus Rufus very much and he
said, 'You could not make up another name? You shall die
for this!' R. Akiba answered: 'What is the difference
between you and the dog Rufus? You eat and drink, as
does also your namesake. You bring up young ones, as

---

[1] v. Clem. Hom. 55–7; Schliemann, Die Clementinen, p. 194.
[2] v. Mekh. 67b; Sifre Deut. § 43; Midr. Tannaim, ed. Hoffmann, p. 20,
Gen. R. 2. 23, and Midr. Ps. 88. 6.
[3] Deut. R. 2. 11; Midr. Ps. 50b. Wertheimer, Bate Midrashot, iv. 12.
[4] Sifre Deut. § 43.   [5] v. above, p. 76.
[6] B. 'Ab. Zarah 55a.   [7] Mal. 1. 3.
[8] A favourite device in these disputes, v. R. Gamaliel II in Gaster's
המעשיות ס', p. 11. R. Akiba, Midrash Temurah, ed. Wertheimer, pp. 15 f.

does also the dog. You perish, likewise the dog Rufus! You are angry with me because I called the dog Rufus, and God, who created heaven and earth, who established the universe, and in whose hands are life and death, should He not hate you, who call wooden idols God, after His name?'[1] The words are identical with those of R. Gamaliel and of the Elders.

2. We learn from these instances that the Haggadists of the first and second centuries, just like the prophets many hundreds of years before them, were forced to point out the futility of idol-worship. Philosophers, priests, and poets also denied the very existence and reality of these gods; general scepticism mocked at the vanity and folly of these idols; yet they graced all the festivals of these gods with their presence. They outwardly observed all the rites, and sacrificed publicly in due season, in order to discharge their official duties and set the crowd a good example, just as the reactionaries of our days conserve senseless customs, either out of convenience or from selfish and low motives. Pliny, who stigmatized idol-worship as 'human weakness', or Seneca, who saw in it an 'abominable game', and many others of their type and convictions, lacked the firmness of will and strength of mind to swim against the stream! Yet they could not prevent the arrival of a new dawn. The mob grew furious against the gods, when Germanicus passed away. In times of national catastrophe the old gods were degraded, neglected, and finally discarded. A very lucrative import of foreign gods began, and foreign priests enjoyed the benefit. The witty Petronius induces a strong Cappadocian to carry away the thundering Jupiter on his shoulders. The Emperor cult was the climax of this madness and killed all traces of piety and reverence which were left. This was due not simply to the fact that men like Caligula and Nero were madmen, immoral and bloodthirsty perverts, since among the so-called deities in the pantheon

---

[1] Tanḥ. (ed. Buber), 1. 108.

many an adulterer or robber was adored and worshipped, but to the origin of these deifications, which opened the eyes even of the uncritical ancient world to the absurdity of the procedure. 'Bread and games' could secure, then as now, the deification even of fools and knaves! The world made some slight progress at this stage. Jewish propaganda lifted up its voice and not wholly in vain.

Owing to this fact, heathen, critics, and students questioned from many sides the doctrine of God's unity, as taught by the Jewish doctors. First of all, they tried to find traces of an older polytheistic stratum in the Jewish religion. This question was put to R. Gamaliel II by an unbeliever (כופר) in the following way: 'You Jews say that wherever ten persons are gathered, there the *Shekhinah* is present? How many gods are there?' Rabban Gamaliel adduces the simile of the sun, which is visible to numerous persons at the same moment, at the most distant places, and still no one would suggest that there are many suns. If that is the case with the sun, which is one of God's servants, why not with God?[1] The interlocutor does not question here a Biblical conception but a Rabbinical statement.[2]

This teaching is certainly older than the age of these Scribes. This is a good illustration, one of many, of the fact that the name of the Talmudist given in the text does not necessarily indicate the date of the saying. The interlocutor was well acquainted with Rabbinical lore and endeavoured

---

[1] Sanh. 39a. On the incident קרייה לשמעיה מחא ביה באפתקא, *v.* the story in המעשיות ס' ed. Gaster, p. 11. As to the simile of the sun, *v.* R. Joshua ben Ḥananya and Caesar (Roman Emperor) B. Ḥul. 59b, 60a, and Midrash Abkir, Yalḳuṭ I. § 396, fragments of which were discovered by the present writer in MS. Adler nos. 638, 3367 and 3692, *v. Catalogue of Hebrew MSS.* in the collection of Elkan Nathan Adler, Cambridge (1921), p. 9; cf. further Yelamdenu, Num. ed. Grünhut, p. 13b; R. Judah bar Ilai' in Tanḥ. (ed. Buber), ii. 98; R. Simon ben Pazzi in Lam. R. i. 23.

[2] Mentioned by R. Ḥalafta ben Dosa of Kefar Ḥananya, a pupil of R. Meir, after R. Gamaliel II. *v.* 'Ab. 3. 6 and 3. 2 in the name of Ḥananya ben Teradyon. They refer to ten such people as are engaged in the study of the law. B. Ber. 6a gives the saying in the name of R. Isaac. *v.* also Mekhilta, p. 73 Mekh. of R., Simon ben Yoḥai, p. 115.

to find traces of polytheism in the theology of the Rabbis. There is another dialogue between R. Gamaliel (according to some readings in the texts) and an unbeliever, which has some bearing on the same problem. 'Why did God reveal Himself to Moses in the thornbush?' R. Gamaliel: 'Supposing He had revealed himself in a fig, or a carob tree, what would you say: "God is not omnipresent"? (i.e. He was only in this place and nowhere else; in other places there are other gods). Learn! God is everywhere present!'[1]

The second objection to the Jewish doctrine of God is attached by the ancient preachers to the words of Cant. 5. 9. 'What is thy beloved more than another beloved?' The nations of the world ask this question of Israel, 'What, is your God more than any other God? Why do you suffer death, why are you slain for His sake, as it is said, "Until death do I love Thee" (cf. Cant. 1. 3), and further it is said: "For Thy sake are we killed all the day long" (Ps. 44. 23). You are so beautiful and brave, come, let us unite.' The community of Israel replies: 'I will make known to you some of His praise, so that you may recognize Him! as it is said: "My beloved is white and ruddy, pre-eminent above ten thousand. His head is as the most fine gold, his locks are curled and black as the raven, etc." ' (Cant. 5. 10–16). As soon as the nations of the world hear this description of the pride and praise of Israel they say: 'Behold, we will join you, as it is said, "Whither is thy beloved gone?" ' (Cant. 6. 1). Israel replies: 'You have no share in Him. I am my Beloved's and my Beloved is mine' (Cant. 6. 3).[2]

---

[1] Pes. (ed. Buber) 2b, Num. R. 12, Cant. R. 3. 16, Exod. R. 4. 1, reads R. Joshua ben Korḥa, v. also Mekh. of R. Simon ben Yoḥai, p. 2, B. 'Ab. Zarah, 55a, Exod. R. 2. 9. This problem gave rise to the view that God has concentrated his Shekhina on a certain place, מצמצם שכינתו, v. R. Yoḥanan bar Nappaḥa, Pes. 20a; Pes. 84b; R. Levi, ibid., 135a; Tractate Aṣilut 71a, Tanḥ. 131a.

[2] v. Sifre Deut. § 343. Midr. Tannaim; Mekh. 37a. R. Akiba figures as the author. A third source, Cant. R. 5. 5, emphasizes the question: 'By what is your God distinguished from all other gods? Your patron from all other patrons?' With some variants in Cant. R. 7. 2 and Num. R. 4. 3, later in the Haggadah of R. Yoḥanan; Pes. 193b; Pes. 106b; Lam. R. 3. 21; Midr. Hagadol, MS. Adler.

These questions and answers are remnants of a dialogue between Israel and the nations of the world. The starting-point of the debate was whether the God of Israel, a national God like that of any other Oriental people, was different from all other gods? There is one impediment to a success-ful assimilation of Judaism and heathendom, and that is: Israel's religion.[1]

The question of nationality would be no obstacle, since the statesmen and soldiers of the ancient world were just as liberal and broad-minded as those of our times. The greatest tolerance prevailed in this respect—as far as it furthered the ambitions and aims of their imperialistic policy. As a matter of fact, Hadrian, in whose days this dialogue was held or composed, tried to bring about such a union of nations as that spoken of in this fragment. The whole dia-logue in the hands of Justin or as miscellanea from the pen of Clement, in Greek garb, would make a long treatise. The taciturn teachers of Judaism, poor in words, rich in thoughts, sketch merely the questions and answers. We can recognize the following main points: (a) In what is the God of Israel different from all other gods? (b) The answer quotes Cant. 5. 10–16. Unfortunately, the compiler of the dialogue satisfied himself with the dry quotation from the Song of Songs. Either the Haggadic meaning of these verses was known to the audience or to the readers, or, more likely, the explanation, for obvious reasons, is missing. (c) The interlocutors make up their minds to embrace Judaism. (d) Judaism refuses their entrance into the Synagogue. Parts of this dialogue are presented with variants in other sources indicated in note 2, p. 83, and in a version of

---

[1] The problem of assimilation is dealt with, Mekh. 9a, 37a; J. Ta'an. 65d; Num. R. 2. 16; Ex. R. 1. 10; Midrash Temurah, ed. Wertheimer, p. 11; M. Lam. (ed. Buber), p. 84; Esther R. 7, Yalkuṭ Makhiri, Psalms, p. 271. The reasons against assimilation are: (1) because the God of Israel is entirely different from the idols of the nations; (2) The descendants of the Patriarchs could not become faithless to their inheritance. (3) The Torah, as a perennial spring of life-giving water, gives Israel the strength of endurance to face all obstacles and hindrances.

the third century. There is no valid reason why we should not suppose this dialogue to reflect the feeling prevailing in the time before the Bar-Kokhba war.

A third attack came from a similar quarter, which may have included atheistic Jews as well. All forms of worship are really the same; all the gods are equal. Whether these thinkers had already reached such a pitch of enlightenment and rationalism as to see in all different denominations the rays emanating from one central light, namely, God, or whether they were atheists who believed all the religions to be nothing but dust thrown in the eyes of the people by priests and humbugs, cannot be fully determined. They make much play with the phrase כל הפנים שוות or, in Aramaic, כל אפיא שווין. Manasseh, one of the archheresiarchs of Rabbinic writings, turns to all the idols in the world for help. He finds a hearing nowhere. Then he turns to the God of his pious father Hezekiah, and says: 'Thou art the God of all. God, hearken unto me; if not, then (I will proclaim) all the gods are the same.'[1] R. Akiba reproduces a prayer of David, saying, 'Lord of the whole world, hearken even unto the most wicked in Israel, should he pray to Thee, so that people should not say: "All the gods are equal!" '[2] The same thought recurs in a saying which explains why Jacob desired to be buried in Canaan and not in Egypt. 'In future they (i.e. the Egyptians), will come and will burn incense before my coffin. God hearkens unto them, I shall be punished; if not, they will say כל הפנים שוות.'[3]

A fourth objection on the part of the heathen was the

[1] Ruth R. 5. 6; R. Levi ben Ḥayta; Deut. R. 2. 13; J. Sanh. 28c, Pes. 162b.
[2] M. Ps. 6a.
[3] Midrash Genesis, published by Dr. Theodor in *Festschrift zum 70ten Geburtstage Jacob Guttmanns* (Leipzig, 1915), 165, ll. 16 f.; cf. Gen. R. 96. 5 and Tanḥ. The expression למחר הן באין ומעשנים לפני ארוני is characteristic. The burning of incense was an ancient magic rite to drive away demons or to enchant them; v. Oldenburg, *Buddha* 3 (1897), p. 21. Ganschienitz, *Hippolytus in Texte und Untersuch.* xxxix, p. 32 f.; Pesikta, p. 39 and paral.; Tobit, ch. 8; B. Ber. 53a; Justin, *Dial.* ch. 85.

invisibility of the Jewish God. This difference between the Jewish doctrine of God and the belief in the gods was dealt with also in the Haggadah of the Amoraim. It may suffice here to draw attention to one or two of these. R. Yoḥanan and R. Simon ben Laḳish commenting on Isa. 8. 20 say: 'God speaks to Israel, "My children, tell the nations, something which is so dark, does it not give you light? The God of the Jews whose existence was denied by the heathen because He cannot be seen, does He not give light to the world?" ' This question, which occupies a prominent place in the dialogues of the first centuries in the Church as well as in the Synagogue, was revived again in the third century. R. Simon ben Laḳish sees in the words of the prophet a reference to idol-worship. 'Your gods are dark, without light, they cannot give light to themselves; how could they give light to others?' The God of Israel requires no light and gives it to others; the idols cannot give light to others, yet need light from others.[1] Or, as R. Judah ben Simon says: 'The idols seem so near, and yet are so very far. God seems so far removed and He is actually so near to all who seek Him. The worshipper keeps his idol in his room, yea in his hands, entreating him for help, until he expires without being heard or helped. Is there, however, a God who is nearer to His creatures than our God?'[2]

R. Samuel ben Naḥman and R. Tanḥuma illustrate this doctrine by various legends and stories. Augustine expresses the same thought when he says: 'The images of the gods cannot guard those who worship them; the latter guard their gods. How could one honour an image as guardian of a city and the citizens, an image which cannot protect itself?'[3]

3. Of the various types of idolatry, the Scribes fought sun-worship especially, and the worship of the planets

---

[1] Lev. R. 6. 6; Apoc. of Abraham, ch. 17.
[2] J. Ber. 9. 2.
[3] *De Civ. Dei*, i. 2.

generally. The sun is emphatically described by some Haggadists as one of God's servants, and not a deity.[1] R. Meir,
in the second century, points out that God is annoyed
when the kings of the East and of the West worship the
sun.[2] In the third century this kind of idolatry spread
greatly in the Eastern as well as in the Western world. It
is, therefore, natural that the teachers of this age should pay
more than usual attention to this aberration. R. Ḥannina
ben Ḥama explains why God created both sun and moon.
'God foresaw that the nations would worship sun or moon.
Had He created either sun or moon, and not both of them,
they would have regarded either of them as a deity. Now,
the existence of the sun refutes the divinity of the moon,
and vice versa.'[3] R. Yoḥanan bar Nappaḥa, another great
teacher of this age, made up a parable to combat the views
of the sun-worshippers. 'Once a king visited a place,
accompanied by his *duces*, ὕπαρχοι and στρατηλάται. The
chief people of the town took counsel. One said: "I will
invite to my place the *duces*." Another said, "I will lodge
this and this ὕπαρχος", and so on. A clever man among
them said, "I will give lodging to the king himself. All
the dignitaries change their title and their influence, but the
king always remains the same." This is the case with the
idolaters. Some among them worship the sun, others adore
the moon, and there are also some who idolize wood and
stone. Israel, however, has chosen God, the maker of all these
things, as it is said: "The Lord is my portion (Lam. 3. 24),
whose unity I proclaim daily" (cf. Deut. 6. 4).'[4] A contemporary of the last-named teacher, the great preacher, R.
Levi, combats in two different sayings the worship of the
sun. In one of these he describes in a picturesque way the
psychology of the sun-worshippers in his days. He compares the inhabitants of Sodom to a city which had two

---

[1] *v.* especially R. Joshua ben Ḥananya, Ḥul. 59b f. and others.
[2] B. Ber. 7a; B. 'Ab. Zarah 4b.
[3] Gen. R. 6. 1; Lev. R. 31. 9; M. Ps. 19. 11; Pes. 42a.
[4] Lam. R. 3. 22. *v.* also *Tanna debe Eliyahu*, p. 5b.

patrons, one of whom lived in the city, the other in the country. The king had some cause of annoyance and decreed the destruction of the city. The king said: 'If I carried out the destruction in the presence of the one and in the absence of the other, the inhabitants would say: "Had X or Y been present, the king would never have done it." ' Therefore, he chose a moment when both were in the city. This is what happened in Sodom. There were worshippers of the sun and also of the moon. God said: 'If I destroy Sodom in the daytime, I confirm the moon-worshippers in their folly; if at night, then the sun-worshippers will triumph.' God chose therefore the 16th of Nisan, the time of the solstice, as it is said: 'The sun was risen upon the earth when Lot came unto Zoar' (Gen. 19. 23).[1] One can easily recognize the use R. Levi made of the arguments quoted above in the name of the earlier Haggadists. In a second Haggadah, R. Levi describes how God has to force sun and moon to discharge their duties. God brings them to trial because they do not like to do their mission. Why? Because they say: 'We are blamed for the sin of the people who worship us!'[2]

There are, however, traces in the literature of the second century of a view which does not condemn this form of worship so much as idol-worship or demon-worship. A Haggadah referring to Deut. 32. 17, 'They sacrificed unto the demons' says: 'If they had worshipped the sun, moon, stars, and planets, which are needed by the world and benefit the same, I would not mind it so much (לא היתה קנאה כפולה), but they worship things like the demons which not only do not benefit but do harm to the world.'[3]

R. Akiba in his discussion with R. Ishmael might be referring to such sayings as those of Pliny[4] or of

---

[1] Gen. R. 19. 23; Gen. R. 50. 22.
[2] Lev. R. 31. 9; M. Ps. 18d.
[3] Sifre Deut. § 318.
[4] In his *Historia Naturalis*, iii. 1. The earth, and whatever that be which we otherwise call the heavens by the vault of which all things are enclosed,

Cicero.[1] R. Akiba had studied in the school of Naḥum of
Gimzo, who used to derive more or less important rules
from such words as אַך, רק, גם, את. He was once interrogated
by R. Ishmael as to the meaning of את in Gen. 1. 1, and
replied, 'Without the את in both cases, people would say that
heaven and earth are gods, and they created the universe.'
R. Ishmael refers his colleague to Deut. 32. 47; 'For it is
no vain thing for you!' R. Akiba says: 'If it is vain, it is
for you, because you cannot explain the Bible without our
method! את השמים includes sun, moon, stars and planets,
ואת הארץ includes trees, grass, and the garden of Eden.'[2]
There can be no doubt that R. Akiba was thinking of the
theories of the pre-Socratic and Aristotelian schools, who
regarded heaven and earth as deities and the creators of the
universe, and incidentally combats the view of the sun-
worshippers, by implying that they were also created. A
created thing, however, cannot be a creator, a God. The
Haggadists spoke also of the king of Babylon as a sun-
worshipper.[3] In the next generation, R. Nehorai, a contemporary of R. Meir, dealt with this subject. He is told by
Elijah: 'When God beholds the idol-worshippers in peace,
and His house destroyed, then He makes the world dark
and shakes it. He says: "The nations annoy me, one wor-
ships the sun, the other the moon; therefore, I make the
earth tremble!" '[4]

The Haggadists dealt also with another and very low
form of ancient idolatry, the worship of animals. It may
suffice to give two or three instances. Jacob's desire to be
buried outside of Egypt is ascribed to the fact that the

we must conceive to be a deity, to be eternal, without bounds, neither created,
nor subject at any time to destruction.
    [1] *Som. Scip.* § 4. 'Novem tibi orbibus, vel potius globis, connexa sunt
omnia; quorum unus est coelestis, extimus, qui reliquos omnes complectitur
summus ipse Deus arcens et continens coelum.'
    [2] Gen. R. 1. 13.
    [3] Esther R. 3.
    [4] J. Ber. 9. 2. Yalḳuṭ Joel. § 536; Tanḥuma, Seder Eliyahu, ed. Friedm.,
p. 4 f.

Egyptians were worshippers of animals, and Jacob was compared to the lamb.[1] R. Ḥanina, in describing the future judgement, makes God say: 'Daily you are being put to shame before me! Some of you worshipped doves, some white doves, others fish, all of them dead in your dwelling places or in the markets.'[2] The view is often repeated that the nations will recognize in the world to come the vanity of idolatry, the helplessness of the gods, and the loathsomeness of animal worship, and they themselves will call their gods to account.[3] 'The idols themselves', says R. Yoḥanan, 'will acknowledge their mistake and recognize their right place.'[4]

Idolatry reached its climax in the deification of individuals. This stage of idol worship represents the greatest depth of immorality to which human folly could descend. A man who could attain to the summit of power without merits or capability, through the stupidity or perversity of the crowd, and with the help of temporal and local conditions, could be deified by the efforts of flatterers or place-seekers, for games or bread. Even the best types among the emperors were not entitled to bear divine names. Vespasian was terrified when called a god, and it is alleged that he exclaimed: 'Woe unto me, I am becoming a god!' Not so the weak ones; weak in mind and heart, they partly believed, partly pretended that they were gods. A characteristic Haggadah deals with this problem. Hadrian, who conquered the whole world, returned to Rome, invited all his friends and officials, and said: 'I desire of you that you shall make me a god!' They told him: 'We cannot do it; you have to defeat one more God, viz. the God of the Jews.' He went to Palestine, destroyed the Temple, carried Israel into captivity, and returned to Rome. Then Hadrian said: 'Now, make me a god!' He had three philosophers. One said:

[1] Cf. Jer. 50. 17; Gen. R. 96. 5.
[2] Tanḥ. 267a (ed. Buber), 16a.
[3] Tanḥ. f. 267. M. Ps. 10a.
[4] Midr. Ps. 26a.

'None can revolt against the King in his own palace; leave his palace and become a god. He created heaven and earth; leave heaven and earth and we will declare you a deity.' The second said: 'None can become a god, as it is said: "Thus shall ye say unto them, 'The gods that have not made the heavens and the earth, these shall perish from the earth, and from under the heavens' " ' (Jer. 10. 11). The third said: 'Sire, I have a ship on the high sea; in it are my gold and silver, everything I possess, and they are in danger.' Hadrian says: 'Very well, I will send my troops and legions to rescue them.' The philosopher said: 'Why should you take so much trouble? You could rescue my ship with one favourable wind!' 'No', said Hadrian, 'that I cannot do!' 'Well', said the philosopher, 'if you cannot command the wind, how can you induce us to make you a god?' Hadrian was very grieved at these answers and went to his wife to take counsel of her. She said: 'I am sure you may become a god; you are a great and mighty king, you are omnipotent. I will advise you. Return to your Creator his pledge, i.e. the soul, and you will be a god.' 'What do you mean?' asked Hadrian. 'Return to him your soul and show him that you are alive without his pledge.' Hadrian replied: 'Then I shall be dead!' 'Well', said his wife, 'if you have no power over your own soul, how can you claim to be a god?'[1] The date of this story can be verified by a parallel passage in the *Tanḥuma* (p. 268b), where R. Eliezer ben Hyrcanus, R. Joshua ben Ḥananya, and their pupil, R. Akiba, are the representatives of the ideas expressed by the three philosophers. The teleological, cosmological, and psychological proofs or arguments exactly fit the age of R. Gamaliel II, who expressed similar ideas in his dialogues with his interlocutors. They represent, generally speaking, the following points of view: the attributes of divinity are: (a) infinitude, there is no limit and no boundary to God's power and being; (b) His creative power is unparalleled;

---

[1] Tanḥ., מעשיות 'ס, ed. Gaster, p. 51.

(c) God is everlasting. Where these attributes, or one of them, are lacking, one cannot speak of a divine being. The historical inaccuracies (for instance, Hadrian destroys the Temple) give rise to doubt as to the truth of the story, but its antiquity is proved by the arguments and the contents.

The Abraham legend attacks the emperor in a more popular manner. Abraham tried sun, moon, images of gold, silver, iron, lead, stone, and wood, without satisfactory result. All these, he found, were created by a higher divine power, and were helpless in distress. He burnt them all together. He was accused and brought before Nimrod, who rebuked him as follows: 'Art thou the man who destroyed my deities? Dost thou not know that I am the lord of all creatures? that I make sun and moon, stars and planets, go their daily course? that I created the whole world?' Abraham replied: 'No, I did not know this, and I should like to know whether what you say is true. I will ask you for something. The sun runs its course from east to west; now let it go to-morrow from the west to the east! Secondly: Could you tell me what I am thinking of just now?' Nimrod and his 365 counsellors were astonished at hearing these words. Abraham said: 'Do not be astonished! You are no god at all, but the son of Kush! If you are a god, why did you allow the death of your father? A god should be able to save his own father, at least, from death!' The legend was meant to settle the old question how Abraham came to his belief in God, and to attack, incidentally, the emperor cult, so fashionable in those days. The Haggadah speaks of four kings who claimed the rights and honours of divinity. These were Nimrod, Sisera, Sennacherib, and Nebuchadnezzar. Hiram, who, according to R. Simon ben Pazzi's Haggadic tradition, was Nebuchadnezzar's stepfather and who was killed by him,[1] also claimed to be a god.[2] Hiram built for himself a palace with seven

---

[1] v. Lev. R. 18. 2. *MGWJ* iii (1854), 384 and 469.
[2] v. Gen R. 9. 6 and Marmorstein, *Midrash Ḥaserot we Yetherot*, note 141.

chambers, corresponding to the seven heavens. God sent
Ezekiel to him and Ezekiel said to Hiram: 'What are you
doing, Hiram; are you not born of a woman? Why do you
boast?' Hiram said: 'I am an immortal god, although born
of a woman. I am a god and act like a god.' Ezekiel said:
'You are like a slave of a king, who made a beautiful garment
for his master. As long as the king was wearing it, the slave
felt proud (and boasted of being a king himself); when,
however, the king tore it, the pride of the slave disappeared.'
Likewise, Hiram, who sent cedar trees to God's Temple,
thought he was a god!

We conclude this account of the campaign against the
emperor cult with a saying of R. Eleazar ben Pedat: 'A
king of flesh and blood has a patron; even if he rules in one
province he has no dominion in another; even if he is a
κοσμοκράτωρ, he can rule on the land but has no power on
the sea. God, however, rules on the sea as well as on the dry
land; He saves on the sea from the water, on the dry land
from the fire!'[1] We see from these passages that the Scribes,
as well as the Hellenistic writers, directed their attacks
against all forms of idol-worship.[2]

III

The second group which opposed the Jewish doctrine of
God's unity consisted of the various sects known by the
name of Gnostics. These sects, however much they differed
from each other in details, agreed in one dogma, to which
they adhered faithfully. They believed in two powers. This
dualistic conception is a characteristic sign of Gnosticism.
Anonymous sayings, the date of which cannot be later than
the end of the first century, if not earlier, point to a dualistic
movement in Palestine. If we may trust Abudarham, a
medieval author who used old and trustworthy sources, the
daily reading of the *Shema'* was introduced as a protest

---

[1] J. Ber. ix. 1.
[2] v. Wendland, *Therapeuten*, 186; *Hermes*, xxxi. 234.

against the adherents of dualism. In those days one of the
Scribes might have applied Deut. 32. 39, 'And there is no
God with me', to the Gnostic teaching, as a reply to the
believers in two powers.[1] Another may have given as a
reason for the statement in Genesis that Adam was created
alone, that this was done so that the Minim should not be
able to say: 'There are many powers in heaven, one created
the male, the other the female!'[2] A Min was recognized, according to the teachers of the Mishnah, by his saying: 'May
the good ones bless thee', implying that there are two powers,
a good and a bad one and meaning, 'May the former bless
thee';[3] further, by repeating מודים מודים, 'we thank thee'.[4]

Aḥer was a Min, because he believed in two powers.[5]
An anonymous sage collected a number of passages from
the Scriptures (Deut. 32. 39; Isa. 41. 4; 44. 6) to refute
dualistic speculations. The same God appeared on the sea
and on the dry land, the God who appeared in the past will
appear in the future, in this world, and that to come![6] The
same God wounds and heals, reveals Himself at the same
moment in the East and in the West, in the North and in
the South, in different places![7] God's revelation takes
different forms[8] but this variety does not in the least imply
the theory of two powers or gods.[9]

There were, however, a few Biblical passages which
apparently supported Gnostic or rather dualistic theories.
R. Gamaliel II was interrogated about Amos 4. 13. The
God, this Min alleged, who created the wind was not the
God who formed the mountains (the argument being based
on the different verbs used: ברא and יצר). The Patriarch
replied that in the story of the creation of man also two

---

[1] Sifre Deut. § 329.   [2] B. Sanh. 37a.
[3] M. Meg. 4. 10. M. Ber. 9; J. Meg. 75c; B. Meg. 25a. Gen. R. 1.
[4] B. Ber. 33b; v. Simonsen, *Kaufmann Gedenkbuch*, p. 115, and Aptowitzer, *MGWJ* lvii. 16.
[5] B. Meg. 15a.   [6] Sifre Deut. § 329.
[7] Exod. R. 28. 3.   [8] Exod. R. 29. 3.
[9] v. Theophilus, iii. 28.

different verbs are used (Gen. 1. 26–7). Then Adam was not created by the Demiurgos alone, but by the 'highest God' as well, who was, therefore, also responsible![1] It cannot be decided whether the interlocutor in this case was a Gnostic or a Christian, for, according to Justin, Christians also believed in Jesus' assistance in the creation.[2] In the Haggadic teachings of R. Simon ben Yoḥai a reference is made to the dualists, again without a clear indication whether Gnostics or Christians were meant. We read the following parable: 'A king built a palace. People come and criticize, saying, "Could these walls not be higher or lower? &c." Yet, is there one man in the whole world, who could say: "Why have I not been given three eyes, three legs, &c." It is not said (Eccles. 2. 12), "what he already did", but "what they already have done", viz. God and His heavenly court. They discussed the details and divisions of the body and they established everything and put thee in thy right place. As it is said: "He hath made thee, and established thee!" (Deut. 32. 6). Now if someone argues, "There are two powers!" answer him, "Is it not written: 'I created thee.' " '[3] The Gnostic of whom Rabbi Simon ben Yoḥai is thinking seems to have argued first of all that man was created by the Demiurgos. Thereupon R. Simon ben Yoḥai makes the obvious but interesting suggestion that God took counsel of the heavenly court. The Gnostic now emphasized with even greater force his dualism. This was refuted by the use of the singular in the relevant verse. A contemporary of this last-named teacher, R. Nathan, surely had Gnostics in mind when he said with reference to Exod. 20. 2: 'This passage provides us with a reply to the Minim, who say that there are two gods. When God said: "I am the Lord thy God", why did none of the alleged heavenly powers

---

[1] B. Sanh. 39a.

[2] The Gospel of John reports that Jesus was punished by the Jews because he called himself God (10. 33); *vide* Hoenecke, *Handbuch der christlichen Apokryphen*, p. 49, und *Theologisch Tijdschrift*, xlix. 361.

[3] Sifre Deut. § 307; Gen. R. 12. 1, ed. Theodor, p. 97; Eccles. R. 2. 12.

rise up in indignation against Him, refuting Him, or contradicting Him? If one argues: "That actually took place secretly", is it not written, "I have not spoken in secret."[1] If there is a higher God above him who gave Israel the law, above the supposed Demiurgos of Gnostic speculation, why did he not interfere?'

These three instances, which by no means comprise the whole material at our disposal in the Rabbinic writings, may suffice to illustrate the struggle of the Tannaim against the Gnostics. The number of combatants, on both sides, must have greatly increased in the third century. To begin with, there is R. Simon ben Laḳish, who proves the unity of God from Isa. 44. 6. God is the first, because He received His power from none else. He is the last, because He does not hand over His rule to anyone else; beside Him there is no God. According to another version R. Simon said: 'א is the first of the letters, מ is in the middle of them, ת at the end. That teaches that God is the first, because He did not receive His power from someone else; beside Him there is no God, for He had no help at the creation, and He does not hand over His rule to anyone else.' There is only one God, teaches this Scribe, neither the Christian God who was supposed to succeed God in heaven, nor the Gnostic God, —creature either of anti-Jewish feeling or of a misreading of Platonic ideas—who can take precedence of the God of Israel. R. Aḥa teaches this same doctrine in connexion with Isa. 42. 8. 'I am the Lord, that is My name and My glory will I not give to another. This is My name, by which Adam called Me. Everything has its fellow, except God!'[2] This argument is, however, much older than R. Aḥa, for the alleged Jew Tryphon mentions it already to Justin.[3] R. Isaac refutes Gnostic doctrines, from Ps. 119. 160 and Jer. 10. 10. 'The beginning of Thy word is truth', i.e. Gen. 1. 1. No one can say 'Two powers created the world', for is it

[1] Isa. 45. 19; Mekh. 66b.   [2] Gen. R. 17. 5.
[3] *Dialogue*, ch. 55; Harnack, p. 64.

not said וידבר or ויאמר or ברא, and never וידברו, ויאמרו or
בראו?[1] R. Isaac adopts the old theory that the angels were
created on the second or on the fifth day, in order that the
Gnostics should not say that they helped God with the
creation.[2]

It cannot be merely accidental that all these verses, for
instance, Isa. 42. 8; 44. 6; Deut. 32. 39, &c., occurring
again and again in undoubtedly apologetic or polemical
sayings of the Rabbis, always recur in the anti-Jewish
polemics of the Church and the dialogues, partly in older,
partly in later sources. Just as the latter repeat and
adopt constantly the arguments and proofs of the older
writings, so the Rabbis of the third century adopted and
referred to the material of former centuries.[3] Originally
these passages were used in the fight against Gnostic
dualism; in the third century they were applied to Christianity, which appeared to the teachers of Israel as a dualistic
creed, so that no distinction could be recognized between
the one and the other.

R. Yoḥanan deals with six passages which apparently
supported the views of the Gnostics and Christians against
the Jewish conception of God's unity (B. Sanh. 28b).
These are: Gen. 1. 26–7; 11. 5–7; 35. 3–7; Deut. 4.
7; 2 Sam. 7. 23; and Dan. 4. 14. In all these verses
the plural form suggests that the Bible speaks of more
than one God, yet in the context the unity is affirmed.
R. Simlai enlarges this list by adding three other passages (Joshua 22. 22; 24. 19; and Ps. 50. 1). Again the verb
has the singular (i.e. דבר) in all cases, and not the more
natural plural (דברו).[4] These Bible questions and difficulties
are so important that one or two of them must be treated
here at some length.

The objections to Gen. 1. 26 occur so often in old anti-

[1] Gen. R. 1. 10.
[2] Gen. R. 1. 1; 3. 11; M. Ps. 24. 1. Tanḥ. (ed. Buber), i. 12 anonymous.
[3] v. Theol. Tijdschrift, xlix, p. 362.
[4] J. Ber. 12d; Gen. R. 8. 9; Deut. R. 2. 8.

Jewish writings from Justin up to the anonymous works of the year 680 that it would take too much of our space to enumerate them.[1] The gist of all these, however, is that all of them saw in the *plural* a proof for Jesus' assistance in the creation of man. There can be no doubt whatever that the Gnostic dualists also availed themselves of these passages generally, and of Gen. i. 26 especially. Theophilus (ii. 18) gave a forced interpretation when he said: 'To no one else says God: "Let us make, &c." but to His logos, to His wisdom.' We find the same solution, as will be seen later on, in the Midrash. Philo served here again as an intermediary between the Haggadists and Christian apologists. At any rate, Philo had to deal with the same difficulty. In Tannaitic sources we find only one reference to this passage, in the list of variants made by those who translated the Bible into Greek for Ptolemy and who put instead of נעשה the singular אעשה.[2] We see thus that all the anti-Jewish forces arrayed themselves against the Jewish doctrine—Heathendom, Gnosticism, and Christianity. As in so many other instances, here, too, we can follow the development of anti-Jewish objections from the pre-Christian period to the beginning of the Middle Ages. Besides R. Yohanan and R. Simlai, we find the following teachers of the third century engaged with this problem. We mention first R. Jonathan ben Eliezer, who deals with it in a legend. He pictures Moses as writing down the Biblical account of the six days of the creation. When he reaches our passage, he is rather astonished and says: 'Lord of the Whole World! You give a good opportunity to the Minim to object to the doctrine of God's unity!' God replies: 'Let him who will go wrong. The man I created, will he not bring forth big and small people? Will not the former say: "Now shall I, who hold this or that rank, obey or ask leave from those who

---

[1] *v.* Justin's *Dial.* ch. 62; *MGWJ* iii. 313; iv. 419; Goldfahn, p. 24; Bonwetsch, *Nachrichten der Kgl. Ges. Wiss. in Göttingen* (1909), p. 152.

[2] Mekh. 15b; cf. J. Meg. 71d; cf. B. Meg. 7a.

rank lower in social or material life than myself?" He must be told: "Look at your Creator, Who took advice of those who were created by Him, i.e. of His ministering angels!" [1] According to R. Joshua ben Levi, God spoke to heaven and earth.[2] R. Samuel bar Naḥman makes God speak to the products of each day of the creation.[3] R. Joshua in the name of R. Samuel advances the view that God addressed the souls of the pious who were already in existence then.[4] The pupils and successors of R. Yoḥanan, R. Ammi, and R. Assi, held that God spoke to Himself, and to no one else.[5] The *Pirke de R. Eliezer* holds that God spoke to the Torah (ch. 9).

Examining the other difficulties, we find several methods in dealing with passages which could be explained by Gnostics and Christians as proving dualistic theories. First of all, we see that the earliest method of overcoming difficulties of this type was to alter the text of the Bible.[6] Secondly, a reference to the context, especially the use of the context, is often utilized to dismiss the superficial interpretations. Thirdly, the Scribes found allusions to the Torah, the Messiah, or the angels in such passages. No wonder that the Gnostic Saturninus, a Syrian, proved from these passages that the God of the Jews is one of the angels, who created the world and man.[7]

In the generation after R. Yoḥanan, we find sayings of R. Ḥiyya bar Abba, R. Abbahu, and R. Tanḥuma in defence of our doctrine. Their defence is not original; they merely repeat the words of their teachers, who, on their part, did the same with the ideas and thoughts of the previous generations. There was, as a matter of fact, very little room left

---

[1] Gen. R. 8. 8. R. Samuel b. Naḥman in his name, also *Ps. Jon. Targum*, Gen. R. 1. 25; R. Ḥanina, Gen. R. 8. 5; and R. Simon ben Pazzi, ibid.
[2] Gen. R. 8. 3.   [3] Gen. R. 8. 3.   [4] Gen. R. 8. 7.
[5] Gen. R. 8. 3; *v.* also Gen. R. 8. 4 for R. Berekhya's view, and R. Levi's, ibid. 8. 8, ed. Theodor, p. 61.
[6] As to Gen. 1. 26, *v.* above, p. 98, as to Gen. 11. 7, *v.* Mekh. l.c. Gen. R. 38. 10; Tanḥ. i. 18.
[7] *Iren. adv. haer.* i. 24, l. 2; Diestel, *Das Alte Testament in der Kirche*, 65.

for originality. R. Ḥiyya bar Abba says: 'If a Min says: "There are two Gods", tell him God is the same on the sea, and on Mount Sinai;'[1] or, according to another version, he lays stress on the singular of the verb.[2] R. Abbahu preaching on Num. 23. 19 says: 'He who says, "I am God", he speaks falsely; "I am the son of man", he will be sorry; "I ascend to heaven", he speaks and will not keep it.'[3] There can be no doubt that R. Abbahu speaks here against Christians who believed in Jesus as being God, the son of man, who ascended to heaven. The same teacher applies to Christians Isa. 44. 6, an old weapon against Gnostics and Christians. A human king has a father, a brother, or a son. The heavenly king has neither, as it is said: 'I am the first', for I have no father; 'I am the last', for I have no son; 'Beside me there is none', for I have no brother.[4] R. Tanḥuma was asked in Antioch about the plural *Elohîm* in Gen. 3. 5. In his reply he points to the singular of the verb, instead of the expected plural (Gen. R. 19. 5, *v*. ed. Theodor, p. 172).

We may conclude this chapter with a legend bearing on our subject. When God was going to hand over the Torah to Israel, the angels protested—in the same way as, in other legends, they protested before the creation of the world and man. They envied the dwellers on the earth the revelation which was to be given to them. God said to them: 'What can the Decalogue teach you? "You shall have no strange gods before Me?" Well, could *you* doubt for a moment that there is only one God in heaven? (Pes. 98a). He who knows the truth can testify that there is only one God in heaven and on earth!'

IV

The Emperor Julian, called the Apostate, asked the Christians: 'Could you show me one passage in the Books

---

[1] Pes. 100b; *v*. Mekh. 37b, 66b; Mekh. of R. S. 6. 7, p. 61.
[2] וידבר and וידברו, *v*. *REJ* lxviii. 170.
[3] J. Ta'an. 65b; Peritz in *MGWJ* (1887), 318.
[4] Exod. R. 39. 5.

of Moses referring to Christ as God?' This question was
raised as early as the middle of the second century, as we
see in the earliest dialogues preserved. It is, therefore, impossible to establish which of the sayings quoted in the
third chapter of this study refer to Gnostics and which
refer to Christians. This could only be done if material
were available to show where Christian and where Gnostic
influence was predominant. In the case of R. Abbahu, e.g.,
we can be sure that the Minim were Christians, because
Caesarea was an important Christian place; his master,
R. Yoḥanan, who taught and lived in Tiberias, where
Christian influence cannot be traced, may have been
thinking of Gnostics. Dualism was a point common to both
sections. There were, however, besides this some specifi-
cally Christian doctrines which could not be reconciled
with the Jewish teaching of God's Unity.

The first dogma, which we shall have occasion to treat
again, is certainly one of the oldest in the Church. Jesus was
alleged to be the son of God.[1] In the Clementine Homilies
we find the saying of Peter: 'Our Lord did not attest the
existence of many Gods, nor did he pretend to be God, but
praised him, who calls him by the name of God's son.'[2]
The common Jew, as well as the ordinary Jewish–Christian,
found the deification of a human being in general unbearable, if not abominable.[3] Both saw in such a doctrine an
unpardonable falsification of the pure Jewish monotheism.
Yet could they themselves not be angry with Jesus for
being called God's son! Every righteous, pious, and good
man was a son of God.[4] Popular feeling and ordinary speech
found no objection to this phrase. Why? All human beings,
good or bad—who has the right to discriminate?—are
God's children. Even those who sat on the judgement seat
and tried to deprive some men of this most noble title,

[1] Marmorstein, *Religionsgeschichtliche Studien*, ii. 87 ff.
[2] xvi. 15; *v.* Schliemann, *Clementinen*, p. 144.
[3] *v.* John 10. 33–5; Hoennicke, *Hb. d. Altchristl. Apokryphen*, p. 49.
[4] Wisd. of Sol. 2. 18; *v.* 15.

'children of God', had to acquiesce. The idea was so popular
and general that no objection was raised in earlier times.
The author of the Epistle to the Hebrews asked: 'To whom
does Ps. 2. 7: "Thou art My son", refer?'[1] Of course, they
could have replied: 'To all children of man.' R. Eleazar ha-
Kappar refers in a lengthy exposition to this point. God
caused Balaam's voice to go from one end of the world to
the other. God foresaw, namely, that the nations were going
to worship sun, moon, stars, wood, and stone; further, He
saw that a man, born of a woman, would rise and endeavour
to make men believe that he is God, thus leading astray
the whole world. Therefore, God vested power in Balaam's
voice so that all the nations should hear him, saying:
'Beware of the man and go not astray, as it is said: "A man
is not God, and (if he asserts his divinity), he lies." If he
says he is God, he speaks falsely. Yet he will mislead people
by asserting that he is going to ascend to heaven and come
back at the end of the days. He says, but he will not fulfil
it. Behold it is written: "And he began a parable saying:
Woe, who shall live when he declares himself to be a God?" '
Balaam meant to say: 'Who will live of those who follow
that man who pretends to be God?'[2] This is one of the
sharpest attacks in Jewish sources against the doctrine of
Jesus' divinity and his second advent. R. Abbahu (v. p. 100)
seems to have repeated this saying in different words.

Not only was the divinity of Jesus rejected, but also his
teaching that he was God's son. The latter doctrine was
based on Ps. 2. 7. An anonymous teacher remarks on this
verse: ' "Thou art My son", here we have an answer to
those Minim who say that God had a son. For, it is not said:
"בן לי" "I have a son", but בני אתה (thou art My son).
Just as a slave, who pleases his master, is called by the

---

[1] I. 5; cf. Ps. 110. 1.

[2] v. Yalḳuṭ, ed. Salonika, Job, § 202; Pent. § 765, missing in the ed.
printed in Christian countries, v. Jellinek בה"מ v. 207 f. omitted in Grünhut's Yelamdenu, Num. 69b. Gr. knew only the version of Bachya who put
Muhammad instead of Jesus.

latter to show his appreciation, "my son" ',[1] in the same way, the words in verse 12, 'kiss the son', נשקו בר were also used as a proof of this doctrine. The sages see in בר not the Aramaic equivalent for the Hebrew בן but the word for 'wheat'.[2] Others saw in בר the law, אולפנא (*v. Relig. Studien.* ii. 88, n. 6). If Isa. 44. 6 was especially made use of to repel these theories, as we saw in the *Agada* of R. Abbahu, *Pirke de R. Eliezer* (ch. xi) adduces it as a support for its teaching that the last of the ten kings is the same as the first, i.e. God. *Midrash Tadshe* (ed. Epstein, p. 14) affirms that God fills the whole universe; He is the first and the last. An anonymous teacher quotes Eccles. 4. 8 to prove the same thing. There is only one, i.e. God (cf. Deut. 6. 4); there is no second, i.e. He has no partner, neither son nor brother. 'Whence do we know that He has no son?' (for are Israel not called God's sons?). 'Out of love He called Israel His children.' (*M. Eccl.* R. 4. 8; *M. Zuta*, ed. Buber, p. 101; Deut. R. ch. 2.)

The problem seems to have attracted general attention in the fourth century. Three Haggadists, contemporaries of the Emperor Julian, who lived after or at the time of the Council of Nicaea, deal with it. These are R. Reuben, R. Berekhya, and R. Ḥilkiyahu. R. Reuben says: 'Multiply not exceeding proud talk' (1 Sam. 2. 3). Nebuchadnezzar is meant by this, 'Who saw four men, and the fourth was like the son of God' (Dan. 3. 25). R. Phinehas ben Ḥama says in R. Reuben's name: 'At this moment an angel descended from heaven and smote his [N's] face saying: Wicked man, retract at once! Has God a son? N. says: Blessed be He who sent His angel. It is not said: "Who sent His son!" (בריה), but, "His angel" (מלאכיה). God has not got a son (*v.* the passages *R.S.* ii. 90).' R. Berekhya refutes this doctrine on somewhat different lines. The wicked assert that God has a son (cf. Dan. 3. 25 'and the

[1] M. Ps., ed. Prague. 4b Targum., ad. loc., and Midr. Ps. (ed. Buber), p. 23.
[2] *v.* Marmorstein, *Relig. Studien*, i. 14; ii. 88, n. 4.

fourth is like God's son'). God says 'Had it been written
דמה לבר אלהין you would be right, but it is written דמה
לברי אלהין; these are the angels who are called בני אלהים
(v. R. S. ii. 90 *Agad. Ber.* (ed. Buber), p. 55, *M. Ps.* ch. 2).
R. Ḥilkiyahu calls those people who speak of and believe
in God's son liars. 'Stupid are those liars who say that there
is a son of God. When God saw that Abraham was about
to sacrifice his child, He said: Do not stretch out thy hand.
If He really had a son who was to be crucified, would He
not have destroyed the whole world?' It is said by Solomon:
'There is One and no second.' He calls Israel, however,
His children, out of love (*Agad. Ber.* p. 64 and *REJ* lxiv.
162).

There are very few references to the doctrine of the
Trinity. It may be that R. Simlai thought of it when he said:
'In the past Adam was created out of the earth, and Eve
from Adam; from now, however, every one shall be in our
image, and after our likeness' (Gen. R., ed. Theodor, p. 63,
1–4). There can be no human being born in an unnatural
way. In a Midrash we read further: 'When the children of
Esau approach you in your exile, saying: "Whom do you
worship? Come to us and let us have one and the same
religion, which will give you a share in paradise!" answer
them: "Our father, Jacob, commanded us not to give up
the belief in *God's unity*. We walk in His ways, and observe
His law."'[1] Julian, the Emperor, rebuked the Christians of
his days for giving up the belief in God's Unity by adopting
the doctrine of the Trinity, whilst the Jews, educated in the
teachings of Moses and the Prophets, kept the teaching of
God's Unity.[2]

If we examine the statements and dialogues of the teachers
mentioned in the foregoing pages, we see that R. Gamaliel
II, R. Eliezer ben Hyrcanus, R. Joshua ben Ḥananya,
R. Akiba, R. Yose ben Ḥalafta, R. Simon ben Yoḥai, R. Meir,

[1] MS. Adler, no. 960. 2B from the Commentary of R. Samuel ha-Nagid, II.
[2] *v. Byzantinische Zeitschrift*, iii. 135.

R. Nathan, R. Eleazar ha-Kappar, and R. Nehorai among
the Tannaim, and R. Hanina ben Hama, R. Yohanan,
R. Simon ben Lakish, R. Simlai, R. Eleazar ben Pedat,
R. Levi, R. Hiyya ben Abba, R. Judah ben Simon, R.
Simon ben Pazzi, R. Abbahu, R. Ammi and R. Assi,
R. Reuben, R. Berekhya, R. Hilkiyahu, and R. Tanhuma
among the Amoraim, combated the various forms of idol-
worship, the various sects and new religious movements,
which either opposed or imperilled the chief teaching of
Judaism, the belief in the Unity of God. There are, of
course, many more sayings on this subject in the anonymous Haggadah, some of which we have mentioned above,
while others we have ignored, because they merely repeat
or expand the arguments brought forward by others.
Mention should also be made of the endeavours common to
the Haggadists and Church Fathers, where their own differences were not involved. Some examples have been quoted,
others can be found in our article, 'Jews and Judaism in the
Earliest Christian Apologies'.[1] We have seen further that
the Rabbis emphasized this doctrine by means of the liturgy,
homilies, and legends, which inspired the synagogues, the
schools, and the home-life of the Jews in the first four
centuries. The greater the intolerance of the State and
Church, the more did the Jews cherish and adhere to their
faith in God. Even in our days, when Judaism is rent in so
many pieces by conflicting emotions and movements, it is
united by the belief in God's Unity.

[1] *The Expositor*, January–February 1919.

THE IMITATION OF GOD (*IMITA-TIO DEI*) IN THE HAGGADAH

I

THE pious teachers of the Haggadah in all their sermons and discourses were filled with one particular holy thought and strove for one particular great ideal. Whether in the diction of prose or of poetry all their linguistic skill was directed to the inculcation of one idea—God. Then, as now, the basis of the religious inspiration, of genuine piety, and of the highest idealism was God. The Haggadists made it their endeavour to bring the divine nearer to man and man nearer to the divine, or in other words to make the recognition of God clearer to the human understanding and to cultivate in man a resemblance to God. This had already been recognized by the old *Dorshe Reshumoth* as the object of the Haggadah, and knowledge of God and resemblance to God were regarded by them as fruits of the study of the Haggadah.[1] This estimate of the Haggadah was, however, not universally accepted. Sharp criticism was levelled at the Haggadah, and voices were raised in condemnation of it. In the centuries which followed the period of the Amoraim harsh judgements were passed on the Haggadah by Geonim and Rabbis. The fountains of Jewish thought and feeling, of religious philosophy and theology, opened up by the Haggadists were more or less neglected. The sermons and homilies constituted an exception; that these, though wrapped up, as they often were, in a philosophical or dialectical covering, contributed anything at all to the explanation of these sources can, with the best will in the world, hardly be seriously claimed. It is to-day universally recognized that, so far as the question can altogether be treated from a scientific standpoint, without a history of the period and some knowledge of the

[1] *v.* Marmorstein, *The Old-Rabbinic Doctrine of God* (London, 1927), p. 7 f.

existing circumstances the whole literature is a book with seven seals. Piety and religious knowledge flow on the one side from man's inner experience, but on the other side also from impressions of the external world around him.

The Haggadah quotes frequently a dictum of R. Yudan ben Simon: גדול כחן של נביאים שמדמין את הצורה ליוצרה[1], 'Great is the power of the prophets in that they compare the creature with the Creator'.[2] Prophets and Psalmists were able without offence to endow God with anthropomorphic features. They knew how to present the knowledge of God, the idea of God's nature and power, in tangible form to the eye and ear of man, and by means of similes and expressions drawn from everyday life to bring it nearer to human understanding. In this respect the teachers of the Haggadah stand not much below the prophets; they attain in many respects the height of the prophetic conception of God. The treatment of the anthropomorphisms in the Bible had from of old been a subject of dispute between opposing schools. The history of this spiritual conflict goes back very far. If this is borne in mind the contradictions between the scholars in the Haggadah

---

[1] Cf. Gen. R. 27. 1. In Eccles. R. 2. 24 and 8. 1 the statement is reported in the name of R. Simon: perhaps instead of א"ר שמעון גדול כח הנביאים שהן מדמין את הצורה ליוצרה we should read שמעון [יהודה ב'ר] א"ר, cf. Midrash Zutta, p. 117. We find א'ר יודן in Tanḥ. (ed. Buber) i, Pes. R. 61b, Tanḥ. Num. חקת 6, Num. R. 19. 4. In Midr. Ps. i. 4 (ed. Buber), the statement is adduced with some variants in the name of Hezekiah b. Ḥiyya אשריהם הנביאים שהן מדמין את הצורה ליוצרה ואת הנטיעה לנוטעה, cf. Amos 3. 8, Ez. 43, 2, Ps. 84. 12 כמד"א כי שמש ומגן ה' אלהים.

[2] The name יוצר or Creator for God is common in the Rabbinic literature, cf. my *Old Rabbinic Doctrine of God*, p. 86. Sometimes we find יוצר עולמים יוצר המאורות, יוצר בראשית and so forth. The parable of the potter, artist, artificer, is much used in order to depict the relation of the heavenly creator to the earthly creature. Philo already warns against esteeming the product above the artist. Stoic piety recognized God from His work. The artist is the creative cause of a work of art, the architect is the creator of a beautiful house, the sailing-ship points to a steersman, and so the world points to a creator, nature to a guide and sustainer, i.e. God, cf. Marmorstein, *Jeschurun*, vii, 1920, p. 98 f., and *Jewish Forum*, 1924, January, p. 18 f.

become much more intelligible. One has only to think of the attitude of R. Akiba and of R. Ishmael to this problem. No harm is done to religion if one designates it as anthropomorphic. All higher religious systems are of this nature. At any rate there are in the so-called higher religions anthropomorphisms which cannot be immediately accepted or justified. On the contrary, they are to a certain extent discarded, antiquated, and regarded as too narrow. An examination of the Biblical anthropomorphisms and the ideas expressed about them in the Haggadah leads to the conclusion that teachers and people in the first four centuries had reached a remarkably high stage of enlightenment in their conceptions of God. A Greek thinker of the sixth century B.C.E., Xenophanes, made the ironical remark, worthy of a Heine: 'If oxen, horses or lions had hands and could draw or produce artistic objects, then horses would have represented their gods in the form of horses, lions in the shape of lions and oxen in the shape of oxen, and given their bodies these forms.'[1]

This observation, which contains much truth, is a somewhat sharp condemnation of all endeavours and productions of the heathen religions at their highest level. Paganism was far removed from anthropomorphism, it cherished the lower stage of theriomorphism. These two ideas must not be confused; they are as far apart as heaven and earth. Men depicted their gods in the form of wild beasts. It is no wonder that these heathen thought they discerned traces of this 'religiosity' in the Jewish conceptions of God also. On the basis of Amos 3. 8, a Roman emperor fancied that he had found this theriomorphism in the religion of Israel also and questioned R. Joshua ben Ḥananya about it.[2] The learned Tanna could not take the question seriously. The religion of Israel was from the very beginning free

---

[1] Diels, *Fragmente*, 15; Burnett, *Early Greek Philosophy*, p. 119; L. R. Farnell, *The Attributes of God*, Oxford, 1925, p. 54 f.

[2] Ḥullin 59b.

from this false doctrine. For this freedom we have to thank the men who recognized God as the beginning and end of all kindness and mercy, of all truth and justice. A holy awe prevented the primitive Israelite from picturing God to himself with form and shape. Nevertheless, Scripture speaks of God as talking or hearing, standing or going, ascending or descending. The scholars endeavoured with their explanations and expositions to bring the idea of God nearer to man and so to lead man to God. Without anthropomorphism the ordinary man with his narrow vision and limited intelligence would not have been able to grasp the belief in God, in His omnipotence and eternity, His universal knowledge and presence.

There were also teachers in the third century who were against carrying anthropomorphism too far in theology or in exposition of the text. Most prominent among them is R. Samuel b. Naḥmani, one of the leading teachers of this period. In a homily on Deut. 1. 1, this verse is brought into connexion with Ps. 50. 21: 'These things hast thou done and should I have kept silence? Thou hadst thought that I was altogether such a one as thyself; but I will reprove thee, and set the cause before thine eyes.'[1] The homily is based

---

[1] Deut. R. i. 3. ד״א אלה הדברים אשר דבר משה זש״ה אלה עשית והחרשתי
דמית היות אהיה כמוך, אוכיחך ואערכה לעיניך מהו אלה עשית והחרשתי? א״ר
שמואל ב״ר נחמן אלה אלהיך ישראל והחרשתי לכם! למה? שהיה משה מפייס
עלי ואומר לי סלח נא ושמעתי לו, דמית היות כמוך, דמיתם את הצורה ליוצרה,
ואת הנטיעה למי שנטעה, אוכיחך ואערכה לעיניך, תרין אמוראין ח״א אעורר כל
לעיניך וח״א אסדור כל לעיניך. Yalḳuṭ Shim'oni Psalms, § 762, reads instead of
R. Samuel b. Naḥman ר' שמואל בר יצחק who belonged to the same period.
The passage runs: א״ר שמואל בר יצחק אלה אלהיך שעשו ישראל במדבר
החרשתי לכם, למה? לפי שמשה מפייס עלי ואומר לי סלח נא ושמעתי לו, דמית
אהיה כמוך דמיתם צורה ליוצרה הנטיעה לנוטעה, אוכיחך ואערכה לעיניך שני
Instead of אמוראים חד אמר אעורר כל לעיניך, וחד אמר אסדר כל לעיניך.
שעשו ישראל we should perhaps read שעשיתם. The words סלח נא do not
require any emendation, as the Haggadist was thinking of Num. 14. 19. The
homily consists of three parts: (a) אלה עשית והחרשתי the sin of the people
in making the Golden Calf, (b) דמית היות אהיה כמוך the idea that God is
like a man, (c) אוכיחך ואערכה, the significance of ערך. The gist of the
homily is in the second part which is explained in the text.

on the threefold occurrence of the word אלה in Deut.
1. 1, Ps. 50. 21, and Exod. 32. 4. You made the Golden
Calf, and still I was silent. Why? Because Moses prayed
for you and said, Forgive the sin, &c. So far all is clear.
But what is the point of the remark about comparing the
Creator and the creature, the plant and him who plants it?
Have we not seen that the prophets were praised because
they understood this art so well? The Psalmist, however,
warns against carrying the comparison too far. God for-
gives and forgets the sin. Is He then forgetful like a man?
'No', says the preacher, 'When the occasion arises I will
reprove thee, and set before thee thy sin and transgression.'

R. Levi uses this verse in the same way, homiletically
connecting Gen. 5. 1 with Isa. 29. 15. He prefaces his
explanation with the simile of an architect who later becomes
the city tax-collector, from whom the foolish inhabitants
try to hide their possessions and themselves.[1] As in the
previous homily the idea that God can be forgetful, so here
the idea that God is not omniscient is reprimanded. It is
quite possible that these teachers considered the anthropomorphic interpretation of the Scripture dangerous and
harmful, because it might incline men to attribute or transfer their faults and weaknesses to God. This brings us to
the history of the *Imitatio Dei* in the Haggadah.

II

Men can speak of God only in human language. Feelings,

[1] Gen. R. 24. 1 (in the name of R. Joshua), ed. Theodor, p. 229. The edd.
have R. Hoshaya. Cf. Midr. Ps. (ed. Buber) 14, 1, p. 111, Tanḥ. 4, p. 30, Num.
R. 9. 1, Yalḳuṭ Shimoni. G. R. reads: כך הוי המעמיקים וגו' הפככם אם כחומר
היוצר יחשב, מדמים צורה ליוצרה נטיעה לנוטעה כי יאמר מעשה לעושהו לא עשני,
הלא עוד מעט מזער ושב לבנון לכרמל לבית מלכות והכרמל ליער יחשב לחורשין
דבני נש ושמעו ביום ההוא החרשים דברי ספר, ספר תולדות של אדם זה ספר
תולדות אדם .M. Ps. reads: אנו חורשין, הרשעים אמרו בלבם, חוקר לב, ד"א
בלבנו כביכול אין הקב"ה יודע מה בלבנו, א"ל הקב"ה ממני אתם מטמינים והלא
כתוב הוי המעמיקים מה" לסתר עצה והיה וכו' אתם סבורים שאני כמותכם שאתם
מדמים הצורה ליוצרה נטיעה לנוטעה הפככם וכו'.

actions, habits, and traits are therefore assigned to God in
order to bring within the scope and conception of man the
highest of all ideas, the purest of all thoughts, the most
elevated of all feelings—God. On the other side we transfer
to man the holiest attributes and qualities of God. This is
done in order to show to poor and suffering humanity the
way to God, to smooth the path to the improvement and
ennobling of the generations of man, to comfort the frus-
trated and sorrowful children of earth, to present to men
and women, old and young, a model of justice and piety,
showing how through spiritual possessions and ethical
values they can enrich and beautify life. In this consists
the teaching of the imitation of God.

How did this teaching arise, and what course did it take
in the first four centuries of the Christian era? The prophets
declared often enough the impossibility of finding comparisons for God. Yet man is able to cultivate a resemblance
to God. In the Haggadah this idea is first expressed by
Abba Saul.[1] When the teachers were once discussing the
explanation of Exod. 15. 2, Abba Saul found in the word
ואנוהו the idea of the imitation of God. 'Be like God',
preached this Tanna, 'as God is gracious and merciful so
be thou gracious and merciful.'[2]

An expanded form of this teaching of Abba Saul is to be
found in an anonymous Haggadah of the Tannaitic Midrash

[1] There are two teachers of this name, an older and a younger. Since the
name is here mentioned in conjunction with the teachers of the pre-Bar-
Kokhba period it is probably the older teacher who is meant.

[2] Mekhilta 37a אבא שאול אומר נדמה לו מה הוא חנון ורחום אף אתה חנון
ורחום. Mekhilta RSbY, p. 60, reads: אבא שאול אומר הדמה לו מה הוא חנון
אבא שאול אומר ורחום אף אתה היה חנון ורחום. Sifra, Warsaw, 1866, 75b:
פמליא למלך ומה עליה להיות מחקה למלך there is a variant which has מחכה instead
of מחקה. B. Sabb. 133b reads אבא שאול אומר ואנוהו הוי דומה לו מה הוא
אבא שאול אומר אדמה לו חנון ורחום אף אתה היה חנון ורחום. J. Peah has
אבא שאול אומר מה הוא רחום וחנון אף את תהא רחום וחנון and Sôferîm 3. 11,
הדמה לו מה הוא רחום וחנון אף אתה רחום וחנון.

On הוא as a name of God cf. Marmorstein, *The Old-Rabbinic Doctrine
of God*, London, 1927, p. 84.

on Deut. 11. 22.[1] The ways of God are the thirteen attributes of God which are enumerated in Exod. 34. 6, and
with them Joel 3. 5 is brought into conjunction.[2] How can
man be labelled with the designations of God? As God is
called חנון ורחום,[3] צדיק,[4] or חסיד,[5] so can the pious man also
become worthy of these names. The man who imitates the
qualities of God can be designated with God's names. An
earthly king would jealously guard his titles and privileges,
but God in His goodness behaves differently.[6] Preaching on
Isa. 61. 8 ('for I the Lord love justice, I hate robbery with
iniquity'), R. Simon ben Yoḥai illustrates the meaning of
the verse with an example. A king is on a journey and
comes with his retinue to a customs house. He says to his
men: 'Pay the officer the customs.' His servants exclaim in
astonishment: 'But the dues belong to you.' To which the
king replies: 'Let all travellers thus learn from me to fulfil
their duty.' In this sense God says: 'I hate robbery with
iniquity, in order that men may take example from Me and
abstain from robbery.'[7] While Abba Saul teaches the
positive side of the imitation of God, R. Simon ben Yoḥai
lays stress on the negative side. What God abhors must
appear contemptible to the pious man also.

The teachers of the third century did not content themselves with the general rule of imitation. They gave practical

[1] Sifre, Deut. § 49. Midrash Tannaim, p. 43, Yalḳuṭ Makhiri (Deut. 11.
22). ללכת בכל דרכיו ללכת בדרכי ה' אלו דרכי הקב"ה [במ"ת הגי' המקום] שנ"א
ה' ה' אל רחום וחנון וכו' ואומר כל אשר יקרא בשם ה' ימלט.
[2] The connexion is made here with the technical expression ואומר,
which in the Tannaitic Haggadah frequently, if not invariably, corresponds
to the Amoraic זה שאמר הכתוב. Cf., for this, Marmorstein, 'Anges et
hommes dans l'agada', in the *REJ*. lxxxiv, 1927, 42–6.
[3] On רחום וחנון as names of God, cf. M. Shebuot iv. 10; Sôferîm 4. 9.
Cf., too, Marmorstein, *Old-Rabbinic Doctrine of God*, p. 41.
[4] Marmorstein, op. cit., p. 95.
[5] Ibid., p. 85.
[6] Tanḥ. (ed. Buber) ii, pp. 22 f., Exod. R. 8. 1. מלך בו"ד אין קוראין בשמו
כמו קיסר אגוסתום בסיליאוס. Cf. also *infra*.
[7] B. Sukkah 30a. R. Yoḥanan ben Nappaḥa in the name of R. Simon ben
Yoḥai, Yalḳuṭ Makhiri Isaiah, p. 256. The text in Makhiri agrees completely
with the Hal. Ged. ed. Hildesheimer, p. 61.

hints of the way in which they thought man might imitate
the mercy, piety, and justice of God. Let us take first
a statement attributed to R. Ḥama ben Ḥanina.[1] The
imitation of the love and mercy of God finds expression in
the following good deeds: clothing the naked, caring for
the sick, comforting mourners, and burying the dead. It
is an interesting fact that the first apologist of nascent
Christianity has borne similar testimony to the Jews.[2] He
writes: 'The Jews imitate God's goodness by beneficence,
they ransom captives, they bury the dead', &c. This apologist is older than the Amora, he is a contemporary of Abba
Saul, whose teaching may already have been widely known
at that time. The following fact also speaks for the early
date and wide dissemination of this doctrine, viz. that the
Palestinian Targum attributed to Jonathan elaborates it in
great detail. On Deut. 34. 6 we read the following homily

.בריך שמיה דמארי עלמא דאליף לן ארחתיה תקני, אליף יתן

(א) למלביש ערטלאין מן דאלביש אדם וחוה

(ב) אליף יתן למזוווגא חתנין וכלן מן דזוויג חוה לות אדם

(ג) אליף יתן למבקרא מרעין מן דאתגלי בחזוי מימריה וכו׳

(ד) אליף יתן למנחמא אבלין מן דאתגלי ליעקב וכו׳

(ה) אליף יתן למפרנסא מסכינין מן דאחת לבני ישראל לחמא וכו׳

(ו) אליף יתן למקבר מיתיא מן משה דאתגלי עלוי במימריה

The introductory words indicate that the Targumist has
here interpolated an ancient discourse. Nos. 1, 3, 4, and 6
appear also in the Haggadah of R. Ḥama ben Ḥanina as
we have it. R. Simlai mentions the beginning and end of

---

[1] B. Soṭah 14a; for the reading cf. Sheiltoth (Dyhernfurth), 3a, 28b, Torath
ha-Adam 52. ואמר ר׳ חמא ברבי חנינא מאי דכתיב אחרי ה׳ אלהיכם תלכו וכי
אפשר לו לאדם להלך אחר שכינה והלא כבר נאמר כי ה׳ אלהים אש אוכלה הוא
אלא להלך אחר מדותיו של הקב״ה מה הוא מלביש ערומים וכו׳ הקב״ה בקר
חולים הקב״ה ניחם אבלים וכו׳ הקב״ה קבר מתים אף אתה.
On the conjunction of these duties in Rabbinic literature cf. also Marmorstein, שבלים, iv, in *Hazofeh*, ix (1927), 34, 35.

[2] Aristides of Athens, *c.* 120, i.e. 100 years before our Amora; cf. Marmorstein, 'Jews and Judaism in the Earliest Christian Apologies', in *Expositor*,
1919, p. 75 f.

I

this statement in his well-known Haggadah.[1] The Targum uses also the word הדרך 'the way (of God)' in Exod. 18. 20, in the sense of care of the sick, disposal of the dead, &c.[2] The interpretation of the Targumist is very close to that of R. Eleazar of Modi'im,[3] as can be seen from the following table.

REM. MII	RJ. II	T.	T. J.	REM. MI	RJ. MII	Text
עריות	גזרות	—	קיימייא	עריות	מדרשות	חקים
גזרות	הוראות	—	אורייתא	הוראות	הוראות	תורות
בית החיים	גזרה	בית חייהם	צלותא	בית חייהם	—	והודעת להם
גמ״ח	—	גמ״ח	בק״ה	בקור חולים	ת״ת	דרך
בקור חולים	—	בק״ח	ק״מ	קבורת מתים	—	ילכו
ק״מ	—	קבורה	גמ״ח	גמ״ח	•	בה

An anonymous Haggadah which is perhaps older than both R. Ḥama ben Ḥanina and Pseudo-Jonathan describes in greater detail than either the ways in which it is possible for a man to imitate God.[4] The lesson is based on Cant. 1. 15: 'How fair art thou, my beloved', and runs as follows: 'Thou art fair in good deeds. My beloved, he who walks in God's ways is called beloved and the friend of God. As God is gracious and merciful, long-suffering and full of love, so be thou also like God, give charity and practise beneficence.'[5] Through doing good man becomes like God.

[1] B. Soṭah 14a and parallel passages.

[2] ותזהר יתהון ית קיימייא ית אורייתא ותהודע להון ית צלותא דיצלון בבית כנישתהון וית אורחא דיבקרון למירעין ודיהבין למיקבור מיתיא ולמיגמול בה חיסדא וית עובדא דשורת דינא ודיעבדון מלגו לשורתא לרשיעין.

[3] v. Mekhilta 59b (= M I), Mekh. RSbY., 89 f. (M II), BK. 18. BM 30b, introduced with תני ר' יוסף (T). RJ is R. Joshua ben Ḥananya, and REM stands for R. Eleazar of Modi'im.

[4] There is a sentence worth noting in the treatise of Tertullian on prayer (ch. xi): 'On dismissing his brothers in order to bring his father, Joseph said to them, "Do not quarrel on the way" (Gen. 45. 24). Clearly enough it is we who are thus admonished by him, for in many other places our discipline and doctrine is called "Way".' In the Haggadah also the word בדרך is taken in this sense, cf. Gen. R. 94. 2, B. Ta'an. 10b.

[5] The passage dealt with here can be found in Midrash Zutta, ed. Buber, Berlin, 1894, pp. 161 f. and Agadat Shir ha-Shirim, ed. Schechter (Cambridge, 1896), pp. 18 f. The discourse specifies: (a) ארך אפים, (b) רחום וחנון,

III

All men have the possibility of becoming like God, but only a few approach the ideal. It is the pious man, the *Ṣaddik*, who most of all resembles his Creator. Noah and Joseph are styled 'just'. Why? Because they sustained the creatures of God. Here the maintenance of the creatures, whether animals or men, is looked upon as an act showing imitation of God.[1] Another teacher illustrates this doctrine with a parable. A king has a rich friend. He is minded to give his friend a present, but does not know what to give, since the friend possesses gold, silver, slaves, &c., in abundance. He resolves at length to hand over his sword to him publicly. God is the king, Abraham the friend. God asks: 'What can I give him?' Be like me. With this we can link R. Simlai's homily, which sees גמילות חסדים both at the beginning and the end of the Torah. God adorns the bridal couple, visits the sick, comforts the mourners, and busies Himself with the dead. Abraham acts similarly, devoting his life to offices of love, and therefore he is like God.[2]

These examples could be greatly multiplied. They would, however, only confirm the fact that in speaking of the imitation of God, one thought first of the pious who attained perfection through acts of loving-kindness. On a point of language it may here be noted that the Tannaim saw in the expression 'to walk in the ways of God' (ללכת בדרכיו or

(c) גומל חסדים and עושה צדקות. These last include feeding the hungry, relieving the thirsty, clothing the naked, redeeming captives, and giving orphans in marriage. Some of these acts have already been mentioned in earlier lists, others are freshly added.

[1] Noah is regularly entitled הצדיק, cf. Yelamdenu, Gen., ed Grünhut, p. 29b, B. Sanh. 108b, cf. מעין גנים, p. 40, Tanḥ. (ed. Buber), נח 6, Tosef. Aboth R. Nathan, c. 16, p. 63, Eccles. R. 9. 3, 17, M. Ps. 58c. Methuselah, Moses, Benjamin, Hannah, Job, Jacob, Miriam, Lot, and Simeon are also mentioned with this appellative.

[2] Tanḥ. (ed. Buber), i. 79, Jellinek, 4. בית המדרש 25. משל למלך שהיה לו אוהב והיה עשיר מדאי אמר המלך מה אתן לאוהבי, כסף וזהב עבדים ושפחות ובהמה יש לו, אלא הריני חוגרו זייני כך אמר הקב״ה מה אתן לך כסף וזהב, עבדים ושפחות ובהמה, כבר נתתי לך, אלא מה אתן לך דייך שתהא כמוני. On the dictum of R. Simlai, cf. Tanḥ., ibid., pp. 83 and 86, Gen. R. 8. 15.

דרכי ה׳) the idea of the imitation of God. They themselves
used in this connexion the verb דמה, to be like or to resemble.
In the Haggadah of the Amoraim we find the noun שותף
used for giving expression to this idea. A few examples may
be mentioned. (1) Abraham is regarded as a שותף because
he shows mercy to God's creatures.[1] אמר הקב״ה לאברהם אתה
קבלת עוברים ושבים מעלה אני עליך כאלו אתה שותף עמי בברייתו של
עולם. (2) He who recites ויכולו on Friday evening is called
God's collaborator in the work of creation.[2] כל המתפלל ע״ש
ויכולו כאילו נעשה שותף להקב״ה במעשה בראשית. (3) Similarly, the
judge who gives a verdict in accordance with the facts.[3]
כל דיין שדן דין אמת לאמיתו נעשה שותף להקב״ה. (4) Also one who
keeps silent when he is cursed, even though he has the
power to defend himself.[4] כל מי ששומע קללתו ושותק וספק בידו
למחות נעשה שותף להקב״ה. Jacob[5] is regarded as a collaborator
of God.[6] Although in early sources the idea that angels or
other beings took part in the creation of the world as God's
helpers is condemned as heretical, yet we see here that the
idea of the pious as God's helpers was quite common.
Apparently the expression שותף במעשה בראשית or שותף לבוראו
signified only an imitation of God.

Voices were indeed raised against this teaching. For
instance, there was R. Simon ben Laḳish, who on the verse

[1] Gen. R. 43, 9, R. Isaac אני לא היה שמי ניכר לבריותי והכרת אותי
בבריותי מעלה אני עליך וכו׳.

[2] B. Sabb. 119b. Cf. Sheiltoth 2c רבא (רב) ואיתימא ר׳ יהושע בן לוי ואמר
רב המנונא.

[3] B. Sabb. 10a; R. Ḥiyya bar Rab from Difti, Wertheimer, בתי מדרשות
iv. 12.

[4] M. Ps. 44c. R. Abba in the name of R. Alexander.

[5] Tanḥ. (ed. Buber), i. 13, 2, שיעקב שותף עם בוראו בכל דבר. Maḥzor
Vitry, p. 367, has a sentence the source of which is unknown to me, which
runs כל הנקרא בשמו של הקב״ה מעלה עליו הכתוב כאלו נעשה שותף להקב״ה
במעשה בראשית, cf. also Pes. 55a–b, Pesik. R. 78b, Exod. R. 19, 3
תהו שותפין לבריוכון.

[6] Cf. also Gen. R. 98. 4, R. Yudan b. Simon and R. Phinehas b. Ḥama
ר׳ יודן אמר שמעו לאל ישראל אביכם ור״פ אמר אל הוא ישראל אביכם מה
הקב״ה בורא עולמות אף אביכם בורא עולמות, מה הקב״ה מחלק עולמות אף
אביכם מחלק עולמות.

'Ye shall be holy' (Lev. 19. 2) remarked: 'Thinkest thou that thou canst be as holy as I am? No, I alone am holy.'[1] R. Levi[2] sides with him when he says: 'Only he who can accomplish My works is like Me', says God. Once a king lit two torches and proclaimed, 'Whoever performs the like shall be called Augustus and I will not begrudge him the title. God has created heaven and earth. Do the same, and then canst thou also be called God, then wilt thou be like Him.'[3] The same idea is carried farther in an anonymous Haggadah. A king goes on a campaign with his troops. He finds himself in the desert with his provisions exhausted. I should be glad, says the king, if someone would give me some bread. When the time arrived for the אריסטון[4] someone gave him a loaf (גלוסקא). In the town he gave him food and

---

[1] Lev. R. 24. 9 אמרש״ל שתי פרשיות הכתיב לנו משה בתורה ואנו למדין אותן מפרשת פרעה הרשע כתוב א״א והייתי רק למעלה יכול כמוני ת״ל רק, וכו' והדין קדושים תהיו יכול כמוני ת״ל כי קדוש אני קדושתי למעלה מקדושתכם.

[2] Tanḥ. (ed. Buber) iii. 111 אמר הקב״ה כל מי שהוא עושה כמעשי יהא דומה לי. אמר ר' לוי משל למלך שבנה מדינה והדליק בתוכה שני פנסים אמר המלך כל מי שמדליק שני פנסים כאלו אני קורא אותו אגוסטה, ואיני מקנא בו, כך הקב״ה ברא את השמים ונתן בהם ב' פנסים וכו' אמר הקב״ה כל מי שיעשה כאלו, יהא שוה לי.

[3] Deut. R. 1. 10, where R. Levi b. Ḥama teaches: ומה מי שעובד ע״ג הרי הוא כמותו שנ״א כמוהם יהיו עושיהם וכו' מי שעובד להקב״ה לא כ״ש שיהיה כמותו, i.e. the doctrine of the Imitation of God. The Haggadist, however, is not the same as R. Levi. There is a similar passage in Philo, who uses the doctrine of the Imitatio Dei to reduce to an absurdity the worship of idols (De Dec. ii, l. 93). Did the Haggadist perhaps know Philo? It is perhaps this R. Levi who is referred to in the passage in M. Koh. Zuṭṭa which runs: א״ר לוי תורה תחלתה וסופה גמ״ח אמר הקב״ה למוד ממני הנחתי שמחה לבני במשכן והלכתי לאבל נדב ואביהו Yalḳuṭ Makhiri has a dictum in the name of R. Joshua b. Levi which also belongs here, and is also a proof that the dicta of R. Levi, as also frequently in this case, were confused with those of R. Joshua b. Levi. R. Simon taught in the name of R. Joshua b. Levi: כל מי שבוטח בהקב״ה זוכה להיות כיוצא בו Yalḳuṭ Makhiri, Psalms (ed. Buber), on Ps. 146. 1.

[4] ἀριστάω means to take breakfast, or simply to take the meal called ἄριστον, which is applied to breakfast, midday meal, and meal in general. The word אריסטון is therefore not to be translated by מי שמאכיל את הסעודה as Buber does (p. 478 note 22) but means that when the time of the meal, which may have been either breakfast or midday, came, then (some man or other) gave him a גלוסקא, a loaf.

drink. When the king returned home he forgot his meal in
the desert. The man who had supplied him reminded him
of it. To reward him the king made him a שלטן. 'Is that all
that you can do for me?' asked the man. The king thereupon made him an אפרכוס. The man was still not satisfied,
so the king said to him, 'Be like me. Do you want more
still?' So God says to the pious man: 'You are like Me, do
you wish perhaps to be even more than I am? (cf. Jer. 15.
19). As I create worlds and revive the dead, do you wish
also to possess this power?'[1] The pious man can resemble
God, but not be greater than God. The power and influence
of the pious have limits which he cannot overstep. There
can be little doubt that these words and the whole character
of the homily have their roots in and are to be explained by
the circumstances of the time.

Actually there is one line of thought in the Haggadah
which contests this capability of the individual personage
and of the *Ṣaddik* to imitate God, and sees this possibility
embodied only in Israel, in the collectivity of the people of
God. The *Kenesset Israel* resembles God. Israel in its unity,
uniqueness, and harmony, in its separation from sin and
impurity, and sanctification by doctrine and precept, comes
nearest to God. God is unique in holiness and purity, in
love and righteousness. This idea is elaborated in a dialogue
between God and the *Kenesset Israel*.[2] The form of this

---

[1] Midr. Ps. ed. Buber, p. 478. I take the concluding words as a question
מה אני בורא עולמות ומחיה מתים אף אתם כן?

[2] Sifre Deut. § 348a, Midr. Tanḥ., p. 221, Midr. Cant., c. p. 16.

I. ישראל אומר אין כאל ורוח הקדש אומרת אל ישורון

II. ישראל אומ׳ מי כמכה באלים ה׳ ורה״ק אומ׳ אשריך ישראל מי כמוך

III. ישראל אומ׳ שמע ישראל ורה״ק אומ׳ ומי כעמך ישראל

IV. ישראל אומ׳ כתפוח בעצי היער ורה״ק אומ׳ כשושנה בין החוחים

V. ישראל אומ׳ זה אלי ואנוהו ורה״ק אומ׳ עם זו יצרתי לי

VI. ישראל אומ׳ כי תפארת עוזמו ורה״ק אומ׳ ישראל אשר בך אתפאר

It is to be noted that instead of ורוח הקדש Midr. Ta'an. reads המקום.
From other passages also we know that רוח הקדש is used in the Rabbinical literature for God, see Marmorstein, *Old-Rabbinic Doctrine of God*,
p. 90, also Midr. Ta'an. reads: אל ישורון.

dialogue is more important for the proper understanding of Haggadic thought than its neglect by modern students would at all lead one to suspect. Israel emphasizes the incomparability of God, while God declares Israel to be incomparable. Israel proclaims the unity of God (Deut. 6. 4), while God proclaims the unity of Israel (I Chron. 17. 21). Why is Israel incomparable and unique? Wherein lies its unity? As the apple-tree which throws no shade is avoided in the heat, so the nations of the world rejected God and the Torah on the day of revelation (Cant. 2. 3). Israel is therefore like the lily which, even though it fades for a time, yet endures perpetually (ibid. 2. 2). God is Israel's leader, Israel is God's people (Exod. 15. 16, Isa. 43. 21). Israel's glory is God (Ps. 89. 18), and God is glorified through Israel (Isa. 49. 3). Nowhere is the resemblance between God and Israel so clearly and eloquently set forth as in this dialogue, even though in our version it is only an outline.

The incomparability and the unity of God are the fundamental doctrines of Judaism. In this the teaching of Judaism differs from that of all other monotheistic religions (with the exception of Islam, although there also the incomparability seems to be somewhat toned down). Israel resembles God in its incomparability and its unique character. This notion differentiates the Jewish doctrine of the Imitation of God from that of the old philosophers and the Christian theologians, both of whom make a prototype of man the object of imitation. There is a wonderful legend in which the Haggadists present the idea we are now considering.[1] God says to Israel: 'Before the creation of the world the angels praised Me and hallowed Me through you.' They said: 'Praised be the Lord, the God of Israel, from eternity to eternity.'[2] When Adam was created the angels asked: 'Is this he in whose name we glorify Thee?' God answered,

---

[1] Tanḥ. (ed. Buber), iii. 72.
[2] 1 Chron. 16. 36.

'No, this is a thief' (Gen. 3. 17). When Noah came they
repeated the question. God answered: 'No, this is a drunkard.' Abraham arrived, and the answer again came, 'No,
this is a wanderer.' 'Isaac loved Esau who hates Me.' But
when Jacob, (i.e. Israel) came, God said: 'Ye are holy as I am
holy.' As in all legends in which the Patriarchs are criticized,
there must here also be some hidden reason of an apologetic
or polemical character, which we cannot now consider. But
at any rate the Haggadah is permeated with the idea that
God and Israel resemble each other in holiness. The Haggadic poet proclaims that the *Kenesset Israel* has come
nearest to perfection, to the highest stage of piety, to the
ideal and the absolute essence of religion, which find their expression in holiness. The teaching and history of Judaism are
nothing more than a long, painful, sad, and inspiring commentary on this resemblance to God. All the sufferings and
joys of the last two thousand years, the light and shadow
of our present and future, are inseparably and eternally
bound up with this idea of holiness. No wonder that the
Kenesset Israel has produced men who were able to come
so near to the ideal of *Kedushah*. Here lies a deep and still
far from exhausted source of true piety, from which present
and future can yet draw much strength and confidence.

In conclusion, may we mention the theory that man can
become like God only after death, in the future world. We
have elsewhere called attention to a similar theory, that
only after their decease can men attain a perfection which
places them above the ministering angels (cf. *REJ* lxxxiv,
1927, pp. 37–50). This idea is expressed in an anonymous
homily on Deut. 1. 10, which runs: היום אתם ככוכבים אבל
לע״ל לרב, אתם עתידין להיות דומין לרבכן. 'To-day you are like
stars, but in the time to come you will be like your Master,
i.e. God.' In another homily on Deut. 4. 4 we read: בעה״ז
היו ישראל דבקים להקב״ה שנא׳ ואתם הדבקים, אבל לעתיד לבא הם
הווים ודומים להקב״ה (Pesiḳta R., ed. Friedmann, 46b). In the
future world you will resemble and be like God. Here in

this world a man cannot be like God, neither the ordinary man, nor the pious man, nor Israel. A new world, an aeon of quite another character, must arise in order to render possible this mighty transformation.[1]

[1] Cf. also, Buber, 'Nachahmung Gottes', in *Morgen*, Jhg. I, 1926, pp. 638–47.

THE HOLY SPIRIT IN RABBINIC LEGEND

OF recent years both theologians and philologists have given much attention to the subject of the Holy Spirit, and quite a number of books and essays have been written on this doctrine,[1] one of the most important for the history of religion. In these works frequent use has been made of the Rabbinic material also; and Fr. Büchsel devotes a special chapter to this subject under the title of 'Der heil. Geist bei den Rabbinern'.[2] Büchsel is sensible of the contradiction which strikes every inquirer in this field and which indeed runs through the whole of Rabbinic literature. Sometimes the gift of the Spirit is spoken of as being denied to the Rabbis, at other times as being vouchsafed to them. This undeniable difficulty is in itself a sufficient ground for going over the sources afresh and examining the whole problem scientifically. In doing so special attention must be paid to the origin of the relevant statement. Every dictum must be separately examined and analysed, with special reference to the date and place of its transmitter. Above all, care must be taken to distinguish between individual views and generally accepted doctrines. Religious points of view and motives must also be considered in their historical setting, which often places them in a fresh light and provides a clue to otherwise insoluble difficulties. We shall thus gain a new and truer idea of the piety which animated the leading figures of that time, or rather of the ideal of piety which inspired and dominated their conduct.

My task is therefore in the first place to examine the statements which have come down to us regarding the cessation of the Spirit in Israel; secondly to bring together

[1] I will refer here only to Volz, *Der Geist Gottes*, 1910; H. Leisegang, *Der Heilige Geist*, 1919; J. Heinemann *MGWJ* lxvi, 1922, 169 ff.; Büchsel, *Der Geist Gottes im N.T.*, Gütersloh, 1926; Hermann Cohen, 'Der Heil. Geist' (in the *Festschrift für Jacob Guttmann*), Leipzig, 1915, 1–21.

[2] Op. cit., pp. 120–35.

the legends on the continued presence of prophecy; and thirdly to describe the replacing of prophecy by the *Bath Kol*, as recorded in the legends dealing with the matter. Fourthly the voice coming from heaven must be compared with other things deriving or falling from heaven. References to non-Rabbinic material for purposes of comparison have been deliberately restricted to as small a compass as possible, the material for this purpose being reserved for the notes.

I

The cessation of the Spirit in Israel is sometimes dated from the destruction of the First Temple (586 B.C.E.), sometimes from the demise of the last prophets. A third view puts it as late as the destruction of the Second Temple (70 C.E.). The first view is represented by certain dicta in which the differences between the First and the Second Temple are specified. According to these, there were certain things in the First Temple which were lacking in the Second, among them the Holy Spirit, i.e. prophecy.[1] On this assumption an Haggadist makes Jeremiah's disciple Baruch say: 'Why am I different from all other disciples of the prophets who received from their teachers the Holy Spirit, like Joshua from Moses or Elisha from Elijah? Why do I not receive it in the same way from my master Jeremiah?'[2] The second view is met with frequently and can be regarded as that of the Tannaim. According to this the Holy Spirit vanished with the last prophets, and thenceforth the *Bath Kol* served instead of it.[3] The author of the First Book of Maccabees must have known this view,[4] since he says: 'Thus there was great trouble in Israel,

---

[1] *v.* the examples in Marmorstein, *Midrash Ḥaserot* (London, 1917), p. 38, n. 158.

[2] Mekhilta 2b.

[3] B. Yoma 9b, B. Soṭah 48b, B. San. 11a, M. Horayoth, 3. 5, M. Soṭah 9. 12; Cant. R. 8, 11. The source may be Tos. Soṭah 13. 2, ed. Zuckermandel, 318, lines 21 ff.

[4] 9. 27.

such as had not been since the time when a prophet last appeared among them.' Thus long before the time of the Maccabees there had been no more prophets in Israel. In contrast with these views, which are almost certainly of Tannaitic origin, we have the following somewhat disrespectful dictum of R. Yoḥanan ben Nappaḥa (before 279 C.E.): 'Since the destruction of the Temple the gift of prophecy has been taken away from the prophets and given to fools and children.'[1] As in all similar dicta, the reference here is to the destruction of the Second Temple, not the First. It is altogether out of the question that the Amora should have denied the existence of the last prophets who were active after the First Temple. Apart from this, his somewhat contemptuous attitude to prophecy is certainly surprising, and difficult for us to explain, though no doubt it was justified by the conditions of the time. We know that R. Yoḥanan on one occasion recognized a power of divination in the utterance of a child.[2] The ascription of a prophetic gift to fools has no doubt something to do with the fact that the term מְשׁוּגָּע frequently used of prophets, is applied also to 'fools'.[3] These two considerations prove the authenticity of the dictum.

Most sweeping is perhaps the dictum of an anonymous teacher who declares: 'In this world there is neither a prophet nor a Holy Spirit[4] (cf. Ps. 74. 9), and even the Shekhinah has vanished on account of our sins (Isa. 59. 2);

---

[1] B. Baba Bathra, 121b. Examples of prophecies by fools and children are given from cases which happened after the death of R. Yoḥanan.

[2] Cf. B. Ḥullin 95b; J. Sabbath 8c. R. Yoḥanan is about to make a journey from Tiberias to Nehardea, in order to visit the spiritual head of the Babylonian Jews, but desists in consequence of a quotation from 1 Sam. 28. 3 (stating that Samuel had died).

[3] Cf. Midr. Ps. 7. 3. For the use of מְשׁוּגָּע v. 2 Kings 9. 11; Jer. 29. 26; Hos. 9. 7. On this designation for the founder of Islam v. Hebr. Bibl. xiii. 59; Steinschneider, Pol. und Apol. Lit., §§ 350, 364, 385.

[4] The distinction made here between prophecy on the one side and the Holy Spirit on the other is rather surprising. Elsewhere they are synonymous, as will be shown in the course of this essay. Perhaps 'Holy Spirit' is added as an explanation of prophecy; or are two readings combined here?

but in the future world a new revelation will be vouchsafed to them.'[1] We note here the distinction drawn between the prophecy and the Holy Spirit; further, that even the Shekhinah is thought of as departed, and finally the restoration of the Spirit in the future. This last idea is one of the basic teachings of the Haggadah. The Golden Age is relegated to the past or looked for in the future, and contrasted with the imperfection of the sinful present, which is unworthy of these favours. In the future world, as R. Ḥanina, an Haggadist of the third century teaches, man will see God with his own eyes.[2] The Haggadah is rich in eschatological promises and fancies, which in this doctrine reach their culminating point. We find the same process in other theological systems also. We need mention only the idea of the *Imitatio Dei*[3] and of the relation of man to the celestial angels[4] to prove the tendency of the Haggadah to place the attainable ideal of the most complete piety, of the most perfect union with God, at the 'end of days', i.e. in the future world. In this world even the prophets of previous days, the pious men of old, have experienced temporary lapses. There were moments in which even men like Jacob, Moses, and Samuel[5] were deprived of the Holy Spirit. Jacob and his sons were prophets, nevertheless, they had no sure knowledge of Joseph's stay in Egypt, because

---

[1] Agadat Bereshit, ed. Buber, p. 47.

[2] Cf. Marmorstein, 'Das Dasein Gottes', in *Jeschurun*, vii, 1920, 174 f., and *Jewish Forum*, 1924, January, 25 ff.

[3] Cf. Marmorstein, 'Die Nachahmung Gottes', in *Jüdische Studien, Joseph Wohlgemuth zu seinem 60. Geburtstag von Freunden und Schülern gewidmet* (Frankfort, 1928), 144–59. [*Supra*, pp. 106–21].

[4] Cf. Marmorstein, 'Anges et hommes dans l'Agada', in *REJ* lxxxiv, 1927, 37–50 and 138–41.

[5] Tanḥuma-Genesis (ed. Buber), 192; Agadat Bereshit, c. 69 (ed. Buber), 138, where the example of Elisha is also adduced. It is taken from the Baraita of R. Eliezer, son of R. Yose, the Galilean. On the withdrawal of the spirit from Jacob, cf. also Gen. R., ed. Theodor, p. 1121; Tanḥuma on the same passage; Pirḳe R. Eliezer, c. 38; Ps. Jonathan-Gen. 49. 1; Abot R. Nathan, 1. 30; Midrash ha-Gadol, ed. Schechter, 672; Pesiḳ. R. 12a. Probably the Rabbis had in mind the idea to be mentioned farther on, that the Holy Spirit can rest only on those whose heart is joyful but not troubled.

the Holy Spirit had been taken away from them. Why? God shows the prophets His strength and their weakness, in order that they may not become puffed up with pride. A similar thing happened to Moses, who did not know what decision to give in the case of the inheritance of the daughters of Zelophehad. Samuel, who was placed on a level with Moses and Aaron, did not know which son of Jesse he should anoint as king over Israel. Some passages also adduce the example of the prophet Elisha, who had no presentiment that the son of the Shunamite was dead. In any case we see from these statements that even in the time of the great prophets a temporary withdrawal of the Spirit could take place.

Apart from the reason already given for this phenomenon, another is adduced which illumines still deeper recesses in the religious consciousness of the Rabbis. R. Akiba[1] taught that God really spoke with Moses only for the sake of Israel, and that during the thirty-eight years that the people was being punished for its sin Moses was not vouchsafed any divine address, any meeting with the Shekhinah, any visit of the Holy Spirit. As long as the wrath of God raged there was no place for the presence and manifestation of God in Israel. For this reason and not on any personal ground it was said that Hillel would have been worthy of the Holy Spirit had not the sinfulness of his age robbed him of its possession.[2] Consequently, it is right and fair that prophets or pious men who commit some sin or error should be deprived of the Holy Spirit, as, for example, Phinehas, who as High

---

[1] v. Mekhilta 2a, and cf. Marmorstein, *The Doctrine of Merits* (London, 1920), p. 9, n. 16 and p. 44. Also Sifra 1. 13, anonym. B. Ta'anit, 30. The same idea is found in the Haggadah of R. Yohanan b. Nappaha, transmitted by R. Abba bar Hana.

[2] v. Tosefta Sotah, 13. 3; J. Sotah 24; Cant. R. 9. 3; cf. Büchler, *Some Types of Palestinian Piety* (London, 1922), p. 8. Very significant is a remark of Hillel about his contemporaries; 'Leave them, the Holy Spirit is upon them, if they are not prophets they are the children of prophets', Tos. Pes. 4. 2, ed. Zuckermandel, p. 163, 2 ff.; cf. also the quotations in the Babli and Jerushalmi of this Baraita.

Priest neglected to release the judge Jephthah from his vow and thus participated in the murder of his daughter.[1]

As already pointed out above, the Holy Spirit can rest only on a glad and joyful heart.[2] This teaching is found in a Baraita and many illustrations of it were adduced by the Amoraim. R. Jonah, a Palestinian teacher of the fourth century, confidently informs us that his namesake the prophet Jonah went on a pilgrimage to Jerusalem, where he took part in the festival of water-drawing and through the pervading joyfulness was vouchsafed participation in the Holy Spirit. The great and joyful festival of water-drawing is constantly represented as having some inner connexion with the outpouring of the Holy Spirit.[3] Since this festival was regularly celebrated till the destruction of the Temple, we have here indirect confirmation of R. Yoḥanan's view about the cessation of the Spirit. Hillel's words can also serve as a confirmation of it. In spite of the great detail with which the ceremonies of the joyful festival connected with the drawing of the water are described, we can form no clear idea of the outpouring of the Holy Spirit.[4] Dancing, singing, and the waving and throwing of torches may well have plunged the spectators and participators into a joyful ecstasy; and this may have given rise later to the idea that a joyful mood is an indispensable preliminary for the possession of the Spirit. With the destruction of the Temple and the loss of the land, and with the hated alien rule on their necks, there was little room for joy. Naturally, thought the Haggadists, the Holy Spirit had departed from Israel.

---

[1] Gen. R. 60. 3, ed. Theodor, 644; Lev. R. xxxvii. 4; Eccles. R., 10. 15; Seder Eliyahu R. c. 4.

[2] J. Sukkah 55a; B. Sabb. 30b; B. Pes. 117b, where instead of רוח הקדש we find the word שכינה. These terms are often interchanged; v. further below.

[3] See especially R. Joshua ben Levi (c. 250), Pesiḳ. R. 1b; J. Sukkah 5. 1; R. Yose, B. Sukkah 50b; R. Hoshaya, Gen. R. 70. 8.

[4] As can be seen from the works of Venetianer, Gressmann, and Feuchtwang, who compare the Eleusinian mysteries, the Adonis cult, and Babylonian rites in order to explain it.

II

Such was the general theory, but, in practice, there were many exceptions. There were teachers who considered possession of the Spirit possible for their own time. One such was R. Aḥa, a Galilean teacher who lived about 300 C.E., and who was distinguished among his contemporaries for the originality and individuality of his views. In his Haggadic sayings he frequently referred to the workings of the Spirit,[1] and one runs: 'He who learns in order to practise what he has learnt, who is able to bring his religious practice into harmony with his doctrine, such a one is worthy of the Holy Spirit.' This teacher was acquainted with the view that the Holy Spirit ceased with the destruction of the First Temple;[2] nevertheless, he considered those of his contemporaries who had reached a certain level of piety worthy of the gift of the Spirit. How is the contradiction to be explained? The uncertainties attaching to oral tradition do not allow us to be sure about the exact form in which the Baraita quoted above was known to our Amora, i.e. whether it definitely reckoned the Holy Spirit among the things which ceased with the destruction of the First Temple or not. But even if the text is quite reliable, it is possible that this Amora adopted an independent view differing from the current one. That the unpleasant contrast between teaching and practice perturbed other preachers of this period also and called forth their censure has been already pointed out by me in another place[3] and need not be repeated here. That R. Aḥa's dictum was meant to be taken literally cannot be denied. Its teaching is expanded in a highly significant passage which we find in Seder Eliyahu

---

[1] Lev. R. 35. 6; also Lev. R. 15. 2; 'The Holy Spirit rests on the prophets only in definite measure'; Lev. R. 6. 1, 'The Holy Spirit speaks in the Book of Proverbs to God and Israel'; and Lev. R. xiv, 2 on Elihu in Job 36. 3.

[2] Cf. Marmorstein, *Midrash Ḥaserot*, p. 38, n. 158.

[3] Id., 'Learning and Work', in *London Quarterly Review*, April, 1925, 217–25.

Rabba:[1] 'I call Heaven and earth to witness that anyone whether heathen or Jew, man or woman, slave or handmaid is capable of possessing the Holy Spirit according to the actions which he performs.' The important thing is therefore the good deed or action, not knowledge. Certainly the value of study is not denied, for the gift of the Spirit is promised in Seder Eliyahu for study also,[2] as was inevitable in a Rabbinic work.

Another contemporary, R. Yudan, teaches as follows regarding the possession of the Spirit by public teachers and preachers: 'Whoever publicly proclaims the words of the Torah is worthy of the Holy Spirit.'[3] It is both chronologically and intrinsically possible that between the dictum of R. Aḥa and that of R. Yudan there is a closer connexion, probably of conscious opposition. R. Aḥa himself had a high opinion of the importance and significance of the public discourse in religious life; nevertheless, he seems to have considered religious action and conduct as more important.[4] Along with teaching and action two other virtues are mentioned in early sources as being capable of procuring the Holy Spirit, namely, beneficence[5] and faith in God and His works, and in His kindness and providence.[6] When one undertakes to carry out a commandment in perfect faith, the Holy Spirit rests on him, i.e. observance of the Law is the preliminary stage to piety of the Spirit. There were among the teachers men of mystic disposition, such as we frequently find in later centuries of Jewish history among the Cabbalists, who felt no contradiction between *pneuma* and *nomos*.

[1] Ed. Friedmann, p. 48. H. Cohen in Guttmann's *Festschrift*, 1915, 21. In the third antithesis I should prefer to read בין בן חורין instead of בין שפחה, so as to make the groups of Paul correspond to those of R. Judah b. Ilai'.
[2] Ibid., p. 8. [3] Cant. R. 1. 8.
[4] Exod. R. 40. 1; cf. Marmorstein, 'Synagogue Sermons in the First Three Centuries', in *London Quarterly Review*, October, 1916, 235.
[5] Mekh. 65b; Sifre Deut. § 352; R. Akiba, Exod. R. 5. 23; Midr. Samuel, ed. Buber, 45; Pirḳe R. Eliezer, c. 33.
[6] Mekh. 33b.

It would be a mistake to form on the basis of these sayings a final judgement on the possession of the Spirit in the Rabbinic period during the first three centuries of the Christian era. Even the long dictum of R. Phinehas ben Yair with its ascending series of 'diligence, cleanliness, purity, holiness, modesty, fear of God, and piety' culminating in 'the Holy Spirit, the resurrection, and finally the appearance of the prophet Elijah', represents rather an ideal than a practical guide to piety.[1] In the Acts of the Apostles[2] also the gift of the Holy Spirit is the promise of the resurrected Jesus. Nevertheless, if possession of the Spirit or pneumatic piety is denied to the Rabbis, wholly or in part, we must see both in this highly significant dictum and in its New Testament parallel only a theory or an ideal to be aimed at, as is actually done by Büchsel.[3] Apparently he is right. Only if one takes the trouble to examine the biography of this extraordinary man, in whom many scholars have sought to discover an Essene among the Rabbis,[4] will he recognize here a picture drawn from life. As will be shown later, R. Phinehas ben Yair belongs to the Sages who possessed the spirit of God and miraculous powers.

In order to judge adequately of the possession of the Spirit among the Rabbis, we must not limit ourselves to what we hear or read about the *Ruaḥ-ha-Kodesh*, but we must also take into account what is said about the working of the Shekhinah. The two ideas and terms have much in common.[5] What is said about the Shekhinah, however, provides far more definite and richer material than what is said about the Holy Spirit. Such expressions as 'receiving the presence of the Shekhinah', 'the Shekhinah rests on someone', and many more of the same kind, give vivid

[1] M. Soṭah 9 ad fin.; B. 'Abodah Zarah 20b; Midr. Tannaim 148; J. Shekalim 47c; Cant. R. 1. 9; Midr. Proverbs 41a.
[2] 1. 8 ff.
[3] l.c.
[4] Cf. esp. A. Epstein, *Jüd. Altertumskunde* (Vienna, 1888).
[5] v. Marmorstein, *The Doctrine of God*, i, 99 and 103 f. (London, 1927).

expression to an intimate communion with the Deity. The
two expressions are often interchanged in the old Rabbinic
texts.[1] Both are frequently used as synonyms for God and
are so to be interpreted in Tannaitic texts. Another point
common to both is that certain sins and transgressions are
described as causing the departure of the Shekhinah and
the Holy Spirit. Correspondingly, certain merits and virtues
qualify equally for the attainment of the Holy Spirit and
the reception of the Shekhinah. R. Hoshaya teaches that
in this world there are only a chosen few who participate
in the Shekhinah—and therefore also the Holy Spirit—
but in the time to come all men will be qualified to receive
the countenance of the Shekhinah.[2] It must, however, be
pointed out that while possession of the Holy Spirit confers
only the gift of prophecy, power of divination, and ability
to see visions, the reception of the Shekhinah signifies much
more. It represents an approach to the Deity, a vision of the
divine glory, a mystical union with God such as only a
pneumatic religion can effect. Naturally, both conditions
often merge into one another. The man who is closely
united with the Shekhinah also possesses the Holy Spirit,
and the one possessing the Spirit also sees the Shekhinah.
Thus, in spite of assertions to the contrary on the part of
certain Rabbis, that in and since certain periods and times
the Holy Spirit has discontinued its activity in Israel, the
Rabbis as a body believed in the presence of the Spirit and
the activity of the Shekhinah in their midst. A similar dis-
crepancy is to be noted in the Rabbinical teaching regarding
the merit of the patriarchs. On the one hand mention is
made of certain periods and certain personages at which
and with whom the working of this merit was exhausted;
on the other hand, the influence of the merit of the patriarchs is depicted as still continuing. We need not see in
this any contradiction. Nor can it be maintained that we are

[1] Cf., e.g., above p. 127, n. 3, and elsewhere.
[2] Lev. R. 1. 14.

dealing here with contradictory views of different individuals. For the same teachers who put a limit to the working of the merits speak of the merits as still continuing and
active.[1] So it is here too. There may have been people who
asked, Why are there no longer any prophets among us,
just as the sceptics asked, Why are there no longer any
heroes? And the theologians answered, 'On account of the
sins', or 'Because of the mourning for the destruction of
the Temple'.

III

We now turn to the Rabbinic legends which show that
the Spirit was thought of as alive and active both among
the scholars and among the masses. For these we rely in
the first instance on the abundant material contained in the
Rabbinic sources, which we have to collect and arrange
under various headings so as to make it serviceable for the
comparative history of religion. For this purpose it is
necessary to draw up a chronological list of persons who
possessed the Holy Spirit. First comes Yoḥanan the High
Priest who heard from the Holy of Holies that the young
men who had gone out to war to Antioch had won a
victory. The prophecy agreed with the event to the minute.[2]
Josephus also reports the prophetic gift of John Hyrcanus.[3]
In the same Rabbinic sources another High Priest is mentioned alongside of John Hyrcanus, namely, Simon the
Pious, who is stated to have lived at the time of the Emperor
Gaius Caligula, and to have been prophetically informed
that the Emperor had died and that his edict, ordering a
statue of himself to be erected in the Temple, had been
withdrawn or annulled.[4] Graetz[5] takes this Simon to be
Simon Kantheras and not, as most others do, the much
discussed and much disputed contemporary of Alexander

---

[1] v. Marmorstein, *The Doctrine of Merits* (London, 1920), 154.
[2] Tos. Sotah 13. 5 and parallel passages.
[3] Cf. Büchsel, op. cit., p. 95.
[4] v. n. 2.   [5] *MGWJ* xxx, 97 ff.

the Great who is also said to have borne the title of ὁ δίκαιος or *ha-Ṣaddik*. The sources are full of the piety of the earlier Simon, but say not a word about that of the latter.[1] However that may be, the form גסקלגוס sounds more like Caligula than any other name. Altogether, before the destruction of the Temple, omens and prophecies accumulated; they are reported by Josephus as well as by the Rabbis.[2] In any case the incidents just mentioned belong rather to the class of omens than to that of prophecies.

A reference[3] to the disciples of Hillel, supposed to have been eighty in number—an exaggerated figure which frequently occurs in other connexions[4]—states that a third of them were of sufficient merit for the Shekhinah to rest on them as on Moses. Samuel the Younger announced beforehand the unsuccessful issue of a revolt organized by Simeon and Ishmael.[5] R. Ṣadok fasted forty years before the destruction of the Temple, foreseeing this catastrophe.[6] R. Yoḥanan ben Zakkai announced to Vespasian that he would become Emperor of Rome,[7] though this prophecy Josephus has ascribed to himself also.[8] R. Eliezer ben Hyrcanus predicted on his death-bed what would happen to R. Akiba and his contemporaries in the Hadrianic persecution.[9] Of R. Akiba himself it is stated that he saw things in the Holy Spirit.[10] The same is reported of R.

---

[1] v. Marmorstein, *The Doctrine of God*, i, p. 29.

[2] v. the latest on this in Weinreich, *Gebet und Wunder*, 105 ff. (Genethliakon W. Schmid, 271 ff.).

[3] Bar. in B. Sukkah 28a; Aboth R. Nathan 29a, b; B. BB. 134a.

[4] Cf. the 80 women in Ascalon who were condemned to death by Simon b. Sheṭaḥ for witchcraft. Sifre Deut. § 221, B. Sanh. 45b; 80 kinds of dishes, Lam. R. (ed. Buber), 65b; John functions 80 years as High Priest, B. Ber. 29a; 80 synagogues in Jerusalem, v. Brüll, *Jahrbücher*, i. 3, note; Menaḥem has 80 disciples, B. Ḥagigah, 16b; J. Hag. 2. 2; 80 High Priests during the Second Temple, J. Yoma 38c, Pesiḳta (ed. Buber), 177a, Pesiḳta Rabbati 131b; R. Ḥanina ben Ḥama attains the age of 80 years and is so active that he can stand on one foot, B. Ḥullin 24b.

[5] For references v. p. 132, n. 2.

[6] B. Giṭṭin 56b and parallel passages.   [7] Ibid.

[8] Josephus, *Life*.   [9] B Sanh. 68a.

[10] Pesiḳta, ed. Buber, 176b.

Gamaliel the Second.[1] R. Akiba's disciple, R. Simon ben Yoḥai,[2] and the latter's son-in-law R. Phinehas ben Yair, whose recipe for attaining the Holy Spirit has been mentioned above, also saw things in the Holy Spirit. It is important to note that some of these possessors of the Spirit appear also elsewhere as wonder-workers famous in their day for banishing spirits, driving out demons, and the practice of magic, and remembered by posterity as such. If so far we have mentioned only a few names, yet it can be safely affirmed that up to the end of the second century—the latest date to which we can assign any of the wonder-workers mentioned—there were 'men of the Spirit' in Israel. That some of them can definitely be classed as 'pneumatic' cannot be denied, especially after a closer examination of their biographies, which have here been only briefly referred to. The unprejudiced inquirer can find no reason for placing Jesus or Paul higher as men of the Spirit than R. Simon b. Yoḥai or R. Phinehas b. Yair. They were equally great as wonder-workers, expellers of demons and magicians, and prophesied more or less in the same manner.

Especially prominent in this field was R. Ḥanina b. Dosa, whose name has purposely been omitted from the above list of scholars. This pious man was one of those who in the second half of the first century were honoured as wonder-workers. He was often called upon to offer prayers in case of illness or some other misfortune, as e.g. when the daughter of a well-digger fell into a pit. This is an interesting fact for the history of religion—that a pious man undertakes the task of praying for others. Even the leaders of the learned world, like R. Yoḥanan ben Zakkai and R. Gamaliel II, do not neglect to send to the wonder-worker when their children are seriously ill in order that he may pray for their recovery. This actually ensues, and what is more, the sup-

---

[1] Lev. R. 37b, B. Erubin 64b and parallel passages.
[2] Pesiḳta, ed. Buber, 90a.

pliant is able to predict the recovery. Certainly the modest
wonder-worker, when asked how he knew this, replies
that he is neither a prophet nor the son of a prophet, but
derives his knowledge from signs. Whether the denial of
the gift of prophecy was merely a conventional show of
modesty we do not know. Certainly the man who could
command the services of angels, who dared to converse
with the princess of the demons Agrath bath Maḥlath, and
to demand from God as much gold as he wished, must have
been a man of the Spirit. What applies to R. Ḥanina ben
Dosa can be confidently affirmed of those prophets among
the scholars who have been mentioned above. It must be
added, however, that we have also accounts of other men
who through their knowledge of magic were able to effect
wonders, and of pious men who in their time were noted
for the efficacy of their prayers for rain or for health, but
of whose prophetical gifts we are told nothing at all, although
such a power may be presumed in some of them. It is hard
to avoid the impression that prophecy and divination sank
to the level of a trade, and that this prompted the Rabbis to
draw a line between past and present. The Holy Spirit of
the old prophets and teachers was after all different from
the divination of the present.

IV

The passage which informs us of the cessation of the
Spirit in Israel speaks also of the activity of the *Bath-Kol*,
literally 'daughter of the voice'. According to some readings the predictions of John Hyrcanus and of Simon ha-
Ṣaddik belonged to this category. According to the Synoptic
Gospels the Voice from Heaven appeared already at the
baptizing of Jesus, only, however, after the Holy Spirit had
descended on him in the form of a dove or like a dove
(Matt. 3. 16, 17, and parallel passages). The combination of
the Holy Spirit with the *Bath-Kol* is certainly surprising.
For so long as the Holy Spirit was operative there was no

room for the *Bath-Kol*. It might seem even more surprising that according to Luke the Voice from Heaven
quoted a passage from the Psalms (2. 7). In the Rabbinic
legend the *Bath-Kol* plays a very important part. We shall
see that it often recites quotations from the Bible. It would
be superfluous here to refer to all the passages which give
us more or less important information on the working of the
Bath-Kol; they are altogether too numerous. They can for
the most part, however, all be classed together as being of
a legendary character. At the most they command interest
and attention as legends, and from this point of view we
shall have something to say of them later on.

We will first take some examples of the *Bath-Kol* which
differ from prophecy or prediction in the fact that they
do not foretell the future but unite the so-called religion
of the law or knowledge of the law with the religion and
reception of the Spirit. The somewhat arid controversy
between the schools of Hillel and Shammai, after lasting
with varying fortunes for many decades, was at length
settled by a 'daughter-voice'. According to the statement
of a well-informed historical authority, R. Yoḥanan bar
Nappaḥa of Tiberias, this voice was heard during the
sitting of the Sanhedrin at Yabne. Its text is given in a
Tannaitic source as follows: 'These and these (i.e. the
teachings of both schools) are the words of the living God,
but the *halakhah* (legal ruling) is as stated by the House of
Hillel.' In another place the statement is reported in the
name of the head of the Babylonian academy of Nehardea,
Samuel, who perhaps drew on an earlier source. The
Babylonian teachers divide their material into the periods
before and after the appearance of the *Bath-Kol*.[1] It is
significant for the character of the tradition, which after all
is built on observance and knowledge of the law, that it
is not the voice of the law and of legal acumen which is

---

[1] J. Ber. 1. 4; J. Yeb. 1. 6; B. Yeb. 14a; B. Erubin, 6b, 13b; B. Pes. 114a;
B. Ber. 52a; B. Hull. 44a.

decisive, but the revelation of the Spirit, for such we can confidently declare the intervention of the 'daughter-voice' to have been. There is obviously no place here for rationalistic explanations, such as that a decision of the majority or something of the sort is to be understood under *Bath-Kol*, since in the absence of more detailed descriptions we cannot form a precise picture of the scene. The ancients took the account literally. A voice from heaven—so they imagined to themselves—came down on that occasion and procured a decision in favour of the school of Hillel. The passage shows clearly that legal piety can well go hand in hand with the gift of the Spirit.

Not without interest, too, is perhaps another occasion on which the 'daughter-voice' pealed forth, again in the House of Study. R. Eliezer b. Hyrcanus was once engaged in a lively halakhic controversy with R. Joshua ben Hananya.[1] Having exhausted all the weapons of dialectic and logic in defence of his view, without being able to convince his opponent of its justice, and being possessed, as we have seen, of prophetic gifts and powers, he betook himself to supernatural means of a very peculiar character. A carob tree was to prove that he was right by being torn away to a long distance from its place, as actually happened. He then caused a watercourse to run in the opposite direction. Next he ordered the walls of the college to bend. Finally, he summoned to his aid a divine voice, which proclaimed that in all points of doctrine R. Eliezer represented the correct view. The prophetically gifted Tanna sets high store by this voice from heaven. Not so, however, the rationally minded R. Joshua b. Hananya, who was familiar with the general culture of the age, though at the same time not ignorant of magic, and who categorically rejected every proof adduced from the *Bath-Kol*. In this case rationalism carried the day against the daughter-voice. The medieval commentators were puzzled to explain how it was that the

[1] B. B.M. 59b.

voice from heaven was listened to in the dispute between
the two schools, while in that of the two individual teachers
no attention was paid to it. The explanation given by the
Tosafists is not at all satisfactory. However this problem
is to be solved, two points at any rate are clear. One is that
the voice from heaven not only announces promises for the
future but intervenes in order to instruct or decide in
learned discussions on practical questions. The same feature
is found in the Old Testament prophecy, as has been rightly
pointed out by certain theologians. The second point is
that there was a rationalistic view which did not believe
in the supernatural power and validity of these revela-
tions.

It was not only in the academy, however, that the *Bath-
Kol* rang out in order to settle discussions and controversies
between scholars, but it intervened also in private life.
R. Dimi brought from Palestine to Babylon a legend about
the patriarch Hillel and his brother Shebna. Hillel devoted
himself to study while Shebna engaged in commerce. The
former lived in great poverty, the latter in tolerably good
circumstances. After a time they made an an agreement that
the merchant should give half his yearly income to the
student and the latter half of his earnings to his brother.
On this occasion a *Bath-Kol* called out the words of
Canticles 8. 7, 'If a man should give all the riches of his
house for love, it would be despised'.[1] Here a Biblical verse
is quoted by the heavenly voice, either to confirm the
agreement or to prevent it. The Gospels also make the
heavenly voice proclaim the relation of God to Jesus
through a Biblical text. I would further call attention to
some statements which attribute to R. Yoḥanan ben
Zakkai[2] the gift of the Spirit in connexion with the *Bath-*

---

[1] B. Soṭah, 21a.
[2] Tos. Hagigah c. 2; B. Hag. 14b. R. Yoḥanan ben Zakkai is also supposed
to have possessed prophetic gifts, since he predicted, or at any rate is said to
have predicted, the destruction of Galilee before 70 C.E., *v.* statement of Ulla
(3rd cent.) in J. Sabb. 15d. Cf. Weinreich, op. cit., 108 (274).

Kol, all the more so in view of the following remarks of Fr. Büchsel about this man (§ 132):

'The Light of Israel, the Right-hand Pillar, the Strong Hammer, Yoḥanan ben Zakkai, dies without the assurance of life. He does not doubt that there is a future existence, but he does not know whether he is destined for life. The consciousness of sin paralyses his faith. He has all his life thought cohortatively, and at the end when he has to reap the fruits he stands empty-handed, sees only a Must, there is no Is in his life. A man of the spirit dies otherwise: I see the heavens open &c.'

The attitude of R. Yoḥanan agrees with the Old Testament idea that no man is free from sin, and with the Haggadic teaching that a man should not believe in himself till he dies. To R. Yoḥanan least of all the scholars can we deny *pneuma*, possession of the Spirit, visions from heaven. When his disciple discussed cosmology with him he saw a fire descend from heaven and surround all the trees of the field, which then broke into a hymn of praise (Ps. 148), and an angel spoke to him from the fire. In another account the master says to his disciples: 'Hail to you, hail to your mother, blessed be my eyes which have seen this. I and you sat in a dream on Mount Sinai, and a *Bath-Kol* called to us from heaven saying: Ascend hither, ascend hither. Great *triclinia* (טרקלין, banqueting couches) with pillows are spread for you. You, your disciples and the disciples of your disciples are destined for the third group.' In virtue of this vision R. Yoḥanan can be regarded as a man of the Spirit. Withal, in spite of the voice from heaven which assures him that even the least of his disciples is destined for the third group, which is reserved for those who will see the Shekhinah, he is in his last hour far from pride, self-righteousness, and arrogance, but awaits his end in humility and devotion.

A closer parallel to the utterance of Stephen (Acts 7. 55 f.) can be found in the account of the martyrdom of R. Akiba,[1]

---

[1] B. Ber. 61b.

where also we hear the voice from heaven announcing that he is qualified for eternal life. In the midst of his agony he joyfully accepts the yoke of the Kingdom of Heaven, and dwells on the word *Eḥad*, signifying the unity of God, in order to give expression in this way also to his love of God. Martyrs die differently from ordinary men. Apart from this we have already seen that R. Akiba became a legendary figure as one endowed with the prophetic spirit. In all the stories about him, mostly legendary, mention is made of approval or recognition on the part of the heavenly power. To complete the survey we may refer to the biographical legend of R. Simon b. Yoḥai, whom we have described above as prophet, expeller of demons, and wonder-worker. This teacher is said to have spent thirteen years—a somewhat mystical number—with his son R. Eleazar in a cave, till at length a voice from heaven, *Bath-Kol*, conveyed to him the message that he could leave the cave without fear of persecution.[1]

From the period of the Amoraim, which is also rich in *Bath-Kol* legends, one case in particular seems to me to be not without interest. R. Yoḥanan b. Nappaḥa, who died in 279 C.E., reports that one year the Israelites failed to observe the Day of Atonement on the 10th of Tishri with fasting, &c. The more pious were afraid that they had forfeited their salvation, but a *Bath-Kol* came and announced: 'You are all destined for the life of the future world', i.e. the salvation of your souls is not in danger. Apparently the preacher intends a reference to 1 Kings 8. 65, where Jewish tradition finds an allusion to a neglect of the Day of Atonement. Whence, however, did he know that the souls of the Israelites at that time were perturbed and troubled or that a voice from heaven calmed them? The clue to this Haggadah is to be found in the frequent practice of the Haggadists, of transferring conditions and relations of their own time to the Biblical period and of reading them into the

[1] Gen. R. 76. 6.

text. So here, too. An historical consideration of the sources leads to the conclusion that we are dealing here with an incident which happened in the time of R. Yoḥanan, when the Jews of Tiberias or of all Galilee were prevented from keeping the Day of Atonement, as I have shown in another place. They were really downcast and troubled in their conscience, and so R. Yoḥanan told them this legend and assured them that in spite of the trespass they were destined for the future life. Here also, as in the legends previously cited, the voice is concerned less with a revelation of the future than with instruction on the right way which a man should go.[1]

This 'daughter-voice' which proclaimed to the contemporaries of Solomon, or rather of R. Yoḥanan, that they were destined for the future life, appears in three legends about the death or the dying hour of certain religious heroes or saints. There was a man named R. Eleazar ben Durdaya[2] who led an extremely immoral life. Once a paramour pointed out to him that there was no longer any salvation for him, and that no atonement on his part would be accepted. He accordingly went into the wilderness and sat down among the hills and mountains and called on them to implore pity for him, but in vain. He then turned to heaven and earth with the same request, but again without effect. Then to the sun and moon, the stars and planets, but still without result. He then placed his head between his knees and wept bitterly till a voice came forth from heaven, saying, 'R. Eleazar ben Durdaya is destined for the future world'. A second case is that of a Roman, Ketiah ben Shalom,[3] whose identity has been the subject of many conjectures among Jewish historians, but who, at any rate, was one of the most prominent Romans who embraced Judaism, and who was perhaps put to death on account of his Jewish sympathies.

[1] Cf. the material collected by Marmorstein, 'Les Persécutions religieuses à l'époque de R. Joḥanan b. Nappacha', in REJ lxxvii (1923), 166–77.

[2] B. 'Abodah Zarah 18a.

[3] Ibid. 10a.

At his death the same voice resounded with the same cry. Thirdly, we hear the same cry at the martyrdom of R. Ḥanina ben Teradyon,[1] whose executioner (קלצונטירי, also קליסטנרי) on seeing the heroic behaviour of the martyr also devoted himself to death, whereupon a voice came forth, 'Ḥanina ben Teradyon and the קלצונטירי are destined for the life of the future world'. Fourthly, we are informed of a 'daughter-voice' which is said to have come forth on the first anniversary of the death of the compiler of the Mishnah and proclaimed that everyone who took part in the mourning for Rabbi was destined for the future life. A certain fuller, who was accidentally away, out of grief threw himself down from a roof and was killed. The voice then proclaimed: 'This fuller also is destined for the future life.'[2] It may be that R. Yoḥanan also brings in the voice for the comfort of the martyrs of that time who suffered death through that persecution.

Reference should perhaps be made here to the account of the death of Yose ben Yoezer from Zereda and his nephew Yakim,[3] since here also we find the persecutor of the martyr sacrificing his life and winning eternal life as in the story of the martyrdom of R. Ḥanina ben Teradyon. The nephew was riding on a horse as the uncle was being led to be hanged. Mockingly he said to his uncle: 'Look at my horse which my master allows me to ride and look at your horse (i.e. the gallows) which your Master (God) is making you ride.' The uncle replied: 'If He does so to those who challenge Him, how much more to those who perform His will?' 'Who has performed His will better than you?' said the nephew. 'If such things happen to those who perform His will,' said the uncle, 'what will be the fate of those who challenge Him?' These words stung him like a

[1] B. 'Abodah Zarah 18a.
[2] B. Keth. 103b.
[3] Gen. R. c. 68. Other examples can be found in my article 'La Participation à la vie éternelle dans la Théologie Rabbinique et dans la Légende' in *REJ* xcix (1930), 305–20.

serpent's bite, and he killed himself with all four kinds of capital punishment. The uncle saw the nephew's death as he was dying on the gallows, and called out that he saw his nephew entering Paradise.

An exact parallel to these voices from heaven is to be found in the martyrologies, especially in that of the widow Julitta and the child Cyricus. A voice from heaven promises mother and son eternal glory.[1] Rabbinic legend shares with the legends of the East the comforting voice from heaven, which is a constantly recurring feature in both.[2]

Along with the 'daughter-voice' there are in the Haggadah many things which are regarded as having fallen from heaven. Chief among these are the fiery objects, such as the Ark, the Table, and the Lamp, all three of fire, which fell from heaven to earth and were received by men.[3] According to R. Simon ben Yoḥai, the bread fell from heaven tied up with the staff, according to R. Eleazar the scroll tied up with the sword.[4] In the second century there must have been current in the circle of these teachers some notion about things which were reckoned as *diipetes*. In conclusion we may in this connexion mention letters from heaven in the earlier and later Rabbinic literature. Rabbah bar Naḥmani's death, which the Angel of Death was able to bring about only with great difficulty, was announced to his contemporaries through a letter from heaven.[5] In the time of Ezra, according to a legend, God announced His concurrence through a letter from heaven containing the word אמת.[6] In the later literature there is mention of several letters from heaven, to which reference cannot be

---

[1] Cf. H. Günter, *Die christliche Legende des Abendlandes* (Heidelberg, 1910), p. 134.

[2] Ibid., p. 148.

[3] Midrash ha-Gadol, Numbers 2d (in MSS.). Fire which has fallen from heaven is particularly prominent in the Hagadah. *v.* Sifre Num. § 44; Sifre Zuṭṭa, 7a; B. Yoma 21b; Exod. R. viii. 1; Pirḳe R. Eliezer, c. 53.

[4] Sifre Num. § 40; Lev. R. 35. 5; Deut. R. 4. 2.

[5] B. B.M. 86a.

[6] B. Yoma 69b (statement of Rab or R. Yoḥanan); B. San. 64a.

made here in detail. A few examples may, however, be mentioned. For the one of R. Samuel b. Kalonymus see *REJ* xlix. 233; for that of Jacob of Marvège, Gross, *Gallia Judaica*, 364; for others, see the *Responsa* of R. Levi b. Habib, no. 75, Lob Karlsburg in R. Mordecai Banet's *Parashat Mordecai* (1820), the biography of the founder of modern Chassidism by M. L. Rodkinson, pp. 140 ff. These letters are a substitute for the vanished 'daughter-voice'.[1]

[1] For the literature, cf. R. Stube, *Der Himmelsbrief*, Tübingen, 1918; also E. Schmidt, *Kultübertragungen*, RGVV viii. 2 (Giessen, 1910), p. 88, n. 3; Otto Berthold, *Die Unverwundbarkeit in Sage und Aberglauben der Griechen*, ibid., xi. 1 (Giessen, 1911), p. 67; O. Weinreich, *Triskaidekadische Studien*, ibid. xvi. 1 (Giessen, 1916), p. 77.

THE DOCTRINE OF THE RESURRECTION OF THE DEAD IN RABBINIC THEOLOGY

THE teaching that there is a blessed life after death, or that the dead will be revived from their graves to a better life, or that there is hope for the soul behind those invisible clouds which divide the past and the future, is a signpost set up on the road of theological speculation to mark a most significant development of religious thinking. The man to whom the idea was first revealed, who conceived it fully and proclaimed it, must be regarded as one of the greatest religious thinkers of all times. There can be no doubt that the doctrine is the climax of belief and the highest development possible in theological thought and speculation. It is quite natural that we should not find the belief in this doctrine until after many centuries of human progress. We may ask such questions as: Whence did it originate? Who taught it first? and How did it develop?—but we find no answer. What we know for certain is that the teaching and belief existed among the Israelites when they settled on Jewish soil. Isaiah speaks of the dead who shall arise and the inhabitants of the dust who shall awake and shout for joy (Isa. 26. 19). Isaiah also teaches that there will be a resurrection, but only for the righteous; the wicked, however, will never leave their homes in the dust (26. 14). It is generally thought that this passage cannot be older than the third century B.C.E. But Ezekiel cannot be understood unless we assume that there already existed among his people the accepted belief in the resurrection. Thus his book says: 'Therefore prophesy and say unto them, Thus saith the Lord God: Behold, I will open your graves and cause you to come up out of your graves, O my people; and I will bring you into the land of Israel. And ye shall know that I am the Lord, when I have

L

opened your graves, and caused you to come up out of your graves, O my people. And I will put my spirit in you, and ye shall live, and I will place you in your own land' (Ezek. 37. 12–14). The prophet who uttered these prophecies must have believed in the resurrection. Daniel agrees fully with the view quoted above from Isaiah, for he says: 'And many of them that sleep in the dust of the earth shall awake, some to everlasting life, and some to shame and everlasting contempt' (12. 2). Other passages from the Scriptures applicable to our doctrine will be mentioned in the course of this article. In the Apocrypha and Pseudepigrapha the belief is repeated in II Maccabees, I Enoch, and the Testaments.[1] In the last two or three centuries before Jesus it was an integral part of the Jewish belief. It is our task to set forth the history and development of this doctrine in Rabbinical theology in the centuries after Jesus.

2. Although the belief was fully established at the time when the first tentative steps were taken in that development of the Jewish religion which resulted in Christianity, we cannot affirm that there was no opposition to it. The Rabbinic sources testify to the doctrine as having been regarded as one of the main teachings of Judaism. On the other hand, we see that there was opposition. It is probable that the Sadducees were the successors of an older school opposing the doctrine of a future life as a part of the reform of the old religion of Israel.[2] We know that the Sadducees were the conservative party in Israel. To abandon a belief held by former generations would contradict the traditions of this party. Josephus relates concerning this point: 'But the doctrine of the Sadducees is this: That souls die with the bodies' (*Ant.* XVIII. i. 4). They denied not merely the belief in a revival after death, but also the doctrine of a blessed future life. It may be that

---

[1] P. Volz, *Jüdische Eschatologie* (Tübingen, 1903), pp. 126–33.
[2] See against this view *Abot de R. Nathan*, ch. 5, and Baneth, *Magazin für die Wissenschaft des Judenthums* (1882), pp. 3 ff. (*Ozar Israel*, iii. 74–5).

Josephus, in accordance with a custom of his, did not like to put their doctrines more clearly, because of his heathen readers. The Gospels support the words of Josephus by saying that the Sadducees came to Jesus stating that there is no resurrection. Jesus proves the doctrine from the passage: 'I am the God of thy father, the God of Abraham, the God of Isaac, and the God of Jacob.' This God cannot be a God of the dead but of the living (Exod. 3. 6; Matt. 22. 23–33; Luke 20. 37–8; Mark 12. 18–27; cf. 9. 10; *Recognitions of Clement* 1. 54). From Acts 4. 1–2 we infer that the idea of resurrection was the main objection to Jesus of the Sanhedrin, which consisted largely of Sadducees who fiercely opposed that doctrine.[1] The Mishnah enumerates them among those who have no part in the future world: 'Whosoever says there is no resurrection of the dead (mentioned) in the Torah, that there is no Torah (given) from heaven, and the Epicureans' (M. Sanh. 10. 1). The point of dispute between Sadducees and Pharisees was therefore whether the doctrine can be proved from the Bible or not. It may be that in those times the prayer was instituted which was afterwards recited by the Jews three times daily: 'Thou, O Lord, art mighty for ever, Thou quickenest the dead, Thou art mighty to save, Thou sustainest the living with loving kindness, quickenest the dead with great mercy, supportest the falling, &c. . . . and keepest Thy faith to them that sleep in the dust. Who is like unto Thee, Lord of mighty acts, and who resembleth Thee, O King, who killest and quickenest and causest salvation to spring forth? Yea, faithful art Thou to quicken the dead. Blessed art Thou, O Lord, who quickenest the dead.'[2] According to Elbogen, the repeated affirmation of the dogma of the resurrection is too marked to be accidental. It was the deliberate institution of the Pharisees to combat the denial on the part of the Sadducees, and was instituted

---

[1] See A. Büchler, *Das Synhedrion* (Vienna, 1902), p. 99.
[2] Singer's *Prayer Book*, pp. 44–5.

during or after the time of John Hyrcanus.[1] It is not impossible that the allusion to Exod. 3. 6 in the answer of Jesus was chosen purposely with the intention of recalling the beginning of the daily prayer (Shemoneh Esreh) which commences thus: 'Blessed art Thou, O Lord our God, and God of our fathers, the God of Abraham, the God of Isaac, and the God of Jacob', meaning that He is a God of the living ones. Then we find another form of benediction: 'Blessed be He who knoweth the number of you all and will hereafter judge you. He will in the future restore you to life. Blessed be He who is trustworthy in His word (promise), the quickener of the dead.'[2] This prayer was said by visitors to the cemetery.[3] Another instance of combating the disbelievers is given in the Mishnah Berakhot 9. 5. All the benedictions in the Sanctuary ended originally with מן העולם, but since the Sadducees (or, according to the Tosefta, the Minim) corrupted their ways and said, 'There is only one world', they (the Rabbis) enacted that people should say: מן העולם ועד העולם.[4] 'Blessed art Thou, O God of Israel, from this world to the other world, O Redeemer of Israel.'[5] It is fairly obvious from these passages that in and before the first century C.E. there was a party among the Jews which did not believe in a resurrection. In Christian circles we find the same movement. 2 Tim. 2. 18 mentions Hymenaeus and Philetus, who were teaching that the resurrection was already accomplished. Paul disputes (1 Cor. 15. 12–34) with those who deny the resurrection.[6]

3. We turn now to the Rabbis of the second and third centuries who endeavoured to prove this doctrine from the Scriptures. The Rabbis were frequently interrogated on

[1] *Geschichte des Achtzehngebetes* (Breslau, 1903), p. 51.
[2] Tosefta Ber., ed. Zuckermandel, 6. 6; J. Ber. 13d; B. Ber. 58b. Cf. Singer's *Prayer Book*, p. 320.
[3] For other prayers see B. Ber. 58a, 60a; B. Megillah, 17b.
[4] See Tosefta, ed. Zuckermandel, p. 17, l. 8; p. 215, l. 28; p. 216, l. 3.
[5] Cf. J. Ta'anit. 65d.
[6] See Hoennicke, *Das Judenchristentum*, p. 153.

the subject by three classes of people: (1) the Minim, who might be regarded in this case as the successors of the Sadducees;[1] (2) the Samaritans (who did not believe in our doctrine, as we know from the *Recognitions of Clement* 1. 54); and (3) the heathen. R. Gamaliel II, about 110 C.E., was asked by the Sadducees: 'Whence do you derive the teaching that the Holy One, blessed be He, will restore life to the dead?' R. Gamaliel quoted from the Torah: 'And the Lord said unto Moses, Behold, thou shalt sleep with thy fathers; and this people will rise up' (Deut. 31. 16); from the Prophets: 'Thy dead shall live, my dead bodies shall arise. Awake and sing, ye that dwell in dust: for thy dew is as the dew of herbs, and the earth shall cast forth the dead' (Isa. 26. 19); from the Hagiographa: 'And thy palate like the best wine, that goeth down smoothly for my beloved, causing the lips of those who are asleep to speak' (Cant. 7. 9). All these proofs were refuted and rejected by them till finally he quoted Deut. 31. 16, or, according to a different reading, Deut. 4. 4 (see B. Sanh. 90b). R. Joshua b. Ḥananya, a contemporary of R. Gamaliel II, wanted to prove to the Romans from the above-quoted passage, Deut. 31. 16, the two doctrines of the resurrection and the prescience of God, but only the latter was accepted by them (B. Sanh. 90b). The same teaching was handed down by R. Yoḥanan (died 278 C.E.) in the name of R. Simon b. Yoḥai (about 160 C.E., B. Sanh. 90b). R. Simon b. Yoḥai declares, with reference to Gen. 3. 19: 'For dust thou art, and unto dust shalt thou return', that there is a hint here pointing to the belief in resurrection, since it is not written 'And thou shalt go', but 'Thou shalt return' (see Gen. R. 20. 26). R. Eliezer, the son of R. Yose, had a dispute about our teaching with the Minim (B. Sanh. 90). According to another source the controversy with the Samaritans is attributed to R. Simon b. Eleazar (Sifre Numbers, § 112).

[1] See on this point A. Büchler, *Das Synhedrion*, pp. 72, 78.

Finally we have to mention the views of two Tannaim, one of whom belonged to the latter part of the second half of the second century while the other lived perhaps about 150 C.E., dealing with the proofs for the doctrine of the resurrection. R. Jacob said: 'There is no commandment in the Torah of which the reward for fulfilling it is mentioned, where the doctrine of resurrection is not implicit, as it is said: "Thou shalt in any wise let the dam go, ... that it may be well with thee and that thou mayest prolong thy days" (Deut. 22. 7). One man climbed to the top of a tree or a building (in order to fulfil this precept) and he fell down and died. Was it well with him and did he prolong his days? Say: "That it may be well with thee" in this world and "that thou mayest prolong thy days" in the world to come.'[1] The other Rabbi, R. Simai, says: 'There is no portion (in the Torah) where the idea of quickening the dead is not mentioned, but we are incapable of finding it, as it is said (Ps. 50. 4): "He shall call to the heavens above, and to the earth, that He may judge his people." "He shall call to the heavens above" refers to the soul; and "to the earth, that He may judge his people" refers to God who judges His people. Whence do you know that we speak here of the resurrection of the dead? Because it is said: "Come from the four winds, O *spirit*." '[2]

In anonymous teachings we find further proofs from the Scriptures for the Biblical origin of the doctrine. Thus from Deut. 32. 39: 'I kill, and I make alive'; 'I have wounded, and I heal.'[3] In the citation from Sifre Deut. the following passages from the Bible are also enumerated: Num. 23. 10: 'Who can count the dust of Jacob, or the number of the fourth part of Israel? Let me die the death of the righteous and let my last end be like his!' Deut. 33. 6: 'Let Reuben live, and not die'; and finally Hos. 6. 2: 'After two days will

---

[1] See Tosefta, ed. Zuckermandel, p. 512, l. 18; B. Ḥullin 142a; B. Ḳid. 39b.
[2] Ezek. 37. 9; Sifre Deut. § 306, p. 132a.
[3] B. Pes. 68a; B. Sanh. 91b; Sifre Deut. § 329.

He revive us: on the third day He will raise us up, and we shall live before Him.' The heretics to support their denial quoted Ps. 103. 16: 'For the wind passeth over it, and it is gone.' But, the Rabbis argued, the verse does not refer to death, but to the evil inclination.[1] Remarkable is the question of an Epicurean who said to a Rabbi: 'Is it possible that the dead will come to life again? Your forefathers did not believe it whilst you do? (See) what is written in the story of Jacob (Gen. 37. 35): "But he refused to be comforted." Had he known that the dead would be quickened would he have refused to be comforted?' He (the Rabbi) said: 'Fool! It was so because he knew by means of the Holy Spirit that Joseph was alive, and we do not accept comfort for the living.'[2] In the third century R. Joshua ben Levi (B. Sanh. 91b) and R. Yoḥanan collected proofs for this doctrine. First from the verse: 'And thereof ye shall give the Lord's heave offering to Aaron the priest' (Num. 18. 28). 'Do you think that Aaron lives for ever? Behold, he did not enter the Holy Land. But it teaches us that he (Aaron) will rise from his grave and the Israelites will give him the heave offerings. This is a proof from the Torah for the doctrine of the resurrection' (B. Sanh. 90b). R. Ḥiyya bar Abba states, in the name of R. Yoḥanan, that we infer this doctrine from Isa. 52. 8. There it is said: 'The voice of thy watchmen! they lift up the voice, together they SHALL sing.' It is not said 'they sang', but 'they shall sing'. Here we have another proof for the doctrine (B. Sanh. 91b). A Palestinian Rabbi of the third century, R. Yoshaya, refuted the heretics from Prov. 30. 16, where the grave (sheol) and the womb are mentioned together (B. Berakhot 15b). We see on one side that the heretics sought verses in the Bible

---

[1] See Midr. Ps., ed. Buber, pp. 348, 437; Marmorstein, *Religionsgeschichtliche Studien*, i. 72 ff.

[2] Yalḳuṭ, 43e; see Tanḥuma, ed. Buber, i. 187. For the use of the word 'fool' in the Polemics see 1 Cor. 15. 35–8; Clement *ad Cor.* xxiv. 5; Tertullian, *De resurrectione* 52; Aphraates, *Hom.* 8. 1, and in the Rabbinic polemics, see Mekh. 57a; Gen. R. 53. 15; 91. 5; Lev. R. vi. 6; Pesiḳta (ed. Buber), p. 281a; Pirḳe de R. Eliezer, ch. l.

from which it could be proved that in the Scriptures there was nothing to rely upon for this doctrine; on the other hand, the Rabbis were on the alert to quote all the verses which might possibly prove this teaching.

4. The resurrection cannot be experienced but may be proved by several passages from the Scriptures. For the believer in ancient times it was quite enough to state that the Bible teaches this or that idea, not for the heathen or the disbelievers. Through the liturgy and the homilies the belief sank deeply into the hearts of the people. In the third or fourth century an unknown preacher praised the Jews— or according to another reading the Jewish-Christians— for believing in this doctrine and blessing the Lord, 'who is trustworthy to revive the dead'.[1] In Judaism the prayer and confession was on all lips: 'We believe and recognize that Thou art the one who restores souls unto dead bodies.'[2] However, the heathen world viewed the doctrine askance, although there are indications that the thinkers of the Old World were familiar with a similar teaching and thought of a blessed future life.[3] Still the Rabbis were asked: 'How will the resurrection take place?' They approached the problem from various points of view.

The first question asked ran: 'Since the dead are but dust, how can dust revive?' This was asked by a man called 'Caesar' (emperor) of R. Gamaliel II. The patriarch's daughter gave the answer on his behalf. We have two versions of it. According to the first version, she gives an illustration of two workmen, one of whom made figures from earth and the other from water. Which is held in higher esteem? The latter one must say: 'He (God) created men of water, how much more then is He capable of forming (the dead) of dust.' According to the other version, she said:

---

[1] Midr. Ps., ed. Buber, p. 240, and Hamanhig, p. 55, by Abraham ben Nathan of Lunel; cf. my *Religionsgeschichtliche Studien*, i. 27 f.

[2] See Midr. Ps., ed. Buber, p. 210; Singer's *Prayer Book*, p. 5; Gen. R. ch. xlviii; Lam. R. ch. 3.

[3] See Friedländer, *Darstellungen aus der Sittengeschichte Roms*. iv. 365 ff.

'A glassblower makes glass which anyone can break, yet he is able to mend it. Surely God, who breathes His own spirit into the human being, has at least the same power.'[1]

A man called Gebiha ben Pesisa, who probably lived before the destruction of the Temple, was asked by a Min: 'You wicked Jews! You say that the dead will revive; (true it is that) the living will die, but how can the dead revive?' Gebiha answered: 'Ye wicked people! Woe to you who teach that there is no resurrection: seeing that those who have not lived live (now), how much more will those who have lived come to life again?' He (the Min) said: 'You call me wicked, wait till after the resurrection and I will straighten your crookedness!' Gebiha replied: 'If you do it, I will call you an experienced doctor and you will receive a good fee' (B. Sanh. 91a).

R. Joshua b. Ḥananya was asked by the Emperor Hadrian: 'How will God breathe life into a human being in the world to come?'[2] A philosopher, Eunamaos of Gadara, wished to refute R. Meir's belief in the resurrection. He was ready to grant a possibility of a spiritual resurrection, and said: '(Do you think perhaps) that all the wool entering the pot comes out of it in the same weight?' (B. Ḥagigah 15b). R. Nathan, a contemporary of R. Meir, asserts that in the world to come the bodies will be clothed in the same garments as those worn at their interment.[3]

R. Ḥanina b. Ḥama (about 220–40 C.E.) dealt with the problem whether those who had bodily defects would rise with or without their old defects. From many statements which we are about to quote it seems that the question was frequently asked, and resulted in a good deal of popular speculation. R. Ḥanina says: 'If one died as a lame man he will revive as such, if he died as a blind man, he will be restored as such,

---

[1] B. Sanh. 91a; cf. *Jewish Review*, v. 69. The same parable is quoted by R. Yose ben Ḥalafta, Gen. R. 14. 8.

[2] Midr. Kohelet R. 197. 2; Lev. R. ch. 18; cf. *Jewish Review*, v. 72, and Gen. R., ch. 28.

[3] J. Kilaim, ch. 9, p. 7.

so that people should not say: Those who died were not the same as those who were quickened.'[1] The same argument is used by an anonymous author in Gen. Rabba 95. 1, where it is said: 'God could heal those with defects, but in order to prevent argument against the doctrine, He does not heal them.'[2] R. Simon b. Laḳish (before 280 C.E.) pointed to a contradiction between Isa. 35. 6 and Jer. 31. 7, and solved it by assuming that the dead will revive with their defects, but they will be healed afterwards (B. Sanh. 91b).

R. Ammi, a Rabbi of the fourth century, answered the question, 'How can dust come to life again?' with the following parable: 'A king once said to his ministers: Go and erect for me great palaces, where there is neither water nor dust. They went and built them, but after a few days the buildings fell into ruins. Then the king said: Go and erect palaces where there is plenty of water and dust! They (the ministers) said: We cannot do it. The king retorted: Where there was neither water nor dust you were able to build, how much more where there is plenty of water and dust.' Then R. Ammi gave the illustration of the mouse, half dust and half flesh, as demonstrating the possibility of the resurrection (B. Sanh. 91a).[3]

From all these quotations we see that the queries of those who doubted the resurrection of the dead took the forms: Is God capable of performing this action or not? How will they revive?

It may be interesting to glance at the kindred literature of the Church, especially at two treatises, that of Athenagoras, and that of Tertullian dealing with the resurrection. Athenagoras and Tertullian are both concerned with the same difficulties which the Rabbis considered in their disputations, which shows that the problem was one of religion in general.

[1] Midr. Eccles. R. to Eccles. 1. 4.
[2] See Tanḥuma, ed. Buber, i. 209; R. Berekhya in Eccles. R. to 1. 16, and Midr. Zuṭṭa, ed. Buber, p. 85.
[3] See Pliny, *Hist. Nat.* ix. 58. 84.

Athenagoras and Tertullian both deal with the following questions: (*a*) Has God the power to revive the dead? (Athenagoras, ch. iii). Athenagoras answers: Yes, God is able to do it. Tertullian goes farther and says: One ought not to think of the lowliness of the material (the body), but rather of the dignity and the skill of the Maker (ch. v). We have seen above how the Rabbis met these questions. (*b*) How can God revive those who were killed or devoured by wild animals or eaten by fish in the ocean or those who were slain on the battlefields or those who perished in famine? (Athenagoras, chs. iii–viii). Tertullian summarized the questions thus: Now you are a shrewd man, no doubt, but will you then persuade yourself that, after this flesh has been withdrawn from sight and touch and memory, it can never be rehabilitated from corruption to integrity, from a shattered to a solid state, from an empty to a full condition, from nothing at all to something, from the devouring fires, and the waters of the sea, and the maws of beasts, and the crops of birds, and the stomachs of fishes, and time's own great paunch itself, of course, yielding it all up again? (ch. iv). In the Jewish apocalyptical literature Elijah points out, no doubt with a polemical purpose, that God will gather the elements of those who have perished in the high sea and have found their grave therein.[1] (*c*) Shall the blind, the lame, the one-eyed, the leper, and the palsied come back again, although there can be no pleasure in returning thus to their old condition? (Tert., ch. iv). It is interesting to draw attention to the numerous statements in the Rabbinic literature which allude to the objections of the heretics which are, of course, also quoted 'in very subdued and delicate phrases, as suited to the character of our style', as Tertullian expresses himself. An anonymous Rabbi states: 'First, as a man leaves this world, so will he return to life: a blind man returns blind, a lame one lame, and so on. Why? Has God no power to

[1] Jellinek, *Bet ha-Midrash*, iii. 67.

heal them? Yes (He has), but so that they (the heretics) should not say: When they were alive, He (God) could not heal them, now after death He has healed them. It would then seem to us that they are not the same people, but quite different people.'[1] R. Simon b. Laḳish (before 278 C.E.) also discussed the question (B. Sanh. 91b), as we saw above. R. Levi states: 'After the resurrection all the mutilated ones will recover, except the serpent' (Gen. R. 20. 5). There seems to have been another question raised: How can there be room in the world at the resurrection for all those who have died since the first man, Adam?[2] (d) In this category we mention the questions put by Tertullian in this way: Will the flesh again be subject to all its present wants, especially of food and drink? Shall we have to suffer pain in our bowels, and with organs of shame to feel no shame, and with all our limbs to toil and labour? (ch. iv). These questions, with which the Church Father deals at length, were considered by the Rabbis as well. We shall give here only a brief summary of their doctrines. After the resurrection there will be no more death, and the revived will live without pain and sin.[3] They will eat and drink joyfully and live in pleasure[4] without any evil inclination, that is, feeling no shame.[5] There can be no doubt that the Rabbis endeavoured to picture the life after the resurrection in this way in order to satisfy all the questioners on these points.

We infer from this fact that the Rabbis as well as the Church Fathers believed in the resurrection. One may add that they did not adopt a spiritual interpretation as did Philo,[6] but believed in a real restoration of the body. Epstein has tried to show that there were many among the

[1] Gen. R. 95. 1; cf. Tanḥuma, ed. Buber, i. 208.

[2] See Tanḥuma, ed. Buber, iii. 20.

[3] See B. Rosh Hashanah 31a; Sanh. 9. 2a; Friedmann, *Seder Eliyahu Rabba* (Vienna, 1902), pp. 7, 20 ff.

[4] Cf. M. Abot, 4. 1; B. Ber. 5a; and see *Seder Eliyahu*, p. 14.

[5] B. Sukkah 52a; *Seder Eliyahu*, pp. 19, 81.

[6] *De cherubim*, i. 159; Josephus, *Wars*, iii. 8.

Rabbis who shared Philo's view. It is a problem still un-
solved whether or not these alleged Essene Rabbis actually
existed. First of all we have to consider R. Phinehas b. Yair's
teaching: 'The holy spirit leads to the resurrection of the
dead' (B. 'Abodah Zarah 20b). We cannot see that there is
a word about spiritual resurrection in this dictum. The
other Rabbi, Ḥiyya bar Abba, had probably never heard
of the Essenes and their ideas. It is impossible, therefore,
to agree with Epstein's theory.[1] It seems clear that the
Rabbis did not hold the view of a spiritual resurrection,
thus agreeing with Athenagoras and Tertullian, although we
find that some of the Church Fathers (e.g. Origen) taught
a spiritual resurrection.[2]

5. The doctrine of the resurrection placed the Rabbis of the
second and third centuries in a difficult position. They were
attacked on one side by Christians who cited the alleged
deeds of Jesus who quickened many to life and who proved
the doctrine by his own resurrection. On the other hand,
there were the Gnostics, who denied the possibility of the
resurrection. Thus we hear R. Judah (after 135 C.E.) preaching: 'If one tells thee that God will restore the dead to life,
reply to him: It was already done by Elijah, Elisha, and
Ezekiel' (Lev. R. ch. 27). This homily cannot be interpreted
except as a polemical argument against those who laid so
much stress on the events related about Jesus. The Rabbi
could not have denied the doctrine of the resurrection,
which, as we saw above, was already established as one of
the fundamental dogmas of Judaism, without being condemned as a dangerous heretic. He wanted to show that
the deeds of Jesus were not at all unique. Such miracles
happened also in the times of the prophets and also after
their time.[3] The Rabbis believed, as many of the Midrashic
legends show, that the pious and righteous are capable of

[1] *Ozar Hachokhma veHamada*, p. 17.
[2] See Harnack, *Dogmengeschichte*, i. 223.
[3] See Marmorstein, *Religionsgeschichtliche Studien*, i. 37.

reviving the dead. The belief in the doctrine of the resurrection is one of the most familiar motives in Rabbinic legends. A few illustrations must suffice. A slave of the Emperor Antoninus died and the patriarch (Judah, the Prince) sent one of his pupils, R. Simon b. Ḥalafta, to restore the slave to life.[1] King David was restored to life for a brief period at the dedication of the Temple in Jerusalem (Exod. R. 8. 1). We know now that such legends influenced in marked degree the legends of the saints in the medieval literature.[2] It is obvious that Jews believed that pious, learned and great men in the past as well as in the present were and are powerful enough to perform miracles which master even the angel of death and thereby overcome even the limits set by Nature herself. This was used as the test in the eyes of many Jews with regard to Jesus' mission, and wherever Paul and the apostles referred to these facts, Jews were silenced thereby.

We have given proofs for the undeniable fact that the Rabbis fought against disbelief in the doctrine of the resurrection. It is a great mistake to assume, as is generally done by historians dealing with the first three centuries, that Jews abandoned their propaganda among the nations of the world and ceased to preach and call on the name of the God who created heaven and earth and lost their courage to fight idol-worship and immoral heathen customs after the first century when the Church was first established. The Rabbis did not give way. They fought bravely, true to their convictions and ancient mission, as their numerous sermons and statements testify. That their voice was not heard as it ought to have been was surely not their fault. The visible effect of their teaching was in no way equal to their great efforts. The reason is quite obvious. They were a small and, moreover, an oppressed minority; and even in

---

[1] See Lev. R. 10. 4.

[2] See about them H. Günter, *Die christliche Legenden des Abendlandes* (Heidelberg, 1910), pp. 25 ff.; cf. Gaston Paris, *Zeitschrift des Vereins für Volkskunde*, xiii. 1 ff.

spiritual matters might unfortunately ousts right. They had also to strive against many political and social hindrances and obstacles. Finally, in the face of foreign influence and the great persecutions to which they were subjected, they had to keep their own people true to their religious ideals, a very difficult task when all the world's hatred and enmity surrounded them. We find opposition to the doctrine of the resurrection in the third century. R. Simon ben Lakish (before 280 C.E.) says: 'If one tells thee that the dead will not revive, tell him there was Elijah, who revived the dead.'[1] The Minim (or heretics) here are surely not Christians ($\kappa\alpha\tau$' $\dot{\epsilon}\xi o\chi\dot{\eta}\nu$) but heretics, as is always the case.[2]

The Rabbis give us the name of a famous heretic, Elisha ben Abuya (about 130 C.E.), who denied the resurrection dogma.[3] But they also give us another type of heretic who opposed this teaching and whom they refer to as 'Esau'. It is a very important point for the understanding of Haggadah generally and the Rabbinic Haggadah in particular that the Rabbis represented the characters and habits of the Biblical personages according to their own view and judgement. The goodness and the saintliness of the pious patriarchs and prophets are glorified to the utmost as models of piety and reverence, while the wickedness and cruelty, the faithlessness and atrocity of those who were condemned by the Scriptures, are depicted in the most glaring colours. Whether this attitude was just or not is not our concern. It reflects, however, the thoughts and ideas of the men who uttered these statements, and the circumstances which produced them. We know that the Gnostics liked such names in the Scriptures as were disliked by pious and good people. Thus Cain, the generation of the Flood, Esau, Korah,

---

[1] See Tanḥuma, ed. Buber, iv. 41; Num. R. ch. 14, Agadat Bereshit., ed. Buber, p. 106.

[2] See the *Hibbert Journal*, vol. iii, No. 1 (1904), p. 196; Professor H. Oort's learned review of *Christianity in Talmud*, by R. Travers Herford (London, 1903).

[3] See Kohelet R. 7, 18.

Balaam, and so on became the heroes of the heretics.[1] We can therefore assert that when the Rabbis speak of Esau as being a man who denied the resurrection,[2] they really meant their own contemporaries, who, whether they chose Esau as their ideal or not, did not accept this doctrine. We do not wish to imply that only this sect did not believe in the resurrection, for we find the denial also attributed to Cain and, of course, to his followers; however, the sect of Esau, so named either by themselves or by the Rabbis, actually existed.

Finally, let us refer to a few of the Rabbinic conceptions as to the resurrection. The resurrection will take place either just before or after the advent of the Messiah. Old Tannaitic sources distinguish between the days of the Messiah and the time of resurrection.[3] The resurrection will be one of the signs heralding the advent of the Messiah, according to the Didache, xvi. 6. This idea is borrowed from the Sybilline Oracles.[4] The Rabbis did not share this view. They held that the resurrection will take place after the appearance of the Messiah.[5] In the later Jewish apocalyptic literature this sign plays an important part. We read that the Messiah comes to the Israelites and reveals himself, whereupon they say: 'Go and revive the patriarchs Abraham, Isaac, and Jacob.' The patriarchs say: 'Go to Adam; he will be the first to be restored to life, then we shall come.'[6] Another remarkable feature of these speculations is that those who are buried in Palestine will be the first to be revived.[7] As we have already said, the mutilated will also be quickened, but with their defects; afterwards God will

[1] See Irenaeus, *Adv. Haer.*, i. 31.

[2] See Gen. R. 63. 20; Pesikta Rabbati 48a, 49b; Midr. Psalms, p. 10a; Ps. Jon. Gen. 36.

[3] See Klausner, *Die messianischen Vorstellungen*, pp. 18 ff.

[4] See Hoennicke, *Das Judenchristentum*, p. 358.

[5] See the material in Klausner's book quoted above, pp. 22–3.

[6] See Jellinek, *Bet ha-Midrash*, iii. 13; Horovitz, *Bet Eked Agadot*, i. 58; Wertheimer, *Leḳeṭ Midrashim*, pp. 6, 12.

[7] See Yoma 71a; Gen. R. 74. 1; Tanḥuma, ed. Buber, i. 214.

heal them.[1] Even those who found their graves in the depths of the sea—a problem dealt with at length by Athenagoras and Tertullian—will be quickened to life.[2] The Pirḳe de R. Eliezer, a very important book of the sixth or seventh century, devotes an entire chapter to our problem (ch. xxxiv). Thus the belief in the resurrection became one of the most important dogmas of Judaism. Fortified by this belief, Jewish warriors, few in number, fought the innumerable legions of Rome (the children of Edom and Esau). Time and again, during their history, Jews bore all their countless sufferings and the indescribable cruelties of martyrdom in many lands. The speculations of philosophers and theologians concerning a bodily or spiritual resurrection mattered very little. What did matter was what the Rabbis taught concerning eternal reward and punishment. Israel believed and felt in its heart that the Day of Judgement would come, when God alone would decide who was right and who was wrong. In our days this is not merely the particular belief of a small community, but, through the teaching of Israel, the majority of believers of all denominations look forward to the great Day of God, when might will give way to right.

[1] See Gen. R. 95. 1; Tanḥuma, ed. Buber, 1. 208.
[2] See Jellinek, *Bet ha-Midrash*, iii. 67.

M

PARTICIPATION IN ETERNAL LIFE IN RABBINIC THEOLOGY AND IN LEGEND

I

IN the time of Plato there was in Greece a class of wandering charlatans who went from house to house giving themselves the pompous title of Orpheo-Celestae. They used to knock at the doors of rich landowners in the towns and villages, and offer for a fee to carry out rites of purification and the like by means of certain collections of writings which they carried under their arms and which they alleged to have been written or collected by Orpheus himself. People thus purified would in this way acquire or assure for themselves a blissful lot in the future world.[1] This is not the first time that we come across aspirations or desires of this nature. Long before Plato and for much longer after him the ancients strove ardently to win the salvation of their souls or their share in the future world; they sought, in any case, to make sure in some way or other that their bodies should remain undisturbed by the demons and the spirits of the dead, that they should be sheltered from the torments and punishments of the underworld, and obtain a share in eternal life. If we turn to the country of the Nile we find in the tombs which have been opened Books of the Dead which were interred with the deceased, in the Saitic period equally with the times of the Ptolemies, and which go back to a very high antiquity. What was the object of this custom among the ancient Egyptians? These Books of the Dead teach the same doctrine as the Orphic documents. Their contents proclaim their object beyond all doubt: they were meant to satisfy the desire for eternal life and to testify to the belief in this life. It is curious to observe that this usage

[1] v. *Republic*, ii. 7; Döllinger, *Heathendom and Judaism*, Eng. edition, i. 105; cf. L. R. Farnell, *Higher Aspects of Greek Religion*, pp. 135 ff.

lasted among the inhabitants of the Nile region far into the Christian era.

The Ethiopian book *Lefafa Zedek* is nothing but a Book of the Dead christianized and translated into Ethiopic.[1] It had the same object as the old Egyptian Book of the Dead. In the early and pre-Nicene epoch of Christianity the dead were similarly provided with certain writings such as the Apocalypse of St. Peter,[2] a document very appropriate for the occasion.

Passing from the religious conceptions of the Egyptians to those of the ancient Persians, we again find hopes and aspirations of the same nature. The believer seeks to recognize his place in Paradise, to make sure of his share in the future life, or at least implores protection against the hostile elements which could or would like to oppose his entry. Certainly the means for attaining these ends are not the same among the Persians as among the ancient Egyptians or their successors the Ethiopians, but the aspiration and the object are similar. This was the significance among the Persians of the ceremony of Narazund. Narazund or the Gheti-Kharid carry the believer up to heaven, and he or his soul sees the place destined for him or it. No ceremony, no good deed or work other than the ceremonies mentioned in

---

[1] Cf. Sir E. A. Wallis Budge, *The Bandlet of Righteousness, an Ethiopian Book of the Dead*, London, 1929.

[2] Traces of this custom can be discerned even in Judaism. In the Talmudic period we meet with the custom of depositing on graves or tombs sacred writings or scrolls of the Law no longer in use. Thus, for example, a scroll of the Law was, according to R. Nehemiah, deposited on the bier of King Hezekiah. B. B.K. 17a; for the contrary cf. B. M.K. 25a, where R. Ḥisda did not allow one to be laid on the bier of R. Huna. Similar usages are mentioned in Semaḥot, ch. 8, cf. also *Wiener Zeitschrift für die Kunde des Morgenlandes*, xii. 62. Obadiah of Bertinoro speaks of a similar custom at Palermo, v. *Jahrbuch f. d. Gesch. der Jüd. und des Judenthums*, iii (Leipzig, 1863), p. 197; cf. also Elijah Capsali with reference to the burial of R. Judah Minz at Padua; Porges, *REJ* lxxix (1924), 40, where similar indications are found. His books were placed by the side of his coffin and part of a scroll of the Law in the shroud under his head; see also Loftus, *Travels in Chaldaea*, 36; Migne, *Dict. des Apocryphes*, ii. 1309; T. W. Hasluck, *Christianity and Islam under the Turks*, Oxford, ii. 1919, 471 ff., note 4 f.

the work, can enable the living part of man to attain to heaven or procure for him his place above.[1] We shall point out farther on the influence of these conceptions on Jewish legend. It is sufficient to remark here that such an influence cannot be denied. R. Reitzenstein has proved the persistence of this doctrine among the Mandeans.[2] As among the Egypto-Ethiopians, here, too, paganism transmitted its ideas and doctrines to nascent Christianity, for Baptism and the Last Supper represent ultimately only similar aspirations and hopes for obtaining life eternal.

We find this desire for eternal life among the ancient Israelites no less than among the other peoples. Even while lying on his death-bed the aged king David is greeted by Bathsheba with the words יחי אדוני המלך דוד לעולם (1 Kings 1. 31). In the royal court of Persia etiquette required the same formula (Neh. 2. 3; Dan. 2. 4 and 3. 9). Certainly all these passages deal only with kings who, according to the ancient idea, resembled the Deity and were nearer to God than ordinary mortals. In the same way we find this idea of the eternal life of the king more or less insistently proclaimed in what are called the 'royal' Psalms,[3] though it certainly did not apply to the masses. However that may be, we do not find among the ancient Israelites any trace of the conceptions which we meet among their Egyptian, Greek, and Persian contemporaries. It would seem that the doctrine and the representations attached to it were intentionally passed over in silence. One easily understands why when one thinks of the practices and magic rites which were closely bound up with this belief; the spiritual leaders of ancient Israel sought to eliminate them, and they were bound to do so at any price if they did not wish to endanger monotheism. Probably these eschatological theories were known in Israel also, but either they flourished in secret or

---

[1] *Sacred Books of the East*, xxiv. 260.
[2] *Die Vorgeschichte der christlichen Taufe* (Leipzig, 1929), 384 ff.
[3] V. H. Gressman, *Der Messias*, pp. 25 ff.

they were the private possession of some chosen spirits who, withdrawing from the crowd, speculated on God and the world, on life and death, on this world and the next, on Paradise and the underworld. They were not much spoken about among the ancient Israelites, and the Scriptures found little among them worthy of being recorded.

It was only when monotheism had definitely consolidated itself and was about to be exposed to more violent storms that the doctrine of the future world was preached vigorously and loudly. At the same time the opposition, too, came out into the open. True to their nature the conservative elements struggled against this new theory of two worlds. As we know from the history of the Jewish religion, they did not carry the day. We find only one brief allusion to the struggles which this doctrine aroused and to the victims which it claimed.[1] Confirmation of the fact, however, is found in the evolution of the meaning of the word עולם, which in the Bible signifies 'eternity' and in the Mishnah 'universe'. The result was to establish a difference between these two worlds, the actual and the future. We will not here go more deeply into the relations between them. A more complete study of this subject, giving our point of view and quoting the sources, will be found in the chapter treating of the relation of God to the universe. We shall confine ourselves here to an examination of the conceptions of man's share in the future world, as they present themselves in the Haggadah and in legend.

II

In the early centuries of Christianity Jews, like non-Jews, often expressed a desire to obtain a share in the future world and inquired how it was to be done. We find this question in the Gospels,[2] but it was also frequently discussed in the ancient schools and in various meeting-places.

---

[1] Mishnah, Berakhot, c. 9, fin.
[2] Mark 10. 17; Matt. 18. 16–19; Luke 18. 18–20.

The disciples assembled round the death-bed of R. Eliezer b. Hyrcanus thus addressed their master: 'Rabbi, teach us the way of life in order that we may have a share in the life eternal.'[1] Similarly, he was asked with regard to a person whose name is not given whether he had a share in the future world.[2] According to the Baraitha there were in the Tannaitic period Jews who used to say, 'I offer a *sela* for charity on condition that my son becomes well again' or 'that I have a share in the future world'.[3] An Haggadah relating to David puts in his mouth this supplication to God: 'Cause me to know which is the great gate through which to pass to the future life.'[4] הודיעני באיזה פילון מפולש לחיי העו' הב', &c.

According to R. Abbahu, who, as we shall see, appears to have interested himself particularly in these matters and to have been well versed in them, questions were addressed to King Solomon on the principles through adherence to which eternal life is to be obtained.[5] The question איזהו בן עוה"ב is very common in the discussions of the *Bet ha-Midrash*. In a written declaration[6] which was sent probably from Babylon we find as an answer to this question the following statement: 'He who is humble and complaisant,[7] who goes about modestly, who constantly studies the law and claims no merit for himself.' On receiving this letter all the Rabbis turned their eyes on Rabba bar Ulla. Our knowledge of the life of this Amora, who flourished at the end of the third century or the beginning of the fourth, is not sufficient to explain how far the message was actually meant

---

[1] B. Ber. 28b, Hal. Ged. Berlin, 40; Dikduke Sôferîm 1. 146; Derech Eretz R., c. 3.

[2] B. Yoma, 66b; Tos. Yeb. c. 3; Ginzberg Geonica ii. 14, קהלת שלמה 542–3; Taussig, *Neve Shalom*, 75–6.

[3] B. B.B. 10b; B. R.H. 4a; B. Pes. 8a.

[4] Pesik. ed. Buber, 179b; Lev. R. 30. 2; Midr. Ps. 16. 10; cf. Yalkuṭ Makhiri, 93, which quotes a Tanḥuma where the question is stated thus; הודיעני דרך שהיא מפולשת לדרך החיים. The phrase is further confirmed by Gen. R. 59, ed. Theodor, 635, where it is ascribed to Abraham.

[5] B. B.B. 10b.   [6] B. Sanh. 88b.

[7] שפל ברך. This quality is also required of a good officiating minister on fast-days.

to apply to him. R. Yoḥanan ben Nappaḥa, who belonged
to an earlier generation, also gave an answer to the question
איזהו בן עולם הבא.[1]

This Amora appears also in a legend in which he promises
a certain matron eternal life. According to the version in the
treatise *Kalla*,[2] he promises the matron, if she will let him
know the desired remedy, לאלהי ישראל מייתינא לך 'I will
bring thee to the God of Israel'. In the *Babli*, however,
this phrase is transformed into לאלהא דישראל לא מגלינא[3]
'I will not reveal the secret to the God of Israel'.

It is easy to see that an attempt was made to place the
Rabbi in as favourable a light as possible. There can be
little doubt, however, that the treatise *Kalla* has preserved
the original version. This view is confirmed by an analogous
dictum of R. Akiba which shows us that the sages were
wont to promise eternal life,[4] for the expression לאלהי ישראל
מייתינא לך corresponds exactly to the words attributed to
R. Akiba, הריני מביאך לחיי העולם הבא as having been addressed
by him to a poor woman selling vegetables to induce her
to communicate her secret about the birth of her son.[5]

All these instances make it clear that among the Jews
also there prevailed an ardent desire to have a share in the
life eternal. We find this desire couched in various expressions such as כדי שנזכה לחיי העה״ב or more simply, מהו לעה״ב,[6]
also איזהו בן עו״ה? באיזה פילון מפולש לחיי העה״ב and finally
מביאך לחיי העו״הב or מייתינא.[7]

---

[1] B. Ber. 4b; B. Sabb. 153a, where R. Eleazar puts this question to Rab.
[2] Ch. ii. 2.   [3] B. Yoma 84a.
[4] Cf. חלק באלהי ישראל. Mekh. 37a, R. Akiba. See also, however, my
Beiträge zur Volkskunde und Religionsgeschichte, i. 5, further B. Ber. 63b,
B. Ned. 50b, J. Sanh. 1. 2, in the exhortation addressed to the nephew of
R. Joshua b. Ḥananya.   [5] Treatise Kallah, c. 2.
[6] Cf. also the account, to which we shall return later, of the death of R.
Ḥanina b. Teradyon, who addresses to R. Yose b. Ḳisma the question,
מה אני לחיי העוה״ב.
[7] These expressions recur in the story of R. Gamaliel, where the Govern-
ment official says to R. Gamaliel אי מעילנא לך מייתית לי לעלמא דאתי,
and the legend quoted in n. 5, where the executioner says, אתה מביאני
לחיי העוה״ב.

There are also other phrases expressing this concept and other notions attaching to it. Above all, we have to explain the basic concept of אין לו חלק לעו׳׳הב or יש לו חלק לעולם הבא, and this will form the subject of the next section.

III

We have almost a whole chapter in the Mishnah of Sanhedrin and even more abundant material in the Tosefta on the individuals and classes who have no share in the future life. This chapter owes its incorporation in the treatise of the Mishnah to a purely external motive, namely, the desire to connect ch. 10. 4 with ch. 9. 1 ff. From the Tosefta and from other sources it is clear that the compiler of the Mishnah did not use all the material of the original Mishnah which dealt with the problem of *ḥelek*. Before we deal with this question, it is necessary to point out that the discussion of the Amoraim relates not to our Mishnah but to a Mishnah which in form was closer to the Tosefta than to our Mishnah. At the head of this Mishnah is a phrase of capital importance for the history of Rabbinical dogma and theology: 'All Israel have a share in the future life', with some important exceptions, among which the Mishnah reckons: (*a*) one who denies the resurrection, (*b*) one who denies the divinity of the Torah, (*c*) the Epicureans.[1] The Mishnah in the Tosefta reckoned four other categories, namely, those who rejected the yoke of the precepts, those who annulled the covenant, those who interpreted the Scripture in an illicit manner,[2] and those who pronounced the Divine Name as it is written.[3] In our Mishnah this dictum is attributed to Abba Saul. In the *Yerushalmi* (Jerusalem Talmud) the so-called additions of the Tosefta are explained at once, while the first two assertions of the

---

[1] The order of the list varies in the parallel passages, cf. B. A.Z. 18a; J. Peah 1. 1; Tanḥ. ed. Frankfort a O., 68b.

[2] Cf. Marmorstein, 'Les Epicuréens dans la littérature talmudique', *REJ* liv (1907), 181–92.

[3] See Marmorstein, *The Old Rabbinic Doctrine of God*, i. 26.

Mishnah are not explained at all. On the other hand, it is
to be noted that the Mishnah as given in the Tosefta agrees
completely with the statement of R. Eliezer of Modi'im,
which puts the profanation of sanctuaries and disregard of
the festivals on exactly the same footing as פורק עול.

The notions of מפר ברית and מגלה פנים are also expanded.[1]
Apparently the Tosefta is more ancient than R. Eliezer of
Modi'im, who, in fact, provides it with a commentary. The
sentence is important because even Rabbis and pious men
who commit these faults are declared to forfeit their rights
to the future world. R. Akiba is represented in the Tosefta
by another phrase, while Abba Saul cites in his name in the
Tosefta a part of the dictum taught by him in the Mishnah.
There must certainly have been different recensions of this
Mishnah.

From a set of four questions in the *Yerushalmi*[2] it is
obvious that the commentators in Palestine could not have
read שלשה מלכים ... אין להם חלק as we find in our Mishnah,
but they had the reading of the Tosefta, ארבעה מלכים ירבעם
אחאב אחז ומנשה.[3] The Babylonian Mishnah had our
reading. As for the question what interest the theologians
can have had in denying the future bliss of four or three
kings, of four private persons, of the generations of the
Flood and of the Tower of Babel and of the people of
Sodom, and in withholding it from the spies, the generation
of the desert, the Korahites, and the Ten Tribes, it is as
difficult to explain this to-day as it is impossible to deter-
mine precisely the motives of the Rabbis who taught the
contrary (for instance, R. Judah ben Bathyra or R. Eliezer
b. Hyrcanus). Most probably these controversies sprang
ultimately from the different conceptions held by various

[1] Abot 3. 12; A.R.N. 26. מלבין פני חבירו seems to be a later addition,
since it is missing in A.R.N.; Sifre, Num. § 112; J. Pes. 33b.
[2] For M. II (a) וכי מה עשה אחז; (c) וכי מה עשה אחז; (b) וכי מה עשה אחאב;
(d) וכי מה עשה מנשה.
[3] *v.* Tosefta 12. 11, ed. Zuckermandel, 433; see also, Abot R. Nathan,
c. 36; Midr. Psalms 5. 8; Num. R. 14. 1; Tanh. and Seder Eliyahu, c. 73.

teachers regarding the characters of the Biblical personages mentioned. The Gnostics of the school of Marcion had condemned certain personages whom the Jews regarded very highly, while others condemned by the Bible were glorified by them. How far this process was carried may be judged from the statement which reports that some wished to include even Solomon among the kings who had no share in the life eternal.[1] This idea certainly did not emanate from the Sadducees or the Hasmoneans,[2] who themselves denied the life eternal or the existence of a future world,[3] but from the orthodox Jews, who found something shocking or even revolting in the large number of Solomon's wives or foreign wives.

Besides these two principal sources there are a number of Tannaim and Amoraim who give certain indications of their views on this doctrine, both on its positive and its negative side. Certain practices and certain principles assure to a man a share in the future world, while others deprive him of it. Expressions to this effect are so numerous and so varied that it is impossible to enumerate them in the space at my disposal. They are, however, of the highest importance for the study of the Haggadah, revealing as they do its inmost nature, and on the historical side throwing valuable light on the religious and intellectual life of their authors, and certain examples therefore particularly deserve to be quoted here.

R. Meir had a saying assuring a share in the future world to anyone who resided in Palestine, who recited the Shema‘ morning and evening, and who spoke Hebrew.[4] This statement is expanded in the *Yerushalmi* with variations.[5] The Haggadah of R. Meir contains other allusions also to this doctrine.[6] But to see the full force of R. Meir's dictum

---

[1] Cant. R. 1. 5 and parallel passages.
[2] *MGWJ* lxxiii, 1929, p. 245.   [3] Ibid. 484.
[4] Sifre, Deut., § 333.   [5] Shekalim, 47c.
[6] On Absalom, *v.* A.R.N., c. 36; B. Sotah 10b; B. Sanh. 113b; further, A.R.N. c. 36, ‏כל מי שיש לו בה״מ בעירו‎.

we have to take something more also into account. He must have been endeavouring after the revolt of Bar Kokhba to fortify the religious and national sentiment by encouraging the colonization of Palestine, the cultivation of the Hebrew language, and the recital of the Shema'. On the other hand, we read that R. Yose b. Ḥalafta, a contemporary of R. Meir, denied the life eternal to him who calculated the time for the advent of the Messianic era.[1] Can we fail to see here an allusion to contemporary history?[2] On the other side we find recorded of R. Yose a number of pious aspirations which make clear to us who it was that he considered worthy to have a share in the future life.[3] To complete the picture we may add that in general the Rabbis of Tiberias extol and emphasize residence in Palestine as a means of obtaining the future life, for example, R. Yoḥanan[4] and R. Abbahu.[5]

IV

We have already met R. Abbahu posing the question about participation in the life eternal. May it not have been his intention incidentally to combat the movement for counting Solomon among the kings who have no share in the future world? This is not impossible. This Rabbi of Caesarea gave proof on various occasions of independence of judgement, but above all in reference to our doctrine. We find in his Haggadah a statement which so far as I know has no parallel elsewhere. He says: 'In the future many will say with astonishment: Where does So-and-so abide who has never studied the Bible or the Mishnah? He actually abides with his ancestors and converses with them! God replies to them: Why are you astonished? It is quite just

[1] Derech Eretz R. c. 11.
[2] Cf. on this subject, Bacher, *MGWJ* xlii. 502 ff.
[3] B. Sabb. 118b.
[4] Pes. B. 113a; Pirḳe, ed. Schonblum ג' מנוחלי העוה"ב הדר בא"י, Midr. Prov. 17. 1; Ruth R. 5, 4; B. Keth. 111a.
[5] Ibid., אפילו שפחה כנענית שבא"י מובטח לה שהיא בת עולם חבא.

that it should be so, because during their lifetime they obeyed Me.'[1] The expression used here is יושב עם האבות. The whole statement seems to be meant as a protest against the pedantry of certain disciples and teachers. Men must not be judged by appearances. Ostentatious piety and arrogant self-complacency are not the best advocates for men before God, even if they succeed in throwing dust into the eyes of the ignorant masses. Humble obedience provides a better title to a place with the ancestors than the swollen pride of the scholars. R. Abbahu was probably led to this conclusion by his strange experience with Pentekaka. This man who, as indicated by his evil nickname, was considered an inveterate sinner, nevertheless received even during his lifetime signs of a divine favour which was not vouchsafed to any mortal in his environment; for it was for him, and in answer to his prayer, that rain fell after a long drought.[2] In this case also it may be regarded as probable that R. Abbahu meant his statement to apply to Pentekaka as one who, though considered by his co-religionists as a despicable person, would in the future abide with the ancestors.

The expression יושב עם האבות may be placed alongside of the phrase חלקו עם אברהם יצחק ויעקב.[3] A Midrashic sentence reads: 'He who practises charity is classed with Abraham, Isaac and Jacob.'

A third variant of this phrase is furnished by archaeology in the inscription of Yudan bar Ishmael, who, as a reward for his gift, expects חלק עם צדיקים 'a share with the just'.[4]

Finally, we have another expression leading back to the conception of which we have just spoken, viz. יושב בחיקו של אברהם אבינו, 'he dwells in the bosom of our father Abraham'. This expression occurs in the Talmudic and Midrashic

[1] Agadat Bereshit, ed. Buber, 163; cf. Marmorstein, *The Doctrine of Merits* (London, 1920), 191, 7.
[2] Cf. J. Ta'anit 64a, and Marmorstein, *Doctrine of Merits*, 190.
[3] Cf. Midr. Cant. Zuṭṭa 18.
[4] See, on this subject, Ury *QSPEF.* 1927, 51, and my remarks; ibid. 101; Sukenik, *Tarbitz*, 1. 150; I. N. Epstein, ibid. 152.

literature about seven times,[1] and much has been written about it.[2] The same phrase occurs in the Gospel of Luke and in other works of the ancient Christian literature.[3] It has been supposed that the expression derives from the conception of the function assigned to Abraham to sit at the entrance of the underworld and save from the fire those Israelites who are provided with the sign of the covenant. This theory, however, takes into account only one of the numerous means of protection against the tortures of the underworld—a subject which by right ought to be dealt with here also, only it would carry us too far.[4] However, this explanation has nothing to do with the place mentioned in the expression, for R. Levi does not in any way say that the circumcised dwell in the bosom of Abraham. On the other hand, this expression can easily be brought into connexion with the phrase 'to sit with the Patriarchs'. 'May they sit with Abraham, Isaac and Jacob in the kingdom of heaven'[5] is an expression well known in the Gospels in general. One can hardly suppose that R. Abbahu borrowed it from the language of the Gospels. R. Reitzenstein[6] has recently called attention to an analogous expression in Mandean, and has endeavoured to explain it as having been forcibly appropriated from the Christian, Egyptian, Hindu, and North German rites. But the Jewish origin of the phrase is as clear as its signification. To abide with the just, to be associated with the ancestors, to sit in the bosom of the fathers, are synonymous expressions, signifying that the deceased has a share in the life eternal.

[1] B. Ḳidd. 72b; Ebel Rabbati, c. 8; Pesiḳ., Buber, 25; Midr. Lam., ed. Buber, 43a; ibid. 85b; Pesiḳ. R. 180b and Tanḥ., ed. Buber V., 39.

[2] Beer, *Leben Abrahams*, 89; Reichmann, *Pesach Davar*, 53; *JQR* iii (1891), 25; vii (1894), 591; I. Levi, *REJ* liv (1907), 138; J. Klausner, *Yeshu ha-Nozri*, 409, 4 and A. Büchler, *Studies*, 197.

[3] Luke 16. 22; cf. A. Geiger, *Jüdische Zeitschrift*, vi. 197; cf. M. R. James, *The Test. of Abraham*, p. 72; *Zeitschrift für Ägyptische Sprache*, 1886, 121; *Apost. Const.* viii. 41 ff.

[4] B. Erubin 19a; Gen. R. 48. 7; Tanḥ. 22a; also the Vision of Daniel, in the Archive of Merx, i. 425.

[5] Matt. 8. 11.

[6] *Pre-Christian Baptism*, 25.

V

It is in the numerous legends relating to our subject that the influence of these conceptions on the people and the scholars is most clearly manifested. Here a 'daughter of the voice' בת קול announces that the hero of the tale is destined for the future life (מזומן לחיי העולם הבא). The following list will give an idea of this conception as a legend-motif.

1. A nobleman (אדון), no doubt a high Roman officer, is sent to R. Gamaliel II to convey to him his sentence of death. From a distance he summons the בעל החוטם,[1] but R. Gamaliel hides himself. At length the envoy meets him in a secret place and says to him: 'If I save you, will you procure me entry into the future world?'[2] R. Gamaliel promises him to do so. Then the Roman commits suicide (he goes up on to a roof and throws himself down), whereupon a *Bath-Kol* (בת קול) exclaims: 'This nobleman is destined for the life of the world to come' אדון זה מזומן לחיי העולם הבא.[3]

2. We find a similar incident in the legend recounting the martyrdom of R. Ḥanina ben Teradyon. The martyr himself tortured by doubts, is asking himself if he is destined for the life eternal;[4] and his executioner says to him: 'If I give you a more speedy death, will you conduct me to the future world?'[5] The 'daughter voice' thereupon announced that both R. Ḥanina and the executioner מזומנין הן לחיי העולם הבא.[6]

---

[1] One might suggest that there is here some confusion between Nasi (נשיא, prince and *nasus* (Lat. nose, Heb. חוטם). Hence the phrase בעל החוטם=*vir nasi*. I seem to remember having seen a similar explanation some years ago in *Hamaggid*.

[2] Cf. *supra* for this expression.

[3] B. Ta'anit 29a.

[4] מה אני לחיי העו״הב, *v. supra*.

[5] אתה מביאני לחיי העולם הבא. It is worth noting that the messenger of R. Gamaliel speaks Aramaic, whereas this one speaks Hebrew.

[6] B. A.Z. 18a.

3. The same thing happened at the martyrdom of R. Akiba, where the voice proclaimed: אשריך ר' עקיבא שאתה מזומן לחיי העולם הבא.[1]

4. Similarly, at the death of Eleazar ben Durdaya, who had lived an immoral life and had ultimately repented, the same *Bath-Kol* echoed: אליעזר בן דורדיא מזומן לחיי העולם הבא.[2]

5. The voice was also heard on the day when Rabbi died, promising eternal life to all who had been present at his interment.[3]

6. A similar announcement was made, according to R. Yoḥanan ben Nappaḥa, by the 'daughter of the voice' to the contemporaries of Solomon who had not observed the Day of Atonement.[4]

7. In the Babylonian Talmud it is said that a blood-letter daily received an assurance that he had a share in the life eternal.[5] The expression employed there is אתי ליה שלמא ממתיבתא דרקיעא which, according to Rashi, is identical with בת קול.

8. R. Eleazar b. Azarya announces after the death of R. Eliezer b. Hyrcanus:[6] רבותי באו וראו שטהור הוא לעולם הבא לפי שיצתה נשמתו בטהרה, 'because his soul departed in purity'. The last word uttered by the dying person is an omen of great importance, a kind of prophecy, like a *Bath-Kol*.

9. There were also people who, while still alive, were already destined for the life eternal, as we learn from the story of R. Berokha Ḥoza'ah, who asked the prophet Elijah in the market-place whether there were any people there with a share in the future world.[7]

---

[1] B. Ber. 61b; Gaster, *Exempla*, no. 286; cf. the variant in Jellinek, *Bet ha-Midrash*, iv. 27, which is certainly more recent; cf. *Hashiloach*, xliv (1925), 229.
[2] B. A.Z. 17a.
[3] B. Keth. 103b.
[4] B. Moed Ḳaṭan, 9a. See my notes in *REJ* lxxvii (1923), 168.
[5] B. Ta'anit 21b.
[6] Abot R. Nathan 625; J. Sabb. 5b; cf. *Hechalutz*, xi (1880), 72.
[7] B. Ta'anit 22a; Maasiyot, Bagdad, no. 70.

10. The conversation between R. Joshua ben Levi and Elijah in front of the opening of the cave of R. Simon ben Yohai also forms part of the legends of Elijah. R. Joshua b. Levi asks the prophet: אתינא לעלמא דאתי, 'Shall I enter the future world?' The prophet thinks that that depends on the consent of this man (i.e. R. Simon ben Yohai).[1]

11. In the legend of Asmodeus[2] we read: ומאן דעבד ליה ניחא נפשיה זכי לעלמא דאתי, 'Whoever gives pleasure to the pious becomes worthy of the future world'.

12. So in the story of Ketia bar Shalom a *Bath-Kol* proclaims קטיעה בר שלום מזומן לחיי העולם הבא.[3]

13. R. Akiba and the Spirit. R. Akiba teaches his son the Shema', the Eighteen Benedictions, and the Grace after meals, by which means the deceased is saved 'from the judgement of the underworld'.[4]

14. A sinner who, before his death, gives an egg to a poor man obtains a share in eternal life (וזכיתי לגן עדן), although he has never done any other good deed during his life.[5]

15. Miriam bath Tanhum and her seven children.[6]

16. Hanina b. Toratha (והיה חלקו עם הצדיקים בגן עדן).[7]

17. Joshua b. Ilem and Namos the butcher[8] who have an equal share and equal seats in Paradise. The Rabbi hears in a dream the words, 'Rejoice, Namos the butcher will be thy companion' (מושבך ומושבו בגן עדן וחלקו וחלקך שוין).

18. R. Meir and the wife of Judah the butcher. R. Meir was inveigled by her into sin. He seeks to do penitence and finds himself confronted with a lion, twice without suffering harm; the third time the lion mauls him and R. Meir

---

[1] B. Sanh. 98a.   [2] B. Gittin 68b.

[3] B. 'Abodah Zarah, 10b and parallel passages.

[4] *Vide* the sources and the bibliography in my *Doctrine of Merits*, 157, n. 17.

[5] Ma'asiyot, ed. Bagdad, no. 17 (1869).

[6] Lam. R. ed. Buber, 34; Pesikta R., c. 43; B. Gittin, 57b; Seder Eliyahu, ch. 30; Gaster, *Exempla*, no. 57; Ma'asiyot, no. 24.

[7] Ma'as., no. 34.

[8] Ibid. no. 39; Gaster, op. cit., 323 and p. 240.

recovers. The story concludes with the words: יצתה בת קול
ואמרה ר׳ מאיר מזומן לחיי העולם הבא.[1]

19. Joseph the gardener[2] at Ascalon, of whom it says:
וישמע קול קורא התבשר חלוק שלך וחלוק של אשתך טובה מחלוקך.

20. R. Amnon,[3] the author of the prayer *U-netaneh
tokef*, appears in a dream to R. Kalonymus b. R. Meshul-
lam and orders him to communicate the prayer to all the
Jewish communities. The story concludes with the words:
ונקרא שמו ר׳ אמנון שהאמין באל חי וזכה למעלה עליונה בגן עדן.[4]

21. A *ḥasid* sees walking about in Paradise[5] his deceased
friend who has not been sufficiently mourned as he deserved,
whereas a sinner who had died on the same day and was a
son of a high official had been honoured with an imposing
funeral.

22. Nathan de Zuzitha[6] and a woman. Through a
sparkling light on his head R. Akiba discerns that he will
have a share in the life eternal (בני על ראשך אור גדול בלכתך
ואני יודע שאתה מיורשי עוה״ב).

23. R. Simon b. Yoḥai and his disciples. They are preparing to go abroad in order to make a livelihood, but the
Rabbi prays and the whole valley is filled with gold pieces.
He says to them, however: כל מי שהוא נוטל עכשיו מתוך חלקו
של עולם הבא הוא נוטל, 'He who takes now takes from his
share in the future world'.[7]

24. R. Simon b. Laḳish and the potter who desired to
have the same share as the Rabbi in the future world
ויהי חולקך עמי לעלמא דאתי or דיהי חולקו חולקך עמך.[8]

These twenty-four examples, to which could be added

[1] Maasiyot, no. 47; cf. for the lion motive Marmorstein, 'Beiträge zur
Religionsgesch. u. Volkskunde, III' (*Mitteilungen*, xxx, 1927, par. 31 ff.).
[2] Ibid. no. 59; Gaster, op. cit., no. 14, 410.
[3] Ibid. no. 64.
[4] *Vide*. I. Davidson, *Ozar ha-Shirah veha-Piut*, ii. 200, where the bibliography should be completed by the indications given in the preceding note.
[5] Ma'asiyot, no. 76; cf. J. Sanh. 23c.; J. Hag. 77d.
[6] Ma'asiyot, no. 108; Gaster, op. cit., no. 35, and bibliogr., ibid., p. 192.
[7] J. Ber. 9. 1; Gen. R. 35. 2; Gaster, Ma'asiyot, no. 151 and parallels,
p. 218.
[8] Eccles. R. 3. 9; Gaster, ibid., no. 195.

many others drawn from the post-Talmudic literature, show that the grant of the life eternal can be known even during the lifetime of a man (Nos. 1, 9). In other cases it becomes certain only at the death of the persons concerned. This same feature is found in the medieval legends, where the heavenly voice plays quite a peculiar part. Thus a *Bath-Kol* appears in the story of the martyrdom of the widow Julitta and her young son Cyricus[1] and promises eternal bliss to the mother and the child. The Church certainly drew this incident from Jewish legend. As these legends are met with in every century of the old Rabbinic period, in Babylon as well as in Palestine, it must be admitted that the conceptions underlying them were at that time deeply rooted in the life of the people.

[1] Günter (H.), *Die christliche Legende des Abendlandes* (Heidelberg, 1910), p. 135.

JUDAISM AND CHRISTIANITY IN THE MIDDLE OF THE THIRD CENTURY

I

RABBI SIMON BEN LAḲISH, who taught in Tiberias about 250 C.E., once raised his voice on behalf of the פושעי ישראל, Jewish transgressors, or apostates. Neither the occasion nor the meaning of his defence of these peculiar people has been properly investigated, and yet there can be no doubt that, for more than one reason, it deserves examination. In attempting to do so I have no apologetic purpose, but hope to contribute some details which should throw light on the darkness covering the relations between early Christianity and Judaism.

Let us first take the saying of R. Simon ben Laḳish.[1] It reads: אין אור של גיהנם שולטת בפושעי ישראל קל וחומר ממזבח הזהב, מה מזבח הזהב שאין עליו אלא כעובי דינר זהב כמה שנים אין האור שולטת בו, פושעי ישראל שמלאין מצות כרמון דכתיב כפלח הרמון רקתך, אל תקרי רקתך אלא רקנין שבך על אחת כמה וכמה: The fire of Gehenna has no dominion over the Jewish apostates. This is a conclusion *a minori ad majus*. If for so many years the fire had no power over the golden altar which did not contain more gold than the thickness of a *dinar*, how much more the Jewish apostates, who are as full of Miṣwot (commandments) as a pomegranate, as it is written:[2] 'Thy temples are like a piece of pomegranate!' i.e. the empty ones in Israel are full of observances; consequently Gehenna cannot have power over them.

What induced this teacher to exempt the apostates from the fire of Hell? Where did these apostates 'full of observances like a pomegranate' live and flourish? What does

[1]. B Ḥag. 27a, B. 'Erubin 19a.
[2] Cant. 4. 3. The preacher understood by רקתך 'the empty one', as in Cant. R. ad loc.: הריקן שבכם רצוף מצות כרמון הזה ואין צריך לומר מבעד לצמתך על הצנועין והמצומתין שבכם.

Rabbinic literature record of these apostates in other sources and places? Finally, can one locate them in literary sources outside Jewish literature? These questions involve more than an idle inquiry into a more or less uninteresting episode of the past. They concern certain religious movements and developments, the attitude of the Rabbis towards which are not without significance, and which should serve as guidance in the problems facing us at present.

To begin with, there are many references, favourable and unfavourable, to the *Posh'e Israel* in Jewish literature. The author of Ps. 51. 15 aims at teaching transgressors (פושעים) God's ways, and hopes to convert sinners (חטאים). Sinners and transgressors form a group. In the book of the prophet Isaiah (1. 28) they are included in the company of those that forsake the Lord (עוזבי ה'). Ps. 37. 38 groups them together with the wicked (רשעים). Both are opposed to the righteous mentioned in the next verse. Similarly in Hos. 14. 10. We can, however, derive from the Bible only very scanty information about the nature of these different groups. In the period of the Hasmoneans the פושעי בתורה, the transgressors against the Torah, must have been well-known, highly detested figures in the then small commonwealth of Judea.[1] The school of Hillel opened the gates of the schools to all who longed to enter, for there had been many transgressors in Israel who, through learning, drew nearer to the Torah and became ancestors of pious and righteous men.[2] The schools of Hillel and Shammai also on another occasion discussed the final destiny of the *Posh'e Israel*[3] It is remarkable that R. Simon ben Laḳish seems to contradict unequivocally the views of those schools, who condemn them to Gehenna, when he says: 'Gehenna has no rule over them!' Further, they do not draw a line between פושעי ישראל and פושעי או"ה, Jewish and Gentile apostates.

---

[1] 1 Macc. 14. 14; 2 Macc. 6. 21.
[2] Abot R. Nathan 2. 9.
[3] B. R.H. 17a, Tosefta Sanh. ch. 13. 3; Abot R. Nathan 1. 41.

The same designations occur in a sentence of R. Eliezer ben Hyrcanus.[1] Finally, the apostates together with the Minim figure in the special benediction of the 'Amidah, which similarly proves the existence of these people in the first century.[2] Apart from the bare names of these *Posh'e Israel* and *Posh'e ummot ha-'olam*, very little information can be gained from our sources.

The school of Hillel draws a line between these Jewish and Gentile elements on one side, and the Minim, informers, Epicureans, those who deny the Torah and the belief in the resurrection, those who separated from the ways of the community, those who spread terror in the land of the living, and, finally, sinners like Jeroboam b. Nebat, on the other side. The *Posh'e Israel* must therefore be distinguished from these eight more serious and dangerous categories of sinners. None of the characteristic faults and shortcomings of these eight groups applies to the transgressors. They are neither Minim in any sense, nor informers on their fellow men. They do not belong to antinomian circles, they do believe in the Torah and resurrection, and are members of the local synagogues and communities, they do not terrorize their fellow men in the land of the living, nor do they preach new creeds and entice people to idol-worship. It would be tempting, if space would permit such an attempt, to depict here the wretched social and religious conditions prevailing in the first century of the Current Era which provided the occasion for this Baraita. In this chapter, however, I limit myself to the Jewish transgressors.

In the first half of the third century, at least in Babylon, the meaning of פושעי ישראל בגופן and פושעי אומות העולם בגופן was not understood by the students of the Baraita, and they asked their teachers for the meaning of these two terms. Rab interprets the former by referring to a man (קרקפתא, lit. a skull, head of a man) who does not put

---

[1] Tos. Sanh. ed. Zuckermandel 434; B. Sanh. 105a.
[2] J. Ta'anit 65c.

on phylacteries, and the latter by referring to a Gentile
who lives in sin (i.e. an immoral life; עבירה, κατ᾽ ἐξοχήν, is
immorality). Though the leader of the school of Sura does
not exaggerate the importance of the law and observance
of Tefillin, it is surprising that he should blame the transgressor for nothing but the transgression of this one law.

The author of the Seder 'Olam Rabba, however, could
not have agreed with Rab's opinion when he defined the
term פושעי ישראל; for he identified them, as we have done,
with people who transgress the Miṣwot, or, according to
a Geniza fragment, who transgress Torah and Miṣwot.[1]
This authority thus judges the transgressors more harshly
than Rab. The view of Seder 'Olam Rabba differs from
the Tosefta in other respects also. The heretics of the alternative group include besides the Minim, Epicureans, and
those who deny resurrection, the following new sets:
apostates (משומדים), blasphemers, Boethuseans, those who
despise the festivals, and those who say that the Torah is
not revealed from heaven. The last-named can be identified
with those who deny the Torah in the Baraita. There
remain merely the informers unaccounted for. Some
manuscripts of the Seder 'Olam have, in fact, the מסורות.[2]
On the other hand, the Tosefta has *Meshummadim*, who
are missing in the Baraita.[3] Anyhow, all texts agree that the
פושעי ישראל have to be distinguished from the others. Yet
even they are here temporarily subjected to the pains of
Gehenna.

R. Simon ben Laḳish, as we have seen, vehemently
repudiated this teaching. Surely he could not have done
so without some cogent reasons, and for some weighty
consideration. Was he the only one who in his independence
of judgement stood aloof from his contemporaries? He is
not the only one who judged so leniently, and showed signs

[1] Seder 'Olam R. ch. 3, cf. ed. A. Marx, p. 9.
[2] Ibid., p. 9, MSS. O and C.
[3] Ed. Zuckermandel 434, l. 21.

of otherwise unusual tolerance. R. Simon the Pious (חסידא),
who most probably lived in the age of R. Simon ben
Laḳish, said: 'Every fast day the service of which is not
attended by the פושעי ישראל is not a proper fast day.'[1]
Homiletically one can twist this sentence into different
meanings,[2] historically it must be taken at its face value.
The 'transgressors' have to join, or to be admitted to, the
services held on public fast days. There, again, they are
considered as belonging to the community in spite of their
faults and blunders. Who and what are they?

One of their dogmas was that the Prophets and Hagiographa were not parts of the Torah, and they did not believe
in them.[3] Secondly, they are depicted by contemporary
preachers, skilled in colouring Biblical narratives and
events with the happenings and experiences of their own
day, as indifferent to the fate of their nation and inclined
to assimilate with their surroundings. They keep the law
of circumcision, but they walk according to the statutes of
the Gentiles.[4] This points to assimilation. Another indication of their indifference is in the next passage, which says
that there were פושעים in Israel who got hold of Egyptian
patrons, acquired fame, wealth, and honour, and consequently did not care to leave Egypt with their brethren.[5]
Thirdly, a complaint is made that these people discourage
or weaken Israel in the performance of the Miṣwot.[6]

---

[1] B. Keritut 6b: כל תענית שאין בה מפושעי ישראל אינה תענית שהרי חלבנה
ריחה רע ומנאה הכתוב עם סממני הקטרת. Cf. Maḥzor Vitry, p. 45, reads
מפריצי ישראל, cf. also Tos. Giṭṭin 19a, Ginzberg, *Geonica*, ii. 379.

[2] Cf. Wolf Jawitz, תולדות ישראל iii, p. 93.

[3] M. Tanḥ. ed. Buber, 5. 19: פושעי ישראל אומרים שהנביאים
והכתובים אינן תורה ואין אנו מאמינים בהם; also *Pugio fidei*, p. 702. Ginzberg, *MGWJ* 1913, p. 675, n. 2, rightly saw that the Haggadist did not have
Samaritans in mind; it will be seen in the course of this essay that there is no
reference to Sadducees either.

[4] Tanḥ. ed. Frankfort a. O. 22a: כופרים ופושעי ישראל והלכו בחקת הגוים
והם מולין.

[5] Exod. R. 19; Tanḥ., f. 74a.

[6] M. Cant. ed. Grünhut, 10a: שהיו מרפין ידיהם של ישראל מן המצות של
תורה.

Finally, they laugh and mock at the Messiah, who spends his time in prison.[1] Occasionally, it is reported that they deny the existence of God.[2] It is, however, doubtful whether such statements are to be taken literally, and if so, whether the report is not exaggerated or biased.

This doubt arises partly out of the attitude taken by men of the type of R. Simon ben Lakish and R. Simon the Pious, as shown earlier, and partly from other statements in favour of these transgressors. An anonymous preacher in expounding Ps. 31. 24 saw in the 'faithful, whom God preserves' our *Posh'e Israel*, who reluctantly utter their Amen, in fact they say: 'Blessed be He who revives the dead.'[3] Their chief doctrine was, therefore, belief in the resurrection, a belief which must have been exceedingly pleasing to the ears and minds of the Rabbis. They further firmly believed and eagerly expected the redemption of Israel, and set great hopes on the rebuilding of Jerusalem. They repeated the Eighteen Benedictions, but whether or not they understood the same things, the same ways and modes of salvation, and the New Jerusalem, we will leave on one side for the present. As a matter of fact, it is recorded that they repaired morning and evening to the Synagogue.[4] The question is seriously discussed whether sacrifices can be accepted from them, and the decision is in the affirmative.[5] A certain פושע ישראל[6] was interrogated by Nekyomanteia[7] together with Titus and Balaam, the representatives of Rome and Gnosticism, as to the attitude one should take or

---

[1] Pes. R. 159b.

[2] M. Ps. 7b: ‏פושעי ישראל שכפרו בהקב״ה‎.

[3] M. Ps. 240: ‏אמונים נוצר אל, אלו פושעי ישראל שהם עונים אמן בעל כרחם‎ ‏באמונה ואומרים ברוך מחיה המתים‎. Cf. Marmorstein, *Religionsgeschichtliche Studien*, i. 28, note, where I read ‏בכל כחם‎, 'fervently'.

[4] Cf. Yalkut Shim'oni's reading 88c.

[5] B. Hullin 5a, 'Erubin 69b, Lev. R. ch. 2.

[6] B. Gittin 57a; cf. M. Friedmann, *Onkelos und Akylos*, p. 97, who erroneously identifies the *Posh'e Israel* with Jesus.

[7] Cf. Marmorstein, 'Die Nachrichten über Nekyomanteia in der altrabbinischen Literatur', in *Zeitsch. für Neutest. Wissenschaft*, xxii (1923), 290–304.

manifest towards Jews. Questioned as to who is honoured in heaven and whether he should become a Jew, he answered: 'Seek their good, and avoid their evil, for he who touches them is as if he had sinned against God',[1] thus displaying a remarkably friendly spirit towards Jews and Judaism.

To sum up, we see that there were friendly and unfriendly views taken of these transgressors; they displayed certain virtues, and yet had shown peculiarities which alienated the Rabbis from them; they surely did not give up their intimacy with the Synagogue, yet they loosened the tie of unity which held Jews together all over the world and through the ages. In other words we find here in the third century a peculiar sect of Jews who retain some laudable characteristics of Jewish religion and life, and yet with one foot stand outside the camp.

II

This material, on which our knowledge of the *Posh'e Israel* rests, was collected by the present writer more than twenty years ago.[2] I suggested then that they represent Jews by origin and customs, who believed in Jesus. Since then I have searched in Jewish and Christian sources, and examined my thesis anew. I have found that the key to the understanding of these problems must be sought in external sources and that the writings of the Church of the first three centuries which hail from the East throw light on the subject.

I studied first the *Clementine Homilies* and *Recognitions* which revealed to me the *Posh'e Israel* in their true character. Apart from the fact that the romance in which the Clementine writings are dressed is the common property of Judaism and Christianity,[3] they possess many Jewish

[1] For the idea, cf. Mekhilta 39a, Sifre Num. § 84, ed. Horowitz, p. 81.
[2] *Religionsgeschichtliche Studien*, i. 26–35.
[3] Cf. the relations of the two stories in my article referred to above, p. 184, n. 7.

elements, and betray Jewish influence and Jewish workman-
ship. Jews and Judaism, Jewish lore and rite, Jewish thought
and life, are the beginning and the end of the Clementines.
It is worthy of note that these literary documents prefer
the name 'Hebrew',[1] whilst Rabbinic sources throughout
favour the term 'Israel' and only occasionally use the name
'Yehudi', mostly in Aramaic fragments or when Gentiles
are speaking of Jews. In the Clementines Mosaism and
Christianity are identical, Moses and Jesus are the only
true prophets. There is no suggestion of the abrogation of
the law, as taught by Barnabas and Paul. One of the greatest
New Testament and patristic scholars of Germany, Prof.
Karl Schmidt, says in his recent work on the Clementines:[2]
'In der gesamten kirchlichen Literatur werden wir verge-
bens nach derartigen Gedanken über die Gleichwertigkeit
des mosaischen Glaubens und des Christentums suchen.'
This assertion is amply borne out by what we are told of
these Jewish Christians. They adhere to the decree of the
Apostles as to the dietary laws and perform the rite of circumcision. They gather in Jerusalem on the Jewish Passover.
Jerusalem is the centre of their unity.[3] They keep the seventh
day, do not travel or make fire. *Quid est ergo, quod nullum
Judaeorum in illa die cogit genesis aut iter agere aut aedificare
aut vendere aliquid aut emere.*[4] The Ps. Clementines lay
much stress on a *propria quaedam nostrae religionis observantia, quae non tam imponitur hominibus, quam proprie ab
unoquoque deum colenti causae puritatis expetitur.*[5] They

---

[1] Cf. *Rec.* 4. 5, *Hom.* 8. 5 f.: What, therefore, was a peculiar gift from God
towards the nation of the *Hebrews*, &c. Since both to the *Hebrews* and to those
who are called from the Gentiles, &c. Neither, therefore, are the *Hebrews*
condemned on account of their ignorance of Jesus, &c.

[2] *Studien zu den Pseudo-Clementinen, Texte und Untersuchungen*, xlvi. 1
(Leipzig, 1930), 251. I take this opportunity to express my deep indebtedness
and sincere gratitude to this scholar for the help which I derived from his
excellent work. I trust that by my treatment of the Rabbinic material his
theory as to the origin and date of the Pseudo-Clementines will be held to be
verified.

[3] Cf. *Rec.* 1. 44, further *Rec.* 1. 10 = *Hom.* 1. 13. Schmidt, l.c. 324.

[4] *Rec.* 9. 28.   [5] Ibid. 6. 10 f., *Hom.* 11. 28.

observed *puritas*, first of all according to the law of Leviticus (*ne menstruatae mulieri misceatur*), secondly, *etiam corpus aqua diluere*, and thirdly the *observantia castimoniae*. They lived and thought as Jews, and were attacked by their fellow-Christians as Jews, and by Jews as apostates. Hence their ambiguous position!

III

Of a totally different stamp is the Syriac Didascalia which preserved a number of the most hostile attacks of the 'Catholic Church' against Jews who believed in Christ but could not sever their Jewish connexions. The Didascalia appeals to Jewish-Christians not to be guided by the Jewish calendar and not to celebrate the Passover on the fourteenth of Nisan.[1] They should not imitate the ways of the Jews as far as the observance of the Sabbath goes.[2] The writer dishes up old[3] objections against the Sabbath: Why did the saints of old not observe the Sabbath? Why does God Himself not keep the Sabbath? He is mightily upset and grieved that men and women in certain unnecessary cases perform their ritual bath[4] or that Jewesses keep away from places of worship during the seven days of the menses.[5] The latter custom prevailed among Jews for many centuries and is still observed in many countries by non-Jews as well.[6]

Yet there were also some ideas common to the Jewish writers of the Ps. Clementines and the Gentile writers of the Didascalia. The latter, for instance, urge the Jews to give up their Jewish practices, e.g. ritual bathing and the dietary laws, to which they still cling,[7] for only the Deca-

---

[1] Cf. Achelis-Flemming 110. 10; 114. 10.

[2] Ibid., 113. 12 ff.

[3] Cf. Marmorstein, 'Juden und Judenthum in der Altercatio Simonis Judaei et Theophili Christiani', in *Theologisch Tijdschrift*, xlix. 360–83.

[4] 139. 1 ff.; 142. 1.

[5] 139. 25 ff.

[6] Cf. Marmorstein, 'Spuren karäischen Einflusses in der gaonäischen Halacha', in *Schwarz-Festschrift* (Vienna, 1917), p. 460 f.

[7] Didasc. ch. 26.

logue is binding, the rest of the Torah was given as a
temporary law, as a punishment for the making of the
Golden Calf, and was abolished with the advent of the true
Prophet. The remainder of the Law is the ' Second Legislation', the *Deuterosis*, which is a heavy burden. This is one
of the Didascalia's pet ideas. Now the term Repetition of the
Law was not known to the Clementine writers, but they
seem to have cherished similar ideas. They speak of the true
prophet, meaning Jesus. All the other prophets are not true
at all. Consequently all the Prophets and Hagiographa are
rejected and even parts of the Pentateuch, for example, the
sacrifices, are objected to. The whole institution of sacrifices
is explained as a concession of Moses to his weak contemporaries, who built the Golden Calf, demonstrating thereby
that they were too much contaminated by Egyptian cults
and examples, of which they could not rid themselves.[1] A
similar idea is represented in the Haggadah by R. Levi,[2] who
was somewhat younger than the probable date of the Ps.
Clementines' source. These points the *Posh'e Israel* shared
with the Gentile-Christians. No wonder that even their zeal
and loyalty to Jewish life and ritual were looked upon as
half-hearted by the majority, and as genuine or wholly
worthy by only a few.

The Didascalia was written with the specific purpose of
frightening away Jewish-Christians from Jewish practices
and usages. Owing to this tendency Jews and Judaism fare

---

[1] *Rec.* 1. 35 ff. Meantime when Moses, the faithful and wise steward,
perceived that the vice of sacrificing to idols had been deeply ingrained into
the people from their association with the Egyptians, and that the root of the
evil could not be extracted from them, he allowed them indeed to sacrifice,
but permitted it to be done only to God, that by some such means he might
cut off one half of the deeply ingrained evil, leaving the other half to be corrected by another, and at a future time.

[2] Lev. R. 22. 5: משל לבן מלך שנם לבו עליו והיה למד לאכול בשר נבלות
 וטרפות אמר המלך זה יהיה תדיר על שולחני ומעצמו הוא נדור, כך לפי שהיו
ישראל להוטים אחרי ע״ז במצרים והיו מביאים קרבניהם לשעירים וכו׳ .... יהיו
מקריבין לפני בכל עת קרבנותיהו באוהל מועד ויהיו נפ־שין מע״ז והם ניצולים.
Cf. also Maimonides, Moreh iii. 32, cf. I. Oppenheim, *Haasif*, vi (1894), 102.

rather badly in that work. The author, whosoever he might
have been, is in many instances indebted to Jewish,
especially Rabbinic, teaching. Korah is depicted as loving
pre-eminence, coveting the High-Priesthood, and cavilling
at Moses' heathen wife, i.e. the Ethiopian.[1] Most probably
the Didascalia is here indebted to some Gnostic critic, who
took the part of Korah, and sided against Aaron.[2] For the
view that Manasseh's sins were forgiven, one can likewise
find authority in the Haggadah of R. Judah ben Ilai' of the
second, or of R. Yoḥanan b. Nappaḥa of the third century.[3]
The admonition to Christians not to let their hair grow,
but to cut it,[4] has a striking parallel in a Baraita which
declares that letting one's hair or finger-nails grow brings
man into trouble or leads to worry.[5] Didascalia as well as
some of the Rabbis at some periods evince hostile sentiments towards the books of the heathen.[6] No inference can
be drawn from parallels between Didascalia and the
Rabbis in ethical and religious views, for they may have
formed them independently, or these may go back to common experience or principles. Thus, when both teach that
one should honour one's master as one honours God,[7]
that sin brings forth sin,[8] that man should practise repentance, and live a clean life for he does not know the day of

---

[1] Didasc. ch. 23; cf. Tanḥ. ed. Buber, 4. 96; ibid., p. 85; Ps. Jonathan,
Num. 12. 1; Book of Yashar, ch. 46, and Chronicles of Yeraḥmeel, transl.
by M. Gaster, London, 1899, pp. 114 f. About Aaron's idolatry, R. Eleazar
ben Pedat, B. Sanh. 7a; R. Jeremiah, Tanḥ. ed. Frankfort a. O. 124b;
Exod. R. 37. 2.

[2] Cf. Irenaeus, *Contra haereses*, i. 31; my remarks *REJ* liv. 190, and 'The
Background of the Haggadah' [*supra* p. 11].

[3] Didasc. ch. 2, M Sanh. 11. 1 and parall. B. Sanh. 103a; cf. also Lev. R.
17, Num. R. ch. 14.

[4] Didasc. ch. 2.

[5] *Pirḳe Rabbenu ha-Ḳadosh*, ed. Grünhut ספר הליקוטים iii. 18, p. 40.
MS. Br. Mus. Add. 22092, 133b. S. Krauss, *Talmudische Archäologie*, i. 191
and note p. 643 overlooked this passage.

[6] Ch. 2, cf. Joel, M., *Blicke in die Religionsgeschichte*, i. 6.

[7] Didasc. ch. 9, cf. R. Eleazar b. Shamua', Abot 4. 12, B. Ned. 41b, B.
Pesaḥim 22b, cf. also Didache 4. 1.

[8] Didasc. ch. 6, cf. Ben Azzai, Abot 4. 2, or the well-known phrase
נעשה לו כהיתר or הותרה הרצועה.

his departure from this world,[1] that a father should teach his son a handicraft which is suitable and leads to the fear of God,[2] this proves nothing more than that there are similarities between the Didascalia and the Rabbis. It is not impossible that the writer of the Didascalia was born a Jew, and as such indebted to the Rabbis in more than one instance. There are many other striking coincidences between the two groups,[3] and it is of some importance for the date of the Didascalia that the similarities can be traced back to Tannaitic material, though the question of priority cannot be treated here. What we have to note is that the agreement is in small matters, in trifles and petty points; this only throws into relief the gulf between them in vital matters, when the author of the Didascalia comes to grips with problems which really matter, with questions of life and death, of being or not being.

The writer, who may or may not have sat at the feet of the masters of Usha or Sepphoris, Tiberias or Meron, finds cruel pleasure in teasing and taunting his poor fellow congregants with the remark that their brethren are a God-forsaken nation.[4] He was not the first to spread this cruel doctrine, and not the last. This teaching is one of the worst fruits of Paul's activity, which has embittered the relations

[1] Didasc. ch. 6, cf. R. Eliezer, Abot 2. 10, B. Sabb. 153a, cf. also Marcus Aurelius xii. 69.

[2] Didasc. ch. 22, cf. the views of R. Judah b. Ilai' and of R. Meir on this subject J. Kid. 4. 12, B. Kid. 82b.

[3] Women have to cover their head, Didasc. ch. 3, cf. Sifre Num. § 11, B. Ket. 72a, B. Yoma 47a, J. Yoma 1. 1, Horayot 3. 3, Pesiḳta, Buber 174a, Num. R. 2. 22, cf. 1 Cor. 11. 3–15. Here again Krauss, *Talmd. Arch.* i. 195 and 652, has to be corrected. One should not go to heathen courts, or receive the testimony of heathen, Didasc. ch. 11. Cf. Mekhilta of MRSbY, ed. Hoffman, p. 112. Didasc. ch. 13 does not like people going to the theatre and circus; the same view is expressed by R. Meir, B. A.Z. 18b.

[4] Didasc. ch. 24, 'God has left the nation and has filled the Church and has considered her the Mount of his habitation and the throne of glory, and the house of exaltation.' Ibid. 23, 'God has removed and forsaken the nation, as it is written in Isaiah, that he hath forsaken the people of the house of Jacob and Jerusalem is fallen, and their tongues are in iniquity, and they have obeyed not the Lord, and behold, your house is left unto you desolate.'

between Jews and Gentiles, Judaism and Christianity, up to this day.[1]

This taunt was born in the pagan mind at the sight of the numerous misfortunes and humiliations of the Jews, even before the final catastrophe in the year 70 C.E., and seemed to receive added justification from the destruction of the Temple and the devastation of the land. Cicero merely asserts that 'while Jerusalem was flourishing, while the Jews were in a peaceful state, still the religious ceremonies and observances were much at variance with the splendour of this Empire, the dignity of our name, and the institutions of our ancestors. And they are the more odious to us now because that nation has shown by arms what its feelings were to our supremacy. How beloved of the immortal gods that nation was, is proved by the fact that it has been defeated, that its revenues have been farmed out, and that it is reduced to a state of subjection.'[2] Jews were consequently hated and forsaken by the gods. This talk, however, impressed the victims very little and did not disturb them. Celsus[3] levels against both Jews and Christians the taunt that the God of both must be very weak in allowing the slaughter of the whole military youth of His people, and the burning of His city. Further he says:[4] 'It is quite improbable that they are specially loved by God, or more beloved than others, or that special angels descended to them from Heaven, &c. For we saw with our own eyes what advantages, what preferences they and their country received!' Origen tells us[5] that Celsus foretold the ruin

---

[1] Cf. as to the early history of this teaching, N. Bonvetsch, *Der Schrift-beweis für die Kirche aus den Heiden als das wahre Israel bis auf Hippolyt*, pp. 1 ff. Further, I. C. Mathes, *De Joden en het Christendom* (Amsterdam, 1913), 1–10, and A. Marmorstein, 'L'épitre de Barnabe et la polémique juive', *REJ* lx (1910), 213–20.

[2] *Pro Flacc.* 28, Oxford text, § 68: 'Quam cara dis immortalibus esset docuit, quod est victa, quod elocata, quod serva facta'; cf. also Posidonius of Apamea in Diodor Sic. 34. 1, Photius, p. 324, and Tacitus, *Hist.* 5. 8.

[3] Origen, *Contra Celsum*, iv. 73.

[4] Ibid. v. 41.

[5] Ibid. vi. 80.

of the Jews, as about to take place in the near future. He speaks in the manner of a prophet foretelling their fate; overlooking all the care which God bestowed upon the Jews, and the revered laws and institutions which He handed down to them; he fails to notice that through their defeat the welfare of the pagans is increased. Celsus is mocking and laughing at God and His followers: Why does He not help you (Christians) and the Jews?[1] Rabbinic sources re-echo similar reproaches and upbraiding on the part of pagans. R. Gamaliel II has a dialogue with a philosopher, who proves from Hos. 5. 6 that God will never return to Israel.[2] R. Joshua ben Ḥananya has a pantomimic dispute with an Epicurean about Israel's being forsaken.[3] Titus is credited with the saying that the God of the Jews has become old and weak, therefore He is unable to help them.[4] The defeats in 70 C.E. and 135 C.E. certainly appeared to the pagan mind as a striking and undeniable proof that the God of the Jews had lost His strength, that He had forsaken His people, as we read in the Dialogue of Tinaeus Rufus with R. Akiba.[5] There must have been theologians who taught that the withdrawal from Israel was merely a temporary one.[6] Paul and Barnabas adopted and adapted this dogma. They based their arguments on passages in the prophets which speak of Israel in terms of disfavour or condemnation. Paul[7] refers to Hos. 2. 25, and Barnabas[8] to the story of the Golden Calf in order to teach that Israel was supplanted by the new Israel, or was forsaken by God, and that Israel never entered the covenant with God. The consequences of these teachings we see before us in the Didascalia. It was the teachers of the third century who felt their danger most keenly. The Tannaitic Haggadah, it

---

[1] Origen, *Contra Celsum*, viii. 39 and 69.

[2] Cf. B. Yebamot 102b, Midr. Ps. 10, Midrash Haggadah Lev. 26. 9, Bacher, *Ag. der Tannaiten*, i. 82. 6. A. Büchler, 'Die Minim von Sepphoris und Tiberias', Cohen's *Judaica* (Berlin, 1912), 280.

[3] Cf. B. Ḥag. 5b.

[4] Gen. R. 10. 8 and parall.

[5] B. B.B. 10a.

[6] Eth. Enoch 90. 28 f.

[7] Rom. 9. 25 f.

[8] Epistle, ch. 9.

is true, could not ignore the taunt that Israel was forsaken,[1]
yet it was by no means so systematically and so often disputed by its teachers as in the age of the Amoraim.[2] Most
of the great apologists for Judaism in the third century
dwell on the doctrine of God's unchangeable love for Israel
on one side, and strongly repudiate on the other side the
idea of Israel being forsaken by God. While doing so, they
mention the latter view expressly as an assertion of the
nations of the world, who are none else but Gentile
Christians. The names of R. Hoshaya,[3] R. Jonathan b.
Eliezer,[4] R. Yannai,[5] Rab,[6] R. Joshua ben Levi,[7] R. Yo-

[1] Cf. esp. Büchler, op. cit., p. 279 as to R. Meir, p. 280 as to R. Joshua
b. Korḥa, p. 281 as to Beruria the wife of R. Meir.

[2] Besides the Didascalia one ought to mention here also the *Carmen
Apologeticum* of Commodian vv. 346–50, where this teaching is so emphati-
cally underlined. Commodian must have written in Jewish surroundings.
The date is approximately settled, the origin still obscure.

[3] A contemporary of the Church Father Origen who lived in Caesarea,
B. Pes. 87b: א״ר אושעיא מאי דכתיב צדקות פרזונו בישראל צדקה עשה הקב״ה
בישראל שפזרן לבין האומות. The exile is not a sign of Israel's rejection on
God's part, but of God's love and justice.

[4] Ag. Ber. ed. Buber, ch. 8, p. 22: א״ר שמואל בר נחמני א״ר יונתן איש
הבירה אמרו ישראל לאו״ה אומר אני לכם במה אנו מתנחמין ולמה אנו
יכולים לעמוד בזעפו, מפני שמכה אותנו וחוזר מיד ובורא אותנו בריה
חדשה וכן ישעיה אומר (42. 24) מי נתן למשסה יעקב, הרי כלו הרי נבוזז, אלא
חוזר מיד ובוראם בריה חדשה, ומה כתיב אחריו (43. 1) ועתה כה אמר ד׳
בוראך יעקב, לפיכך אמרו ישראל בדבר זה אנו רואין ומתנחמין שבורא
אותנו מיד [צ׳ להוסיף בריה חדשה] זה הוא שאומר ירמיה זאת אשיב אל לבי
(Lam. 3. 21). Israel's reply to the taunt of the nations is: God smites us, and
creates us as a new creature. The latter term may be used purposely as a
retort against the Epistle to the Romans.

[5] Cf. Midr. Ps., ed. Buber, ch. 36. 11.

[6] B. Ta'anith 20a: אמר ר׳ יהודה אמר רב לברכה כנדה מה נדה יש לה היתר
אף ירושלים יש לה תקנה, כאלמנה ולא אלמנה ממש אלא כאשה שהלך בעלה
למדינת הים ודעתו לחזור עליה. Cf. also his saying B. Ber. 3a, God mourns
because of Israel's absence and affliction.

[7] B. Soṭah 38b, Pes. 85b, Pes. Rabbati 85b: אפילו מחיצה של ברזל אינה
מפסקת בין ישראל לאביהם שבשמים :B. Menaḥot 53b אמר ר׳ יהושע בן לוי למה
נמשלו ישראל לזית לומר לך מה זית אין עליו נושרין, לא בימות החמה ולא בימות
.Cant הגשמים אף ישראל אין להם בטילה עולמית לא בעוה״ז ולא בעוה״ב
R. 1. 5: ר׳ ברכיה וריב״ל למה נמשלו ישראל לנקבה, — כך ישראל משתעבדין
ונגאלין משתעבדין ונגאלין וחוזרין ונגאלין ושוב אין משתעבדין לעולם.

ḥanan,[1] R. Simon ben Laḳish,[2] R. Ḥama b. Ḥanina,[3] R. Isaac,[4] R. Levi,[5] R. Samuel b. Naḥmani,[6] and R. Abba b. Kahana[7] are witnesses for the frequency with which Jewish teachers took up the defence against the charge of the Didascalia.

Even more eloquent is the anonymous Haggadah on this question. The scoffers declare: מי שהגלה אתכם עוד אין משיב אתכם (He who exiled you will never bring you back, i.e. to Jerusalem).[8] These people base their idea on the Scriptures, e.g. Lam. 4. 16. In this connexion a religious persecution is spoken of, forbidding circumcision, Sabbath observance, and the reading of the Law, probably earlier than the prohibitions of Justinian.[9] Israel was accompanied by God into exile.[10] Job 39. 27 is a reply to those who assert that the Temple will never be built again.[11] A preacher expounded Ps. 3. 3 f. applying the verses to Israel. The

---

[1] Lev. R. ch. 6. 5 נתנו ביניהם שאינו (compromises) אמר ר' יוחנן קופרמסאות; Pesiḳta, ed. Buber, 142a ר' אחא בש"ר יוחנן כופר בהם והם אינם כופרים בו. הרבה צדיקים העמידה בחורבנה יותר מצדיקים שהעמידה לי בבנינה. Israel produced more righteous men after the destruction of the Temple than before. How can such a nation be forsaken?

[2] God cares for Israel even in distress and in poverty, J. Ber. 13b, and Midr. Ps. 4. 2. God's love to Israel is expressed by three verbs: דבק, חשק, and חפץ, Gen. R. 80, M. Ps. 22. 22.

[3] B. Ber. 32a: אלמלא שלש מקראות הללו נתמוטטו רגליהם של שונאי ישראל. Cf. also B. Sukkah 52b; the three passages are Mic. 4. 6, Jer. 18. 6, Ezek. 36, 26.

[4] Eccles. R. 1. 4: ישראל עומד לעולם, Midr. Ps. 36. 11, Pesiḳta 165a, Cant. R. 1. 6: אור מוני לישראל ואומרים אומה זו המירה כבודם. Cf. Marmorstein, Rel. Studien i. 17. God is with Israel even in exile, Exod. R. 15. 16. The idea occurs also in the Haggadah of the Tannaim M. Cant. ed. Grünhut 9b.

[5] Pes. R. 85b, Cant. R. 7. 1.

[6] Lev. R. 17, 4, Cant. R. 8. 7, Pes. R. 15b.

[7] Lam. R. 66b, Pes. (ed. Buber), 139b.

[8] Midr. Ps. (ed. Buber), p. 495.

[9] Cf. Marmorstein, 'Les Persécutions religieuses à l'époque de R. Johanan b. Nappacha', REJ lxxvii (1923), 166–77, further, דורו של ר' יוחנן ואותות המשיח Tarbiz, iii (1932), pp. 161–80; cf., however, Graetz, Geschichte, v, 3rd ed., pp. 20 f.

[10] Pes. R. 141a: מיד אמר להם הקב"ה אני אהיה זיווגך ואני אעלה אתכם. Cf. also ibid., 143b, 144a, 162a.

[11] Pes. R. 190b: שאומרים הן שאמר הקב"ה אני בונה ביהמ"ק בנה אותו וחטאתם והחריבו ועוד אינו בונה.

nations of the world (i.e. רבים, the many) rejoiced when
Israel made the Golden Calf, and spoke about them, saying:
'Henceforth there is no salvation and existence left for
them!'[1] Here we meet in the Haggadah, not for the first
time, as will be shown later on, the view that Israel lost its
claim on God, and God gave Israel up on account of Israel's
sin. In a homily on Ps. 4. 3 God repeats the words of the
nations of the world who say: 'God has left them, forgotten
them, and He will never return unto them.' This argument
is not true. God has not forsaken and never will forsake
Israel.[2]

The compiler of the Midrash on Exodus uses many older
homilies and fragments of Midrashic works in which this
problem was treated at greater length. In one passage we
read: 'Israel dwelt in Zion, God was among them. When
they sinned they were cast out. Yet, when He sees that they
persevere in the performance of the commandments, then
God repents of what He wrought against Zion, and pleads
Zion's cause and contemplates the return of the exiles.'[3]
Secondly, when Israel was exiled from Jerusalem, and the
enemies carried them away in chains, then the nations of
the world said: 'God does not like this nation! as it is said:
Reprobate silver they shall call them' (Jer. 6. 30). Silver
can be melted and used for making vessels, once or twice,
or more times, but finally one breaks it and it becomes
useless; similarly, Israel was described as a fallen people
which had no hope to rise any more,[4] God having rejected

---

[1] Pes. ed. Buber 10b: אומה ששמעה מפי הקב״ה בהר סיני וכו׳ . . . יש להם
אין לאלו עמידה ולא. Pes. R. 39a reads תשועה? אין ישועתה לו באלהים סלה
ישועה. Tanḥ. Exod., Midr. Ps. ch. 3.

[2] Pes. R. 147b: מה אתם מרדפים אחר דברים של ריקנות ואומרים עזבו
הקב״ה שכחו אין שכינה חוזרת שם. Pes. (ed. Buber), 134b, M. Ps. ch. 4.

[3] Exod. R. 30. 8: כך ישראל היו בציון והקב״ה שרוי ביניהן, וכיון שחטאו
טרפה אף היא השליכה בניה עליו וכשהוא רואה לישראל שעושים מצוותיו מתנחם
על מה שעשה בציון ומבקש לה זכות וגו׳.

[4] Exod. R. 31. 10: והיו או״ה אומרים אין הקב״ה חפץ באומה זו and כן ישראל
היו אומרים להם תקומה שאין, cf. also Num. R. 16. 23, Tanḥ.
(ed Buber) iv. 71.

them. When Jeremiah heard this, he said: 'Lord of the world! hast Thou really rejected them?' (cf. Jer. 14. 19, 'Hast Thou utterly rejected Judah? Hath Thy soul loathed Zion? Why hast Thou smitten us, and there is no healing for us?'). It is to be compared to a man who was in the habit of beating his wife. Her *Shushbin* said to her husband: 'How long are you going on like that beating her? If you want to drive her away, beat her to death, if not, why do you beat her?' He says: 'Even if the whole of my palace is to be destroyed, I will not divorce her!' Thus says Jeremiah: 'If you intended to drive us away, beat us to death (cf. Lam. 5. 22), if not, why do you beat us without healing?' God replies: 'Even if I destroy my whole world I will not drive Israel away' (cf. Jer. 31. 36, 'If heaven above can be measured, and the foundation of the earth searched out beneath, I will cast off all the seed of Israel for all that they have done'). God will never sever his connexion with his people. The author of this homily must have come across missionaries in Galilee who propagated the Gospel of Israel's rejection, and of the Jews being forsaken by God, as taught in the Didascalia.

A third homilist preached on Exod. 25. 1, and, according to the way of preaching in his age, connected his text with Ps. 68. 19. He finds that the words 'that they take for me an offering' have a bearing on the verse in Psalms: 'Thou hast ascended on high, thou hast led captivity captive!' How did the preacher bring out the connexion? 'Thou hast ascended', that is Moses (cf. Exod. 19. 3 and 20. 21). 'Thou hast led captivity captive'; a king is grieved when his armies are led away captive. Thou wilt say that the same is the case with God? The text therefore continues: 'Thou hast received.' Further, when a man sells some of his property, he is grieved. (Perhaps the same happened with God?) Therefore it says: 'Gifts among men.' God said to them: I consider it as if I had given it to you as a present. 'Among the rebellious': God spake to Moses: What do

those idolators say: 'will I not return to them because they
worshipped idols' (cf. Exod. 32. 7–8, Deut. 9. 12)? No, even
if they were rebellious I do not forsake (leave) them, and I
do dwell among them, as it is said: God dwells among the
rebellious.[1]

Let us turn to another compilation of homilies on Canticles,[2] in which the compiler of the Midrash collected
many sermons on the same subject. Thus on Cant. 8. 14[3]
he comments: 'On the day the Temple was destroyed my
Beloved fled, and became like a hart. Just as a hart runs
from one end of the world to the other and returns to its
place, so Israel, even though they are scattered in the whole
world, will in future return', cf. Hos. 2. 9. Further, in a
parable to Cant. 6. 2, we read: 'Israel is like a *matrona* who
rebelled against the king and was divorced and driven out
of the king's palace. People called her the divorced queen.
She said: "It is true that the king drove me out of his
palace. Yet he did not repay me my dowry, and his name
is still on me, i.e. I bear his name." '[4] In a third place a
sermon of R. Yoḥanan[5] is concluded with Deut. 30. 9 and 3,
containing the promises of God to restore the exiles to the
Holy Land.[6]

Anti-Jewish polemics went even farther than this. 'God

---

[1] Exod. R. 33. 2: כל, עלית למרום שבית שבי, ד״א ויקחו לי תרומה הה״ד
עלויך לא היה אלא מן המרום ומשה עלה אל אלהים ומשה נגש אל הערפל שבית
שבי מלך ב״ו בשעה שחיילותיו נשבים הוא מיצר תאמר אף כאן כך ת״ל לקחת.
ובשעה שאדם מוכר הוא מיצר [תאמר אף כאן כך] ת״ל מתנות באדם. אמר להם
כך אני מעלה עליכם כאילו מתנה נתתיה לכם. אף סוררים, אמר הקב״ה למשה מה
עכו״ם אומרים שאיני חוזר עמהם על שעבדו עכו״ם שנא׳ סרו מהר, אפילו סוררים
מה עכו״ם. Instead of הן איני מניח אותם ועמהם אני דר שנא׳ אף סוררים וכו׳
one ought to read מה אומות העולם אומרין, cf. Yalḳuṭ Makhiri Psalms (ed.
Buber), p. 335, where the reading is או״ה.
[2] מדרש שיר השירים ed. Grünhut (Jerusalem, 1897).
[3] P. 48b: אף ישראל אע״פ שנתפזרו בכל העולם עתידין לחזור שנא׳ אלכה ואשובה.
[4] P. 42b, the text is fragmentary, the application missing.
[5] Cf. Pes. (ed. Buber), 139b, Pes. R. ch. 4 Lam. R.
[6] P. 21a.

hates Israel!' is a saying attributed to the nations of the
world by a teacher of the third century, R. Shemaya.[1]
They try to sow hatred between God and Israel by their
decrees and persecutions, by death and torture, yet they
are unable to extinguish the mutual love between God and
Israel.[2] These assertions of Israel's degradation and humilia-
tion correspond word for word to the words of the Didascalia. The author of this document clearly voices the feelings
and expresses the attitude of Gentile-Christianity, with a
double point, first of all against Jews, and secondly against
Jewish-Christians, the פושעי ישראל. The latter have been,
it is true, converted to the belief in Jesus. That is not
enough. They are under the curse of the Law, especially
the Repetition of the Law. Why is Israel forsaken, hated,
and rejected? On account of the Law. Paul and Barnabas
could not find words strong enough to condemn the Law.
The Law was given as a sign and as a punishment for Israel's
Golden Calf. The Didascalia follows the teaching of these
religious leaders most faithfully. Did their teaching find
adherents in the Jewish communities of Galilee, or was their
preaching restricted to the churches? Surely, the latter
was not the case, if we interpret correctly the numerous
homilies on this subject contained in the Haggadic literature.

IV

In the sermons, anonymous and otherwise, cited in the
previous chapter, we have frequently come across the idea
that the rejection of Israel was due to the sin of the Golden

---

[1] Agadat Bereshit (ed. Buber), p. 27. R. Aḥa in his name: לפי שאו״ה
מבקשין לבא על ישראל לומר שונא אותם הקב״ה נלך עליהם.
[2] Ibid., p. 164: כמה נתקעו או״ה להטיל שנאה בינו לבינינו ואין יכולין לבטל
שנאמר מים רבים לא יוכלו לכבות את האהבה אלו האומות שנמשלו כמים, כמה
או״ה הורגין בהן בישראל בשביל להחזירם מאחר הקב״ה, וכנסת ישראל אומרת
להן אין אני יכולה לכפור בו. Cf. also Midr. Psalms 15. 4, ed. Buber 117:
מים רבים אלו או״ה לכבות את האהבה זה האהבה שבין ישראל לבין הקב״ה.

Calf.[1] This view of the Didascalia was shared by the Church Fathers as well.[2] On this subject, too, there is little to be gleaned from the Tannaitic literature; either the arguments were not known to the Tannaim, or, if known, were considered of no importance whatsoever. They are concerned with Moses' action in breaking the tablets, whether he did so at the command of God, or by his own will.[3] There are some, not very numerous, sayings on this subject by Tannaim, which in style and tone differ greatly from those of the Amoraic period. Some of the former may be cited here. R. Akiba, who defended Moses for breaking the tablets,[4] seems to have pleaded also for Israel. He agrees with the school of R. Yannai, who blamed the sin on the prosperity of Israel; the abundance of gold and silver was the cause of the making of the Golden Calf.[5] R. Yose, the Galilean, remarks: 'Come and see how great is the mischief wrought by sin. Before Israel committed that sin (i.e. the Golden Calf) there were neither people with issues, nor leprous among them, but afterwards there were.'[6] In the days of the teacher of these sages, R. Eliezer b. Hyrcanus, a wise woman asked a question about the three different

[1] Cf. pp. 194, n. 4; 195, nn. 1–2; 197, n. 1.

[2] Cf. esp. Tertullian, adv. Judaeos, ch. 1; cf. Justin, Dial. ch. 21, 22, and 27; Harnack, Dogmengeschichte i. 3. 579; Diestel, Geschichte des A.T. in der christl. Kirche (Jena, 1896), 55. 'Die Hauptstrafe für diesen Abfall seien die Ceremonialgesetze.'

[3] Cf. Abot R. Nathan, ch. 2. R. Yose the Galilean, R. Judah ben Bathyra, R. Eleazar ben 'Azarya, R. Akiba, and R. Meir endeavour to explain Moses' extraordinary action in breaking the two tablets. It is a veritable apology for Moses, but the burden of the accusation against Israel, as taught by the Church from the middle of the second century and onwards, is not yet discernible.

[4] Cf. previous note: לא שבר משה את הלוחות אלא שנאמר לו מפי הגבורה שנ' ואתחפש בשני הלחות במה אדם תופס במה שיכול.

[5] Cf. B. Ber. 32a, B. Yoma 86b, B. Sanh. 102, further Tos. Yoma, ch. 4. 19, cf. also the reading in Ginzberg's Geonica, ii. 374, ll. 16 ff., where the words כדר' ינאי דאמר ר' ינאי are omitted.

[6] Sifre Num. § 1, ed. Friedmann, 1b: בוא וראה כמה קשה כחה של עבירה שער שלא פשטו ידיהם בעבירה לא היו בהם זבים ומצורעים ומשפשטו ידיהם בעבירה היו בהם זבים ומצורעים.

punishments meted out to the worshippers of the Golden Calf, but there is in it no trace of the dogma taught by the Church Fathers.[1]

Turning to the teachers of the post-Bar Kokhba period, one notices the same attitude towards this problem. R. Meir, who defended Moses in his action,[2] has a word also for Israel. They sinned whilst they were in a state of drunkenness.[3] This lame apology was rightly rejected by R. Judah b. Ilaiʿ. We may finally cite R. Simon ben Yoḥai to illustrate our observation on the distinction between the Tannaitic and the Amoraic treatment of this problem. This Tanna, on the lines of R. Yose the Galilean,[4] draws a psychological difference between Israel before the sin and after. Before they were fearless, afterwards they were frightened of Moses.[5] In the time of the Mishnah this outcry against Israel on account of the Golden Calf was still so mild and insignificant that no objection was raised to the reading and Targum of Exod. 32. 1 f. Exod. 32. 21 f. was read, but not translated.[6]

How different is the outlook and the situation in the Amoraic Haggadah! Here we again come across the same names as those whose bearers lodged a lively protest against the saying: God has forsaken, or rejected Israel. We meet R. Hoshaya,[7] R. Joshua ben Levi,[8] R. Yoḥanan,[9]

---

[1] B. Yoma 66b, Gaster, *Exempla*, No. 27, p. 20.

[2] Cf. above, p. 199, n. 3.

[3] Cant. R. 2. 13: אמרה כנסת ישראל הושלט בי יצר הרע ביין ואמרתי לעגל אלה אלהיך ישראל.   [4] Cf. p. 199, n. 6.

[5] Sifre Num. 1, p. 1b: בוא וראה מה כח עבירה קשה שעד שלא פשטו ידיהם בעבירה מה נאמר בהם ומראה כבוד ה׳ כאש אוכלת לא יראים ולא מזדעזעים משפשטו ידיהם בעבירה מה נאמר בהם וירא אהרן וכל בני ישראל והנה קרן עור פניו ויראו מגשת אליו; cf. Num. R. 7. 6.

[6] M. Meg. iv. 10, B. Meg. 25b, J. Meg. iv. 11, where, in the Talmud, different portions are assigned to the second מעשה עגל.

[7] B. Ber. 32a: משל לאדם שהיתה לו פרה כחושה ובעלת אברים האכילה כרשינין והיתה מבעטת בו א״ל מי גרם ליך שתהא מבעטת בי אלא כרשינין שהאכלתיך. The defence is on the same lines as that of R. Akiba and the school of R. Yannai, cf. above, p. 199, n. 5.

[8, 9] *See opposite page.*

R. Eleazar,[1] R. Levi,[2] R. Isaac,[3] R. Samuel b. Naḥmani,[4]

[8] Eccles. R. 4. 5, Exod. R. 41. 12, in Midr. Eccles. z. p. 100, the passage is quoted in the name of R. Simon ben Yoḥai. Yet it is more probable that R. Joshua ben Levi is its author. Moses did not move from his place until he was granted forgiveness for Israel. A similar defence is put up by R. Abbahu, B. Ber. 32a: אלמלא מקרא כתוב אי אפשר לאומרו מלמד שתפסו משה להקב״ה כאדם שהוא תופס את חבירו בבגדו ואמר לפניו רבש״ע אין אני מניחך עד שתמחול ותסלח להם. In another saying, R. Joshua ben Levi pleads: לא עשו ישראל את העגל אלא ליתן פתחון פה לבעלי תשובה. The making of the Golden Calf was not the source of a curse, i.e. the law, but of a great blessing, to provide a justification for repentant sinners. I wonder who is more human, more enlightened, Paul, Barnabas, the Church Fathers on one side, or R. Joshua ben Levi, who may have followed an older saying of R. Simon ben Yoḥai? Cf. B. A.Z. 4b, cf. also Exod. R. 46. 6.

[9] B. Ber. 32a: אמר רבי חייא בר אבא אמר ר׳ יוחנן משל לאדם אחד שהיה לו בן הרחיצו וסכו והאכילו והשקהו ותלה לו כיס על צוארו והושיבו על פתח של זונות מה יעשה אותו הבן? This apology tallies with the view cited above from the Ps. Clementines, p. 188, n. 1, and that of R. Levi, cf. p. 188, n. 2, cf. also Exod. R. 43. 8, where the same idea is expressed by R. Huna, in the name of R. Yoḥanan in a somewhat fuller and clearer manner: משל לחכם שפתח לבנו חנות של בשמים בשוק של זונות, המבוי עשה שלו, והאומנות עשתה שלו, והנער כבחור עשה שלו, יצא לתרבות רעה, בא אביו ותפסו עם הזונה התחיל האב צועק ואומר הורנך אני, היה שם אוהבו א״ל אתה איבדת את הנער ואת צועק כנגדו, הנחת כל האומניות ולא למדתו אלא בשם והנחת כל המבואות ולא פתחת לו חנות אלא בשוק של זונות, כך אמר משה רבון העולם הנחת כל העולם ולא שעבדת בניך אלא במצרים שהיו עובדים טלאים ולמדו מהם בניך ואף הם עשו העגל. A similar apology is taught by R. Abin in the name of R. Simon ben Yehozadak, Exod. R. 43. 10, the application of which reads: כך כשעשו ישראל אותו מעשה בקש הקב״ה לכלותם אמר משה רבון העולם לא ממצרים הוצאתם ממקום עע״ז ועכשיו נערים הם המתן מעט להם ו׳לך עמהם ועושין לפניך מע״ט הוי אשר הוצאת. R. Yoḥanan further asserts that God's vow was dissolved by Moses, as a scholar annuls vows of people. Hence R. Simon ben Laḳish explains the fact that Moses was called איש האלהים, the man who annulled God's vow, Exod. R. 43. 5.

[1] Cant. R. 2. 11 defends the worship of the Calf by assuming that Israel was not liable for punishment until the Law was expounded to them in the Tent of Meeting: כך אע״פ שהתורה נתנה בהר סיני לא נענשו עליה עד שנתפרש אע״פ שנתנה תורה סייג לישראל מסיני לא: להם באוהל מועד. Cf. Lev. R. 1. 10: נענשו עליה עד שנישנית באוהל מועד—כך אע״פ שנתנה תורה לישראל מסיני לא שמשם נתחייבו; cf. also Cant. R. 3. 4: נענשו עליה עד שנישנית להם באוהל מועד ישראל (anonymously), further Cant. R. 8. 2, where R. Berekhya says: א״ר ברכיה למה קוראין לסיני בית אמי שמשם נעשו ישראל כתינוק בן יומו. The idea is that the erection of the Tabernacle wiped off the sin of the Golden Calf. Thus R. Berekhya goes a step farther in the defence of the מעשה עגל.   [See pp. 202-4 for notes [2], [3], [4].

[2] R. Levi defends the deed of Israel in different ways: God forgave Israel and has not rejected his people, Lev. R. 1. 3: בן אביתר שויתר הקב״ה על ידיו מעשה העגל. Of a similar type is his saying in Lev. R. 27. 7, כל פעולות טובות ונחמות שהקב״ה עתיד לעשות עם ישראל אינם אלא בשביל פועה שפעיתם לפני בסיני ואמרתם כל אשר דבר ה' נעשה ונשמע וכו' תועבה יבחר בכם אותה תועבה שכתוב עשו להם עגל מסכה מאותו התועבה הביאו לפני קרבן. The very sacrifice shall remove the sin of the Calf. Ibid. 27. 8, after a parable of a suspected *matrona*, R. Levi quotes the saying of the nations of the world: כך אומות העולם מונין להם לישראל ואומרים להם עשיתם את העגל ובדק הקב״ה בדברים ולא מצא בהם ממש. Here R. Levi in his apologetic zeal is inclined to treat the whole crime as a meaningless suspicion. This is surely exaggerated; cf., however, Exod. R. 49. 2, שחורה אני בשור and שנ' וימירו את כבודם בתבנית שור ונאוה אני בשור, שור או כבש או עז Cant. R. 1. 15. In a third homily R. Levi preaches that God foresaw at the revelation at Sinai that Israel was going to commit that crime of idolatry, Cant. R. 1. 15: ר' פנחס בשם ר' לוי היה לפני הקב״ה שעתידים ישראל להמיר כבודו באחר שנ' וימירו כבודו שלא יהא אומרים אלו הראנו את כבודו א״ר לוי וכי לא היה גלוי. Cf. also Exod. R. 29. 4: ואת גדלו היינו מאמינים לו לפני המקום שאם הוא מראה כבודו לישראל ... שאינן יכולין לעמוד אלא צפה הקב״ה שהן עתידין לעשות עכו״ם שלא יהו אומרין וכו'. Exod. R. 41. 3. R. Phinehas b. Ḥama, in the name of R. Levi: אלא שהיה צפוי וגלוי לפני הקב״ה שעתידין ישראל אחר מ' יום לעשות העגל וכו'. Since no apology is attached to this sermon, which is somewhat surprising, most probably R. Levi elaborated an older saying. The term מקום for God corroborates this idea. There is a long sermon in which the two ideas of Israel's rejection and the sin of Israel are defended, written either by R. Levi or by R. Simon b. Lakish, cf. B. Ber. 32b; cf., however, Yalkuṭ Makhiri on Isaiah, p. 179. There Israel says before God: 'Lord of the Universe! A man marries a second wife and remembers the first one. Thou, however, hast forgotten and forsaken me!' God assures Israel that the whole universe was created for Israel's sake, how can He forget all the sacrifices of Israel in the wilderness? Since there is no forgetfulness before God perhaps He still remembers the incident of the Golden Calf. No, this is forgotten. Since there is forgetfulness before God He might have forgotten the event at Sinai? No, this I will not forget. The latter doctrine is ascribed to R. Hoshaya (cf. p. 193, n. 3), taught by R. Eleazar (cf. p. 201, n. 1).
Finally, in a homily of R. Levi we read: יסכר פיהם של או״ה שהיו אומרים לישראל שאין השכינה חוזרת אלינו לעולם שנ' רבים אומרים לנפשי וגו' אלו עד שלא עשו את העגל בא הקב״ה ושרה אצלם משכבעם עליהם אינו חוזר עליהם. Tanḥ. f. 134a. The reply is again that the building of the Temple is an eloquent proof that God has forgiven Israel. Here, again, the rejection of Israel and the incident of the Golden Calf are closely connected, as in the Didascalia.

[3] Deut. R. 1. 2: בשעה שעשו ישראל את העגל ביקש הקב״ה לכלות שונאיהן של ישראל, א״ל משה רבש״ע העגל הזה טוב הוא לסייע לך. א״ל הקב״ה מה מסייע לי? א״ל אם אתה מוריד גשמים הוא מפריח טללים אתה מוציא את הרוחות והוא מוציא את הברקים. א״ל הקב״ה אף אתה טועה בעגל? א״ל רבש״ע למה יחרה

אפך בעמך, ולישראל אמר אתם חטאתם חטאה גדולה. The sin, alleged by the nations of the world to have broken God's covenant with Israel, is not so weighty as assumed. A similar homily is given in Exod. R. 43. 6, in the name of R. Nehemiah, from a source which bears all the characteristic features of the Yelamdenu, especially אלהים as the name of God, reading: בשעה שעשו ישראל אותו מעשה עמד לו משה מפייס את האלהים אמר רבון העולם עשו לך סיוע ואתה כועס עליהם, העגל הזה יהיה מסייעך אתה מזריח את החמה והוא הלבנה, אתה הכוכבים והוא המזלות, אתה מוריד את הטל והוא משיב רוחות, אתה מוריד גשמים והוא מגדל צמחים, אמר הקב״ה משה אף אתה טועה כמותם והלא אין בו ממש א״ל אם כן למה אתה כועס על בניך הוי ה' למה יחרה אפך. Num. R. 2. 15 copies merely a part of the homily, without mentioning either the name of R. Isaac or that of R. Nehemiah: אמר לו משה זה העגל שעשו ישראל עכשיו הוא מסייעך הוא מוריד גשמים ואתה מפריח טללים א״ל הקב״ה וכי יש בו תוחלת? א״ל משה ואם אין בו ממש למה ה' יחרה אפך בעמך וכו'. Cf. also Pes. Rabbati 46a, Cant. R. on 1. 6. R. Isaac relates the following story: מעשה בקרתנית אחת שהיה לה שפחה כושית שירדה למלאת מן העין היא וחברתה אמרה לחברתה: חברתי למחר אדני מגרש את אשתו ונוטלני לאשה! אמרה לה: למה? בשביל שראה ידיה מפוחמות, אמרה לה: אי שוטה שבעולם ישמעו אזניך מה שפיך מדבר ומה אם אשתו שהיא חביבה עליו ביותר את אומרת מפני שראה ידיה מפוחמות שעה אחת רוצה לגרשה את שכולך מפוחמת ושחורה ממעי אמך כל ימיך עאכו״כ כך לפי שאו״ה מונין לישראל ואומרים אומה זו המירו כבודם שנ' וימירו את כבודם, אומרים להם לישראל ומה אם אנו לשעה כך נתחייבנו אתם עאכו״כ. Gentile-Christianity cannot reproach Israel for 'once' making an idol, since it is steeped in idolatry, cf. also a fragment of a Midrash in Jellinek's *Bet ha-Midrash*, v. 160 f.

[4] R. Samuel ben Naḥmani often reverts to this subject. He defends Israel either in the name of his teacher, or in his own name. In the name of R. Jonathan b. Eleazar he teaches, Exod. R. 43. 1: כך בשעה שעשו ישראל את העגל היה השטן עומד ומקטרג בפנים ומשה עומד מבחוץ. מה עשה משה, עמד ודחף את השטן והוציאו לחוץ ועמד במקומו. R. Samuel b. Naḥmani expounds and develops this theory even further by increasing and exaggerating the anthropomorphic tendency of the Haggadah, saying: כך בשעה שעשו ישראל אותו מעשה ישב הקב״ה עליהם בדין לחייבם, ולא עשה... אלא בא לחתום גזר דינו, מה עשה משה? נטל את הלוחות מתוך ידו של הקב״ה כדי להשיב חמתו, כך עשה משה. It is obvious משה כיון שעשו ישראל אותו מעשה נטל את הלוחות ושברן וכו' that R. Samuel b. Naḥmani availed himself of R. Yose the Galilean's defence of Moses. Cf. p. 199, n. 3. There, however, the defence of Moses' action in his breaking the tablets is the chief aim, while here it is the defence of Israel against the nations' verdict. Here again we note a remarkable contrast between the aims of the teachers who preached in the first decades of the 2nd century C.E. and the tendency manifested by those of the 3rd century C.E., the explanation being that there is a full century between them, in which Christianity made great headway in its opposition to Judaism. The second apology of this teacher is also most remarkable in its tendency as well as in expression. It is a flat denial of Israel's guilt. Israel did not commit that

R. Simlai,[1] R. Abbahu,[2] R. Judah b. Simon,[3] R. Abba b.
Kahana,[4] R. Assi,[5] and R. Judah bar Shalom,[6] most of them

terrible crime at all for which the nations of the world, Apostolic and Church
Fathers, condemned their descendants in their own day. The latter are not
responsible for the Calf, but the proselytes and strangers within their midst.
R. Huna and R. Idi say in the name of R. Samuel b. Naḥmani: מוצלים היו
ישראל מאותו מעשה, שאילו עשו את העגל היה להם לומר אלה אלהינו ישראל,
Tanḥ. Lev. אלא הגרים שעלו עמהם עשאוהו ואמרו לישראל אלה אלהיך ישראל
(ed. Buber), 94. Cf. also Lev. R. 27. 8, Pesiḳta. In a third homily, God's
forgiveness is emphasized, in contrast with the character of a human being,
Tanḥ. Frankfort 27a: וכן אתה מוצא אחר שעשו ישראל את העגל ובקש עליהם
משה רחמים מה הקב״ה א״ל וידבר ד' אל משה לך עלה מזה וכו', א״ל הק' משה
איני כב״ו שאומר ליתן מתנה וחוזר בו הוי לא איש אל ויכזב. מהו אומר ולא יעשה
אם אמר בשעת כעסו להביא רעה שכן אמר חוזר שכן למשה הרף ממני וגו', ולא
עשה אלא וינחם על הרעה וכן ועתה הניחה לי ויחר אפי בהם ולא עשה אלא ויאמר
ד' סלחתי כדבריך א״ל הקב״ה איני כבשר ודם שאומר לעשות רעה ומתגאה לעשותה.
I wonder whether R. Samuel b. Naḥmani ever read the Epistle of Paul to the
Galatians 3. 15 ff.: 'Brethren, I speak after the manner of men: Though it
be but a man's covenant, yet when it hath been confirmed, no one maketh
it void, or addeth thereto', &c. R. Samuel b. Naḥmani's words might have
been directed against Paul. In a fourth homily again the building of the
Tabernacle is adduced to disprove that God has not forgiven Israel for the
deed of the Calf: עדות היא לבאי העולם Tanḥ. Frankfort 136b. The term
באי העולם is here intentionally used, to indicate the objections of the
nations of the world; similarly, in the application of the parable, where one
reads: אמרו הגוים (או״ה) שוב אינו חוזר אליהם. Finally, there is a fifth
homily of R. Samuel b. Naḥmani, which cannot be understood without
bearing in mind the anti-Jewish attacks on the part of the hostile Church.
He says: בו ביום שעשו ישראל את העגל בו ביום ירד להן המן ולא עוד אלא
שנטלו ממנו והקריבו לע״ז שנא' ולחמי אשר נתתי לך סלח וכו', Tanḥ. Frkft.
264b. Although Israel used the manna for idolatry, nevertheless God's gifts
never ceased; so his covenant was not annulled, cf. also Tanḥ. Frankfort
123a f., where the homily is fuller than here, and Exod. R. 44. 2 and 7.

[1] R. Simlai sees in Isa. 53. 12 a characteristic of Moses: והוא חטא רבים
נשא שכיפר על מעשה העגל, B. Soṭah 14a; consequently Moses achieved
Israel's atonement for the deed of the Calf.

[2] Cf. above, p. 201, n. 8.

[3] Tanḥ. Frkft. 122a. The payment of the Shekel atoned for the sin of the
Calf. Num. R. 7. 4 they were punished with leprosy for the deed of the Calf.
Cf. above, p. 109, n. 6. M. Deut. Zuṭṭa (ed. Buber), p. 11: כך כיון שחטאו
ישראל שבעם עליהם הקב״ה וביקש לכלותם שנ' הרף ממני ואשמידם, also Exod.
R. 43. 9 in the name of R. Levi b. Parta.

[4] Cf. Lev. R. 10. 3.

[5] Eccles. R. 9. 3, 11: אין לך כל דור ודור שלא נטל אונקי אחת של עגל, Exod.
R. 43. 2.

[6] Exod. R. 43. 9, Tanḥ. Frankfort 148b.

familiar to the readers of these pages.[1] Reviewing the teachings of these teachers, given fully in the footnotes, one is
surprised by many quaint and unusual features. These
teachers of the third century seem compelled to wipe off
from Israel's history the sin of the Golden Calf. This white-
washing sounds strange when we remember the narrative
of the Bible. The attempt to throw off all responsibility
for that not too glorious deed and to lay the burden on the
strangers who joined the camp of Israel sounds more like
the fancy of a learned antiquarian and an eloquent preacher
than true history. Even those Haggadists who do not shut
their eyes to the truth are inclined to invent legends and
situations proving the pardon granted by God to Israel.
There can be little doubt that the polemics of Christian
fanatics prompted these sayings. The dark clouds of mis-
representations, the gloomy spirit of fanaticism in the new
sect or sects used the Bible as a cruel weapon of humilia-
tion and subjugation, which poisoned and embittered the
relationship between Judaism and Christianity. It is,
naturally, impossible for a Christian to be quite impartial in
judging that colossal fight between the two religions, which
are so near to, and yet so far from, one another. Yet any
impartial reader of the Bible will nowadays smile at the
attack of the Church more than at the defence of the Haggadists. The latter, however unsatisfactory their views
might appear from the historian's point of view, are nearer
to the modern approach to the Holy Scriptures. This
defence was of particular importance for the Galilean Jews
of the third century, since it was there chiefly that, with the
acceptance of the theory that Israel was forsaken as a
consequence of the Golden Calf, the doctrine of the abrogation of the Law penetrated into the hearts of Jewish-

[1] Sifra, Shemini 1. 4: יבוא שור ויכפר על מעשה שור יבוא עגל ויכפר על
מעשה עגל תדעו שנתרצה המקום על עונותיכם עבירה שאתם מתיראים ממנה.
Sifre Zuṭṭa, ed. Königsberger, p. 1: נגד כל האומות שהם מרננין אחריך
במעשה עגל ואומרין שאין להם מחילה לעולם, Cant. R. 5, 5.

Christians and Jews. The traces of this struggle for the law will be the subject of the next chapter.

V

It was no doubt humiliating to the Jews to be told that God had forsaken Israel and that the Shekhinah was far removed from their community. It must have been intensely annoying to them to hear it said that Israel's covenant with God had been broken or had never been effective. But the statement that the Law was a curse, a cruel punishment, was a calumny which passed their comprehension, as it still passes ours. Could an impartial mind, one not blinded by hatred, a religious leader or teacher not perverted by selfish motives, really preach that the Law was closing the door to seekers after God? The author of the Book of Jubilees must have had in mind some such opposition to the Law even before Jesus and Paul arose, when he said that Israel's precepts and ordinances, moral and ritual alike, are not the ephemeral expression of the moral consciousness of a particular age, but are valid for all eternity (2. 18, 15. 27). The eternity of the Law is taught also by other writers of Pseudepigraphical literature.[1] That these writers were confronted by antinomian tendencies can be shown not by one but by many passages in their works.[2]

It was, however, left to the writer of the Epistle to the Galatians to invent the theory that the Law is of divine origin but was given as a punishment to the Jewish people for their wickedness and sins.[3] From Justin Martyr[4] onwards we find in Christian writers a disposition to collect Biblical passages which show that God needs nothing, whence it is inferred that all, or some at least, of the institutions of the Jews cannot represent God's will. Here Justin

[1] Cf. I Baruch, 59. 2.
[2] Enoch 94. 3, Jub. 1. 9, 1. 20, 6. 37, Baruch 41. 3, IV Ezra 7. 21-5; cf. also Mark 13. 31, Matt. 5. 18.
[3] Gal. 3. 19 f.; F. C. Baur, *Geschichte*, i. 111.
[4] Diestel, *Das AT in der Kirche*, p. 85; cf., however, earlier Enoch 45. 3.

coincides with the old Jewish polemics against the gods and their needs on one side, which have a close parallel with Epicurean thought, and with Marcionite polemics against the Bible on the other side. Some writers of Early Christianity stigmatize the Sabbath, circumcision, and the dietary laws as ridiculous and absurd.[1] Tertullian does not treat these matters in the frivolous manner of the Alexandrian and Roman anti-Semitic literature, but parades the familiar question, how is it that people, who did not keep the Sabbath, or practise circumcision, were called friends of God?[2] Clement of Alexandria adopts an exceptional standpoint in acknowledging the educational value of the Law,[3] which is, naturally, not entirely denied by writers like Tertullian[4] and some others, who became conscious that the earlier radical view of the abrogation of the Law was detrimental and contradictory to the teaching of the Church about the divinity of the Holy Bible. Only later, when the Gnostic flood abated, did the preachers and teachers of the Church revert to their antinomian attitude.[5] So much so that after the consolidation of Christianity, Jewish ceremonies and observances became a laughing-stock on the part of clergy and laity. The Church vied with the ancient satirists and comedians of Rome in feeding the prejudices and keeping alive the ancestral hatred of the new converts.

I can hardly think that there are many bishops or professors of theology in western Europe who believe to-day that Moses spoke in spirit, that is, in a spiritual sense, and hold that the Jews, as the writer of the Epistle of Barnabas asserts, were led into error by a bad angel and adopted the carnal and literal meaning of the Mosaic laws and injunctions which

---

[1] Epistle to Diognetus, ch. 4.

[2] Tertullian, *adv. Judaeos*, ch. ii; Eusebius, *Hist. Eccl.* i. 4, 8.

[3] Cf. Diestel, p. 56.

[4] Cf. Wirth, *Die Lehre vom Verdienst*, p. 26.

[5] Cf. Asterios of Amasea, Bretz, *Studien und Texte zu Asterios von Amasea*, TuU. xl. 1. 84. Cf. Harnack, *Diodor von Tarsus*, p. 93; about the dietary laws, p. 92: Why are some animals clean, and others unclean? All are created by God!

concealed the spiritual truths, and that thus the entire ceremonial system was a result of a deplorable misconception.[1] Nevertheless, I find some definite misconceptions of Christian theologians about the Jewish attitude to the laws of Moses, especially when Schürer teaches in his history:[2] 'wie die Motive im wesentlichen doch äusserlicher Art sind, so ist auch das Resultat eine unglaubliche Veräusserlichung des religiösen und sittlichen Lebens.' On a similar misunderstanding is based the opinion of Keim:[3] 'Es wiederholte die jüd. Gesetzgebung, aber je ernstlicher es ihren sittlichen Inhalt herauskehrte und die geforderte Heiligung des äussern und noch vielmehr des innern Lebens schärfte, um so mehr überschritt es die notdürftigen Buchstaben des Gesetzes, um so mehr ignorierte es jede rituelle und ceremonielle Äusserlichkeit.' Here breathes Pauline spirit and Marcionite bias against the Law.

Jewish-Christians, however, taught differently and thought otherwise. The Epistle of James[4] admonished Jewish-Christians in a spirit quite in agreement with Rabbinic lore: 'Whosoever shall keep the whole Law, and yet offend in one point, he is guilty of all.' Jewish teaching and Rabbinic thoughts are echoed by the writer of the Clementine homilies[5] when he says: 'For he is a worshipper of God, of whom I speak, who is truly pious, not one who is such only in name, but who really performs the deeds of the law that has been given him.' 'If he, who is of another tribe, keeps the law, he is a Jew; but he who does not keep it is a Greek. For the Jew believes in God and keeps the law.' 'But he who keeps not the law is manifestly a deserter through not believing God; and thus is no Jew, but a sinner.' Those here called Jews are the Posh'e Israel of R. Simon b. Lakish[6] and of Simon the Pious.[7] The authorities of the Church had a difficult task

[1] Ep. of Barnabas, ch. 10 ff.   [2] Geschichte, ii[4]. 548.
[3] Rom und Christentum, 133.   [4] 2. 10.
[5] Hom. xi. 16.   [6] Cf. above, p. 179, n. 2.
[7] Cf. above, p. 183, n. 1.

to entice Jews and Gentiles alike from the Law. Synods and pulpits encouraged all their incumbents and representatives to threaten with the fire of hell and with the disabilities of the Church all those who adhered to the law of Moses and his successors.

How were these calumnies received by the Jews? And how were they refuted by the teachers of the Synagogue? Apart from the group, by no means small, of Posh'e Israel, who must have been mightily disturbed by this fight against the Law which was still sacred and dear to them, the community of real Jews deeply felt this onslaught on the most vital fortress of their very existence. Teachers of the second century raised their voices against the doctrine that the Law was given to Israel as a punishment and chastisement. No! the Law was the most eloquent sign of God's love for his people, Israel. The Tannaitic Haggadah preserves a number of sayings intended to bring home this truth.[1] The Miṣwot have no other function than to increase man's holiness. This was emphasized[2] by a teacher of the second century, Issi ben Judah, who heard, or read, that some people taught abominable ideas about the law. R. Ḥananya b. Akashya, another sage of this time, said that the Law was given in order to enable Israel to acquire merit.[3] The

---

[1] Sifre Deut. § 36, 75b: חביבין ישראל שסיבבן הקב״ה במצות תפילין בראש ותפילין בזרוע מזוזה בפתחיהם וציצית על ד׳ כנפות כסותך. Cf. B. Menaḥot 43b, Tos. Berakhot, ch. 1, B. Sabb. 130a, Midr. Ps. 6. 1, Tanḥ. (ed Buber), iii. 110 and iv. 73. The latter passages reveal clearly the apologetic tendency underlying them. Midr. Ps. concludes with a peroration against the Minim and *Posh'e Israel*, who deny the existence of God; their share will be the fire of hell. It is doubtful whether פושעי ישראל is correct, perhaps it refers to apostates of a later period. Tanḥ. iii has: אם תקיימו מצוותי מניח אני את העליונים וארד ואשכון ביניכם. The law could not be so bad, if God makes it a condition of His dwelling in Israel's midst. Tanḥ. iv has the teaching that Torah and Miṣwot assure Israel's share in the world to come, זרע הקב״ה את התורה ואת המצות לישראל להנחילם חיי העולם הבא. God did not leave a single thing without Miṣwot. Surely this could not be meant for punishment, or to deprive them of future bliss, salvation, or nearness of the Shekhinah. Just the reverse, in order to draw them near to the Divine Presence.

[2] Mekhilta 98a.   [3] Abot R. Nathan 141; Makkot iii. 16.

Babylonian Rab must have had some special idea in his mind in teaching that God commanded the Law in order to cleanse mankind.[1] It is remarkable that Rab considers the Miṣwot binding and effective in the case of all creatures, without distinction of race or creed, nationality or religion. Some copyists or editors of the Midrashim, for example, those of Midrash Psalms,[2] Leviticus Rabba,[3] Midrash Samuel,[4] read 'Israel', but in the Tanḥuma[5] the reading 'creatures' coincides with that of Gen. Rabba. These teachers must have been aware of the attacks made against the Law, without or within the community, which could not be allowed to pass in silence. The Law is not an abomination as was taught in the Churches, it is the means of cleansing and purifying from sin. It is not a source of contamination, but an ever fresh well of holiness and sanctification. Finally, it is a sign of God's love, and not of His hatred.

Even more emphatic are the teachers of the third century (especially after 240 C.E.), who protested against the Church Fathers' allegations that God had forsaken Israel, and that the sin of the Calf still counted against them. They had to take up the cudgels against pernicious and perverted ideas which were engendered by accusations against the Synagogue now generally recognized as false. R. Jonathan ben Eliezer says: 'Whosoever performs a commandment in this world, the same precedes him and goes before him in the world to come.'[6] The Miṣwah is an agent for salvation, and not for perdition. R. Jonathan ben Eliezer must have been perturbed by people who argued with him that the performance of the commandments deprives man of his future life. Where are these people to be sought, if not in the

---

[1] Gen. R. ch. 41. 1 (ed. Theodor), 424: לא ניתנו המצות אלא לצרוף את הבריות בהן.
[2] Ed. Buber, 18. 25, correct ישראל to בריות.
[3] Ch. 13.   [4] Ed. Buber, ch. 4.
[5] Lev. שמיני (ed. Buber), § 12, cf., however, תזריע, § 7.
[6] B. Sota 3b. R. Samuel b. Naḥmani in his name: כל העושה מצוה אחת בעוה"ז מקדמתו והולכת לפניו לעוה"ב.

Gentile-Christian camp? R. Joshua ben Levi faced the same antagonists of the law when he preached in his synagogue in Lydda: 'All the commandments that Jews perform in this world will rise and testify for them in the world to come.'[1] Or when the same teacher uttered his saying: 'He who performs Miṣwot is as if he had received the Shekhinah.'[2] Observances draw men near to God, and do not drive them far away from Him. These sayings are closely connected with the anonymous teaching cited previously,[3] that God has sown Torah and Miṣwot in order to make Israel inherit a share in the future life. The preachers in Tiberias in the sixties and seventies of the third century, R. Levi and R. Isaac, show in some of their homilies and other utterances a special concern for our problem, which is shared by others as well, for example, R. Samuel b. Naḥmani, who says: 'All the good things and blessings which the prophets saw in this world were the result of their obedience to the law.'[4] On similar lines is the teaching of R. Isaac: 'He who performs a Miṣwah as it ought to be performed will never hear evil tidings, and if evil decrees are passed on him God will nullify the same.'[5] He further makes God say to Israel: 'I did not trouble you for observances.'[6] The observances are not given as a burden, as an unbearable yoke, but as a joy. Similarly: 'He who loves Miṣwot never gets satiated with them',[7] i.e. the lover of the commandments longs for more and more; all the talk about precepts and ordinances being a burden does not apply in reality to law-abiding and God-fearing Jews. Let us now turn to R. Levi, in whose

---

[1] B. A.Z. 2a: כל מצות שישראל עושין בעוה״ז באות ומעידות להם בעוה״ב.

[2] J. Ḥag. 76a: כל המקיים מצות כאילו מקבל פני שכינה.

[3] v. p. 209, n. 1.

[4] Eccles. R. 1. 27: כל טובות וברכות ונחמות שראו הנביאים בעוה״ז לא לחנם ראו אלא ע״י שהיו הוגין ועושין מצות וצדקות.

[5] B. Sabb. 63a, according to MS. Brit. Museum Or. 1389, 4b, our text has: R. Ḥinnana b. Idi. כל העושה מצוה כמאמרה אין מבשרין אותו בשורות רעות ואפי׳ אם גוזרים עליו גזירה המקום מבטלה.

[6] Lev. R. 27. 6, Tanḥ. (ed. Buber) iv. 128.   [7] Deut. R. 2, 18.

Haggadah, as we saw,[1] the perverted theory of the Golden
Calf was more than once refuted. What good comes of observing the Law and doing good deeds? seems to have
been a question openly asked during the second half of the
third century in religious meeting-places of Tiberias.[2]
Here again, just as in the saying of Rab,[3] the use of the
term בריות 'creatures', and not 'Israel' is most noteworthy
to the student of universalistic thought in Rabbinic
theology. To the view of the Church that ceremonies and
ritual commandments are a punishment for the making of
the Golden Calf, the reply is given that the Calf actually
caused a shortening of many precepts and the omission of
others, which were originally intended to be given to
Israel.[4] Through the making of the Calf they lost festivals
and Miṣwot, and it is not as the Fathers of the Church
teach that these were imposed upon them as a burden.
One may have one's own views as to this method of homoeo-
pathic apologetics, but one thing is sure, that R. Levi knew
the theories attached to, or derived from, the Bible narrative of the Golden Calf.

The author of the Didascalia endeavours to convince
Jewish-Christians, who, in common with those from whom
the Clementine writings emanated, thought very highly of
the Sabbath and its uniqueness, and who knew and kept
the minutiae of its observance (Rec. 9. 28), of the futility
of this observance. The following are his two arguments:
First of all, if the Sabbath was God's will, then, why were
not the old saints of the Bible, before the revelation on
Mount Sinai, entrusted with the same? Secondly, why
does not God Himself observe this law.[5] These questions

---

[1] v. above, p. 200, n. 4.
[2] Eccles. R. 1. 4: ‏מה הנאה יש לבריות אשר מסגלות במצות ובמע״ט‎.
[3] Cf. p. 210, n. 1.
[4] Pes. R. 200b: ‏אמר ר׳ לוי כך עלתה על דעתו של הקב״ה ליתן לישראל רגל‎
‏אחד בכל חודש שבקיץ בניסן פסח, באייר פסח קטן, בסיון עצרת ועי״ עבירות‎
‏ומעשים רעים שעשו את העגל שהו בידו שלשה‎.
[5] Didascalia, l.c. 136. 3 ff.

are of importance for the elucidation of many Haggadic passages and teachings. Yet, before turning to these, it may not be uninteresting to point out a few Christian writers who developed a similar quibble[1] with reference to the law of circumcision. In the dispute between the Jew Simon and the Christian Theophilus,[2] which is contemporary with the Didascalia and the Clementines, the same objection is raised. Why are not Enoch, Noah, Job, or Melchizedek, or even Adam commanded this rite? Because all that God wants is the circumcision of the heart! The answer to this interpretation of the covenant, which is an old argument against Judaism, was given as early as the beginning of the second century C.E. by R. Ishmael and R. Akiba.[3] The anonymous Haggadah enumerates a number of persons, among whom the aforementioned Biblical personages are to be found, who are said to have been born circumcised.[4] Why was the law of circumcision not given to Adam, or included in the Decalogue? was asked by heathens of many Rabbis. So, by Tinaeus Rufus of R. Akiba,[5] by Akylas of R. Eliezer b. Hyrcanus,[6] by the Matrona of R. Yose b. Halafta,[7] and by a philosopher of R. Hoshaya in Caesarea.[8] In another homily Abraham asks this question of God.[9]

In any case we may see in this argument against circumcision a pagan inheritance on the part of the Church, which lingered on in the polemics against Sabbath-

---

[1] Cf. Carl Schmidt, *Studien zu den Pseudo-Clementinen*, 253. Note: 'In echt rabulistischer Weise sucht er (the author of the Didascalia) &c.' There is no reference in the text of Schmidt's work to the authors mentioned above.

[2] Cf. Marmorstein, 'Juden und Judentum in der Altercatio Simonis Judaei et Theophili Christiani', in *Theolog. Tijdschrift*, xlix, 1915, pp. 360–83.

[3] Cf. Marmorstein, op. cit., p. 377.

[4] Cf. ibid., p. 378, esp. note 1 and M. Friedländer, *Talmudische und Patristische Studien*, p. 73.

[5] Pes. R. 116b f. בעשרת נתנה לא מה מפני הקב״ה לפני מילה היא וחביבה הואיל הדברות?

[6] B. B.B. 10a.   [7] Pes. R. 117a.

[8] Gen. R. ch. 11 (ed. Theodor), p. 94 and Pes. R. 116a (Rabbi).

[9] Gen. R. ch. 46 (ed. Theodor), p. 480.

observing Jewish-Christians and Christians up to the turn
of the fourth century. No wonder that the same argument
is advanced by the author of the Didascalia against the
Sabbath. Why did not the saints and heroes of the Bible
observe the Sabbath? One reply can be found in the theory
developed in the Haggadah, that the patriarchs of old kept
all the minutiae of the law.[1] The Sabbath was not given as
a burden, but, like all the observances for man's welfare
and happiness, it increases holiness.[2] The second point of
the Didascalia about God's observing Sabbath was raised
by a Min, a Gnostic Jew, who attended a Sabbath service
in Rome, during which R. Gamaliel and his colleagues
from Palestine preached on the subject: Whatever God com-
mands others to do, He does Himself. Thereupon the Min
objected: Your God does not keep the Sabbath![3] R. Akiba
proves to Tinaeus Rufus[4] that Nature rests on the Sabbath.
An anonymous preacher exclaims in his sermon on the
Sabbath: 'Is it possible that God did work on Sabbath?'[5]
These instances may suffice to show that both arguments
against the Sabbath have been drawn by the author of the
Didascalia from pagan sources; also that they are preserved
in the Haggadah to defend the Jewish standpoint.

VI

Strenuous efforts were made by the Church to fight
Jewish-Christians and also Christians who could not free
themselves from the 'yoke of the commandments'. Whether
the Rabbis defended the law against Christians for their
sake or in order that the poison of antinomianism should not
penetrate into synagogues and schools is another question.

---

[1] Cf. a fuller treatment of this Haggadic idea in my article: 'Quelques
problèmes de l'ancienne apologétique juive', in *REJ* lxviii (1914), 161–74.
Cf. further Num. R. 14. 9, Joseph observed the Sabbath before the Giving
of the Law; Midr. Ps. 52 (ed. Buber.), Adam was reprieved on account of
the Sabbath; Exod. R. 5. 18, Israelites kept the Sabbath in Egypt.

[2] Mekh. 109b, Deut. R. 3. 1, R. Ḥiyya b. Abba.

[3] Exod. R. ch. 30. 6.

[4] Gen. R. ch. 11, ed. Theodor.   [5] Pes. R. 187a f.

All Rabbis were not so tolerant towards the Posh'e Israel as were R. Simon b. Laḳish and R. Simon the Pious, for, in spite of their faithfulness to the Law, they succumbed to Christian teaching in other respects, apart from their belief in Jesus. Their attitude towards the Holy Scriptures was not the correct Jewish standpoint as taught and dogmatized by the Synagogue. As we can see from the Clementines, which are the most reliable witnesses for the doctrines and feelings of the Palestinian-Syrian Jewish-Christians of the third century, they did not accept the Canon of the Holy Scriptures in its entirety. Even parts of the Pentateuch were eliminated as forgeries. Some objectionable stories in the life of the forefathers were simply ignored. A conception similar to the teaching of the Didascalia that the law of God comprises only the Decalogue and the statutes issued before the making of the Calf crept into the Clementines (*Rec.* 1. 36). No adherent of the Jewish synagogue would go so far as to say: 'Or, supposing the expressions in the Scriptures which are against God and are unjust and false, to be true, they did not know His real divinity and power' (*Hom.* 18. 19). It may be remarked in passing that the Rabbinic sources show various attitudes towards the Holy Scriptures to have been adopted during the Tannaitic and Amoraic periods. By some a distinction was made between the Decalogue and the rest of the Mosaic legislation, the natural laws on one side and the ritual laws on the other side. Some others accepted the Pentateuch with the exclusion of narratives and stories which for some reason or other did not appeal to them. A third group found it necessary, or convenient, to eliminate Prophets and Hagiographa. A fourth group accorded approval to the Canon of the Holy Scriptures, but did not accept the authority and binding power of laws and traditions outside these books.[1]

[1] For a fuller treatment of these movements cf. my article: 'Ein Fragment einer neuen Piska zum Wochenfest und der Kampf gegen das mündliche Gesetz', in *Jeschurun*, xii (1925), 34–62.

In view of this fact it is not surprising that R. Simon ben Laḳish emphatically deduces from Exod. 24. 12 that the Ten Commandments, the whole Pentateuch, Prophets, and Hagiographa, all commandments in the Mishnah, and the Talmud, all were given to Moses from Heaven.[1] Since we know R. Simon ben Laḳish's attitude towards the Poshʻe Israel, we can appreciate the motives underlying his elaborate defence of all parts of the Bible and post-Biblical literature. He surely wanted to convince these straying members of the Jewish community that their treatment of the Bible, their differentiation between the different parts of the Torah, is not according to the spirit of the Law. How far, if at all, he succeeded with his persuasion and with his tolerance, is not recorded. Another teacher of this age, whom we know as a spokesman on all problems affecting relations between Judaism and Christianity in the third century C.E., R. Joshua ben Levi,[2] affirms the same idea. Bible, Mishnah, Halakhot, Talmud, Tosefta, Haggadot, even a stray saying by a qualified pupil before his master, are of Sinaitic origin.[3] This saying, surely an exaggerated one, must be taken in the apologetic sense in which it was uttered. This teacher's life was, as we know,[4] made miserable by Minim, who wearied him with their Bible difficulties, blasphemies, and taunting questions, all amounting to the one argument that the Torah has discrepancies, some of which cannot be reconciled. His reply was this declaration. In an anonymous sermon, R. Joshua ben Levi's teaching is deduced from Exod. 34. 27 connected with Hos. 8. 12, the very words of the teacher in Lydda being quoted without his name.[5]

A full treatment of this subject is contained in a Midrash, which was until lately buried in the dust of the Geniza.

---

[1] B. Ber. 5a.
[2] Cf. above, p. 200 f.
[3] Eccles. R. 1. 29, 5. 7, p. 104, J. Pea 2. 4, Ḥag. 1. 8, Lev. R. 22. 1.
[4] Cf. B. Ber. 7a, our text reads צדוקי, MSS. have מינא.
[5] Tanḥ. (ed. Buber) 116, Exod. R. 47. 1, Yalḳuṭ Exod. 405.

Dr. L. Ginzberg[1] has recently published a Midrash fragment, which he furnishes with the title, 'A Tanḥuma-like Midrash to the section לך לך'. He overlooked the fact that the author of the *Or Zarua*, R. Isaac ben Moses of Vienna,[2] knew this Midrash. Further, that pages (*a*) and (*b*) belong to the Pesiḳta, a Cambridge fragment of which was discovered and published in an article referred to above.[3] This Piska, as far as it can be reconstructed, treats the following matters: (1) How many Torot are there? Answer: Two; (2) Differences between the two laws; (3) God offered the Torah to all the nations of the world; (4) (*a*) Israel accepted the Torah, consequently the covenant is made with them; (*b*) both are threefold (Pentateuch, Prophets, and Hagiographa on one side, Midrash, Halakot, and Haggadot on the other side), all of Sinaitic origin.

So far the contents of the Piska. No teacher or Haggadist is mentioned in our fragment, which may be a matter of accident owing to its fragmentary state. Its date, however, can be fixed by the fact that it deals with the problem which agitated the teachers mentioned above, e.g. R. Joshua ben Levi and R. Simon ben Laḳish, and their contemporaries. This century saw among Jews, or Jewish-Christians, a movement which had many forerunners as well as followers, of those who picked and chose, according to their religious beliefs and theological preferences, among parts of the Scriptures, or within a section of them. Needless to say, the radical wing of these factions did away in its entirety with the Oral Law, although the Clementines as well as the Didascalia on the one hand and the Dialogues on the other hand seem to suggest that some Soferic or Rabbinic extensions of some of the laws were observed among the Jewish-Christians whose conduct was a thorn in the sides of some anti-Jewish writers. And some kind of an opposition, most likely as a result of these agitations, crept into even Jewish circles and groups, homes and schools.

[1] *Ginze Schechter*, i. (1928), 18–22.   [2] i. 7a.   [3] *v.* p. 215, n. 1.

There has to be mentioned a rather strange sentence of R. Adda b. Ḥanina according to the Babylonian version, or of R. Ḥunya according to the Palestinian version. The first reads[1] אלמלא לא חטאו ישראל לא ניתן להם אלא חמשה חומשי תורה וספר יהושע בלבד שערכה של ארץ ישראל הוא, the second[2] שאילו זכו ישראל לא היו קורין אלא חמשה חומשי תורה ה' ספרים בלבד. The former sentence implies that the books outside the Pentateuch and Joshua were given because of Israel's sin; the latter puts it that were Israel free from guilt they would read no more than the Pentateuch; Prophets and Hagiographa can be considered as punishment for Israel's sin. There can be no doubt, to judge from the passages cited previously, that the sin κατ' ἐξοχήν was the sin of the Calf. In spite of the differences between the two texts and the names of the teachers we can connect them with the teaching of the Didascalia which saw in the 'Repetition of the Law' a punishment. These teachers[3] must have heard of the anti-Jewish teachings about the effect of the Golden Calf, and the law being a punishment. Just as the contemporary teacher, whose view was recorded before,[4] says that not Sabbath and festivals were the punishment, but the deprivation of additional festivals, so these teachers deny the doctrine of the repetition of the law, and consider the Prophets and other books, some of them the very basis and only justification of the Gospels and Epistles, the consequences of that sin. It may be taken for granted that the Posh'e Israel rejected Prophets and Hagiographa—the scarcity of quotations from these parts of the Scriptures in the Clementine writings bears out quite eloquently the observations of the Jewish teachers that these people ignored these parts of the Holy Bible.

As a result of our investigation, we may establish the following facts. Around the chief seats of Jewish learning

---

[1] B. Ned. 22b.   [2] Eccles. R. I. 34.
[3] Cf., however, Bacher, *Agada Pal. Am.* iii. 655, who tries to identify them and saw in Eccles. R. I. 34 a modification of the Talmudic passage.
[4] Cf. above, p. 212, n. 4.

and communal activities, like Tiberias and Sepphoris, Caesarea and Lydda, there were scattered about smaller or larger settlements of Jewish-Christians. These stood between two fires; on the one side Jews attacked them for their partly separatist position and Christian leanings, on the other hand they were condemned by Gentile-Christians for their Jewish observances and Jewish leanings. These latter consisted in the first instance of more or less scrupulous observance of Sabbath and festivals, circumcision and the dietary laws, and the laws of purity and impurity, for which they earned the highest praise in a Jewish teaching of the third century, where they are called, 'full of observances as a pomegranate'. Their interest in, and attachment to, their Jewish brethren is manifested by their longing to share the official fast-day services, from which, probably, some fanatics wanted to exclude them. They most probably took part in the ordinary public services as well as in Synagogue life. On account of all these virtues they were disliked by teachers and bishops of the Church, which was quite natural. The Didascalia follows herein the tradition laid down by Paul and some of the more intolerant Apostolic Fathers. The polemics against these Jewish-Christians continued in an unbroken line from Paul to the Didascalia, just as the Jewish-Christians kept to their old traditions from the earliest days of the Church. In this essay we are confining ourselves to the task of investigating and describing the position of the Jewish-Christians of the third century with regard to the threefold attack of the Gentile-Christian Church, that the Jewish nation was forsaken by God, that the making of the Calf deprived the Jews of the privileges granted to them and their forefathers in the Holy Scriptures, and, finally, that the Law was given as punishment and chastisement for the transgression and wickedness of the people. Our material shows clearly that on the whole these points of accusation and attack are a legacy of pagan anti-Jewish polemics and anti-Semitism, grown on the poison-breeding soil of Alexandria, Caesarea, and other Greek cities. They were adopted and adapted by Christian teachers, who supplied chapters and verses from the Bible. Jewish-Christians, rank and file, certainly disliked this method, and defended themselves, as Jews, against these highly pernicious, and, if judged impartially, quite unhistorical and unfair doctrines and views. There is not much preserved of their endeavours, and what is left has come to us in a Gentile-Christian garb and shape. I mean the Clementine writings and the so-called Apostolic constitutions. These reveal the very interesting fact that Jewish-Christians did not give way without a struggle but held in reverence their old traditions and the hallowed forms of their ancestors' liturgy, until they disappeared, either returning to the Synagogue or assimilating with the main body of Gentile-Christianity. Smaller or larger Jewish-Christian assemblies may have survived in Transjordania or in Syria for some generations, even after Christianity became the successor to pagan gods. We know nothing of them. Anyhow, this possibility accounts for the remarkable fact that preachers and luminaries of the Church harangued their audiences to refrain from visiting Jewish places of worship, from celebrating Jewish festivals, from observances, &c. The jealousy of the triumphant Church cannot be explained otherwise. Eloquent and honey-mouthed orators become stammerers full of gall when they mention Jews or refer to Judaism in their pulpit utterances or letters.

It is no wonder that the preachers of the Synagogue took up the cudgels in this fight for their sacred religion. Since at least some of their sayings evince interest in these stray members of the Jewish religion, one has a right to assume that teachers were not indifferent about the present attitude and future fate of these Jewish-Christian communities. They hoped to bring them back to the fold, and tried to prevent their drifting away. The misconception of Israel's relation to God, and God's attitude to Israel, of Jewish history and observances, of Scriptures and of expectations, could not leave them cold and indifferent. If the Rabbis did not think of the partly alienated Jewish-Christians in the first instance, they perceived the danger looming in the near future for the whole house of Israel. The destroyer was not distant, but very near and able to carry discord and apostasy into Jewish family life and the Synagogues. Two independent witnesses bear out the historical fact that this agitation against which the teachers of Judaism fought did not remain without serious consequences. A member of the distinguished family of Hillel, which nominally ruled in Judea and Galilee, was so much attracted by Christian doctrines or the advantages accruing to those professing them that he embraced Christianity and forsook the religion of his fathers. Similarly, another writer of the Church speaks of the conversion of noble and distinguished Jews about the middle of the third century, and of assisting a bishop in baptising them. These facts fit in well with the reports to be found in the contemporary *Carmen Apologeticum*, a work which breathes pagan and Christianized hatred of Jews and Judaism because high-standing, influential Jews, either in Rome or in the provinces, agitated against Christianity. This must not be understood to mean that Jews instigated a movement for the persecution of Christians, but that they may have protected, or at least tried to safeguard, the best interests of their fellow Jews against apostates and their satellites on the one hand, and against overzealous missionaries on the other hand.

In spite of this vehement opposition to Jewish customs and to the Law on the part of many foes and antagonists, the attraction of Jewish observances continued for a considerable time in Christianity, though we cannot say whether they were the result of Jewish influence or a more or less shadowy legacy of defunct Jewish-Christianity. Every honest student of Rabbinic sources must be puzzled by a saying of R. Simon ben Lakish, in whom we have recog-

nized a protector and defender of the Posh'e Israel, or
Jewish-Christians, that a pagan who rests on the Sabbath is
deserving of death.[1] How could this teacher derive such a
harsh law from Gen. 8. 22 ('day and night shall never
cease')? Who were those pagans and where were they to
be found, who endeavoured to observe the Sabbath by
resting? Finally, what real objection can be raised to Sabbath observance on the part of Gentiles? To add to our
perplexities, we find recorded of R. Yoḥanan, the leader of
this age, and a colleague of R. Simon ben Laḳish, whose
name has been mentioned more than once in the course of
this essay, a similarly strange and puzzling statement about
Gentiles engaged in the study of the Torah.[2] Yet in spite
of this unfriendly attitude towards Gentile students of the
Torah, which, by the way, must be taken as a proof that
non-Jews tried to study the Torah, the Written and Oral
Law, R. Yoḥanan opposes R. Simon ben Laḳish on the
subject of the observance of the Sabbath by Gentiles.
One can further recall the strange remark in the *Epistle of
Peter*, that no one who is not circumcised can study the
Law,[3] which is paralleled by an exactly similar saying of
Akylas in his dialogue with the Emperor.[4] R. Yoḥanan
uttered the saying: 'He who observes the Sabbath according
to its rules, even though he be an idolator like the generation
of Enosh, is granted forgiveness of sin.'[5] From the point of

---

[1] B. Sanh. 58b, ואר״ל עובד כוכבים ששבת חייב מיתה שנ׳ ויום ולילה לא
ישבתו, cf. Yalḳuṭ Gen. § 61 where the full name is given.

[2] B. Sanh. 59a: עכו״ם שעוסק בתורה חייב מיתה, cf., however, B. Ḥag. 13a.
R. Ammi, a pupil of and a successor to R. Yoḥanan says: אין מוסרים דברי
תורה לעכו״ם; further, the view of R. Meir about the pagan who studies
the Torah, that he ranks higher than an ignorant High Priest, B. Sanh.
59a and parall., finally R. Jeremiah, Sifra on ch. 18, Warsaw, 1866, p. 75b.

[3] *Clem. Hom.* Epistle of Peter to James, ch. 4: 'We should not communicate
the books of his preaching . . . but to one who is good, etc., and who is circumcised and faithful.'

[4] Tanḥuma (ed. Buber), ii, p. 82.

[5] B. Sabbat, 118b: ר׳ חייא בר אבא בשם ר׳ יוחנן כל המשמר את השבת
כהלכתו אפי׳ עובד ע״ז כדור אנוש מוחלין לו. Cf. Midr. Ps. 92. 2. Pirḳe R.E.
ch. 18, cf. Marmorstein, 'Eine liturgische Schwierigkeit', *Jeschurun*, xii
(1925), p. 202.

view of historical and theological studies, it would be futile
to read new ideas into these quotations, or to minimize
their actual contribution to the knowledge of contemporary religious conditions. The fact cannot be disputed
that Sabbath observance was popular even outside the
Jewish communities in Palestine as well as in the Diaspora,
where it attained a special significance for the Jewish
communities.[1] This attraction of the Sabbath and the
attitude of the pagan world to it was viewed differently by
different teachers of the third century. It may have been
a matter of temperament, but more likely they were guided
by actual events, considered and judged in the light of
contemporary history. However that may be, we are surely
right in assuming that Sabbath observance penetrated
beyond the not very wide boundaries of the Jewish congregations.

How popular the Sabbath was can be deduced from the
limitations of work on Sunday on the one hand, and the
application of Jewish laws of Sabbath observance, which is
condemned and considered as the crime of 'judaizare',
on the other. The age of Constantine was strongly attracted
by the law of refraining from manual labour and work. In
the year 538 C.E. the Jewish mode of observance by not riding
on Sabbath, not preparing food, or avoiding any adorn-
ments of the house, was officially condemned. Many synods
and councils disapproved of the celebration of the day from
evening to evening. Altogether the Christian Sunday re-
tained or received a Jewish character, and was considered as
a successor to the Sabbath of the Old Testament. Some
went even farther, and made of it a weekly Day of Atonement.[2] That the criticism levelled by Early Christianity

---

[1] Cf. Marmorstein, שמירת השבת בגולה בסוף תקופת האמוראים in *Hator*
(Jerusalem), viii, 1928, No. 11.

[2] Hans von Schubert, *Geschichte der christlichen Kirche im frühen M. A.*
(Tübingen, 1920), p. 664. Attention may here be drawn to M. Friedländer,
Synagoge und Kirche in ihren Anfängen (Berlin, 1908), pp. 34 ff., who adduces
convincing evidence that the observance of the Sabbath gained a popularity

against the Law generally as well as particularly did not prevail is shown by the fact that the Church had to fight against the translation of the Jewish Sabbath into the Christian Sunday for nearly the whole of the first millennium of its existence. To Judaism the strict adherence to the Law gave life and strength to endure, whilst for the Church, in her war against her Law-abiding sections, the victory meant a return to barbarism and paganism.

among pagans in the third century C.E. which was looked upon with considerable disfavour by the teachers of the Church. It may be that R. Simon ben Lakish and R. Yoḥanan also had occasion to express their views on this subject. Friedländer would have found confirmation of his theory in the material discussed in the text.

INDEX

שגם מצות סוכה נחשב למצוה ששומרת מן המזיקין וגורמת להשיג חיי
עוה״ב.[1] ובלי ספק היה ידוע להם זכות התורה והשבת והמועדים,
ושכדי להיות האדם משומר מן השדים ולהיות זוכה לחיי העלם הבא
היו מתאווים היהודים בזמנם.

---

[1] סוכה לצדיקים לעתיד לבא: פסיקתא רבתי קפ״ו ע״ב. ועיין השקפה צרפתית
חלק מ׳ ע׳ 163 דברי רבי לוי שם בפסיקתא גם ויקרא רבה ה׳ ב׳.

של שמירת המצוות בתוך עמי הארצות, שנית הידיעה מועלת גם כן
להבנת הדרשות וההלכות אודות הגרים בעשרות השנים האחרונת ובמאה
השלישית קודם ואחר מותם של ראשי הדור רבי יוחנן ורבי שב"ל
וחביריהם ותלמידיהם.

טרם שאסיים דברי אני צריך לאחוז את ההזדמנות זו כדי לפרש
בדרך השערה למה חבבו הגוים מצות הללו כמו תפילין ציצית מזוזה,
מתאוים לתורה ושומרים שבת ומועדים? גם דברי ההלכה מעידים שעשו
כן ממה שפסקו בדינים אם מעשי הגוי בכתיבת ס"ת, או תפילין ומזוזה,
סוכה וציצית, מה דינם. אם נדקדק במצות הללו שזכרנו נכיר שמצוות
הללו מסוגלות להבריח מזיקין או להביא את עושיהם לחיי העולם הבא.
דוגמאות פרטיות יספיקו להראות זאת. כבר ראינו לעיל כי התפילין
וכן ציצית ומזוזה משמרים את האדם מן החטא והקב"ה אומר לישראל,
קיימו מצות תפילין ומעלה אני עליכם כאלו אתם יגעים בתורה יומם
ולילה.[1] הרעיון שהתפילין מגינים על האדם כנגד החטא מבורר גם
מתשובה שהשיב רבי ירמיה בר אבא לרבי זעירא ,,תפילין מנחנא''.[2]
גם רב הונא בשם רבי אחא מדגיש באגדה שלו שהתפילין מגינים, באמרו
על האנשים שלחמו במדין: שלא היה אחד מהם מקדים תפילין של ראש
לתפילין של יד, שאילו הקדים אחד מהם לא היה משה משבחם ולא
היו עולין משם בשלום.[3] אדות מצות ציצית אנו שומעים מתנאים
ואמוראים שמי שזריז או זהיר בהן זוכה ומקבל פני שכינה.[4] הרעיון
התפשט בדורות הללו שכמו התפילין שומרים את האדם מן הפורענות
וכן מן העבירה,[5] כן הציצית, כמו במעשה דנתן דציצית.[6] וכן שמירת
מצות מזוזה מבריח את המזיקין מן הבית.[7] האמונה הזאת היתה רגילה
עוד בזמנו של הרמב"ם כמו שנראה מדבריו הברורים[8] ונוסף עוד

---

[1] מדרש תהלים הוצ. באבער ע' 15.

[2] ברכות ל' ע"ב, מדרש תהלים שם ע' 511.

[3] שה"ש רבה ו' י"ב ועיין גם ירוש' חגיגה ב', ב' וירוש' סנהדרין ו' ט'.

[4] מדרש תהלים ע' 394. וגם מנחות מ"ג ע"ב ירוש' ברכות א' ב'.

[5] עיין תוספתא חגיגה פ"א, מנחות מ"ג ע"א סוכה מ"ב ע"א.

[6] עיין ס' המעשיות של גסטר סי' ל"ה, ושי"מ.

[7] עיין דברי רבי לארטבן ירוש' פאה א' א', שבת ל"ב ע"ב, בעון מזוזה וכו
ע"ש גם לענין תפילין וציצית. ע"ז י"א ע"א, מנחות ל"ה ע"ב, ב"ר פ' ל"ה. וס' רזיאל
המלאך, ח' ע"ד. ושי"מ ואכמ"ל. [8] הל' תפילין ומזוזה ה' ד'.

יוחנן – אולי הם דברי רבי שמעון בן לקיש שלפיה ,,להודיעך שכל
הגוים עובדי ע״ז הן ואין בין זה לזה״.י יש לתמוה בדברי המאמר,
מהו ,,ואין בין זה לזה״? המוציא לאור את המדרש החשוב הזה לא
הרגיש מהו ,,ואין בין זה לזה״ ודברי המדרש צריכים פירוש והבנה.
לפי דעתי רצה לומר בעל המאמר, שאין הפרש בין גויי הארץ ובין
גויי חוץ לארץ, כולם נחשבו לעובדי עבודה זרה, בניגוד לדברי רבי
יוחנן שרצה לחלק ביניהם.

ה) עוד בסוף המאה הרביעית, כשכבר תקפה הנצרות על יושבי
מלכות אדום, וכבר גברו ההגמונים והכומרים שלטו על האומות היו
אוכלסים מן הגוים משמרים מצוות פרטיות. אם מצב כזה שלט אחרי
ההתנצרות, שלא יכלה לעקר את שרש העבודה מקרבם, כל שכן קודם
לזמן ההוא במאה השלישית שהשכינה את נצחון הנצרות. יש לנו עד
אחד שהוא כמו מאה עדים ושמעיד על מה שהוכחנו כבר במאמר זה,
שהרבה גוים שמרו את המצוות, והוא, הדרשן המפואר יוחנן כרסוסטומוס,
שחי בסוף המאה הרביעית באנטוכיא.² מדבריו מוכח שהגוים שכבר
התנצרו עוד החזיקו במנהגים ושמירת מצוות שלמדו מן היהודים בעודם
בגיותם. אוזענער סובר שהרופאים העברים שביניהם שלטו בגוים הללו
והכריחו אותם לקבל עליהם את עול המצוות שעל ידי כן יתרפאו
מחלים או לדרוש את אלה, שיבקרו בתי כנסיות בתור incubatio. אבל
אין לדבריו שום יסוד, ואין לו על מה לסמוך לפי המקורות המסורתיים
שפתוחים לפנינו. בודאי האיש הזה בשנאתו את היהודים, שמסכים בזה
עם שאר אבות הכנסיה, השתמש בעלילות כאלו כדי להמשיך את לבות
שומעיו בכנסיה שלו כדי להבאיש את ריח היהודים בפני הנוצרים.
בודאי כמו שהיה באנטוכיא, כן בכמה עיירות בא״י ובמזרח ובמערב
תחת ממשלת הרומיים, בכל מקום הגוים ישבו עם היהודים יחד והגוים
למדו ממעשי היהודים, והיהודים למדו ממעשי הגוים. ההשפעה לא
פסקה כמה דורות אחרי קונסטנטין. כמה גברה קודם לזמן הזה?
הידיעה הזאת פותחת פתח כפתחו של אולם להבנת מצב הגוים והתנועה

_____

י מדרש שיר השירים הוצ. גרינהוט י״ט ע״ב.
² עיין אודותו ועל ידיעות שבתוך דרשותיו ספרו של Usener, Das
Weihnachtsfest: הוצאה שניה, בון, 1911, ע׳ 245-235, וגם דברי קרוים
שקפה האנגלית, ח״ו.

בפניהם בסתם ,,יום השביעי'', זה השם ידוע אצל כל העמים שבעולם,
אולם הסבה עצמה לקריאת השם נעלם מהם. רבי שמעון בן לקיש
פגש באנשים כאלו שחושבים שהם שומרים את השבת ורעה בעיניו
המעשה שראה, כי העושים זאת מהפכים את האמת לשקר, ואת השקר
לאמת, באמרם שיכול האדם להיות עובד עבודה זרה וגם לשמור את
השבת. על כן קם כנגדם ואמר שהשבת סימן ליחידו של עולם ואינו
עולה יחד עם עבודה זרה. מי שיש בידו מצות שבת ירחיק את עצמו
מן האלילים ופסילים. ולפלא, שחבירו רבי יוחנן דעת אחרת עמו
בענין זה,[1] כי רבי חייא בר אבא מוסר בשמו: ,,כל המשמר שבת
כהלכתו אפילו עובד ע''ז כדור אנוש מוחלין לו כל עונותיו'', כלומר אם
מצאנו בני אדם מן הגוים ששומרים את השבת כהלכתו, ובודאי ראו
גוים כאלו בטבריא בזמנם, יש להם מחילה. ויש לשער כי נגד ,,שומרי
שבת'' הללו התקינו אולי כבר במאה השלישית או במאה הרביעית את
המאמר בעמידה של שחרית לשבת: ולא נתתו ה' אלהינו לגויי הארצות,
ולא הנחלתו לעובדי פסילים, וגם במנוחתו לא ישכנו ערלים, כי לישראל
עמך וכו'. הרעיון הזה בודאי גם בתפלת ,,אתה אחד'' למנחה,
,,יום מנוחה וקדושה לעמך נתת''. ומסדר התפלה אחז בשיטת רבי
שמעון בן לקיש כנגד רבי יוחנן.[2] כל התפלה אין לה שחר אם לא היו
גוים עובדי ע''ז דוחקים את עצמם לשמור את השבת. הן מדברי
כותבי הכנסיה הנוצרית והן מדברי רבי יוחנן ודברי רשב''ל יש ללמוד
שהיו עובדי ע''ז אלו בזמנם ובסביבותם. רק זאת אין לכחד כי פלא
הוא שרבי יוחנן מתנגד ללימוד תורה שלמה ומוותר על שמירתם את
השבת? אולי שיטתו תלויה במה שמציינו בשמו במקום אחר שאמר שגויי
חוץ לארץ אינם עובדי ע''ז כל עיקר אלא שמנהג אבותיהם בידם,[3]
אולי עשה הפרש בין גויי ארץ ישראל ובין גויי חוץ לארץ או, אולי,
חשב שלימוד תורה גנאי הוא להם, ושמירת שבת זכות הוא להם? יהיה
זה איך שיהיה, במדרש מזכירים דעה אחרת המתנגדת לדברי רבי

---

[1] עיין שבת קי''ח ע''ב. עיין גם מדרש תהלים צ''ב, ב' ושם הגירסא: כל מי
ששומר את השבת הקב''ה מוחל לו כל עונותיו, ופרקי דר''א, פ' י''ח, ועיין גם מאמרי
Eine liturgische Schwierigkeit בישרון י''ב, 202, 1925.

[2] עיין את המאמר שרשמתי בהערה הקודמת.

[3] חולין י''ג ע''א, גם כן המוסר את המאמר רבי חייא בר אבא.

במקום. באגדה אחת אנו קוראים: ולא ממה שאתם מרובים מכל
האומות, ולא ממה שאתם עושין מצוות יותר מהם, שהאומות
עושין מצוות שלא נצטוו יותר מכם והם מגדלים שמי יותר
מכם וכו׳,[1] והוא פלא. אלא ודאי מה שהוכחנו כבר שהאומות
משמרים מצוות שהבאנו לעיל הוא בנוי על אדני האמת. אחד מן
האמוראים שהתנגד לשימור מצוות בידי הגוים היה רבי שמעון בן לקיש,
ואחת המצוות ששמירתה לא היתה ישר בעיניו היא מצות שבת. הוא
אומר שגוי ששבת חייב מיתה.[2] גם כאן כמו בדברי חבירו רבי יוחנן
בלימוד תורה, הלשון „חייב מיתה" לאו דוקא, אולם מראה באצבע
שגם רבי שמעון בן לקיש היה מתנגד לשימור המצוה בידי הגוים. יש
לנו חומר חיצוני שהגוים בזמנו של רשב״ל קיימו מצוה זאת ומשתדלים
לשמור את השבת, על פיהם יש להבין את דברי האמורא באר היטב.
אב הכנסיה טרטוליאן, שחי לערך 200 למספרם, אומר: כיוצא בו, אם
אנחנו מתענגים ביום הראשון טעם עונג שלנו משונה כל עיקר ממה
שעושים עובדי השמש ואנו דומים לאותם האנשים שנמצאו בקרבכם
שמקדשים את יום השביעי לעונג ולתפארת, אף על פי שהם מרוחקים
ריחוק גדול מן היהודים, הם שומרים את השבת אף על פי שאינם
יודעים באמת את מנהגי היהודים.[3] עם קצת שנויים כותב האב הזה
דבריו גם במקום אחר באמרו: אף אתם פונים אל מנהגים זרים ומניחים
מנהגי אבותיכם לגמרי, כמו שאתם שומרים את השבת ואת מנהגי
הטהרה[4] הם מנהגי היהודים. ועוד היהודים מתנהגים במנהג הדלקת
הנרות, ותעניות ותפלות, ואתם אוחזים את מעשיהם בידכם! כאן הוא
אומר בפירוש כי שמירת השבת בידי הרומיים לוקחה ממנהגי היהודים.
אם נפן עוד אל כותב אחר של הכנסיה, כלומר Theophilus, שחי
במזרח בעיר הגדולה אנטוכיא במאה השלישית,[5] יתקיים הדבר בבירור,
וכן הוא אומר: הם (האומות) נושאים על שפתם את זכר יום השביעי,
יום זה שגור ורגיל בפי הבריות בכל מקום, אולם רק מעט מהם יודעים
את מקורו של השם הזה. מה שקוראים העברים בסתם „שבת", נקרא

---

[1] תנחומא, הוצ. באבער דברים ע׳ 17, וגם דפוס פפד״א ע׳ רפ״ז ע״ב.

[2] ב. סנהדרין נ״ט ע״א.

[4] Ad nationes i. 13   [3] Apologia c. 15

[5] Theophilus ad Autolicum, ח״ב, פרק י״ב, ועיין M. Friedländer, *Synagoge*
und Kirche, וויען, 1908, ע׳ 35.

אהובים לפניך אהבה גמורה בין שהוא לטוב בין שהוא לרע להם.[1]
אי אפשר להאמין שחכם שדורש כזאת חשב שיש למנוע תורה מאו"ה,
או שאין תורה באו"ה, או שאין מוסרין להם דברי תורה.

גם בענין חלק לעולם הבא של האומות לא היו הדעות שונות כל
עיקר. למשל מאמר סתמי מגיד: או"ה אומרים לישראל מי יתן לספות
עמכם באותה טובה של עוה"ב! וישראל אומרים להם: בכמה צרות
ובכמה שעבודים, בכמה הריגות מסרנו עצמינו על קדושת השם.[2] או
במקום אחר אומר הדרשן: אף האומות מבקשין לבוא תחת כנפי
השכינה – כבר בעולם הזה – בשעה שישראל עושין את רצונו של
המקום.[3] ועל פי שלשה עדים יקום דבר. רבי יעקב בשם רבי אבהו –
שראינו כבר שמליץ בעד אותם ששמעו לדבריו של הקב"ה בעוה"ז
אע"פ שלא קראו ולא שנו מ"מ הם יושבים אצל האבות – מזמור לתודה:
אמר הקב"ה, יודו בי כל האומות ואני מקבלם,[4] כלומר שגם הגוים יש
להם חלק לעוה"ב ובאים תחת כנפי השכינה אם הם מקבלים עליהם
את האמונה ביחידו של עולם. גם זה מגיד שהגוים מתאוים ליקח חלק
בעוה"ב, ויש אפשרות לפניהם אם יודו באלהי ישראל. עוד יש לחבר
עם דברי הדרשן הזה את דבריו במקום אחר. רבי אבהו מבאר את
דברי הנביא ישובו יושבי בצלו אלו הגרים, שבאים וחסים בצלו של
הקב"ה ונעשו עיקר בישראל.[5] הדרשן מצייר בדברים מעטים הללו
את מצב בני מקומו ובני דורו בקיסרין. שם נתרבו הגרים הבאים מן
החוץ לקהל ישראל, ויוצאו חלציהם נעשו עיקר בישראל. אין בדעתי
כאן להאריך בענין קבלת גרים והשתתפותם לכנסת ישראל אולם זאת
אפשר להחליט מתחלה פה שרבי אבהו היה הולך אחר השיטה שמחבבת
את הזרים בנגוד להחכמים שראו בהם ספחת ולא ברכה. גם בדין
חלקם של או"ה הוא אוחז את שיטת הליברלים בידו.

כלל גדול יש לנו להוציא מדברים הללו כי בקירוב ובסביבות
האמוראים נולדה תנועה וגם נראה השתדלות בין הגוים שמקרבים את
עצמם לתורה ולמצות ולחיי העולם הבא. יש מחכמים שהחזיקו ידי
הגוים הללו, ויש שהיו מתנגדים בנגוד גמור לתנועה כזאת שנתפשטה

---

[2] מדרש תהלים הוצ. באבער ע' 47.
[4] מדרש תהלים הוצ. באבער ע' 424.

[1] ויקרא רבה ב' ז'.
[3] אגדת בראשית פ' ט"ו.
[5] ויקרא רבה א' ב'.

א.   ב.

ד"א אם יתן איש וכו' אם פותחין   ד"א אם יתן איש וכו'. אם פותחין
כל או"ה את כל תוסביריאות שלהן   או"ה כל תסבירואות שלהן בדבר
ונותנין ממונם בדבר אחד מן התורה   אחד מן התורה ונותנים כל ממונם
אינו מתקשר בידם לעולם.   בדמיו של ר"ע וחביריו אין מתכפר
                                       להם, בוז יבוזו לו.

כבר הרגיש המפרש שהלשון השני מיותר, אולם ברור הוא שהמסדר
השתמש והרכיב שני מאמרים או שתי נוסחאות יחד. ושניהם מאוחרים
למאמרו של רבי שמואל בר נחמן. במדרש תהלים[1] מביא זה הלשון
שאם מתכנסין כל אלה ונותנים כל ממונם בתורה, אינם יכולים לכבות
את האהבה שבין הקב"ה וישראל. הדרשן וגם לוקחי דבריו ידעו בלי
ספק כמה גוים שהיו מתאוים בלבותם לקנות ולהשיג ידיעות בתורה.
הרי שבסוף המאה השלישית למספרם וכמו בדורו של רבי שמעון בן יוחי
ובימי רבי מאיר וכמו שראינו כבר לעיל מזה, היו כמה מאו"ה
שהשתדלו לקנות תורה, יש לשער כי מספרם של אוהבי תורה מן
האו"ה רבה כל כך שגדולי החכמים כמו רשב"ן, ולפניו רבי יוחנן
עמדו בפומבי ומתנגדים לתועעה כזאת ורצו לסגור את הדלת בפני הגוים
הללו, שלפי דעתם ידיעת ולימוד התורה אצל או"ה סכנה גדולה לקיום
היהדות. בתוך המתנגדים לעסק בתורה באו"ה יש למנות גם את תלמידו
של רבי יוחנן וממלא מקומו בישיבת טבריא, כלומר רבי אמי, שאמר
אין מוסרין דברי תורה לגוי.[2] האמוראים השפיעו על בני דורם שלא
ילמדו את הגוים שרוצים לקנות תורה, שלא תהיה להם הזדמנות
ואפשרות להשיג את התורה.

ד) עד כאן רמזנו כי רוב החכמים התנגדו לאו"ה, ומונעים מהם
תורה ומצות, וגם אוחזים בשיטה פשוטה שאין חלק לאו"ה, בעולם הבא.
זאת אומרת שהם מתנגדים לדברי רבי מאיר שמגלה בדבריו שיטה
והשקפה אחרת. אולם גם נמצאו חכמים שאחזו בשיטתו ונתנו להם
מקום בדרשותיהם. למשל בעל אגדה אחד מדגיש בדרשה שלו, בודאי
בניגוד לרבי יוחנן שגוי שעוסק בתורה חייב מיתה, באמרו: ואפילו או"ה
מכירין בחכמה בדעת ובתבונה ובהשכל מגופין לגופה של תורה, היו

[1] מדרש תהלים מזמור ט"ז, הוצ. באבער ע' 117.
[2] ב' חגיגה י"ג ע"א.

שלהם ובין שאר דברי תורה. אם האמת עמהם ולא דחוי בעלמא,
הדבר קשה מאד למה לא תרצו, כאן בגוי שאינו עובד ע"ז (רבי
מאיר), וכאן (רבי יוחנן) בגוי שעע"ז?. אלא ודאי יש כאן הוכחה
גמורה לפנינו שהדורות, ועמהם גם הדעות, נשתנו לגמרי. מתוך סבות
הידועות להם נדחקו להחליף את שיטתם בענין הלז. דברי התנא ר'
מאיר מפיצים אור גם על דברי בן דורו, רבי שמעון בן יוחאי, שאומר
שג' דברים, כלומר תורה א"י ועולם-הבא שנתן הקב"ה במתנה ואו"ה
מתאוים אותם.[1] בין החומר שהבאתי כבר נכיר את אמיתת דבריו של
רבי שמעון בן יוחאי שבלי ספק הגוים שבדור התנאים והאמוראים
בארץ-ישראל היו מתאוים ליטול חלק לעולם הבא או לירש גן עדן.[2]
עתה אנו רואים שגם התורה היתה חביבה בעיניהם כל כך שהיו
מתעסקים עמה כפי כחם. ולא עוד אלא שהרהיבו עוז בנפשם לומר
שהתורה אצלם. לפי זה יש לפרש את דברי בעל אגדה שאומר: אם
יאמר לך שיש חכמה באו"ה תאמין, אבל אם יאמר לך שיש תורה
באו"ה אל תאמין.[3] הרי שהאו"ה מבקשים לומר שהתורה אצלם, ולא
בישראל. וזה אי אפשר בלא לימוד ובלא עסק בתורה. ונחקור גם
על מאמר אחד שמובא בשם רבי שמואל בר נחמני[4] שדרש את הפסוק
אם יתן איש את כל הון ביתו כו' באהבתה של תורה. ואמר: שאם
מתכנסין כל או"ה ואומרים אנו מוכרין את ממונינו ועושין את התורה
ואת המצות, הקב"ה משיב להם: אפילו אתם מוכרין את ממונכם
לקנות את התורה בזיון הוא לכם,[5] לפני מסדרו של מדרש שיר השירים
רבה היה המאמר סתם ובשתי נוסחאות, כזה:

---

[1] עיין ספרי דברים סי' ל"ב, מכילתא דרשב"י ע"ג. וגם ספרי דברים פי' שמ"ה
וש"ם.

[2] עיין מאמרי La participation à la vie eternelle dans la théologie rabbin-
nique et dans la légende בהשקפה הצרפתית, חלק פ"מ, ע' 305 והלאה [ולעיל ע'
162 והלאה].

[3] מדרש איכה רבה הוצ. באבער ע' 144, מדרש אלה הדברים הוצ. באבער
ע' 28 וגם מאמרי ברבעון London Quarterly Review שנת 1935, ע' 363 והלאה:
Judaism and Gentile Christianity in the Third Century.

[4] עיין מדרש שיר השירים רבה ח' ז', וגם הלשון בילקוט מכירי הושע הוצ.
גרינוף ע' 150.

[5] אולי צריך לגרוס מוסרין את ממונינו, וגם מוסרים את ממונכם, במקום
מוכרים? מהו מוכרים את ממונינו? עיין להלן.

שהתגייר משום שראו אותו יוצא ביום הכפורים במנעל פחות, ואלו
אומרים שמשם אין שום ראיה שכן אפילו יריאי שמים יוצאין בכך![1]
והרי שגם גוים מגויי הארצות בא״י שמרו את יום הכפורים, וכן בודאי
גם את ראש השנה וגם מצות סוכה.

ג) גם בתקופה שלפני דיקליטינוס עמדו גוים מגויי הארצות ונתאוו
ללמוד תורה או לשמור את השבת, וגדולי המנהיגים הרוחניים שבזמנם
מתאמצים להרחיק אותם מזה. רבי יוחנן אמר שגוי שלומד תורה חייב
מיתה, וחברו רבי שמעון בן לקיש גוזר ומחייב מיתה לגוי ששומר את
השבת.[2] בודאי הלשון ,,חייב מיתה'' אינו בדיוק אלא בלשון הגזמה,
הפלגה והעברה. לא היה כח ביהודים שבארץ בזמן ההוא לחייב את
הנכרי שמתעסק בלימוד תורה או ששומר את השבת. בכל זאת מבלי
סבה ידועה וטעם חמור לא היו חכמי ישראל באים לגזור גזירות כאלו
על בני זמנם. לרגל מלאכתי אני לומד מזה שכמה גוים התאוו
והתאמצו ללמוד תורה וגם לשמור את השבת. למה רצו לקבל עליהם
את עול התורה או את עול השבת, לא נודע לנו. בודאי חשבו
שיכולים להשיג על ידי קיום המצות חלק לעוה״ב, או אולי עלה בלבם
לחקות את היהודים, יושבי הארץ. כבר בזמן הבית וסמוך לחורבן
הבית והלאה במשך הדורות כמה מההגמונים והשרים, הפלוסופים
והמטרוניות שהתוכחו עם חכמי ישראל הקדמונים היו יודעים את המקראות
וגם השקפות שהיו מאוחרות לכתבי הקודש וילידי רוח הסופרים לא
נעלמו מהם, והמתוכחים כמובן מתוך דבריהם ומסגנונם לא היו נוצרים,
אלא גוים עובדי עבודה זרה. ידיעת התורה בקרב המחנות הללו
היתה פשוטה כל כך שאין להרבות ראיות לדבר זה. ונוסף על זה יש
לרמוז על דברי רבי מאיר שאמר: גוי העוסק בתורה הרי הוא חשוב
ככהן גדול בישראל[3] וכמאה שנה אחריו בא חכם צעיר שחי גם כן
בטבריא ומכריז כנגדו: גוי העוסק בתורה חייב מיתה וסמך את דבריו
ודינו על אסמכתא קלושה? הסתירה היתה כל כך גלויה לפני בעלי
התלמוד ששקלו וטרו בדבר, שדחקו את עצמם לחלק בין ז' מצוות

---

[1] ירושלמי מגילה א, י״א. עיין קרוים, *Antoninus und Rabbi*, Vienna, 1910, ע׳ 59
והלאה.

[2] ב. סנהדרין נ״ט ע״א.

[3] ב״ק ל״ח ע״א, ע״ז ג׳ ע״א, סנהדרין נ״ט ע״א.

להשיג חלק זה, הקב״ה נותן להם מצות סוכה. אולי, לפום רהטא,
יש להטעים את סוכות כדי לחוג את חג שלהם.[1] אך יותר נכון יש
לשער כי על ידי השפעת היהודים שדרים בסביבתם היו באמת שומרים
את המצוה בעצמה. כי בידינו עדיות שמהן יש ללמוד שכמו ששמרו
מצות תפילין, ציצית ומזוזה, כן קיימו את המועדים ואת השבתות. בלי
ספק אינה מקרי שמסדר של מדרש תהילים מחבר מצות תפילין עם
מצות סוכה בין הז׳׳, מצוות שנצטוו בני נח, וזה לשונו: ננתקה את
מוסרותימו, אלו תפילין שביד, ונשליכה ממנו עבותימו אלו תפילין
שבראש. ד׳׳א ננתקה את מוסרותימו אלו שבע מצוות שנצטוו בני נח.
ונשליכה ממנו את עבותימו אלו שלש מצוות שהן קולעין בהן כגון
סוכה ולולב שהן נקראו עבות.[2] הרי שמצות סוכה ניתנה אצל חכמי
הזמן בתוך השלש מצוות, ובלי כל ספק יש לחבר את האגדות הללו
יחד. הרעיון של ז׳ מצוות בני נח נשנה על ידי מר רב הונא בשם רב,
לפי הנראה לא היה ידוע לרבי יוחנן עד שאמרו לו תלמידיו בשם רב.[3]
והדברים הללו מפיצים אור בהיר על אגדה אחרת שדומה כמו חידה
בלא פירוש. דרשן מאוחר, רבי אבין, אומר שאו׳׳ה וישראל מתוכחים,
וכל אומה תובעת נצחון בדין לפני הקב״ה–כאן בכל שנה ושנה ולא
לע׳׳ל. עבר ראש השנה ועדיין לא נגלה מי נוצח, ישראל או או׳׳ה,
עבר יום הכיפורים ועדיין הדבר תלוי, אולם ביום הראשון של החג כל
ישראל לוקחים לולב ואתרוג, ודבר זה מוכיח שישראל נוצחים.[4] אע׳׳פ
שאין לנו רשות להשיב על האגדה, אולם בודאי יש לנו רשות לשאול,
למה לא יראה על ידי תקיעת שופר, ותענית יוה׳׳כ ועשיית סוכה
שישראל מסוגלין בהן כמו בשמירת מצות לולב, שהניצוח שלהם, ולא
של או׳׳ה. אלא ודאי מזה יש ללמוד שגם הגוים בארץ ישראל שמרו
את הימים האלו. בהמשך זה יש להזכיר את המשא ומתן שהיה להם
בבית המדרש, אם אנטונינוס התגייר או לא נתגייר. אלו מביאים ראיה

---

[1] עיין ע׳׳ז Fowler בספרו *The Religious Experience of the Roman People*
ע׳ 473.

[2] מדרש תהלים הוצ. באבער ע׳ 26 והלאה, ועיין גם דברי קרויס בהשקפה
האנגלית חלק ו׳ ע׳ 259.

עיין ירושלמי ע׳׳ז מ׳׳ב, א׳, חולין פ׳׳ט ע׳׳א, ב׳׳ר צ׳׳ח, ט׳, ואכמ׳׳ל על זה.

[4] עיין מדרש תהלים הוצ. באבער ע׳ 128, ויקרא רבה ל. ב׳ וגם במכירי ע׳ 32.

חלפתא, ורבי אליעזר בן יעקב הוא הצעיר בן דורו של רבי מאיר
ורבי יוסי, אז יש לקרות דבריו גם בניגוד לדברי ציורו של רבי יוסי
שאומר שהגוים לע"ל מנתקים את המצוות ומשליכין אותן אחרי גוום.
מזה יש ללמוד שכבר במאה השניה, אחרי חורבן ביתר, אם חשבונינו
מקויים, היו גוים בא"י מתחזקים בקיום מצוות הללו. גם בדור הראשון
של האמוראים דורש רבי הושעיא בקיסרין, עיר שרובה גוים: [1] עתידין
בני נח לקבל עליהם כל המצוות ולבסוף עומדין לחזור בהן; גם הוא
נותן לדוגמא את מצות ציצית ותפילין. מכאן יש לשער כי ממאה
השניה עד מאה הרביעית נתפשטו מצוות הללו אצל הגוים בארץ
ישראל.

ב) ויש שהסיבו את הפתגם של רבי יצחק על אגדה אחרת מעניינת
השייכת גם כן לנושא שלנו, שממנו נלמוד על מצוה אחרת, כלומר
מצות סוכה שהיתה גם כן רגילה אצל הגוים בזמן ההוא. [2] הדברים
מיוחסים לרבי חנינא בר פפא, ולפי אחרים לרבי שמלאי. לפי האגדה
הקב"ה עתיד ליטול את ס"ת בחיקו ואומר למי שרוצה יבוא ויטול
שכרו. מיד כל הגוים באים, אולם אין הוא רוצה שיבואו בערבוביא
כאחת, אלא כל עם ועם יבוא בפני עצמו. בראשונה באה מלכות רומי
וחוזרת בבושה ובכלימה, ואחרי כן מלכות פרס, וכן כל עם ועם מן
אומות העולם. לבסוף הקב"ה נותן להם מצוה קלה, כלומר מצות
סוכה, ומיד כל אחד ואחד מן הגוים הולך ועושה לו סוכה בראש גגו.
והקב"ה מקדיר עליהן חמה כבתקופת תמוז, וכולם מבעטים במצותה
והולכים להם. על זה אומר רבי יצחק–לפי הנוסחא הזאת–שאין לו
להקב"ה צחוק בעולמו אלא אותו היום בלבד. עד כאן תוכן האגדה
בקיצור נמרץ שמגדת בבירור שהאומות מצפות לקבל שכר לעולם
הבא, והרי הוא, שרוצים בחיי העולם הבא או ירושה בגן עדן. כדי

<hr />

[1] ר' חייא בר לולייני בשמו, עיין ירוש' נדרים פ"ג, מ"ג ע"ב ובקיצור לשון
במדרש תהלים ב' ה', ע' 26.

[2] עיין ב' ע"ז ב' ע"ב והלאה. אולם בתנחומא הוצ. באבער, דברים ע' 32
המאמר בשם ר' חמא בר חנינא. בפסיקתא דר"כ, הוצ. באבער, ע' קפ"ה ע"ב,
הגירסא כמו בבבלי. ועיין עוד מש"כ על האגדה הזאת הח' י"ל בלוי במאמרו
Une homélie sur le Jugement des Nations בהשקפה הצרפתית ח' 80, ע' 207
והלאה.

שרואין מלחמת גוג ומגוג ואומרים להם : על מה באתם? והם משיבין
על ה׳ ועל משיחו, מיד הגוים הללו משליכין מהם את מצותם והולכים
להם, על זה אמר רבי יצחק שאין להקב״ה שחוק בעולמו אלא באותו
יום בלבד. יש להכיר כי יש יחס בין דברי התנא רבי יוסי ובין דברי
האמורא רבי אחא, אולם האחרון מזכיר רק מצות ציצית, והראשון
כולל ציצית עם תפילין ומזוזה כנהוג בדברי החכמים. ועוד, רבי יוסי
אומר שהגוים מתגיירין ורבי אחא מספר שהגוים משתמשין בציצית. וזו
השיטה יותר נכונה, כי אם מתגיירים הם חייבים בכל המצות, ומה לנו
לסגל רק מצות הללו שנזכרו. יהיה זה איך שיהיה, בפסוק אין שום
רמז מיוחד על המצות הפרטיות שמזכיר התנא. אולי כבר בימיו
משכו המצות הללו, מטעם פנימי שצריך עוד בירור, את לבות הגוים
וקרבו אותם תחת כנפי השכינה. מה ששייך לעניננו הוא שרבי יצחק
נקט גם הזדמנות זו בידו כדי לפרש התנגדות כזו להרעיון שיש גוים
שעל ידי שמירת המצות יכולים להשיג חיי העולם הבא, ואין זה אלא
שחוק והבל בעלמא. עוד צריך להוסיף כאן גרגיר או שני גרגרים
להבנת דברי רבי יוסי. בראשונה אולי יש להחליט, כי האגדה אינה
לרבי יוסי הגלילי אלא לרבי יוסי בר חלפתא. אם זאת ברור אז
נרויח לקבע את זמנה של האגדה. רבי יוסי הגלילי מקלס ומשבח את
הגוים בני דורו שהם מחזיקין ביראתם ואינם נוחים להמיר אותה באמונה
אחרת, וגם אדוקים בנימוסיהם הדתיות.[1] מי שאמר דברים הללו אינו
מסוגל להמציא אגדה שהגוים יבואו ויתגיירו ויחבבו בפרט מצוות אלו.
אולם זאת אומר רק בדרך השערה בעלמא. שנית, מצוות הללו נמנו
בין אותן המצוות שעל ידיהן חביבין ישראל לפני המקום. ר׳ אליעזר
בן יעקב חולק על זה ואמר שכל מי שיש לו תפילין בראשו וציצית
בבגדו ומזוזה על פתחו הכל בחזוק שלא יחטא,[2] זאת אומרת שלא רק
ישראל מצויינים במצות הללו, אלא כל מי שהוא, בין ישראל בין גוי,
ימלט על ידי שמירת מצוות הללו מן החטא. רבי אליעזר בן יעקב
מתנגד לא רק לדברי התנא שמדגיש שרק ישראל חביבין ומצויינים ע״י
מצוות הללו, אלא גם הגוים. ועוד, אם רבי יוסי הוא רבי יוסי בר

6

לאור עולם בשנים האחרונות בא״י,[1] כי שגורות הן בפיות הבריות.
משמעות המליצה ברורה שעשו מבקש לישב בגן עדן. מלבד אלו
האמוראים יש לנו עוד בעל אגדה מצויין שרומז באצבע על התנועה
הזאת, והוא רבי יצחק בן דורם של הנזכרים. כדי להתנגד לדעות
ורעיונות כאלו של בני עשו יש להם חלק לעו״ה, משתמש רבי יצחק
בויכוח (דיאלאג) בין הקב״ה ובין יצחק שמעניין מפני צורתו החיצונית,
אולם ביותר מפני כחו הפנימי. וזהו לשונו:

יצחק: ״יחן״, כלומר תן חנינה לעשו בני.

הקב״ה: ״רשע״, כלומר אינו ראוי לחנינה מאתי.

יצחק: ״בל למד צדק״, ז. א. אין מי שילמוד עליו זכות?

הקב״ה: ״בארץ נכוחות יעול״, כלומר, החריב את המקדש
ואין זכות או למוד זכות מועילים לו כלום.

יצחק: ״אל יראה גאות ה׳״, כלומר אין לו תקוה.[2]

דברי האגדה הם תשובה לגוים שמקוים שיהיה להם חלק בחיי
העולם הבא, שאפילו אם יצחק, אבי עשו בא להיות מליץ בעדו וילמד
עליו זכות, הקב״ה אינו מקבלו. אע״פ שרבי יצחק הלביש רעיונותיו
ודעותיו בכסות משונה מזאת של רבי אחא ורשב״ן, מ״מ דעתו
ותכליתו שוה עם חביריו. לכל הפחות מצאנו שלשה בעלי אגדה והם
מצויינים, שחשבו להקהות את שיניהם של הגוים שאומרים שיש להם
חלק לעולם הבא.

גם במקום אחר[3] נשאר לנו זכר משיטתו של רבי יצחק. באגדה
זאת רבי יצחק מתאים עם רבי אחא לא רק בנקודה זאת שהתהאמצות
האו״ה להשיג חיי עולם היא הבל, אלא גם בנקודה אחרת שהגוים
שומרים את המצות, כלומר תפילין, ציצית ומזוזה. והשייכות בין שתי
הנקודות, כמו שנראה לפנינו היא, שעל ידי שמירת המצוות הללו הגוים
חושבים שיש לאל ידם להשיג בקשתם. רבי יצחק מוסיף לדברי התנא
רבי יוסי שאמר שלעתיד לבא הגוים באין ומתגיירין ומניחין תפילין
בראשיהם ובזרועותיהם, ציצית בבגדיהם ומזוזות על פתחיהם, כיון

---

[1] עיין מש״כ על זה ב-PEFQS, בחלק LXV, עמוד 101.

[2] ב׳ מגלה ו׳ ע״א.

[3] ב׳ ע״ז נ׳ ע״ב ועיין במכירי תהלים ע׳ 16, ושם גרס רבי יוסי הגלילי במקום
רבי יוסי סתם (בר חלפתא) וגם מדלג את הקושיא ואת התירוץ והוא אין מקבלים
גרים וכו׳.

באמת, הרעיון שהגוים בדור זה מתאמצים לישב בין הצדיקים חוזר
גם באגדות רבי שמואל בר נחמני,[1] ואלה הם דבריו: אמר הקב״ה
ליעקב, אל תחת ישראל! כביכול אפילו אתה רואה את עשו יושב
אצלי משם אני מורידו. שניהם מדברים, ובודאי היו דבריהם נחוצים
לדורם מטעם שאמרנו, שעשו ישב או בין הצדיקים או אצל הקב״ה
ושניהם מתאימים בהגשמה שהקב״ה מורידו וגוררו משם. מי שיודע את
רוח האגדה העומד למעלה מן החידות יכיר מיד שגם רבי שמואל בר
נחמני הרגיש בבני דורו מזרעו של עשו שגם הם מבקשים חלק לעולם
הבא או לישב אצל הקב״ה. וכאן חסר העיקר מן הספר שרבי שמואל
בר נחמני שותק ואינו מגיד על מה תקותם בגויה. אולם מדבריו אנו
לומדים דבר חדש שלא נשנה בפירוש בדברי רבי אחא, כלומר
שישראל מתירא מזה. בכלל, שניהם מתנגדים להשתדלות הגוים להשיג
חיי עולם או לשמור את המצות בגיותם. שניהם הלכו בשטה אחת
בזאת השאלה, שהיתה לפי דעתם, ראויה לישא וליתן בה בפומבי לפני
באי בתי כנסיות.

כאן המקום לעמוד על הסגנון ,,לישב אצל הקב״ה״ או ,,לישב
בין הצדיקים בגן עדן״ שפגשנו במאמרי האמוראים לעיל. מענין
השינוי שנמצא במאמרו של רבי אבהו, שמשתמש בלשון: ,,לישב עם
האבות״. הוא אומר: ,,לעתיד לבא להיות הכל מתמיהין כנגד מי
ששמעו להקב״ה, ואומרים: מהו כך פלוני שיושב (כלומר אצל האבות)
והרי הוא לא שנה ולא קרא מימיו הרי הוא יושב עם האבות ומשחק
עמהם״.[2] והקב״ה אומר להן: מה לכם תמהין? לא זכו אלו אלא
מפני ששמעו לי בחייהן! החילוק בין רבי אבהו מצד אחד ובין רבי
אחא ורבי שמואל בר נחמני מצד אחר הוא, כי האחרונים מדברים על
או״ה, ורבי אבהו על ישראל שכל חבריו חושבים שאין ראוי לירש גן
עדן.[3] הסגנון בדברי רבי אחא דומה להלשונות שנמצאו במדרשים;
כמו ,,עמד זה בחבורה של צדיקים״, או, ,,ליטול חיים וכבוד וחלק
עם הצדיקים״.[4] מענין כי לשונות אלו או אלו נשתמש בכתובות שבאו

[1] עיין פסיקתא דר״כ קנ״א ע״א, תנחומא ויצא, ויקרא רבה כ״ט, א. ילקוט
מכירי עובדיה הוצאת גרינוף ע׳ 10.
[2] אגדת בראשית הוצ. באבער ע׳ 163.
[3] עיין מש״כ בחיבורי The Doctrine of Merits, London, 1920. 191-2.
[4] קהלת רבה א, ל״ו.

את המלכות לנצרות. פלא בעיני שעדיין חוקרינו לא נתנו לב לשאול,
אם מקורות שלנו, התלמודים והמדרשים, אינם מכילים חומר או ידיעות
הרומזות על המאורע הלז; היתכן שתנועה כזאת שבודאי עשתה רושם
גדול על לבבות בני אדם בארץ ישראל ובמדיניות הסמוכות לה, עברה
על ראש בני עמנו ועל המנהיגים הרוחניים שבתקופה הזאת מבלי
להשגיח עליה? וביותר יש להדגיש, כי השתנות כזאת, זאת אומרת
התנצרות המלכות, לא באה כהרף עין וצריכה זימון גדול ותמידי.
ולזה בידינו ראיות באגדה של הדור הזה.

יפה לברור ליסוד הבנין שאני עסוק בו היום מאמר אחד של רבי
אחא[1] שמצייר כי לעתיד לבא עשו הרשע מעטף טליתו ומשתדל
לישב עם הצדיקים בגן עדן, אולם הקב״ה גוררו ומוציאו משם. באמת
אגדה זרה בפי דרשן מפואר אע״פ שסמך את דבריו על הפסוק
בעובדיה, ודורש אותו כזה: אם מגביה (עשו), זאת אומרת שעשו
מגביה את עצמו לשמים ושם קנו בין הכוכבים, כלומר הכוכבים
שנמשלו לצדיקים (עיין דניאל י״ב, ג׳) משם אורידך, אמר הקב״ה.
אולם אין בפסוק זכר או אסמכתא שעשו מתעטף בטלית או בציצית,
כדי שישב בין הצדיקים, ומתאווה לחלק עולם הבא. אשער כי הדרשן
משחק בדרך היתול על בני דורו בין הגוים שבסביביו שהם חושבים
שעל ידי שמירת מצות ציצית יש לאל ידם להשיג חיי העולם הבא.
אין אני יכול לחשוב כי בלי מעשים כאלו שאירעו בכל יום ויום בין
הגוים בארץ ישראל יבא רבי אחא ומצייר דברים שלא היו ולא נבראו
בקתדרא של משה בבית הכנסת שבעירו! אם נניח שעשירות של כח
הדמיון ורוח הפיטני גרמו לו לרבי אחא לצייר דבר מה, האם אפשר
שלוקחי דבריו שמעו זאת בלי ערעור ובלי מחאה? אלא ודאי יש לנו
רשות ללמוד מזה שגויי ארץ ישראל, – לא נוצרים אלא גויים אמתיים
– בדור הזה שמרו מצות ציצית וקוו שעל ידיה ישיגו חלק בעולם הבא.
אם השערה הזאת אמתית היא, אז צריכים אנו לתור ולדרוש, אם
נמצאו עוד עדים אחרים שמעידים על תנועה הזאת. כי אי אפשר שרק
רבי אחא הרגיש בה, ולא אחרים; או, שרק בסביבתו התנהגו הגוים כן
ולא במקום אחר.

[1] ירוש׳ נדרים ג׳ ח׳, ועיין הגירסא ברמזי הפטרות לרוקח ב׳ ע״א שגרס במקום
טליתו „ציצית שלו", ובירוש׳ צ״ל רב הונא בשם רבי אחא, ולא ר׳ אחא בשם
רב הונא.

מאמר על ערכה ההיסטורי של האגדה

א) במאמר זה, שמוקדש לכבוד הפרופיסור דר׳ שמואל קרויס שבכמה מחבוריו וחקירותיו השתדל להוציא מן האגדה לאורה ידיעות היסטוריות הן בקורות ארץ ישראל הן בדברי ימי ישראל בכלל, בדעתי לסדר לפני החברים שתים או שלש דוגמאות מערכה של האגדה בתור מקור לדברי ימי ישראל.[1] בפרט, ברצוני להפיק אור על אגדות הכי תמוהות שבהן מדובר על אומות העולם, או עשו, או אדום או מלכות רומי שהיו משתדלים לשמור מצות פרטיות. האפשר שהתנאים והאמוראים בעלי האגדה בדו מלבם שהגוים מדקדקים במצות תפילין וציצית ומזוזה, לומדים תורה, משמרים את השבת ומועדים, בפחות או ביותר, מבלי שיהיה לדבר זה יסוד או בסיס ריאלי בחיים? אם אגדות הללו אינן רק דברי פיוטין של מה בכך שאין להם אפילו סמך מן המקראות, מה אמרו התלמידים והשומעים את הדרשות לזה? בלי להאריך בכללות, נרד לפרטיות.

התקופה שבין דיקליטינוס ובין קונסטנטין, היא הכי נכבדה וחשובה בהיסטוריה העולמית. בתחלת התקופה הזאת נפלו כמה עריצים מן כסאם, ובסופה נולד דבר חדש, כלומר התנצרות מלכות רומי. במעשה זה יש להכיר את הסבה האמתית שבעבורה נתקיימה הכנסיה; בלעדה, הנצרות, עם מיסדה היתה נשכחה מן הלב, כמו שאבד זכרו של מרקיון וכנסיה שלו או מגי וכנסיה שלו, וזה האחרון משל כמו אלף שנה בארץ מולדתו בפרס ובבל ותורתו הגיעה עד מצרים ומערב מצד אחד, ועד כינה והודו מצד אחר, והראשון שמשל במדינות של הים התיכוני כמו ארבע מאות שנה, שניהם עשו חיל ובכל זאת נידונו לאבדון. בודאי גם תורת ישו ותלמידיו היתה מצפה לדין זה אילולי שקם קונסטנטין והפך

<hr>

[1] קרויס במאמרו החשוב והיסודי, *JQR.* חלק ה׳ וחלק ו׳ The Jews in the Works of the Church Fathers מסיים דבריו בזה הלשון: It is to be hoped that an investigator will soon arise, who will treat the immense field of the Haggadah according to requirements of historical criticism. בדעתי למלאות כאן בקיצור, כפי שידי מגעת, קצת מבקשתו וחפצו. כמה חבורים יצאו לאור על השואות שבין האגדה ובין פירושי אבות הכנסיה, אולם ערך ההיסטורי של האגדה עוד לא ניכר ומבורר כל צרכו.

בלי ספק כמה חוגים בתקופת האמוראים חשבו שהגואל אינו בן
אדם פשוט או מסוגו אלא כדמות אור או רוח ומתגשם ונצמח או נגלה
בתואר אנושי כמו אם אומרים שהוא נצמח משערי רומי (אגדת בראשית
פ' כג, מב עמוד 47).

באגדת רבי יהושע בן לוי אנו מכירים דו־פרצופין של הגואל
והגאולה. במקום אחד הוא אומר – כמו שרמזנו כבר בפרק הקודם –
שאם זכו ישראל אחישנה ואם לא, בעתה. ועוד: אם זכו יבא בעָני
שמיא, ואם לאו עני ורוכב על החמור. ורבי יהושע בן לוי ראה בעצמו
את המשיח שישב על פתחא דקרתא רבתא דרומי ושאלו אימת אתא
מר? וא"ל: היום, וכיון שלא בא היום, קסבר שקורי קא משקר בו.
ואולי שעל עובדה זו מיוסד הפתגם: זכו אחישנה, לא זכו בעתה (עיין
ב' סנהדרין צח, ע"א). ואין כאן סתירה בדבריו כי המשיח מזומן
ומעותד מבריאת העולם ובזמן קצוב וידוע וגלוי לפני הבורא. ורעיון
זה שולט גם בפתגמים אחרים מחכמי הדור. מצד אחד אין לנו שום
רשות להטיל ספק בדבריו האומר שהוא היה ברומי – זה מוסכם גם
ממקומות אחרים באגדה שלו – ששם ראה את הגואל וגם דבר עמו כאיש
המדבר אל רעהו, ואין כאן פטומי מילי בעלמא, אלא שכמה פרטיות
מהתנועה המשיחית הזאת היום מכוסות ממנו ורק בדרך השערה יש
להחזיר את המאורעות ליושנן, כמו שהשתדלתי לעשות במקום אחר.

הרשעה, ורוחו של משיח מרחפת עליהם. הוי אומר: שהמשיח או הגואל
חי ורוחף על כולן (ב״ר ב, ה הוצ׳ תיאודור עמוד 16). ז. א. לפי
לשון האגדה שרוחו של המשיח מנהיג את הגאולות שהיו בימי בבל מדי
ויון ויעמוד גם אחר מפלת מלכות הרשעה להגן על עם ישראל. דברי
רשב״ל כאן עומדים ותלויים במאמר אחר שמציינו בשמו בתנחומא
(שמות, הוצ׳ מהרש״ב, עמ׳ 114). על דברי כנסת ישראל שאומרת
לפני הקב״ה: רבש״ע! חושבת אני ומחשבת לכמה שנים גאלתנו ממצרים,
לכמה שנים גאלתנו מיון (צריך להשלים מבבל וממדי) ואומר חלותי
היא שנות ימין עליון – אמר רשב״ל אם חולים הם יכולים להרפאות,
כלומר שרוח אלהים מרחפת על המלכיות והוא מביא רפואה למכתה
של כנסת ישראל. פתגם זה מראה בעליל את אישיותו הבולטת של
רשב״ל ותקותו החזקה לגאולה. דבריו עשו רושם גדול על האגדה
בדורות האחרונים עד כדי כך שהדרשנים היו מסיימים את דרשותיהם
ברעיון זה. משל אחד מן הדוגמאות שנשארו לנו בכתובים בתנחומא
(בראשית ה׳ ב׳, סט ע״א) בתור פראורטיאה (סיום הדרשה): א״ל הקב״ה,
בעוה״ז עשיתי לכם פלאים, וגאלתי אתכם משעבוד מצרים (בודאי
צריך להוסיף גם כן, משעבוד בבל, משעבוד יון) כך אני עתיד לגאול
אתכם לעתיד לבא משעבוד אדום ולעשות לכם נפלאות שנא׳ כימי צאתך
וכו׳. הרי הדורש תוקע בלב העם את האמונה ומטעים דברים של נחמה
בפי הקב״ה כדי להרים את הלבבות המדוכאים בצער ובשעבוד וביאוש
מן הגאולה. בכלל יש לראות ברעיון הגאולה של רשב״ל דבר שמתקיים
ועומד מבריאת העולם עד סוף כל הדורות. על כן אין להתפלא אם
אנו שונים באגדה שהמשיח סובל כל השמדות והצרות והיסורין והגזרות
שבאות על עמו ומצטער עמהם בכל שעבוד ושעבוד (פסיקתא רבתי
קמו, ע״ב). אם המשיח מתיסר ביסורים בכל דור ודור מפני עונות
הדור א״כ בודאי הוא חי וקיים בכל הדורות והוא בריה למעלה ומחוץ
לטבע האנושי.

בשיטה זו אוחז גם רבי אבא סרונגיא, שרואה בפסוק בדניאל ב,
כב (ונהורא עמה שרא), זה אורו של מלך המשיח (ב״ר א, ח, עיין
גם איכה רבה לא, טז) ואור שכנסת ישראל מצפה זה אורו של מלך
המשיח (פסיקתא רבתי קסא, ע״א). האור הזה קיים ועומד להודיע
לגאולת ישראל. ועל אישיותו האלהית של המשיח יש ללמוד מן האגדה
שהקב״ה נותן לבושו למלך המשיח (תנחומא מב, במדבר עמוד 44).

ביום השני אינה נכבה לעולם. גם בעל אגדה כרבי שמואל בר נחמני
אוחז בשטתו (עי׳ ב״ר פרשה טו, עמוד 137). בעל ספר מעלות
המדות השתמש במדרש או במקור קדום שבו יצא המחבר ללחום נגד
הדעה שג״ע וגיהנם נבראו קודם לבריאת העולם, כמו ששנינו בבבלי,
ואלו דבריו: מהו מקדם? שמא אתה סבור קודם לבריאת העולם, אינו
כן אלא קודם לבריאתו של אדם הראשון, ע״כ. קשה להחליט למה
ובמה חלקו הקדמונים בענין זה. אבות הכנסיה, כמו תיאופיל (בחיבורו
ב, כג) אוחז השיטה בידו שג״ע וגיהנם נבראו או ביום הששי או ביום
השביעי.[1]

נחזור לעניננו. אנו רואים שבכל הנוסחאות שמו של משיח נמנה
בין הדברים שנבראו קודם לבריאת העולם, אם כן גם הרעיון קודם
לבה״ע, רוצה לומר כי אחד מן התנאים שעליהם מיוסד בסיס העולם
שהיה צריך למשיח או גאולה, זה היה צפוי מראש. בפתגם אחד מובא
הרעיון הזה, בזה הלשון: מלמד שצפה הקדוש־ברוך־הוא במשיח
ובמעשיו קודם שנברא העולם (פסיקתא רבתי קסא, ע״א וע״ב). על
כן לא רק שמו של משיח אלא גם מעשיו ופעולותיו היו צפויים ועומדים
מראש. הדרשן מוציא את הלימוד מן הפסוק וירא אלהים את האור
כי טוב (בראשית א, ד). בפתגם שני באותו מדרש (קנב, ע״ב) מדגיש
הדרשן ביתר שאת ובכוונה גדולה את הרעיון: אתה מוצא שמתחלת
בריתו של עולם נולד מלך המשיח שעלה במחשבה להבראות עד שלא
נברא העולם. לפי זה שמו של משיח עלה במחשבה להבראות קודם
לבה״ע. אבל מלך המשיח נולד מתחלת בריתו של עולם. ההפרש
הגדול בין האגדה התנאית ובין האגדה האמוראית גלוי לעין כל.
בראשונה מדייקים בכל המקורות כי שמו של המשיח נברא קודם לבה״ע.
באחרונה המשיח עצמו צפוי ועומד קודם לבריתו של עולם. אם נטייל
ארוכות וקצרות בשדה האגדה היהודית נפגוש במראות ובהשקפות שונות
לנושא שלנו.

רבי שמעון בן לקיש מפרש את הפסוק ורוח אלהים מרחפת על פני
המים (בראשית א, ב) זהו רוחו של מלך המשיח. הוא פתר את המקרא
בד׳ מלכיות: תהו זו בבל, בהו זו מדי, חשך זו יון, תהום זו מלכות

---

[1] עיין גם האפוקריפן בארכיוון של א. מרכס עמוד 425: באותה שעה מגלה
הבורא את הגן עדן ואת הגיהנם שברא קודם לבה״ע.

מעולים ומצויינים מכל היו קודמים ג״כ בבריאה, אם בבריאה ממשית
או רק שעלו במחשבה תחלה להבראות. אף על פי שחכמי ישראל גזרו
ואסרו לדרוש במעשה בראשית,[1] ומ״מ ראו לנכון לנקוט את הדברים
שנבראו או שעלו במחשבה להבראות קודם שנברא העולם. המאמר
נשנה בכמה מקומות ונוסחאות, נחפש בראשונה בנוסחת בראשית רבה:
ש׳ דברים קדמו לבריתו של עולם, יש מהם שנבראו ויש מהם שעלו
במחשבה להבראות, התורה וכסא הכבוד נבראו, בסוג השני מונה האגדה
את האבות, ישראל, בית המקדש, שם המשיח. רבי אהבה בר זעירא
שהיה שונה ברייתות, מוסיף אף את התשובה. בבבלי (פסחים נד, ע״א)
מביא הברייתא בנוסח אחר ובסדר אחר; כולל את דברי רבי אהבה
בר זעירא ומונה שבעה דברים שנבראו קודם שנברא העולם (ואינו מחלק
בין הדברים שנבראו ממש ובין הדברים שעלו במחשבה להבראות), ואלו
הן: תורה, תשובה, גן עדן, גיהנם (לא נזכרו בב״ר כל עיקר), כסא
הכבוד, ובית המקדש, ושמו של משיח. וכן הוא הנוסח והסדר גם בבבלי
נדרים לט, ע״ב. הבבלי מפיק אבות וישראל ומעייל במקומם גן עדן
וגיהנם. וזה חולק וסותר את השיטה הירושלמית שלפיה גן עדן וגיהנם
לא נבראו קודם לבריאת העולם. כמו״כ בב״ר פ׳ ד עמוד פד, נמצא:
רבי יוחנן תני לה בשם רבי יוסי בן חלפתא: (למה לא נאמר טוב ביום
השני) וביום השני נברא גיהנם. ועוד שם פ׳ כא עמוד 263 נמצא: ד״א
מקדם קודם לגן עדן נברא גיהנם, גיהנם בשני וגן עדן בשלישי, הדעות
עתיקות ומשונות אם ג״ע וגיהנם נברא קודם לבריאת העולם או אחר
כן. מחברו של ספר עזרא הרביעי מדגיש שגיהנם נברא קודם לבריתו
של עולם (א, ז), ומתאים לפי זה עם נוסח הבבלי, גם בספר גן עדן
(ע׳, בה״מ, ג, קלב). מסכים לדעה זו. כנגד זה מצינו בפרקי דרבי
אליעזר פ׳ ד, את דעתו של רבי יוסי ברבי חלפתא ויש למצוא אותה
גם בברייתא בתוספתא ברכות ז, יא ששם אומר: אש גיהנם שנבראת

---

[1] גם חנוך פרק מח, פסוק ב וג׳ יודע שהמשיח או יותר נכון שמו של משיח
נברא קודם לבריאת העולם. הדברים מעניינים וכדאי להביאם כאן במילואם:
פסוק ב. באותה שעה נקרא שמו של בן האדם בפני אדון הרוחות ושמו
קדם לראש הימים.

פסוק ג. באמת, קודם שנברא השמש והאותות, טרם שנעשו כוכבי השמים,
הוא נקרא בשם לפני אדון הרוחות. כאן הוא המקור העקרי והיותר קדום לדברי
הברייתא ששמו של משיח נברא קודם לבה״ע.

האפוקלפטיקא? אולם המצב הכלכלי והמדיני היה באמת שפל וגרוע
במאוד מאוד. ואין להכחיש הדברים כהוייתם. שרבי יוחנן עמד תחת
השפעת האפוקלפטיקים מוכח ממה שמובא בשמו בכמה מקומות „שאין
מלך המשיח בא עד שיבראו כל הנשמות שעלו במחשבה להבראות".[1]
הרעיון תופס מקום מיוחד וחשוב בספרי החוזים, כמו שהוכיח כבר ג.
האלשר.[2] עוד סימן שלישי נמצא באגדת רבי יוחנן בענין זה שאמר:
משם, ז. א. מטבריה עתידין להגאל שנא' התנערי מעפר עמי,[3] או
בלשון אחר: טבריה היא משלמת למינים שנא' תרמסנה רגל רגלי עני.[4]

על העניות הכוללת רומז מאמרו של רבי חנינא בר חמא שאמר:
אין בן דוד בא עד שיבקשו דג לחולה ולא ימצאו.[5] בנו רבי חמא בר
חנינא אוחז בשטה שיסודה ג׳׳כ בצאן ברזל של האפוקלפטיקא: שהגאולה
תבוא כשתכלה מלכות הרשעה מישראל.[6] ודומה לזה השקפתו של רבי
אחא ברבי חנינא שהקב׳׳ה נקרא ראשון, עשו נקרא ראשון, בהמ׳׳ק נקרא
ראשון, ומשיח נקרא ראשון. יבא ראשון ויבנה ראשון ויחריב ראשון.[7]

ח.

בחבור עם ההשקפות שדברנו עליהן בפרקים שלמעלה יש לנו
לחקור על הדעות המפוזרות באגדה, שהמשיח נברא קודם לבריאת
העולם. בהשקפה זו תלויה שאלה יותר עמוקה והיא: אם הגואל הוא
בשר ודם כשאר בריות או משונה מהם לגמרי. עלינו להראות בראשונה
את המקורות שעליהם מיוסד הרעיון. באגדה אחת – קדומה שהיא כעין
ברייתא – נמנה שמו של משיח בין הדברים שעלו במחשבה להבראות
קודם שנברא העולם עם שאר דברים אחרים (ב׳׳ר פ׳׳א, הוצאת תיאודור
עמוד 8). השקפה שמי שגדול מחבירו בחשיבות ובמנין צריך גם להיות
קדום ממנו בזמן ובמנין הולידה את הרעיון שהדברים היותר חשובים

---

[1] ב׳׳ר פ׳ כד, תיאודור עמוד 233, קהלת רבה א, וב.

[2] עיין מאמרי מרעיונות הגאולה ב„מצודה" חלק ב תש׳׳ד.

[3] ב׳׳ר לא, יג.

[4] עיין ילקוט שמעוני בראשית, קסא. וייליניק, בית המדרש ח׳׳ב, ע׳׳ט ומש׳׳כ
במאמרי בישרון, הנ׳׳ל, תרפ׳׳ד עמ׳ 337–340.

[5] סנהדרין צח, ע׳׳א.   [6] שם.

[7] פסיקתא דר׳׳כ, קפה ע׳׳ב, ועיין דברי רבי יצחק שהגאולה בזכות הלולב
שנקרא ראשון.

ברומו של עולם! אם המשיח כבר בא או לא? רבי לוי רוצה לומר
אפילו תימא שכבר בא, כמו שחשב רבי יהושע בן לוי – שיושב על
שערי רומי – או רבי יוחנן שהשעבוד אינו ראיה שלא בא עדיין, מ״מ
נתכסה מבני אדם דוגמא לגואל ראשון. ורבי יצחק· שהוא מתכוון
בהתנגדותו לכנסיה הנוצרית ולכל דעותיה מדגיש שהמשיח שמאמינים בו
הנוצרים אינו המשיח האמתי, כי סימני המשיח האחרון הם הם עצמם
סמני הגואל הראשון, עני ורוכב על החמור, המן והבאר, – סימנים שלא
באו עדיין·

מסוג של מאמרים אחרים ג״כ לשפוט ולדון על המצב הרוחני
השולט בקהלות ובבתי מדרשות· הנקודות ששמנו לבנו עליהן היו
לקוחות מהחיים הפנימיים של העם, כמו באיזה זכות הגאולה באה, ואם
הגואל כבר הופיע ומהותו וכוחו, אולם גם החיים החיצוניים שלטו בהם,
בפרט הכח הפוליטי של רומי, המלחמות והערבובים שבדורות ההם
עשו רושם אדיר על התפתחות הרעיון שאנו מדברים בו· למשל, רב
אמר: אין בן דוד בא עד שתפשוט מלכות רומי בכל העולם כולו
תשעה חדשים (בבלי יומא י, ע״א)· עדיין לא נתברר כל צרכו על
איזה מאורע רמז רב במאמרו זה, ולמה מדבר מט׳ חדשים? גם רבי
יוחנן בר נפחא נותן כמה סימנים לביאת בן דוד שהם לקוחים מחיי זמנו
וכוללים חיי הרוח, הפוליטי והכלכלי כאחד, מזה שראה בעיניו:

א) תלמידי חכמים מתמעטים,

ב) והשאר עיניהם כלות,

ג) ואנחה וצרות רבות,

ד) גזרות קשות מתחדשות,

ה) עד שהראשונה פקודה,

ו) השניה ממהרת לבוא,

ז) ייתי ולא אחמינה·[1]

רבי יוחנן תופש כאן לשון החוזים בעלי האפוקליפטין שדבריהם
כבר נשנו ונשלשו בחזיונות התנאים· בקיצור, סימני הגאולה הם: מיעוט
התלמידים, – וזהו אינו מתאים עם המצב הרוחני בזמנו של רבי יוחנן
שבדורו אם לא היה מספר התלמידים מרובה מן הדורות שלפניו, לכל
הפחות לא היה גרוע ממנו! אולי נקודה זאת שייכת לצאן ברזל של

---

[1] סנהדרין צז, עא·

לכפול הבטחון שבגאולה האחרונה השלימה לא יוסיף לבוא עוד שעבוד? אולם עוד יש בכוחנו להפיץ אור על המאמר הזה משני צדדים. מצד אחד ראינו שנתפשטה האמונה שכבר נולד המשיח, שאם לא כן אין שום תועלת במעשיות כמו של אגדת רבי יהושע בן לוי או במעשה המשיח שנולד בט׳ באב. בודאי האמינו חוגים רחבים באומה בזה, או בניגוד לדעות שהכריזו בכנסיה הנוצרית על עם ישראל. מצד זה יש להוכיח שבני דורו של רבי יוחנן, הדרשנים רבי לוי ורבי יצחק באגדות שלהם מביעים דעתם על המשיח שהוא קיים בעולם. פגשנו כבר שניהם בעניני גאולה. מדבריהם יש להשיג כי גם הם היו מעונינים בשאלה זאת, שהיא היתה שאלה יומית ועממית. ונוסף לזה מצינו באגדת רבי לוי המאמר, שאמר הקדוש־ברוך־הוא לישראל: חייכם! אף הגואל שאני מעמיד לכם לעתיד לא יהיה לו אב ואם (אסתר רבה פ׳ו, יח ע״א), ז״א, או שהוא יהיה יתום או שיוולד מחוץ לטבע הרגיל. נצרף לזה עוד מאמר אחד שלו שאומר: שהגואל הראשון, כלומר משה, והגואל האחרון, כלומר: המשיח, יהיו שווים, כמו שמשה נגלה ונתכסה, כך זה נגלה ונתכסה. נעיין במקורות שלפנינו מה שיש להביא על דברי רבי לוי וגם חבירו ר׳ יצחק בענין זה. במדרש רות רבה (ה׳ ו׳) מביא מאמר רבי לוי, רבי ברכיה בשמו, כגואל הראשון כן גואל האחרון, מה הגואל הראשון נגלה וחזר ונכסה מהן, כך הגואל האחרון נגלה ונכסה מהן. בקהלת רבה (א, כב) מביא רבי ברכיה דברי רבי יצחק שמדמה את שני הגואלים ומעמיד אותם בשלש השוואות: א) מה גואל ראשון נאמר בו ויקח משה את אשתו ואת בניו וירכיבם על החמור, כך גואל אחרון, שנאמר עני ורוכב על החמור; ב) מה גואל ראשון הוריד להם את המן כך גואל אחרון יוריד להם את המן; ג) מה גואל ראשון העלה להם את הבאר, אף גואל אחרון יעלה להם את הבאר. בפסיקתא רבתי (פט״ו הוצ׳ מהרמא״ש עב צ״ב) מביא דברי רבי ברכיה בשם רבי לוי. משם יש להשלים את המאמר ברות רבה, שחסר שם הדמיון: כך גואל אחרון נגלה להם וחוזר ונתכסה מהם. בשיר השירים רבה (ב, כב, בפסוק דומה דודי לצבי) מביא המאמר בלי שם רבי לוי, סתם ובקצת שינויים, מה צבי זה נראה וחוזר ונכסה, נראה וחוזר ונכסה, כך גואל הראשון נראה ונכסה וחוזר ונראה.

מה רצו בעלי אגדה הללו לומר בהשוואות כאלו? בודאי עלינו לשער כי חלופי הדעות שביניהם הוא בדבר ממשי ריאלי שעמד בימיהם

הרעיון הזה שהוא אוחז בשיטת רבי אליעזר באמרו שהגאולה באה על
ידי התשובה (עיין מדרש איכה רבה). מכל זה אנו רואים שבתקופת
האמוראים התעסקו בשאלה באיזה דבר תלויה הגאולה, אם בתשובה
בלחוד, או בתשובה וקץ, או בשמירת מצות מיוחדות. אולם גם להרעיון
שפגשנו כבר בדור התנאים שהגאולה תלויה בחסדו של המקום, נמצא
מקום בתקופה זאת. רבי יוסי ברבי חנינא מטעים את הרעיון בדרשה
יותר מפוארה שראויה להעתקה כאן: בשעה שבקש הקדוש־ברוך־הוא
לשלוח את משה למצרים, מה אמר משה? ואמרו לי מה שמו. א״ל
הקב״ה למשה: אין אתה יודע מה שמי? בוא ואומר לך: אהיה אשר
אהיה, אהיה שלחני אליכם, אתה מוצא שלש פעמים כתוב אהיה, אמר
הקדוש־ברוך־הוא:

ברחמים בראתי את עולמי.

ברחמים אני עתיד לנהוג.

וברחמים אני עתיד לחזור לירושלים.

כיון שהלך משה ואמר להם, אמרו: מה יש עלינו לומר לצדיקו של
עולם? שהוא טוב (מדרש תהלים הוצ' רש״ב ע״ב ע' 344). הרי שהבטיח
המקום בשמו שברחמים יגאל את ישראל.

עתה נפן אל השקפה אחרת של רעיון הגאולה שנשאו ונתנו בה
חכמי הדורות. זהו שהגואל כבר קיים ושרוי בעולם, ויש יודעים באיזה
מקום הוא יושב, ויש מהם מפרשים למה הוא מכוסה מעיני הבריות, ויש
מהם נותנים טעם לדבר למה ישראל בשעבוד למרות שהמשיח כבר
בעולם. נתחיל עם רבי יהושע בן לוי ששאל את אליהו הנביא: אימתי
אָתי משיח? אמר ליה: זיל שייליה לדידיה! א״ל: והיכא יתיב? אמר
ליה: אפיתחא דרומי, א״ל: ומאי סימניה? א״ל: יתיב בין סובלי
חולאים ונגעים והוא ג״כ מנוגע. הרי שבימיו נתפשט הרעיון של המשיח
המנוגע שיושב על שערי רומי. לפי דברי רבי יוחנן בר נפחא אמר
הנביא לישראל: דוגמא שלכם דומה ליעקב אביכם. מה יעקב אביכם
עד שלא נשא אשה נשתעבד, משנשא אשה נשתעבד, אף אתם, משלא
נולד גואל נשתעבדתם, ומשנולד גואל אתם משתעבדים (ב״ר ע' יח.
וגם ילקוט מכירי הושע, ע' 207). מה היתה דעתו של הדרשן בהשוואה
זו בין יעקב אבינו ובין בניו? על איזה גואל רומז כאן? האפשר שבדעתו
לפרסם הרעיון שפגשנו כבר בפרקים שלפנינו שבגאולות הראשונות
שעבוד בא בכל פעם אחרי כל גאולה וגאולה? א״כ בודאי היתה ראויה

רבי יוחנן שיקר הוא מצד עצמו, באמרו: כל צרה של ישראל עצמן
אינה צרה, של ישראל ואומות העולם שותפין בה היא צרה, ועל זה
דרש: כמו צרתן בשושן הבירה, שלא היתה אלא לישראל, שנאמר: אבל
גדול ליהודים, מיד הצמיח להן הקדוש־ברוך־הוא ישועה שנאמר:
ליהודים היתה אורה. בדורו של רבי יוחנן נתנסו בצרות ומחבבים
להזכיר בשעה כזאת את צרת המן. על כן מבטיחם ומזרזם הדורש
ואומר להם: מיד יצמיח לכם הקדוש־ברוך־הוא ישועה לצרה כמו
תשובה וקץ, אחת מחמשה דברים שמביאים את הגאולה, כמו שראינו
כבר בדרשת ר' אלעזר בן פדת. גם רבי שמעון בן לקיש נתן סימן
הדומה לזה באמרו: אם ראית שהצרות מכסות אתכם באותה שעה אתם
נגאלין (מדרש תהלים יט, עב). רבי לוי – מצות פרטיות ששמירתן או
העוסק בהן מקרבים את הגאולה, כמו תלמוד תורה. העוסק בתורה
לשמה מקרב את הגאולה (ב. סנהדרין צט, עב). או מצות שמירת
שבת, אם ישראל שומרין את השבת כראוי מיד בן דוד בא (שמות רבה
כה, טז). רבי יצחק כופל דבריו של רבי יוחנן ורשב"ל, שהצרות
מביאות את הגאולה והוא אומר: אם ראית צרות שהן ממשמשין ובאין
על הארץ, תראה בהן סימני הגאולה (במדרש קהלת רבה, אם ימלאו.).
גם מדגיש את זכות נטילת לולב ברעיון הגאולה, הקדוש־ברוך־הוא
נקרא ראשון, בהמ"ק נקרא ראשון, אדום נקרא ראשון, אם אתם נוטלים
לולב בראשון, יבא הקדוש־ברוך־הוא הנקרא ראשון ויגאלכם מיד אדום
הנקרא ראשון ויבנה לכם ביהמ"ק שנקרא ראשון (ב"ד, פ' סג, הוצ'
תיאודור עמוד 687 ורבי חגאי בשמו). דברי רבי יצחק שמדגיש את זכות
לולב, מתאימים עם דרשה אחת של רבי יהודה בר סימן באותו נושא
עצמו (שה"ש רבה ב, א) כך אמר משה לישראל: אם מבקשין אתם
להגאל בדבר קל אתם נגאלים. אמרו לו: משה רבינו הדא מיסרתא
דאזובא (אגודת אזוב) בכמה היא טבא? בד' מיני או בה' מיני? א"ל:
אפילו בחד, והיא גרמה לכם לירש את ביזת מצרים וכו', לולב שהוא
עומד לו לאדם בכמה דמים ויש בו כמה מינים על אחת כמה וכמה.
אם מין אחד כמו אזוב שהוא דבר קל הביא לכם גאולה ממצרים,
על־אחת־כמה־וכמה – אומר הדרשן – שתזכו לביאת הגואל על ידי
שמירת מצות לולב שאתם מקיימים כראוי וכהלכתה בכל שנה ושנה,
שתראו בנחמת ציון וירושלים.

יש עוד להוסיף את דברי רבי אחא שתופס מקום מיוחד בתולדות

וליתן לפני היהודים שהיו חשודים או קרובים להמשך ברשת הכנסיה
ציור יהודי מלידת המשיח האמתי. זמן המעשה בודאי נופל לאחר זמנו
של רבי שמואל בר נחמני שדברו נעשה לבסיס המעשה שלא היה מעולם,
אלא משל בעלמא. ויותר מזה מצינו באגדת רשב״ן שהיה מאמין שהגאולה
באה לא על ידי גואל פרטי, איש מצויין, רק הקדוש־ברוך־הוא בכבודו
ובעצמו יבא ויגאל את עמו מן המלכיות והגליות, ויקבץ אותנו מארבע
כנפות הארץ לפיכך קשה הוא ליחס לו עובדות ומשלים כאגדת לידת
המשיח.

מכל אלו המאמרים יוצא לנו ציור שלם מרעיון הגאולה באגדת
רשב״ן. הוא מאמין באמונה שלימה בתורת הגאולה העתידה לבא,
ולהביא בכחה את הסרת שעבוד מלכיות או גליות, קיבוץ הגליות ובנין
ירושלים, הגאולה תהיה בחסדו ובחמלתו של מקום, ואפילו יאוש מן
הגאולה אינו מעכב אותה, והגאולה האחרונה לא תהיה על ידי אמצעי,
גואל ומושיע, אלא הקדוש־ברוך־הוא בעצמו יגאל את ישראל.

נפן עתה אל דעות שאר האמוראים בענין זה, הן שחיו לפני רשב״ן,
הן שהיו בני דורו, הן הבאים אחריו.

ז

השפעת האגדת התנאית ניכרת גם בתורת הרעיון הזה אצל האמוראים.
גם בתקופה זאת שמו לב להשאלה אם הגאולה תלויה בתשובה או בקץ,
או בחסדי השם? כבר פגשנו את שיטתו של רבי יהושע בן לוי, מובא
בשמו על ידי רבי אחא שמפרש הפסוק בעתה – אם לא זכו, אחישנה –
אם זכו (ירושלמי תענית א, א, ועיין לעיל בפרק שני).[1] מרכיב את
רעיון התשובה שראויה להחיש את הגאולה, ואם לא, תמתין עד שימלא
הקץ כראוי. נציג לזה את דברי רבי יוחנן בר נפחא שדורש ג״כ שהקץ
עומד והגאולה באה בין אם חוזרין ישראל או לא חוזרין. אבל אם
עושין תשובה הגאולה מקדמת לקץ (שמות רבה כה, יב). עם זה
מתאים מאמרו הידוע שאין בן דוד בא אלא בדור שכולו זכאי, זאת
אומרת, קודם הקץ, או בדור שכולו חייב, כלומר – אחר הקץ.[2] ואולם
גם מתוך צרה צרה נגאלין. במדרש דברים רבה (ב, יד) נשאר מאמרו של

---

[1] עי׳ עמוד כג–כה.

[2] בבלי, סנהדרין צח, ב. בילקוט מכירי ישעיה עמוד 246 מיוחס המאמר לר׳
יהושע בן לוי.

דבר מלידת המשיח כל עיקר. למשל ויקרא רבה י"א. יז: והיה כאשר
נלכדה ירושלים, אמר להן אף היא אינה צרה שבו ביום נטלו ישראל
איפופסין על עוונותיהם, דא"ר ישמעאל (צ"ל ר' שמואל) בר נחמן,
איפופסין שלימה נטלו ישראל על עוונותיהם ביום שחרב בית המקדש
הה"ד תם עונך בת ציון לא יוסיף להגלותך. השמות איפוכי ואפופסין
משתמשים ביוונית בבתי המשפט בתור מחיקת חובות או שטר־זכות. על
כן גם כאן אמר הדורש שעל ידי חורבן המקדש באה להם לישראל
גאולה של מחילת עוונת. לידת המשיח לא נזכרה כאן אפילו באות
אחת. וכן במקום אחר, בב"ר פ, מב הוצאת תיאודור ואלבק עמוד
405, אפוכי גדולה נטלו ישראל על עוונותיהם ביום שחרב בית המקדש,
(שנאמר) תם עונך בת ציון. גם כאן נפקד הרמז על לידת המשיח.
ודאי אם הרמז על לידת המשיח שייך בעקרו לרשב"ן כי אז לא היה
מעלים עינו מדבר זה לפרש את השמחה שבאה לישראל ביום שחרב
בית המקדש, בזמן שכל האומה היתה מצפה לביאת המשיח? שלישית
מצינו את המאמר בפסיקתא רבתי, הוצ' מהרמא"ש כ כ ע"א, על הפסוקים
ירמיה לח, כח, ואיכה ד, כב, כמעט באותו לשון עצמו: שלא נתן
הנביא איפוכי לישראל אלא הוא כמו שכתוב תם עונך בת ציון.[1]

מזה יש לשער, כי בעקרו תפס רשב"ן ברעיון שחורבן בית המקדש
הביא מחילת עוונת לישראל, על כן אין זה צרה אלא שמחה, ולא נתן
מקום או זכר ללידת המשיח, רק אחרי כמה דורות שהרכיבו איזו
חכמים את הרעיון של ביאת המשיח עם מחילת עוונות נולדה האגדה
שביום שחרב בית המקדש נולד המשיח, שהיה מגשים, לפי רוח הזמן
של אותם חכמים, את האפוכי של ישראל ... על כן הרכיבו, ואולי
להוציא מלבם של הנוצרים, – את שני הרעיונות. ידוע, מתוך ספרו של
אוזענער, ,,דאס וויהנאכטס פעסט" שרק בזמן מאוחר החליטו שישו
הנוצרי נולד בכ"ה לחודש דצמבר. במאות הראשונות היה הדבר תלוי
בספק בכנסיה, יש מהם שחשבו באמת שנולד בקיץ, כמו בחודש יולי
וזהו בקרוב ליום ט' באב. בודאי בכדי ליחס את האגדות והחשבונות
אלו לאלו וזה מביא אותנו לתכלית הבולטת מהאגדה של לידת המשיח
שהזכרנו בפרק הקודם. במעשה זה רצו להקהות שניהם של הנוצרים

[1] עיין עוד על מאמרי רשב"ן, באריכות במאמרי: 'Einige messianologische
Vorstellungen des dritten Jahrhunderts neu beleuchtet', Jeshurun, XI, 1924,
323–342.

מסור בידך בשעה שתראי אותו תדעי שאני בא ואני קרוב – כך ישראל
מצפין, משעמדה מלכות אדום אמר להם הקדוש־ברוך־הוא: הסימן הזה
יהא בידכם אם עשיתי לכם תשועה באותו הלילה היו יודעים שאני
גואלכם, ואם לאו אל תאמינו, שלא קרבה העת (מדרש שמות רבה, פ'
יח. עיין גם ילקוט ישעיה עמוד 246). כאן רואה רשב"ן את
עיקר הגאולה בהסרת שעבוד רומי מעל שכמם, ושנית שמזהיר את בני
דורו שלא ילכו אחרי סימנים מובהקים שאינם מובהקים ונתפרסמו על ידי חוזים
מבוהלים ומבהילים את העם.

ז) רשב"ן מתנגד לשיטתו של שמואל שאמר אין בין העולם הזה
לימות המשיח אלא שעבוד מלכיות, לשיטתו יש להבדיל בין העוה"ז
והעוה"ב. בעוה"ז ישראל הולכין ומשתמשין לאור החמה ולאור הלבנה,
משא"כ לעוה"ב, אין צריכים להן מפני שהולכין לאורו של הקדוש־
ברוך־הוא (מדרש תהלים. הוצ' מהרש"ב, 521. ילקוט מכירי ישעיה
ע' 246). דברי רשב"ן אלו מתאימים עם דברי רשב"י שאמר שדור
המדבר לא היה צריך לאור החמה ביום ולאור הלבנה בלילה וכו',
ואף לעתיד לבא יאיר להם כן שנאמר והיה לך ה' לאור עולם, ואומר
קומי אורי (ילקוט מכירי ישעיה ע' 214, שם פרקי מלאכת המשכן, עיין
ברייתא דמלאכת המשכן פ' יד).

ח) לפלא שבכל המאמרים לא נמצא רמז פרטי או כללי למשיח
עצמו, שמו או אישיותו, מעשיו או צדקתו, ובכל זאת רבי ברכיה מביא
בשמו פירוש על החסירות במלים תולדת (תולדות): אף על פי שנאמרו
הדברים על מליאתן כיון שחטא אדם הראשון עוד אינן חוזרין למקומן
עד שיבא בן פרץ, אלה תולדות פרץ (בראשית רבה פ' יב, הוצ'
תאודור ע' 104). ועיין במדרש חסירות ויתירות שלי. בלשון אחר
הובא המאמר על ידי ר' יודן בשם רבי אבין (רות ד, יח). תולדות
חסרין בר מן פרץ (רות ד, יח). תולדות, והדין (בראשית ב ד, ב"ר
שם ע' 101).

לפלא יש לחשוב על כן המאמר שבא בסוף הפרק הקודם שבו
ביום שחרב בית המקדש נולד המשיח. מקור לרעיון זה, כמו שראינו
בא בצירוף עם המעשה של לידת המשיח. באסתר רבה פתיחה א.
מרכיב דעה זו עם רעיון אחר, כלומר שחורבן בית המקדש אינו צרה
לישראל אלא שמחה שעל החורבן נטלו אפוכי שלהן, כלומר מחילת
עוונות. מעניין כי בכל המקומות האחרים שהובא רעיון זה לא נמצא

5

אעפ״י שידע בשעת הגאולה שיכעיסוהו במדבר: הדבר הזה שפט עתניאל
בן קנז לפני הקדוש־ברוך־הוא, אמר לפניו רבון העולם, כך הבטחת
את משה בין עושין רצונך בין לא עושין רצונך אתה גואלם. הרי שלפי
רשב״ן הגאולה אינה תלויה בתשובה או במעשים טובים, אלא בהקדוש־
ברוך־הוא עצמו.

ד) פסיקתא דר״כ פ׳ החודש, נב ע״א. נמצא מאמרו: אילולא
שאסר הקדוש־ברוך־הוא עצמו בשבועה, לא היו ישראל נגאלים, דכתיב
לכן אמור לבני ישראל וכו׳. ואין לכן אלא לשון שבועה. הרי גם כאן
רצה הדורש להחליט שאין ישראל נגאלים על ידי זכות או בשכר צדקתם
אלא מפני שהקדוש־ברוך־הוא נשבע למפרע שיגאל אותם.[1]

מאמרו של רשב״ן, מסורת אגדה היא שאין ירושלים נבנית עד
שיתכנסו כל הגליות, אם יאמר אדם שנתכנסו כל הגליות ואין ירושלים
נבנית, אל תאמין, שנאמר בונה ירושלים ה׳ נדחי ישראל יכנס. אמרו
ישראל לפני הקב״ה: רבש״ע! לא כבר נבנית ירושלים וחרבה? א״ל
על ידי העוונות חרבה ונגליתם מתוכה, אבל לעתיד אני בונה אותה
ושוב אינה נחרבת לעולם. הרי גם כאן, כמו בפרק שלפני זה, מדגיש
שהגאולה ובנין ירושלים יהיו ע״י הקדוש־ברוך־הוא בעצמו ושוב לא
יהיה שעבוד או חורבן אחר.

ה) רבי אחא מביא בשם רבי שמואל בר נחמני המאמר: בג׳ מקומות
מצינו רוח הקודש סמוך לגאולה. הפסוקים שהביא רומזים על השקפת
הדרשן על הגאולה וגם על ביאורו של ,,רוח הקודש׳׳. א) ישעיה ס,
כב, הקטן יהיה לאלף והצעיר לגוי עצום אני ה׳ בעתה אחישנה. וכתיב
בתריה (שם סא, א), רוח אדני ה׳ עלי וכו׳. ב) שם לב, יד וט״ו משוש
פראים מרעה עדרים, עד יערה עלינו רוח ממרום. ג) איכה ג, מט, וג,
עיני נגרה ולא תדמה מאין הפגות, עד ישקיף וירא ה׳ משמים (איכה
רבתי ג, מט, וילקוט מכירי על ישעיה ע׳ 247).

ו) עוד מצינו דרשת רשב״ן על הפסוק ויסעו בני ישראל מרעמסס,
שאמר: כיון שיצאו אפו בצק שלשו, דכתיב ויאפו וכו׳, משל לאשה
שהיתה מצפה לבעלה שהלך למדינת הים אמר לה: הסימן הזה יהא

---

[1] בתנחומא, נח, הוצאת מהרש״ב, עמוד 43 מביא בהמשך להאגדה שהקב״ה
נשבע לציון ג׳ שבועות, בבריתו של אברהם אבינו, בשבת, ובתורה שיבנה את
ירושלים.

ממקורות הפתוחים לפנינו בתלמוד ובמדרש אנו יודעים, שבימיו של רבי
שמואל בר נחמני היו כפנא ומותנא בעולם (עיין בבלי תענית ח, ב).
ויותר ממה שנמצא מזה בתלמודים ובמדרשים מגידים לנו מקורות
חיצוניים על הרעב והמגפה בדורו של רשב"ן. בפרט ההיסטוריון
Zosimus[1]. בשנות 260 עד 268, שלטו בכל המלכות, מבול של מים,
רעשים ורעמים, חושך ואפילה וכל מיני רעה, אולם יותר קשה מכולן
היה הרעב שצער את העולם. הרעב בא מסיבה אחת: המלחמות
וההרגות. אלו גרמו שזרע שזרעו לא נקלט, או שלא היו יכולים
לקצרה אם זרעו. לרגל הרעב באה המגפה הכללית. במגפה מתו
כמה וכמה אוכלוסין בכל המדינות של מלכות רומי, בכל העיירות
לא עשו שום דבר אלא קברו את מתיהם. על כן אמר רבי שמואל בר
נחמני: היכי נעביד ליניצל מצרה כפולה כזאת, דבר ורעב? (עיין גם
ילקוט מכירי, תהלים קמה עב). אנו מבינים, איפוא, מדוע העריץ רב
שמואל בר נחמני את גודל כוחה של הפרנסה.

גם חכמים אחרים מחכמי הדור, כמו: רבי יוחנן בר נפחא ורבי
אלעזר בן פדת, מחשבים את היחס שבין פרנסה וגאולה, אולם רבי
שמואל בר' נחמני עולה עליהם.

ב) על הפסוק ,,ותשכח ה' עושך'' (עיין בפסיקתא רבתי קנז, ב)
דרש רבי שמואל בר נחמני: ,,בצרת המן הכתוב מדבר, ראוים היו
שלא ליגאל מצרת המן על שנתיאשו מן הגאולה, אילולי שהסכימו לדעת
יעקב אביהם, יעקב ששמע מפי הדיבור ,,והנה אנכי עמך'' ונתירא
מעשו, ,,וַיִירא יעקב מאד''. כבר בספרות התנאים ראו ביאוש מן
הגאולה חטא גדול ועכוב (עיין בפרט ספרי במדבר פי' עח, מחלון
וכליון נענשו מפני שנתאישו מן הגאולה, ספרי דברים, פי' שכו). רשב"ן
מוכיח מחייו של אבינו יעקב שיש בכוחו של הקדוש־ברוך־הוא לגאול
את ישראל אפילו אם מתיאשים מן הגאולה על־ידי צרות ושמדות.

ג) שמות רבה ג, ד מביא מאמר בשם רבי שמואל בר נחמני,
בחיבור עם הגדה שלפניה שהקדוש־ברוך־הוא גאל את ישראל ממצרים

---

[1] Zosimus, *Hist.* I. 26, 36, 37, 46, 47; Theodor Reinach, *Rev. Ét. Gr.*
XIX (1906) 142; M. Rostovtzeff, *The Social and Economic History of the
Roman Empire* (Oxford, 1926) 619; Gibbon, *Decline and Fall* I, 455;
ועיין עוד במאמרי: המצב הכלכלי בגליל בדורו של ר' יוחנן בר נפחא ובדור
שלאחריו בספר היובל לכבוד הרב יעקב פריימן, ברלין תרצ"ו, עמוד 81–92.

טעם – לשבח או לפגם – באגדה זו ורואים בה את האופטימיסם של
היהדות. בעל האמונה או בעל הבטחון באלהית חיים לא יבוא לידי
יאוש אפילו בשעת חורבן בית מקדשו ויצפה לגאולה. אין אנו רוצים
כאן להשיב על הדרש, ואם אנו רוצים להכניס ראשינו בתשובות – עלינו
לחבר את דעתו של בעל אגדה מפואר זה עם שיטתו ברעיון הגאולה
בכלל. באמת: הרעיון תופס מקום חשוב באגדת האמורא שלנו וחייבים
אנו לקבוע לו פרק מיוחד בפני עצמו כדי לברר ולהאיר את אחורי
הפרגוד של דרשותיו.

מלבד דעה זו מצטיין אמורא זה בשיטה מעניינת מאוד. הוא אומר,
שהגאולה העתידה לא תבוא על ידי שליח ולא על ידי אדם מיוחד,
אלא הקדוש־ברוך־הוא בכבודו ובעצמו יבוא ויגאל ויפדה ויושיע את
ישראל מגלות ומשיעבוד. עוד נראה אם דעה זו מקורית היא באגדתנו
ואם נודעת מחכמים וחוזים, שקדמו לו במקום ובזמן, ומהי השפעתה על
הדורות שבאו אחריו. אולם כדי לירד לסוף דעתן של האגדות אנו
צריכים לחבר באופן סידורי את מאמריו בעניין הגאולה.
ואלה הם:

א) מקום רחב וחשוב תופס באגדה המאמר ש„גדולה או יותר קשה
הפרנסה מן הגאולה". פעם הוא מדגיש: רצונך לידע מה כוחה של
הפרנסה (בנדפס: הפרוסה), זו שאדם נותן לתוך פיו שהיא קשה מן
הגאולה· מניין? אתה מוצא בשעה שהקריב יוסף את בניו לפני אביו
שיברכם תלה את הגאולה במלאך, אבל כשיבוא לברכם בפרנסה אמר
האלהים הרועה אותי וכו'.[1] במדרש תהלים[2] הובא המאמר בקיצור
בשם רשב„ן, שהפרנסה גדולה מן הגאולה. וכן בסדר אליהו רבה (ד):
בכל יום עושין לי גדולה כיוצאי מצרים, ז. א. פרנסה.[3] מי דחקו ומה
הביא את ר' שמואל בר נחמני לידי כך להגדיל את כוח הפרנסה וכנגד
זה להחליש את כוח הגאולה? אולי יש לנו רשות לשער, שהמאמר תלוי
במצב הכלכלי, היותר גרוע ושפל, ששלט בדורו. מצב זה משמש פרגוד
לכמה דעות ומאמרים שהובעו בתקופה שאנו עומדים בה. כי אין כוח
ביד העם, אפילו מנהיגיו, לברוח מן הכחות הגשמיים השולטים בעולמם.

---

[1] פסיקתא רבתי קנד, עא.

[2] הוצאת ר' שלמה בובר, עמ' 521, ועיין גם ב„ר הוצ' תיאודור עמוד 192.

[3] הוצ' מהרמא„ש, עמוד 8.

והטיבך והרבך מאבותיך. לעתיד לבא ואומר: אבותיך ירשו ארץ
של ז׳ עממין, ואתם עתידים לירש של עשר עממין. אבותיך אעפ״י
שנגאלו חזרו ונשתעבדו, אבל אתם משאתם נגאלים עוד אין אתם
משתעבדין. אולי גם דבריו במקום שלישי מאירים את שטתו, באמרו:
כתיב ויברח יעקב שדה ארם. דוגמא שלכם דומה ליעקב אביכם. מה
יעקב אביכם עד שלא נשא אשה נשתעבד, משנשא אשה נשתעבד, אף
אתם משלא נולד גואל נשתעבדתם, משנולד גואל אתם משתעבדים.[1] מה
היה בדעתו של רבי יוחנן כשבא להשוות את חייו ושעבודו של יעקב
אבינו עם לידת הגואל ושעבוד ישראל? ומה רמז יש ללידת הגואל
בימיו? אולי רומז על לידת משיח הנוצרי? או ללידת משיח שקר בימיו
ונמצאו כמה יהודים שהלכו אחריו? יהיה זה איך שיהיה, ברור הוא
שהולך הוא לשטתו שגואל בשר ודם אינו יכול להסיר את עול השעבוד
משכמם.

מלבד רבי יוחנן יש לנו עוד בעל אגדה אחד בתקופה שקודמת
לרבי אהא שנקט שטה זאת בידיו, ומדגיש הרעיון באופן הכי מסוים
ומוחלט, והוא, רבי שמואל בר נחמני, אגדת הדרשן הזה – כמו שנראה
עוד בפרק מיוחד – עשירה בדעות ובדרשות המקיפות את רעיון הגאולה
והמשיח, הוא אומר: הנביאים קוראים אותנו גאולי ה׳, פדויי ה׳, ואינם
משתמשים בסגנון ,,גאולי אליהו״ או ,,פדויי משיח״ אלא גאולי ה׳,[2]
לפי שאין להם לישראל גואל אלא הקב״ה בעצמו. אולי יש לשער שרבי
הלל,[3] שאמר אין משיח לישראל שכבר אכלוהו בימי חזקיהו, הוא רבי
הלל בנו של רבי שמואל בר נחמני, והבן הלך בעקבות אביו שהגואל
הוא הקב״ה, ולא אחר.

ו.

דברי רבי שמואל בר־נחמני האחרונים, שביום שחרב בית המקדש
נולד הגואל, או המשיח, צריכים ביאור. מטיפים ומגידים, דרשנים
מינים ממינים שונים, הן בדורות שעברו והן בדורות שלנו, הן שרוח
חדש מדבר מתוך גרונם והן שמרצים בסגנון עתיק, הן שקורין את עצמם
אורתודוכסים והן שמכנים את עצמם בשם רפורמים, משתדלים ליתן

---

[1] בראשית רבה י״ח.   [2] מדרש תהלים הוצ׳ מהרש״ב ע׳ 61.

[3] ב. סנהדרין צ״ט, ע״א.

ואינם משתעבדים עוד״. אולם מצד אחר נמצאו גם במדרש זה
סתימות שבהן מדגישים את הגאולה על ידי המשיח.[1]

במדרש אגדת שיר השירים או במדרש זוטא על שיר השירים, שהוא
מלא וגדוש רעיונות משיחיות ורעיון הגאולה, נמצא העניין שאנחנו מדברים
בו בזה האופן: כל השירים לשעבר היו בלשון נקבה, מפני שהגאולות
הולידו אחריהם שעבודים חדשים, אבל לעתיד לבא תהיה הגאולה ע״י
הקב״ה בעצמו ואין אחריה עוד שעבוד. על כן הוא בלשון זכר, בשיר
חדש.[2] יש בכח הדמיון לצייר בדעתנו את המצב הרוחני שבו חיו
השומעים לדרשות הללו. בודאי הוכיחו את המורים שלהם בטענות על
רעיון הגאולה, מה תועלת יש לנו בגאולת ישראל? הרי אנו רואים שכמה
וכמה פעמים גאל אותנו, וכל הישועה לא היתה אלא לשעה קלה.
אחרי הישועה בא שעבוד, וכל שעבוד ושעבוד היה יותר קשה ממה
שהיה לפניו. הרי טוב לנו לעבוד בשעבוד מלטעום טעם גאולה לשעה!
באותו מדרש עצמו נמצא מאמר חשוב שמפיץ אור בהיר על הדעות
והאמונות ששלטו באומה בזמן הדורש.[3] הדרשן סומך את עצמו על
הפסוק: משכני אחריך נרוצה, ואומר הקב״ה לכנסת ישראל:
להודיע שכל הימים שהייתם מסורין ביד המלכות שהיו משעבדים אתכם
הייתי מקצר את ימי השעבוד ומקרב את ימי הגאולה לפני
שאתם חוזרים לשעבוד אחר, אבל עכשיו משכתי לכם את הגאולה
ומשתגאלו בפעם הזאת אין שוב אתם חוזרים לשעבוד מעתה. הרי לפי
הדרשן הזה השעבוד החדש אינו תלוי בגאולה על ידי גואל בשר ודם,
אלא באורך הגלות עצמו. אולם גם הוא מסכים לדעת חבריו שאחרי
הגאולה האחרונה לא יהיה עוד שעבוד אחר. הוא נותן טעם לדבר למה
לא היתה הגאולה שלמה בפעמים הראשונות, מפני שנתקצר הקץ.
השעבוד והגאולה הם עניינים התלויים זה בזה שעבוד שלם מביא גאולה
שלמה. לא כן שעבוד בלתי שלם.

רוב המאמרים שאספנו עד כה הם סתמיים, מלבד דברי רבי רבי אחא
ולפניו דברי רבי יוחנן. יש לנו עוד חזוק שרבי יוחנן נקט שטה זאת
בידו. רבי חלבו ושמעון בר אבא מביאים בשמו[4] פתרון על הפסוק

---

[1] עיין שם קפ״ב, ע״ב, רבי ברכיה בשם רבי אבא בר כהנא.

[2] הוצ׳ שכטר ע׳ 10. עיין גם בהמנהיג דפוס ברלין כ״ז ע״א, ובמכילתא פ׳ שירה.

[3] שם ע׳ 13.

[4] ירושלמי שביעית ו׳, א׳.

א) פיסקא ט':[1] הדרשן מסיים בתפלה א: רבש"ע בנה ביתך
ושכנינו בתוכו מקצה הארץ! ז. א. בנין המקדש וקבוץ גלויות.

ב) פיסקא י"ג:[2] הקב"ה אומר לישראל, בעוה"ז אמרתי לכם
למחות את שמו של עמלק, אבל לעתיד לבא השבט שהשכינותי לו הוא
פורע ממנו ומוריש ביצתן מן העולם.

ג) פיסקא כ"א:[3] לשעבר הייתם עבדים לעבדים, אבל לע"ל
עבדיו של הקב"ה.

ד) פיסקא כ"ו:[4] בעולם הזה בשר ודם בונה אותך ובשר ודם
מחריבך, אבל לע"ל אני בונה אותך.

נעמיד נגד אלו הסתימות שאינן מזכירות את המשיח, את הסיומים
המשיחיים.

א) שם קנ"ט, ע"ב. בזכות הנשים הקב"ה מגין עליהם ומוליכם
דרך ישרה, וגואל אותם. מה ת"ל הוי לימות המשיח, הוי לעולם הבא,
ואין אחר עמו, ואויביו אלביש בושת ועליו יציץ אלו החולקים עליו, עליו יציץ
נזרו, "עליו ועל הדומים לו". הסיום מתנגד לאותם שחולקים על
המשיח, ומחזק ידי הדומים לו, כלומר רעיו ובעלי בריתו.

ב) שם קס"ה, ע"ב. באותה שעה הקב"ה מבהיק אורו של מלך
המשיח ושל ישראל, וכל או"ה בחשך ואפלה. והולכים כולם לאורו
של משיח ושל ישראל, שנאמר והלכו גוים לאורך, ובאים ומלחכים עפר
תחת רגלו של מלך המשיח, ובאים כולם ונופלים על פניהם לפני משיח
ולפני ישראל ואומרים לו נהיה לך ולישראל עבדים.

הנגוד הזה בין הסיומים נמצא גם בפסיקתא דר"כ, ק"ו, ע"ב,
משתמש בתור חתימה במאמר סתמי שנמצא במדרש תהלים על הפסוק
ישראל נושע בה', עם הפסוק כי עמך מקור חיים[5] שאולי הוא מרבי
יוחנן (עיין לעיל). הדרשן חותם בזה הלשון:

"בעוה"ז נגאלו בני ממצרים ונשתעבדו בבבל,

מבבל למדי, ממדי ליון, מיון לאדום, ומאדום הקב"ה גואלם.

[1] הוצ' מהרמא"ש ל"ג ע"א (ולא יהיה עוד חורבן).

[2] שם, נ"ו, ע"א. רגיל הוא בחתימות להתנגד להעולמות זה כנגד זה ואכמ"ל.

[3] שם ק"ג, ע"ב.

[4] שם קל"ב, ע"א.

[5] עיין לעיל הערה 7. עיין גם הנוסחא שמובא ממדרש בכת"י ב', מ', סי' 2853
נ"ג, ע"א.

נשתעבדו באדום הרשעה אמרו ישראל: הרינו נתיגענו משתעבדין ונגאלין וחוזרין ומשתעבדין עכשיו אין אנו מבקשים לגאולת בשר ודם. אלא גואלנו ה' צבאות קדוש ישראל, אין אנו מבקשים שיאיר לנו בשר ודם, אלא שיאיר לנו הקב"ה.

אם באמת רבי יוחנן הוא בעל המאמר אז יש בידינו להחליט כי כבר באמצע המאה השלישית למספרם נתפשטה שטה זו בבתי כנסיות ובתי מדרשות בגליל. בקשת העם שהגאולה הסמוכה לבא לא תהיה על ידי בשר ודם, אפילו הגון ומצוין כמשה רבינו או דניאל וכו', אלא הקב"ה בעצמו יבא ויגאל את עמו מתוך צרותיהם וגלותם. עוד יש לחקור אם יש עוד עדים או רמזים בקורות הזמן או בדברי החכמים בני דורו של רבי יוחנן שהדבר כן הוא, ולמה הדגישו הרעיון של גאולת ישראל בלי סרסור של בשר ודם?

מקור שני פתוח לפנינו בתנחומא שמורה על התפשטות של השטה הזאת. כבר הראתי במקום אחר,[1] שהמסדר של המדרש תנחומא משתמש בסוף הדרשות והמלוקטות מכמה קובצים של דרשות, בחתימות שהיו חביבות ומצוינות בזמנו או בזמן המקורות ששאב מהם. אם נשער כי החתימות נולדות או במאה הרביעית או במאה החמישית למספרם, אז נוכל להכיר כי מלבד רבי אחא גם הבאים בדורות תלמידיו ותלמידי תלמידיו חבבו ביתר שאת להדגיש הרעיון שאנחנו עומדים עליו כאן. בכמה מן החתימות מסיים הדרשן בנחמות וברכות לחזק את הלבבות האומללות והמתיאשות שהקב"ה בעצמו יבא ויגאל את ישראל, הוא בעצמו יבנה את ירושלים, הוא בעצמו יקבץ את נדחי עמו, הוא בעצמו יכסה האומות באפל ובחשכה ויאיר לישראל, ועוד מה שדומה לזה, ולא זו בלבד אלא אף זו שבחתימות הללו לא נמצא שום רמז לא על שמו ולא על פעולותיו של גואל בשר ודם. הלא החסרון הזה דבר הוא!

דבר חדש יש ללמוד אם נדקדק בחתימות שבפסיקתא רבתי! נראה שבחתימות עד ע' קי"ט, ובסימנים שאחרי זה. בחלק הראשון מסיים הדרשן בגאולת ישראל ע"י הקב"ה ובחלק שני בגאולת משיח. נסדר החתימות כסדרן.

---

[1] עיין מאמרי „פרקים באגדה" ב„הסוקר" שנה רביעית תרצ"ז—צ"ח ע' 138—141.

מסדר המדרש[1] מביא על הפסוק ,,אמונים נוצר ה'" אגדה
סתמית שהיא נפלאה במינה: אלו ישראל שהם מאמינים בתחיית המתים
ועדיין לא חיו המתים ואומרים ברוך אתה ה' מחיה המתים. שנית
מאמינים בגאולה ואומרים בתפלה בא''י גאל ישראל ועדיין לא נגאלו,
שלישית אומרים בתפלה בא''י בונה ירושלים ועדיין לא נבנית, ועוד
חרבה ושממה, הרי גודל אמונת ישראל. האגדה מסיימת בדברי הקב''ה
לישראל: אתם מאמינים בגאולה! ועדיין לא נגאלו גאולה שלימה אלא
לשעה, וחזרו ונשתעבדו, אבל לעתיד לבא אני גואלם, כלומר: גאולה
שלימה שאין אחריה שעבוד אחר. גאולת הקב''ה גאולה שלמה היא,
והיא בהא תליא שאין אחריה שעבוד ולהיפך בגאולת בשר ודם. הדרשן
נקט בידו אלו העיקרים מעיקרי הדת, האמונה בתחיית המתים בגאולת
ישראל ובבנין ירושלים, שגם הנוצרים האמינו בהן, והלא כל מה שהם
חושבים ודורשים תלוי באמונה שמיסד דתם קם מן המות והביא גאולה
לעולם, ובנה את ירושלים שלמעלה למטה, אולם הם מאמינים באלו
מפני שחושבים שכבר נתקיימו, אולם ישראל הם מאמינים באלו הדברים
אף על פי שעדיין לא באו, מ''מ הם מתפללים בכל יום בתפלה שלהם
על אלו שלשתם. באגדה שלפניה יש נוסחא שהאמונים נוצר ה' אלו פושעי
ישראל שהם אומרים בעל כרחם ברוך מחיה המתים, אולי צריך
להוסיף, גאל ישראל ובונה ירושלים? והם אומרים אמן בעל כרחם, ז''א,
שמוכרחים להאמין באלו האמונות, כי בכפירתם בטל כל בנינם.

שלישית מחריז דרשן אחד את הפסוק בתהלים קוה קויתי
עם ישעיה כ''ה, ט'[2] (זה ה' קוינו לו ויושיעֵנו) ומצא בהם הרעיון: אין
ישראל מקוה לבשר ודם שיגאלם אלא הקב''ה בעצמו יבא ויגאלם,
בשכר קוה קויתי.

עוד יש לנו לרמוז על מאמר אחד שמדבר בענין זה. המאמר
נשנה בהמשך עם אגדה אחת של רבי יוחנן, אולם הדבר אינו ברור אם
הדברים עצמם שייכים לרבי יוחנן או אם נתוספו למאמרו.[3] הדרשה
עצמה מיוסדת על הפסוק ,,כי עמך מקור חיים וכו'" הדורש מוסיף
למשל בזה הלשון: כן ישראל נשתעבדו במצרים עמד משה וגאלם,
נשתעבדו בבבל, עמדו דניאל וכו' וגאלם, נשתעבדו בעילם פרס ומדי
ועמדו מרדכי ואסתר וגאלום, נשתעבדו ביון באו חשמונאי ובניו וגאלום,

---

הכי מצוינה, באגדה זאת מצינו הרעיון שכבר פגשנו באגדת התנאים,
שהקב"ה מביא את הגאולה למען שמו, אפילו אם אין צדיקים באומה
עכשיו כמו שהיו צדיקים בדורות הראשונים. ולא עוד שישראל לא
בוטחים בגואל אחר אלא בהקב"ה שהוא הגואל האמתי. הדרשן מחריז
את הפסוק בתהלים ל"א, ב' עם הפסוק בישעיה מ"ה, י"ז (ישראל
נושע בד' תשועת עולמים). כנסת ישראל שהיא שרויה בבושה ובכלימה
בין הגוים, מתאוננת ומבקשת: ,,גאל אותנו''! הגאולה תהיה להסיר את
הבושה והכלימה מבני האומה! התשובה על דברי הצועקים לפני הקב"ה
נשארה לפנינו בב' נוסחאות, ,,כשם שגאלתי אתכם לשעבר – אומר הקב"ה
לשעבר, כן אני גואל אתכם להבא'' ז"א שהגאולות הראשונות היו באמת
על ידי הקב"ה בעצמו, כן תהיה הגאולה העתידה לבא. הדרש מיוסד
על דברי הפסוק: אל תירא כי גאלתיך (ישעיה מ"ג, א) הבורא
והיוצר הוא הגואל האמתי ולא הבשר ודם הנברא והנוצר. הוא אומר
דבר ונעשה מעשה. לא כן בשר ודם שהיום כאן ומחר בקבר. בלי
ספק רמוז בזה על משיח הנוצרים, בהתנגדותם להגואל בזה האופן לא
חשו כל עיקר שגם רעיון הגאולה בישראל מדבר מגואל בשר ודם, כמו
משה רבינו ואחרים כמותו, אולי מטעם זה באמת הדגישו בהגדה של
פסח שגאולת מצרים לא היתה על ידי משה או על ידי מלאך, אלא
על ידי הקב"ה בכבודו ובעצמו.

סגנון התשובה משונה, וגם תכליתה משונה. בנוסחא האחרת שלפנינו
הקב"ה מבטיח את ישראל שהוא יפדה אותם מגלותם (עיין ירמיה ל"א
י' כי פדה ה' את יעקב). אמרו לפניו ישראל: רבש"ע! הלא כבר
גאלתנו פעמים רבות על ידי משה ויהושע ואחרים, ואח"כ חזרנו
לשעבודינו כבראשונה, והיינו בבושה ובכלימה כאילו לא נגאלנו כל
עיקר? על זה אומר הקב"ה: לא כגאולה ראשונה האחרונה! הראשונה
היתה על ידי בשר ודם שהיום כאן ומחר בקבר, על כן בא שעבוד
אחר גאולה, אולם האחרונה תהיה על ידי גאולה שלימה, ואין אתם
חוזרים לשעבוד. בשר ודם יכול להביא רק גאולה שהיא לשעה, לא
כן הוא, מביא תשועת עולמים.

בכל הנוסחאות מדגיש הדרשן – כמו שעשה רבי אחא – שהגאולה
העתידה לבא תהיה על ידי הקב"ה ולא על ידי בשר ודם. אף על
פי שבעצם הדבר אין חילוק בין התשובות, בטעם יש הפרש
ביניהם.

הצליחו גמרו בלבם שאין תועלת לפנות לכאן ולכאן, תקות הגאולה
אינה תלויה בבשר ודם, אלא בגואל יחידי והוא היושב בשמים. רבי
אחא מדגיש זאת באמרו: לאותו הקלע אנו מצפים שנא׳ אשא על גוים
וכו׳,[1] רבי אחא אחד מן החכמים שמחבב לדרוש את הכתובים כמשמעם,
ואינו רואה את עצמו להרחיק דבריו מן ההתגשמות. רבי אחא גם אינו
אורגינלי בשטתו אלא, כמו בעקבות אחרים השייכים לתורת הגאולה
כמו שראינו כבר וכמו שנראה עוד לפנינו, אוחז בשטתו בדעות
עתיקות שנמצאו בדורות הראשונים, תכף לחורבן הבית, אחרי
שקמו ועמדו משיחים ממינים שונים בישראל, אחזו מורי התורה שטה זו.
אולי התפתחות הכנסיה הנוצרית עם הרעיון המרכזי של ביאת המשיח,
והאמונה במשיחת ישו הנוצרי, גרמו לזה שהיו מלמדים לעם שאין משיח
בשר ודם לישראל, אלא הגואל האמתי הוא הקב״ה. מחברו של ספר
עזרא הרביעי נושא את קולו נגד המבשרים והמאמינים שבשר ודם יבוא
ויגאל ויפדה את ישראל.[2] אינו ידוע אם החוזה הזה היה הראשון מהחוזים
שדרשו כן ואולם בודאי לא היה האחרון מאוחזי שטה זאת. בודאי רק
טעם עמוק הניע את החכמים להדגיש רעיון כזה ולבטל את האמונה
העממית שיבא איש אחד, מלאך או שליח שיפדה את ישראל. מלבד
התנגדות להכנסיה החזיקו גם טעמים אחרים את ידי המורים לפרסם
דעה זאת בתוך העם. כדי להבין את הדברים על בורים ובאמתת
ענינים יש לסדר את המאמרים עצמם ולחקור אותם.

הרעיון נכפל ונשלש במדרש תהלים כמה פעמים. המדרש הזה
עשיר הוא בחומר הנוגע לרעיון הגאולה. אולי יש לראות בשטה זו רמז
על זמנו ומקורו של המדרש. ועוד מקור אחר עשיר הוא בחומר כזה.
רצוני לומר החתימות והסיומים שהשתמשו בהם הדרשנים או קובצי
אגדות בסוף דרשותיהם כדי לנחם את העם בנחמות ובברכות. עשו
זאת כדי לעורר את הלבבות המדוכאים בצרה ובשעבוד ובשמד שיהיו
מצפים לישועה שתבוא במהרה בימיהם, החתימות האלו מענינות הן מצד
עצמם, כי לומדים על אופני הדרוש בתקופות הקדומות, הן מצד סגנונם
ולשונם.

נפן עתה אל פרטי הדברים:

א) על הפסוק ,,בך ה׳ חסיתי״ נשארה במדרש תהלים[3] אגדה

---

[1] גם כן שם ד׳, ו׳.   [2] פרק י״ג, פסוק כ״ז.   [3] הוצ׳ באבער עמוד 237.

שמחברם כותב: לעשו אין לו ישועה בעולם מפני שפרק עולו של מקום ממנו.

כל זה די להראות על השיטות המתנגדות אלו ואלו בנושא זה. בודאי אוחזות הכתות דעות הפוכות בשאלה זו, וגם מקרי הזמנים הביאום לחוות דעתם, בין לטוב בין לרע, אם יש לאו"ה חלק בטובה שהיא צפונה לצדיקים ולישרים או לא. כי לא רק באו"ה, אלא גם בישראל היו הדעות מחולקות ביניהם, אם יש לפושעים ולרשעים חלק בעוה"ב או בגאולה או לא. אולם זה שייך לפרק אחר מן תולדות הרעיון שאנו עומדים בו.

ה.

מתוך ההרפתקאות שעברו על ראש עמנו מימות חורבן בית שני עד דורו של רבי אחא, במאה הרביעית למספרם, באו חכמי ישראל לידי מסקנה: שאין לו גואל אחר אלא הקב"ה בכבודו ובעצמו יגאל את עמו מתוך השעבוד. קצים בלי מספר שחשבו מחשבי קצים ודוחקי קצים עברו ולא בא הקץ. משיחים שונים עמדו בישראל והוברורו להיות משיחי שקר וכזב. מי ישתומם אם דרשו הדורשים בהקתדראות שלהם בבתי כנסיות ומדרשות שאין גואל משיח לישראל. גם רבי אחא אחד מהדרשנים הללו שפתחו פיהם לומר שהגואל האמתי של ישראל הוא הקב"ה, ולא אחר, הוא ואין זולתו יקבץ נדחי ישראל מקצות הארץ, הוא ולא אחר יפדם מכל צרותם, הוא בעצמו יגאלם משעבודם, בשביל זה אומרת כנסת ישראל לפני הקב"ה בדרשת רבי אחא,[1] נפניתי לכאן ולכאן ואין לי גואל אלא אתה! בין המלות נפניתי לכאן ולכאן מכוסות כמה תנועות משיחיות שנאבד זכרם מתוך העם, כמה השתדלות לדחוק את הקץ, כמה תחבולות וחשבונות עמוקות להביא את הגאולה במהרה, או על ידי איש פרטי ומסוגל: או על ידי מרידות והתקוממות נגד המושלים הרודים בעם, נגד העריצים שעבדו בהם בפרך. כולם לא עלתה בידם לפרוק עול הגוים מעל צואריהם. כיון שלא

ובל יראה גאות ה' לעולם הבא! שאנוכי הוא לי לפרוע לו הכבוד שכבדני, מיד תלה עשו עיניו למעלה ובכה. שנא' וישא עשו את קולו ויבך. בב"ר פ"ז ה'. המאמר בשם רבי שמלאי וא"ל בשם רבי אבהו. ושם הגירסא עתיד הוא להפשיט ידו בבית המקדש.

[1] מדרש תהלים י"ח, י' הוצ' רש"ב, עמוד 129 ע' 47, רב הונא בשמו.

המאמרים הללו נולדו בזמנים שונים, ובתקופות רחוקות זו מזו,
וצריכים בירור וליבון שאין כאן מקומם. מטרתנו רק להראות את הרגשת
העם כנגד אדום, והן היו גורמות שהיו מחזיקים באמונה ובדעה שמלכות
כזאת אינה ראויה להתקיים ואין לה ישועה עולמית. הרגשה זאת נגד
אדום מצאה לה מקום בשאלה ששאלה כנסת ישראל: היאך אנו יכולים
לראות פניך? הלא נמסרים אנו בידי מלכות זאת?[1] אי אפשר שיהיה
חלק ונחלה למלכות רשעה כזאת בתוך הנגאלים. באמת הרעיון של
הגאולה דומה רק לחוכי וטלולי – בעיני כל הבריות אם רשעים הללו
יבואו בתוך הנגאלים לעתיד. ועולה על כל החטאים הללו, חטאו של
אדום שהרב את המקדש, פשטו ידיהם בזבול, והחריבו את הארון.
חטאו של אדום בחורבן נדגש באגדה אחת של רבי יצחק. בעל האגדה
מצייר את יצחק אבינו עומד בתפלה ותחנונים ומבקש רחמים בעד עשו
בנו. ז"א, בעד מלכות רומי, שיהיה לו חלק לעולם הבא, אולם
הקב"ה משיב לו, איך ירש עשו את העולם האמיתי, שהרב את המקדש,
העיר והארון? ויצחק חייב להודות על האמת.[2] הויכוח (דיאלוג) בין
יצחק אבינו והקב"ה. נמצא בזה הלשון:

יצחק: יוחן, כלומר תן חנינה לבני לעשו!

הקב"ה: רשע. ז"א, אינו ראוי לחן וחסד מפני שהוא רשע?

יצחק: בל למד צדק. ז"א, אין שום אדם או דבר ללמד זכות
עליו?

הקב"ה: בארץ נכוחות יעול, הוא החריב את המקדש ואין זכות
או מעשה עולה לו להסיר את העולה את העולה שעשה.

יצחק: אל יראה בגאות ה', כלומר, בודאי – אין לו תקוה או
תקנה! הדעה של עשיו אין לו ישועה – אולם לא מטעם האחרון – קדומה
היא, ונמצאת לה מקום גם בספרים הגנוזים, בפרט בספר היובלים[3]

---

[1] שמות רבה ט"ג, י"ח.

[2] עיין ב' מגלה ו' ע"א, ועיין מאמרי על ערכה ההיסטורי של האגדה
ע"ז והלאה.

[3] פ' ל"ה, פסוק י"ד, וגם פ' כ"ג, פסוק ל"ד. דברי רבי יצחק בבבלי מפורשים
ביותר בתנחומא, הוצ' מהרש"ב, בראשית, 143, וראוי להעתיק האגדה כאן בצורתה
ובלשונה. התחיל (יצחק) להתפלל ולומר: בל יוחן רשע א"ל בל למד צדק. א"ל
זה אתה מבקש לברך? עשו שהוא שהחריב את ביתי? ולערבב הארצות
והמדינות? שנאמר בארץ נכוחות יעול. א"ל (יצחק להקב"ה) תן לו בעולם הזה!

חכמי ישראל תפסו בידם הכלל שאין גאולה בלי פרעון לאוי״ה.
אין הקב״ה עתיד ליפרע – אנו מוצאים במכילתא¹ – אלא ברוח קדים,
כמו שעשה למצרים. נושא חשוב ופופולרי היה בידי הדרשנים לדרוש
בזכותו ובחטאו של אדום. למה זכה מלכות הרשעה לגדולה? ומה
היתה בידה ליפול ולהשיג פורענות ולעשות שנוי בפני המקום והבריות?
בשאלה הראשונה נחלקו גם חכמי האומות וראשי הכנסיות הנוצריות.
שאול שהתנצר לפאול דרש כי ברצונו של המקום נתנה הגבורה
והממשלה לרומי, ואין להרהר בדבר, וכל ירא אלהים חייב להשתעבד
לה. אחרים אמרו שלא מצדקת האומה השיגו הרומים לכל הכבוד
שהשתמשו בו, אלא מחמת העון והגזל וכל הדברים אכזריים שנהגו בהם.²
גם חכמי האגדה שהאמינו בפתגם שאין שכר בלא מעשה, לפיכך אין
גדולה וכבוד בלי זכות, שאלו ודרשו באיזה זכות זכה אדום או עשו
או רומי לגדולה בעולם הזה? ואמרו בזכות שקיים מצוות כבוד אב.³
ושגור בפי הבריות השאלה: מלכות הרשעה אימתי נופלת?⁴ ומצפים
למפלתה של אדום.⁵

נפן עתה בקצור אל החטאים שמיחסים לאדום! מלכות הרשעה
מחרפת ומגדפת,⁶ שנית שלא קבלה את עולו של הקב״ה ואת התורה,⁷
הורגת את הצדיקים ואת החסידים,⁸ גוזלת וחומסת את ישראל ומיצר
בניו של המקום,⁹ ואינה מניחה את ישראל לעשות את התורה ואת
המצוות,¹⁰ לבסוף, מלכות הרשעה קיימת בניגוד למלכות שמים.¹¹

---

¹ הוצ׳ מהרמא״ש ל׳ ע״ב.

² ‏‎403 ‏ע‏ P. Wendland, *Hellenistische u. Römische Kultur*, ‏ועוד לענין פאול
‏‎Minucius Felix ‏בנוגע לדברי ‏*Apologeten* *Zwei Griech.* ‏Gettreu ‏‎243 ‏עʼ ‏‎92.

³ הרעיון הזה נתפשט בכל האגדה ואתן בפנים רק פתגמים אחדים, ולא כולם
שאינם שייכים בפרט לענין שלנו אלא בכלל. עיין בפרט חיבורי ‏‎Doctrine of
‏‎Merits ‏עʼ ‏‎19 ‏ושʼʼמ.

⁴ עיין ב״ר, ס״ה ב׳.

⁵ רבי יהושע בן לוי, קהלת רבה י׳, י״ד.

⁶ עיין ויקרא רבה ז׳ ו׳.

⁷ ירושלמי ר״ה, נ״ט ע״א. כשמואל בר נחמני, עזבו את התורה, פסיקתא רבתי
ס״ב ע״ב. מדרש משלי ט׳ ע״ב.

⁸ במדבר רבה ד׳ ו׳.

⁹ שמות רבה ל״א, י״ח. בראשית רבה ס״ה א׳ תנחומא שמות הוצ׳ באבער עʼ
‏‎84, רבי לוי, קהלת רבה א׳ כ״א, כל הממון אינו עולה אלא למלכות אדום, ומלכות
אדום אינה מתמלאת. אודות המסים עיין למשל פסיקתא רבתי ל״נ ע״ב וש״מ
שאין כאן המקום לפורטם. ¹⁰ מדרש תהלים ל״ג, ע״ז וש״מ.

¹¹ שיר השירים רבה, עיין ילקוט מכירי ישעיה עʼ ‏‎195 ‏והלאה.

דברי בעל אגדה שרק ישראל חיים וקיימים לעולם בלי מיתה, אבל יש
מיתה לאו״ה. בסעיף זה יש לסדר הדעות שמהן אחדות יותר קשות
מן הראשונות, ומהם שמראים באצבע על העובדא שכל זמן שהאומות
בעולם – או בכלל או בפרט המלכיות ואדם[1] אין מקום למלכות שמים
בעולם, או לא השם שלם ולא הכסא שלם כל זמן שעמלק בעולם.
המה החזיקו בכלל – ואמיתת הרעיון מודגשת בחיי הדורות ובחיי כל
יום ויום בזמנינו – אין לצפות לישועה בדור של חייבים ורשעים בעולם.
מלכות ש-ד-י ומלכות הרשעה אינן יכולות לעמוד ולהתקיים זו בצד
זו. יש רק ברירה אחת, או זו, או זו.

מקובלת היתה בעיניהם התקוה שכשם שהביא המקום מכות על
מצרים – קודם הגאולה ע״י משה – כן מביא מכות גדולות על המלכיות
קודם הישועה.[2] ולא עוד אלא שישראל מכלין לאו״ה.[3] גם בתקופה
הראשונה של הכנסיה הנוצרית שלטה התקוה ונתגבר הרעיון שהגאולה
העתידה לבא תביא את מפלתה של רומי, כליון של אדום, והאומה
תראה את הריגתה של החיה הרעה ששפכה דם צדיקים וקדושים. אולם
ה״אבות״ שלה, או מתוך יראת המלכות, או מתוך שייכותם להאומות
החליפו ושינו את דברי החזיון וזייפו אותם כפי רצונם ודעתם.[4] לא כן
בישראל. האומה החזיקה באמונה הקדומה שאין הגאולה אמתית כל
זמן שאדום שולט בעולם, מסופו ועד סופו. כמו בדורנו כן היה בזמנם.
כל מי שאינו מוכה בסנורים היום – יהיה מי שיהיה – יודע, שכל הימים
שהמלכות הרשעה קיימת, שהרצחנים והחיות הרעות שגרמו שמד והריגה
בעולם ידם רמה וקיימת בעולם, האמת נעדרת, הדין מעוות, והשלום
לא יחזור בשום פנים לבריות, כן חשבו גם בני עמנו בדורות התנאים
והאמוראים – לכל הפחות רובם אם לא כולם.

אולם חוזי העתיד לא הסתפקו כל עיקר במפלת אדום ביום הדין.
נצחון התורה וישראל מרחף לפני רוחם, לא יכלו להכחיד מעיניהם
שיהיה הבדל גדול בין אותם האומות שהיו משתעבדים בישראל ובין
אותם שלא השתעבדו בהם. הראשונים יטלו את שלהם מתחת כס הדין,
והאחרונים יהיו מרוצים להגאל.

---

[1] עיין מדרש חסירות ויתירות שלי בהערה, ששם רשמתי את כל המקומות
השייכים לענין.

[2] תנחומא דפ׳ פפד״א ע״ז ע״א.   [3] שמות רבה, י״ב, י״ב.

[4] עיין על כל זה דברי W. Bouset בספרו *Der Antichrist*, ע׳ ע״ד.

ז) מלך המשיח מקבל כל האומות אפילו עובדי עבודה זרה
אולם רק אם לא שעבדו בהן בישראל.[1]

ח) המשיח מביא שש שש מצוות לבני נח, או לפי נוסחא אחרת ז'
מצות. רבי תנחומא מונה י' מצוות, כגון סוכה ולולב ותפילין.[2]

ט) ביאת המשיח תהיה לעין כל, גלוי לכל ישראל כמו לאו"ה.
כמו השמש והירח נראים לכל באי עולם, כך גילוי המשיח.[3] והוא
עושה שלום בין הקב"ה ובין כל בריותיו, והקב"ה פושט ידו לקבלם
כמו שעשה במעמד הר סיני.

י) או"ה מביאים דורנות למלך המשיח, על ידי זה מקבלים
עליהם את עול מלכותו ויהיו משועבדים לו.[4]

יא) ירושלים נעשה קסולפנס לאומות העולם, כלומר שכל
הגוים ילכו לאורה של ירושלים.[5] או בלשון אחר שירושלים תהיה
מטרפולין לכל האומות.

אלו המאמרים והעתידות והשקפות מראים בבירור שלפי דורשי
האגדה חלקן של האומות גדול פחות או יותר בפעולות ובטובות שיבואו
לעולם בזמן הגאולה. ברחב דעתם לא יכלו למנוע מהם הברכות
והנחמות שנתנבאו נביאי ישראל, והיעודים שיעדו החכמים בחזיונות
ובפירושים בענין זה. שנים העדים שרשמנו מעידים כמאה וכמאתים
עדים שהאומות נכללו בטובת הגאולה.

נפן עתה לאידך גיסא! נחפש במקורות על הדעה המתנגדת לשטה
זו. בודאי אנו פוגעים בכת של חכמי ישראל שמצדדים בשיווי זכיות
של האומות עם ישראל בגאולה ובמשיח אחר התשובה אל הקב"ה, יאוש
מן העבודה זרה, והסרת השעבוד מישראל שהן כולן הזמנות לקבלת
מלכות שמים, אבל כת אחרת מדגישה סימנים יותר מצוינים וקשים
שמוטלים אם רוצים להכנס תחת ממשלת המשיח. כבר ראינו שהתנא
רבי נחמיה חושב שביאת המשיח תהיה חד לאו"ה ורך לישראל, או

[1] פסיקתא רבתי ב' ע"א.

[2] מדרש תהלים הוצ' באבר ע' 177. ירוש' ע"ז ב' י"א. ב"ר צ"ח ט' ב'. חולין
צ"ב ע"א. אולם לפי דברי רב הונא בשם רב מדבר משלשים מצוות שעתידים
בני נח לקבל על עצמם.

[3] מדרש שה"ש הוצ' שכטר ע' 42.

[4] ב"ר ע"ח ט"ז, ובמדרש תהלים דפוס פראג, מ"ה, ע"ג.

[5] מדרש תהלים ל"ג, ו', פסיקתא ב' קמ"ד ב'.

נחמיה שהוא חד לאומות העולם ורך לישראל. אולם יש גם שטה
אחרת. ד״א מלך המשיח שעתיד להדריך כל באי עולם בתשובה
לפני הקב״ה.[1] הרי, המשיח מקרב את כל האומות להקב״ה, ע״י
התשובה, כי – זה כלל גדול בכל השקפות האגדה – בלי תשובה אין
גאולה.

ב) רבי לוי אומר שלעתיד הכל מתרפאין חוץ מנחש וגבעונים.[2]
משמע שהקב״ה מביא רפואה לכל באי עולם בעת הגאולה. כנגד זה
מצינו[3] בשם רבי לוי שעתיד הקב״ה להוריד את או״ה לגיהנם, משום
שהיו קונסים את ישראל. אולם הם מתנצלים באומרם: היו בהם
שאמרו לשון הרע, נוטל אלו ואלו ומורידם לגיהנם. אין בין המאמרים
סתירה, כי הגיהנם מרפא את ישראל ואת או״ה מעוונותיהם.

ג) לפי דברי רבי יהושע בן לוי אין מיתה לעתיד לבא. לא
בישראל ולא באומות העולם, נגד דברי רבי חנינא בר חמא, שזהו
דבריו ״יש מיתה בבני נח״[4] בכל זאת רבי יהושע בן לוי אומר:
שהקב״ה עתיד להשקות כוס תרעלה לאומות העולם, ממקום שהדין
יוצא על ד׳ מלכיות.[5]

ד) עתידין כל אומות העולם באים באוכלסין שלהם ונשבעין
שבועה חמורה להמקום ולמשיח שלא יעבדו עוד עבודה זרה.[6]

ה) המקום מבטיח את ישראל אם שומרים מצוותיו ועושים רצונו,
ריחן הטוב נודף מסוף העולם ועד סופו כשמן הטוב, ואו״ה מדבקים
בהם באהבה ובחבה.[7]

ו) האו״ה מקבלים עליהם בחרם שלא לגזור גזירות על ישראל,
ושלא לרדוף אותם ברדיפות ובשמדות בכל מקום שהם.[8]

---

[1] עיין ילקוט מכירי על זכריה הוצ׳ גרינוף ע׳ ע״ה, על פי שיר השירים רבה ז, י.
[2] בראשית רבה ד, כ. הוצ׳ תאודור ע׳ 189.
[3] שם פ׳ כ ע׳ 182 וש״מ. באגדה סתמית מרחיב הדבור בזה העניין בפתגם: בא
וראה כל מה שברא הקב״ה בעולם הזה, מתרפא לעתיד לבא, ומונה את העורים,
הפסחים, האלמים, ומביא ראיות מן הפסוקים על כל אחד ואחד מהם (תנחומא
בראשית באבר ע׳ 208) וכולל גם או״ה בתוך המתרפאין לעתיד.
[4] שם פ׳ כ״ו ע׳ 245 וש״מ.
[5] שם פ׳ ט״ו ע׳ 145 והלאה וש״מ.
[6] מדרש שה״ש הוצ׳ שכטר ע׳ 40.
[7] שם ע׳ 12.
[8] ע״ל הערה 1.

4

ד.

מה יהיה גורל האומות לעתיד לבא? איזה חלק יקחו הגוים לימות
המשיח? מה יהיה סופו של אדום ועשו בזמן הגאולה? היהיה עוד
מקום לפירוד האומות בתקופה של גאולה שלימה? איך יתקיים עולם
חדש אם מלכות הרשעה עוד שולטת? שאלות כאלו הולידו שטות
שונות בקרב החכמים, ואיחד להם פרק מיוחד כאן. אולם, טרם
שאתחיל לסדרם ולבררם, מוכרח אני לפנות לספרו של דזון גיליל,
סופר אנגלי במאה הי״ז והי״ח. בימים ההם היה המנהג באנגליה –
אחרי שבאו היהודים מכמה ארצות ונתיישבו ברשות המושלים בארץ
האי – להוכיח להם בראיות ברורות וקלושות שהמשיח כבר בא.
השאלה היתה מעניינא דיומא, וכמה פומפלטים נשארו בידינו מאותה
תקופה עצמה שמאירים על מצב היהודים באנגליה, בעשריות הראשונות
אחרי קרומוויל עד המאה הי״ט. הסופר גיליל כתב פירוש על
האונגליון מיוסד על אדני התלמוד והמדרש. כותב אחד מן המאפילים
את האור רדפו בבזיון וכלימה. בספר הנוכחי שנדפס בלונדון בשנת
1728 בשם Prophecies of the Old Testament respecting the Messiah
הוא כותב: ,,קרוב לזמן ביאת המשיח, ז״א, ישו הנוצרי, התוכחו
בית הלל ובית שמאי, ז״א אם המשיח מביא ברכה או תועלת
לאומות העולם או לא? רובם הסכימו וגמרו שלגוים אין להם חלק
בביאת המשיח, רק מעוטם כגון שמעון הזקן ואחרים ידעו שהוא
יהיה אור הגוים, וכבודם של ישראל: גיליל אינו מודיע לנו את
מקורו שממנו שאב את ידיעותיו אודות מחלוקת של בית שמאי ובית
הלל, וגם הכחיד תחת לשונו מי הוא שמעון הזקן וחבריו. הוא רומז
רק ל־Lightfoot מחבר ספר Horae על יוחנן י״ג יב, אולם שם לא
נמצא דבר אודות זה העניָן. ועוד, דבר פלא הוא, למצוא מחלוקת
כזאת בזמן קדום כזה. באמת, בפרטיות הדברים בטלים ומבוטלים,
ואין להם יסוד, אולם בכלל יש למצוא חלוקי דעות בין בספרות
התנאים ובין בספרות האמוראים, על שאלה זאת. אסדר קודם כל את
דעות המטיבים לאו״ה, ואח״כ המשמאילים ועליהם יש לבנות את
מקור הדברים.

אלו יעמדו להעיד בזכותם של האומות:

א) בפירוש המלה ,,חדרך״ (זכריה ט׳ א׳) חולקים רבי יהודה
ורבי נחמיה, לפי רבי יהודה מקום הוא שנקרא חדרך, לפי רבי

דרשן סתמי מרכיב רעיונות התשובה והקץ ביחד כשאומר: והגפנים
סמדר נתנו ריח, אלו הנשארים שעשו תשובה ונתקבלו. קומי
לך רעיתי יפתי ולכי לך שהרי הגיע זמן הגאולה.[1] אלו הלשונות,
שנמצא כפלי כפליים בתלמודים ובמדרשים, מגידים שהרעיון של הקץ
היה שגור בפיהם ובדעתם.

טרם אסיים פרק זה צריך אני להוסיף את מאמרו של רבי
אלעזר בן פדת שבשמו נשאר לנו מאמר יותר מסויים וחשוב בענין
הגאולה בכלל, ובאופני הגאולה בפרט, ,,אין ישראל נגאלין אלא מתוך
חמשה דברים: מתוך צרה, ומתוך תפלה, ומתוך זכות אבות, ומתוך
התשובה, ומתוך הקץ''.[2] המאמר נמצא עוד בירושלמי תענית, ובפסיקתא
רבתי, ודברים רבה בשינויים, ויש לעורר ולברר וללבן את הנוסחאות.
בירושלמי תענית א, א, הגירסא, מתוך הקץ, מתוך צרה, מתוך צוחה,
מתוך זכות אבות, ומתוך תשובה נגאלו ישראל ממצרים. שם הדרשן
חסר, אולי מפני שהמאמר הקודם לו מסיים איסתלק לו רבי אליעזר.
והחסירו המעתיקים את שמו של רבי אלעזר בן פדת. גם בפסיקתא
רבתי ה' מא''ש, קפ''ד ע''ב מביא המאמר בסתם ובשינויים: חמשה
דברים מביאים את הגאולה: מתוך צרה, מתוך קץ, מתוך תשובה,
מתוך רחמים, מתוך זכות אבות. אין הסדר במקור אחד דומה
לחברו. וגם יש לעורר כי בפסק''ר מביא רחמים במקום תפלה.
ועוד מקור רביעי פתוח לפנינו בדברים רבה, פ' ב' סי' י''ג ושם
הסדר: אמר ר''א כשנגאלו ישראל ממצרים לא נגאלו אלא מתוך
חמשה דברים אלו: מתוך צרה, מתוך תשובה, ומתוך זכות אבות
ומתוך רחמים, ומתוך הקץ. ואף לעתיד לבוא אין הקדוש ברוך הוא
גואלם אלא מתוך חמשה דברים אלו, ודוד פירש אותן. אולי הסדר
היותר נכון הוא במדרש תהלים. הקב''ה מביא צרה על ישראל קודם
הקץ, הצרה מעוררת את ישראל לתפלה, וחלק גדול מתפלה מכיל
את זכותם של אבות, וכולם: צרה, תפלה, וזכות אבות מביאים לידי
תשובה, והתשובה מביאה את הקץ. הרי שבעל אגדה זו מחבר את
הקץ עם התשובה ומצמד את הדברים של הגאולה. וזה מביא אותנו
לשאלה: אם הגאולה ההיא כללית או פרטית, שנדבר עליה בפרק הבא.

[1] תנחומא במדבר, הוצ' רש''ב, ע' 133.
[2] מדרש תהלים, קג, ט, הוצ' רש''ב ע' 457.

בקטע של מדרש,[1] מצינו אזהרה ואיסור לעסוק בעניינים אלו: ,,אם יאמר אדם לחבירו:

יודע אני אימתי תידון.[2]

אימתי הקץ בא.

אימתי משיח בא.

אימתי גאולה באה.

נתקצרו ימיו. שכבר בקשו אחרים(?) לעמוד על הקץ ונטלו(?) נשמתן''. הרי שחשבון הקץ מקצר ימיו ושנותיו של אדם. כמה מבני אדם שהתעסקו בעניין זה נקטפו מארצות החיים בעונש זה. אם זה היה מצב הדברים וההרגשה בקרב החכמים אין לתמוה אם דרשן מאוחר ובעל מוסר שחיבורו מפורסם גם בקרב המון העם, בעל ספר שבט מוסר מזהיר את שומעי לקחו וקוראי תוכחתו ,,שלא יוציא אדם זמנו לבקש קיצין, ולומר בזמן פלוני תהיה הגאולה'' (פ' נ''א). חכמי ישראל הקדמונים דחו בקש את שואליהם בעניני קיצין, כמו רבי שמעון בן לקיש שאמר: אם יאמר לך אדם ,,מתי קץ הגאולה''? אמור לו כי יום נקם בלבי.[3] ראוי לעורר כאן על מאמר אחר של רשב''ל שמפיץ אור על רוחו ועל שטתו. לפסוק חשבתי ימים מקדם מביא מסדר התנחומא אגדה סתמית:[4] אמרה כנסת ישראל לפני הקב''ה: רבש''ע! יושבת אני ומחשבת לכמה שנים גאלתני ממצרים, לכמה שנים גאלתני מיון ,,חלותי היא שנות ימין עליון''. אמר רשב''ל אם חולים הם יכולים להתרפאות. בני דורו ישבו וחשבו את הקץ ועדיין לא בא, הגיעו לידי יאוש מן הגאולה בהתדמם את אורך הגלות של מלכות הרשעה עם שנות הגאולה במצרים, ביון ושאר מלכיות. אמר להם רשב''ל: אל תתיאשו, באמת חולים אנחנו, ז''א מן הגלות, אבל רוב חולים מתרפאים ואינם מחוייבים למיתה.

בכל זאת לא נמנעו חכמי האגדה ליתן מקום מיוחד להרעיון של קץ בדרשותיהם. כמו רבי לוי באמרו: אמר הקב''ה, פעמים אמרתי בעצמי בשבועה שאני מביא את הקץ וגואל אתכם משעבוד מלכיות ואף כשיבא גוג ומגוג לעתיד לבוא אני נלחם עמו.[5]

[1] יצא לאור ע''י רש''א וורטהימר בבתי מדרשות שלו חדר ד' ע''ב.

[2] כלומר: אימתי יהיה יום הדין.

[3] מדרש קהלת רבה, ל''ב, ט'.

[4] שמות, הוצ' באבר ע' 114.

[5] מדרש תהלים, פ' י''ז. ו. הוצ' רש''ב ע' 133.

הנותן את הקץ אין לו חלק לעולם הבא.[1] רב"ז בכר,[2] חשב
כי דברי רבי יוסי בן חלפתא מוסבים על יהודים המאמינים בישו
המיסד כת הנוצרים. ראיותיו קלושות ומיוסדות על השערות שאינן
מתקבלות ללב. כי הלשון ,,אין לו או להם חלק לעוה"ב" אינו
מגיד כלום על מהות המינים והפושעים שמדברים בהם במשניות או
בברייתות. בכר סומך את עצמו על דברי ר"י גוטמן שלפי דעתו
המינים שנזכרו במשנה סנהדרין י' א' ובדברי רבי אליעזר המודעי
באבות ג' י"א הם נוצרים. בודאי לא כן הוא כי הסימנים שנתנו
במשניות אינם מסוגלים ומיוחדים לבעלי הברית החדשה. מה כח ביד
חכמים לאיים על הנוצרים שאין להם חלק לעוה"ב? והלא חלקם –
כך ישיבו לחכמים – בטוח להם באמונתם בישו הנוצרי? ועוד, כי בכל
מקום שהשתמשו בלשון אין לו חלק לעוה"ב רמזו על מינים ממינים
שונים? העונש מוטל גם על בני ישראל שאינם נוהגים כשורה או עושים
כהלכה. בלי ספק יש לסדר דברי רבי יוסי עם דברי רבי יונתן בן
אליעזר והדומים להם שראו סכנה גדולה בחשבונות כאלו. יש להבדיל
בין אלו שחשבו את הקיצים ובין אלו שהאמינו וחיכו לקץ. בשם רבי
יוסי ברבי חלפתא עצמו נשאר לנו מאמר שראוי לשימת עין ולחקירה
משני צדדים. מצד אחד שאומר שמי שנותן את הקץ מפסיד חלקו של
העולם הבא, ומצד השני באופן צורתו הדומה למאמרו של רבי אחא
שהבאתי למעלה בזה הפרק. מצינו: כל מי שהוא יודע כמה שנים
עבדו ישראל עבודה זרה, ,,הוא יודע אימתי בן דוד בא".[3] ריב"ח
שידע את ,,סדר העולם" שמיוחס לו בקל היה יכול להוציא מן
הכתובים את מספר השנים שעבדו ישראל עבודה זרה. אולם גם הוא
רצה לומר, שאין שום טעם ותכלית ליתן את הקץ, ודבר שוא והבל
הוא לאבד את הזמן והשכל בדברים הללו. כמו שחשב גם רבי אחא
באמרו, שמי שיודע לחשוב את הימים שישב יעקב אבינו בשלוה עם
עשו יודע את ימי הגלות, אעפ"י שחכמי ישראל[4] השתדלו למצוא את
החשבון, מ"מ יותר נכון לשער כי גם רבי אחא כמו רבי יוסי ברבי
חלפתא התאמץ להגים הדבר, כדי להרחיק בני אדם מחשבונות הללו.

---

[1] מס' ד"א רבה פ' י"א.

[2] ירחון אשכנזי, חלק מ"ב, ע' 505 והלאה.

[3] מדרש איכה רבתי, פתיחתא סי' כ"א, הוצ' רש"ב ח"ב ע' 16.

[4] עין דברי רב"ז בכר בהערות שלו ב,,הגורן" ח"א.

לגלות את הקץ, והם מחשבי קיצין, כמו רבותינו או רבי שמלאי, או
רבי עקיבא, או בני אפרים. נגד זה מצינו באגדה שהקץ נגלה רק
לשני בני אדם, ואלו הן: יעקב ודניאל. וגם הם לא קבלו רשות
לגלות את הקץ, יעקב אבינו בקש לגלות את הקץ קודם פטירתו –
ונסתם ממנו.[1] תכלית האגדה היתה להרחיק את בני הדור מן הקיצים.
סבה זו עצמה גרמה שידרשו ברבים שגם שלמה, החכם מכל אדם
בקש לעמוד על הקץ ולא יכול, ק"ו לשאר חכמים ואי-חכמים.[2]

כל אלו השבועות לא השיגו את תכליתם, כי לא היו החכמים
יכולים לבטל ולהפסיק את החשבונות, כמו שלא עלתה בידם להפליג
את דעת העם מן הגאולה.

רבי אחא, – אחד מגדולי בעלי האגדה במאה הרביעית למספרם
– נותן סימן לבני דורו, כל מי שיודע לחשוב ימי הגלות ימצא שיום
אחד ישב יעקב בצלו של עשיו.[3] רב הונא – בדורו של רבי אחא,
אומר:[4] לפי ששני פעמים תינוקות אומרים בבית הכנסת אחת בבוקר
ואחת בערב הושיענו ה' אלהינו, לפיכך הקב"ה אומר ב' פעמים
מי יתן ישועות, מי יתן שיגיע הקץ ויקרב גאולתכם! הרי
שהקב"ה בעצמו מתאוה לגאולתן של ישראל ולקרב את הקץ!

אגדת רב הונא מאירה את דברי הירושלמי:[5] רב אחא אמר כל
הברכות אחר חותמיהן ואילין דאמרין צהלי ורוני בת ציון וגו' אין
בהם משום ברכה פסוק. מענין מאד שכאן בחרו את הפסוק צהלי
ורוני שהוא כעין נחמה וגם תפלה על הישועה הקרובה לבא. עוד
נראה בפרק אחר שדבר גדול מקורות העתים רמוז כאן.

בכלל יש להסיק מדברי האמוראים שרובם, אף אם לא כולם,
לא הביטו בעין יפה בבני אדם שחושבים את הקץ, ומגלים את הקץ,
קל וחומר לאותם שלא עמדו על הקץ אלא שגם דחקו את הקץ.
גם בספרות התנאים יש למצוא סעד על תנועה כזאת אולם שם שגור
הסגנון ,,נותן את הקץ''. רבי יוסי, זהו רבי יוסי בן חלפתא, אומר:

───────────────

[1] בראשית רבה, צ"ח ב'. ותנחומא ויחי ח'. פסיקתא רבתי פ' כ"א. אגדת
בראשית ר' פ"ט, מדרש תהלים פ' ל"א, וגם ב. פסחים נ"ו ע"א. נושא המאמר
רבי יודן בשם רבי אליעזר בר אבינא, עיין גם האסיף חלק ה, ע' ה'.
[2] קהלת רבה יב, י.   [3] בראשית רבה ס"ג, ח.
[4] פסיקתא רבתי קע"ר, ע"א.
[5] ברכות א', ח'. עיין גם מגילה י"ז ע"ב.

חנינא בכתובות מובא הלשון שלא יעלו ישראל בחומה. הלשון קשה
הבנה. על כן העתיקו אותו כבר בתנחומא: כשיעלו ישראל מן הגולה
לא יעלו המונים המונים. חכמי ישראל בדור שלפנינו נתחבטו בפירוש
הלשון, וקשה להחליט אם ירדנו לסוף דעתם של הקדמונים שהשתמשו
בלשון זה. גרטץ,[1] ורב"ז בכר,[2] חשבו שהלשון מזהיר את ישראל
שלא יעלו בחיילות ובעלי מלחמה מן הגולה לארץ-ישראל, אם פשט
זה נכון ומקויים אין להבין ההבדל בין השבועה שלא ימרדו ובין
השבועה שלא יעלו בחומה, והלא אין לך מרידה קשה מזו? וגם יש
לפקפק אם שמוש לשון זה עולה בכל המקומות שהשתמשו בסגנון זה.[3]
כדי לברר הוראת הסגנון לאמיתתו נחוץ להשוות את שימוש הלשון גם
במקומות אחרים שנמצא שם.

הלשון מורגל בפי רבי שמעון בן לקיש, כשראה את הבבליים
,,מצמתון'', אמר להם בדרו גרמיכון! אמר להם: כשעליתם לא
עליתם חומה, וכאן באים לעשות חומה![4]

גם רבי שילא משתמש בלשון זה באמרו: אלו ישראל עלו חומה
מן הגולה לא חרב ביהמ"ק פעם שנייה.[5] ועדיין אנו צריכים למודע
ולקשר נכון על הדרוש שדרשו רבנן על הפסוק אחות לנו קטנה
שמוסב לפי דבריהם על עולי גולה, וזה לשונם:

אחות לנו קטנה, אלו עולי גולה,

קטנה, שהם דלים באוכלסין.

ושדים אין לה, אלו חמשה דברים שחסר בית אחרון מן
הראשון, מה נעשה, ביום שיגזור כורש,

אם חומה היא, אלו ישראל העלו חומה מבבל לא חרב ביהמ"ק
פעם שנייה.[6] לפי האגדה הזאת ברור שעליית חומה מובן בהוראת
עליה מן הגולה באוכלסין, לפיכך כשאמרו שלא יעלו חומה
אזהרה שלא יתקבצו בגלות הקץ. להלן עוד נראה אם הוראת הלשון
בדיוק או לא.

ה) שלא יגלו את הקץ. נזכר בדברי רבי לוי, וגם באגדה סתמית
במדרש שיר השירים, ממנה אנו רואים שבני הדור היו מתאמצים

נגד המלכיות. מ״מ באותו מדרש עצמו נמצאת האזהרה עצמה בין השבועות שהשביע הקב״ה את ישראל (מדרש שה״ש הוצ׳ גרינהוט, כ״ח, ע״א). כאן יש להעיר שדברי רבי יוסי ברבי חנינא נשארו לנו בב׳ נוסחאות, מלבד הנוסחא בבבלי שרמזנו עליה לעיל: בשה״ש רבה ב׳ ע׳ הוא אומר: ב׳ שבועות יש כאן אחת לישראל, ואחת לאו״ה, נשבע לישראל שלא ימרדו על המלכיות, נשבע על המלכיות שלא יקשו עול על ישראל, שאם מקשים עול על ישראל הן גורמים לקץ לבוא שלא בעתה. (עיין מה שכתבתי על זה בישורון, חלק י״ג, ע׳ 22). בבבלי נתוספה שבועה אחרת: ב) שלא ידחקו את הקץ. סימן זה נתן בדברי רבי חלבו.[1] מדברי רבי אוניא יש ללמוד מה שהבינו הקדמונים במובן ,,דוחק את הקץ״ שהמשלים שהביאו על דוחקי הקץ אין מניחים שום ספק על זה, ואולי גם הלשון שהמלכיות גורמים לקץ לבוא שלא בעתה על ידי גזירות ושמדות שמכבידים עולם על ישראל, שייך לכאן.

ג) שלא יגלו מסתורין שלהם לאו״ה. כן בדברי רבי חלבו, אולם בדברי רבי יוסי ברבי חנינא בבבלי גרס: שלא יגלו הסוד לעכו״ם. הלשון קשה וצריך בירור למה ולאיזה צורך יגלו ישראל את הסוד שלהם הכמוס אתם וחשוב בעיניהם כ״כ – לאויביהם הרשעים? ומה תועלת להם בסודם של ישראל? אם לא שיחזרו בתשובה ויתגיירו בעת בא הקץ? ומה בכך ולמה להשביעם על זה. אולי צריך לגרוס באמת כמו שגורס במדרש שה״ש של גרינהוט (כ״ח, ע״א) ,,שלא יגלו סדר העבור״ ובקל נשתבשו המלות מ,,סדר העבור״ ל,,סוד לעכו״ם״ אעפ״י שיש כאן לבעל הדין להרהר ולומר: איפכא מסתברא, מעתיק המדרש שה״ש לא הבין את הלשון ,,מגלה סוד לאו״ה״, או ,,מסתרין לעכו״ם״, ועשה ממנו ,,סדר העבור״? ואם כן אז הוא הפשט: שלא יגלו תורה שבע״פ לאו״ה.[2] זה בוודאי אפשר, אולם מי יבטיח לנו שמעתיקי התלמוד והתנחומא ראו זאת בשימוש הלשון הזה, אולי הבינו בסוד או במסתורין את חשבון הקץ?

ד) שלא יעלו חומה מן הגולה, כן הלשון בדברי ר׳ חלבו. במדרש שה״ש גרס: ושלא יעלו לא״י בחומה. בדברי רבי יוסי ברבי

---

[1] עיין גם תנחומא דברים׳ פ״י ע׳ 4.

[2] עיין מש״כ בחבורי Religionsgesch. Studien II על זה.

מחשבי קיצים. שהיו אומרים כיון שהגיע הזמן והגאולה לא באה, שוב
אינה באה, אלא חכה לו.[1] שיטת רבי יונתן ברבי אליעזר גלוייה
וברורה גם מאגדה אחרת, שהוא היה ממחכי קץ הישועה והתנגד
למחשבי קץ מפני שהחשבון מביא לידי יאוש מן הגאולה. רבי ברכיה
משום רבי חלבו, ורבי שמואל בר נחמני בשם רבי יונתן אומר:
ראויים היו ישראל כלייה בימי המן אילולי נסמכו על דעתו
של זקן שאמרו מה אם יעקב אבינו שהבטיחו הקב"ה וא"ל הנה אנכי
עמך ושמרתיך בכל אשר תלך ונתיירא, אנו על אחת כמה וכמה, הוא
שהנביא מקנתרן ואומר להן השכחת ה' עושיך, נטה שמים ויסד ארץ?
אנשיתון מה דאמרית לכון אם יומדו שמים וכו'. ראיתם שמים שנימודו
והארץ שנתמוטטה? מנטיית שמים וארץ היתה לכם ללמוד, אלא תפחד
תמיד כל היום מפני חמת המציק.[2] ברור הדבר שבעל האגדה מוכיח
את בני דורו על שהיו מקטני אמונה, וכשבא הקץ והגאולה לא באה
היו מתפחדים ושכחו את ההבטחות שהבטיחו להם הנביאים
.

עתה נשוב אל השבועות שמצאו חכמי ישראל ברמיזה במגלת שיר
השירים. אם נדייק ונעיין בהם נראה שהן שש: א) שלא ימרדו
במלכיות, אזהרה זאת מובאה גם בדברי רבי לוי בתנחומא[3] בסגנון
משונה ממה שאנו שונים בבבלי. ,,ד' פעמים כתוב השבעתי אתכם
ולמה? כנגד ד' מלכיות שלא ימרדו באחת מהן". במדרש זוטא לשיר
השירים[4] הובא בסתם ,,השביעם הקב"ה שלא לעמוד כנגד מלכיות".
בוודאי היתה השעה צריכה לכך בימי הדרשנים האלו כדי לאיים על
העם שלא יעמדו או ימרדו במלכיות. אולם יש להטיל ספק בדבר
אם הרעיון הזה נתקבל בכל העם, או אם עשה רושם על כל חוגי
האומה שלא התנגדו לו? באמת במדרש אחר לשיר השירים[5] אנו
קוראים על אותו ענין עצמו: אם תעירו אם תעוררו את האהבה אשר
ביני וביניכם עד שתחפוץ המלכות למסור החרב בידיכם דכת' ונתתי
נקמתי באדום ביד עמי ישראל. דרשן זה בוודאי חולק על הדרשנים
שהובאו לעיל, ואומר כי חרב נוקמת תנתן ביד ישראל ובידם ללחום

---

[1] ב. סנהדרין צ"ב ע"ב.

[2] פסיקתא דרב כהנא הוצ' מהרש"ב ק"מ ע"א. עיין גם פסיקתא רבתי קנ"א
ע"ב. ובראשית רבה ע' ג. וישורון, חלק י"ג, ע' קע"ב.

[3] דברים הוצ' מהרש"ב, ע' 4.   [4] הוצ' מהרש"ב.

[5] הוצ' גרינהוט, כ"ב, ע"ב.

ושלא יגלו מסתורן שלהם לאויב,

ושלא יעלו חומה מן הגולה.

אם כן למה מלך המשיח בא? לקבץ גליותיהן של ישראל.

ב) רבי אוניא אומר: ד' שבועות השביען כנגד ד' דורות שדחקו

את הקץ ונכשלו ואלו הן:

אחד בימי עמרם

ואחד בימי דיני

ואחד בימי כוזיבא

ואחד בימי שותלח בן אפרים

בדברי ,,יש אומרים'' גורס במקום ב': דורו של שמד.

ג) רבי יוסי בירבי חנינא:[1] ג' שבועות הללו למה?

שלא יעלו ישראל בחומה,

שלא ימרדו באו"ה,

לאו"ה שלא ישתעבדו בישראל יותר מדאי.

ד) רבי לוי: שש שבועות הללו למה? תלתא הנך דאמרן.

ואינך, שלא יגלו את הקץ.

ושלא ידחקו את הקץ.

ושלא יגלו הסוד לעכו"ם.

בכל המאמרים, חוץ ממאמרו של רבי יוסי בירבי חנינא, נמצא
השבועה שהשביע הקב"ה את ישראל שלא ידחקו את הקץ. בודאי
היו בני דורם של החכמים הללו נצרכים לאזהרה ולשבועה כזאת, כי
כל השבועות הללו רומזות שהסיתו את העם למרוד במלכיות או
באומות העולם. מי יפלא על מראה כזו? אם עמדו משיחים או נולדו
תנועות של גאולה בזמן שהשמדות וגזירות קשות רעות באו על הדורות?
כל פרקי קורות בני עמנו מלאים מהם, ובלי ספק גרמו לפעולות כדי
לשבור עול הגלות מעל צואריהם. אולם חכמי ישראל המתונים בדין
ראו בדחיקת הקץ סכנה גדולה ונמרצה, והראו באצבע על תנועות
כאלו בעבר, ושיותר טוב להתרחק מהם בהוה. אלו החכמים בודאי
היו בברית עם רבי יונתן בן אליעזר שרוחו לא מצא נחת במחשבי
קיצים, אף על פי שלא נתיאש מן הגאולה והיה עם מחכי קץ ישועה
בכל לבבו, באמרם דברים קשים על מחשבי קיצים: תיפח רוחן של

---

[1] ב. כתובות קי"א ע"א.

כרבותינו שהיו דורשין „עד עדן ועדנין ופלג עדן", ולא כרבי
שמלאי שהיה דורש „האכלתם לחם דמעה ותשקימו בדמעות שליש",
ולא כרבי עקיבא שהיה דורש „עוד אחת מעט היא ואני מרעיש את
השמים ואת הארץ".[1] מי הוא זה רבי נתן? בודאי אינו רבי נתן הבבלי,
כי אי אפשר לו להזכיר את רבי שמלאי שחי כמעט ג' דורות אחריו.
גם האמורא הבבלי שידוע בשם זה אינו יכול להיות כי נזכר בשם רבי
ולא בשם רב נתן. אלא ודאי הוא אמורא ארצי ישראלי שחי במאה
הרביעית למספרם שמונה את כל החשבונות של הגאולה וגם התנועות
המשיחיות שהיו בזכרון האומה עד ימיו. מהן נודעו לנו רק התנועה
שנתפשטה בימי רבי עקיבא והולידה את בר כוכבא. אולם מי היו לו
רבותינו, ומה טיבו של רבי שמלאי בענין זה לא נתברר כל עיקר
מדברי רבי נתן. המדרשים מתאמצים לחשוב חשבונות שיש להוציא מן
הכתובים. אם אנו מקבלים דבריהם אז רומזים החשבונות לזמנים שונים
יותר מאוחרים מדורו של רבי שמלאי או רבי נתן עצמו. בכל אופן
מה ששייך כאן הוא שרבי נתן לא היה מסכים לא עם רבותינו – שאולי
היו בזמנו – ולא עם רבי שמלאי או עם רבי עקיבא שקדמו לו בזמן.

מעניין מאד כי גם חכמי ישראל במאה השלישית למספרם מונים
מלבד שותלח בן אפרים ובר כוכבא, תנועות משיחיות שעדיין לא נודעו
לנו. במקור אחד[2] נמנו א) עמרם, ב) דיניי, ג) כוזיבא, וד) שותלח.
במקור אחר החליפו במקום דיניי את דורו של שמד. לפי שאי אפשר
להאמין שהמקור יכפיל מארע אחד פעמיים ובודאי צריך להבדיל בין
התנועה של כוזיבא ובין התנועה של השמד. יכול להיות שהמקור מסדר
את התנועות המשיחיות באותו סדר שנמצא גם באגדת רבי נתן: מקדים
את המאוחר, ומאחר את הקדום. ויתכן שהחשבונות הרגילות בימי
רבותינו מראים על מעשה עמרם, ודברי רבי שמלאי על דיני, או דורו
של שמד, ומכאן ראיה שהחשבונות היו מחוברים עם תנועות משיחיות.
החשבונות וגם התנועות הללו לא מצאו חן בעיני הדרשנים. נראה
בראשונה מה שאמרו חכמי האגדה על דוחקי הקץ, ואלו הם:

א) רבי חלבו אומר: ד' שבועות יש כאן, השביע הקב"ה לישראל:

שלא ימרדו על המלכיות,

ושלא ידחקו על הקץ,

---

[1] בבלי, סנהדרין צ"ז, ע"ב.   [2] שיר השירים רבה ב', י"ח.

תפלתם? כשם שהגבלת בסיני, הקרב הקץ ותייחד אלהותך בעולמך!
ובאגדה אחרת[1] אומר הקב״ה לישראל שהיו מתפחדים שיהיו לקוחים
למיתה ולהריגה – בימי המן – אולם מוסב גם על בני דורו של הדרשן
ונתיאשו מן הגאולה: שכחתם מה שאמרתי לירמיה: כה אמר ה׳ אם
ימדו שמים מלמעלה ויחקרו מוסדי ארץ למטה גם אני אמאס בכל
זרע ישראל (ירמיהו ל״א ל״ו), ואתם רואים את השמים במקומם ואת
הארץ במקומה, ואתם מתיראים? זאת אומרת שאין להם לישראל
להתיאש מן הגאולה. שמים וארץ עדים נאמנים שהקב״ה לא ימאס
בכל זרע ישראל.

בכל זאת נמצאו במדרש זה – שהוא חשוב לתולדות הרעיון שאנו
מדברים בו – רמזים אחדים על התנגדות גמורה לחשבון הקצים. דרשן
אחד אומר,[2] אחרי שמביא משל של איש שהיתה לו מכה שכל הרופאים
לא יכלו לרפאותה עד שאמרו לו: לך אצל רופא קבוע שלך הוא
יודע רפואה למכתך, כך הנביא אמר: כל מה שאתם מפליגים
דעתכם מן הקץ! עשו תשובה והקב״ה גואל אתכם משעבודם של
מלכיות שהוא הוא שהכה והוא הוא שמרפא! הרי שבעל אגדה זה
מצדד עם שיטתו של רבי אליעזר שהתשובה מביאה את הגאולה ואין
שום תועלת לחשוב קצים וזמנים: כל מה שאתם מפליגים מן הקץ,
שֶׁם בפי הנביא לישראל, תוכחות הן כדי להפליג דעתם ולהסיח
דעתם מן החשבונות ומן העניינים הדומים להם. הם הם הדברים שאמר
רבי זעירי לחבריו בבית המדרש כשמצא אותם עסוקים בחשבונות או
בפירוש הפסוקים שרומזים על ביאת המשיח: בבקשה מכם אל תעכבו
את ביאת המשיח במעשיכם ובדרשות שלכם, כי הגאולה באה בהיסח
הדעת, או בלשון המדרש: הפליגו דעתכם מן הקץ! מכל זה יש להכיר
בבירור כי בחוגי העם היו כמה וכמה מחכי קץ ישועה וגם מחשבי
קיצין.

נראה עתה את החומר התלמודי והמדרשי המפיץ אור על מחשבי
קיצים ועל אותם שהיו מתנגדים להם. נפן בראשונה למאמר היותר
חשוב שנשאר לנו בשם רבי נתן, שאמר על הפסוק בחבקוק: „עוד
חזון למועד ויפח לקץ ולא יכזב אם יתמהמה חכה לו כי בא יבא לא
יאחר" (חבקוק, ב׳ ג׳), שהפסוק הלז „נוקב ויורד עד התהום". ז״א

[2] שם, קנ״ג ע״א.　　　　　　　　[1] שם, קנ״א ע״ב.

בדרך. וחטא זה נקרא בלשון המכילתא ,,עברו על הקץ", כלומר:
שרצו למהר את הקץ קודם שבא.

כאן המקום להעיר על אגדה אחת הכי מעניינת ומפיצה אור על
העניין שאנו דנים בו.[1] ישראל שואלים את בלעם ואת נביאי ישראל
על הקץ. בלעם מרחק את הקץ – נביאי ישראל מקרבים את הקץ.
נעיין בדברי המדרש, כפי ששואלים את בלעם ואת נביאי ישראל:

שאלו את בלעם:

יש להם קץ של ישועה?

א״ל הן.

א״ל אימתי הוא?

א״ל רחוק הוא ואראנו ולא עתה וכו'.

מרחיק את הקץ.

שאלו לנביאי ישראל:

אמרו קרוב הוא, כי קרוב יום אידם.

בא ירמיהו ואמר הילילו כי קרוב יום ה'.

בא מלאכי ואמר קרוב הוא כי הנה היום בא וכו'.

בא יואל ואמר כמוהם, תקעו שופר בציון וכו'.

אמר דוד הנה רחוקין יאבדו זה בלעם וחבריו שהרחיקו את

הקץ, יאבדו מן העולם.

האגדה מיוסדת על הרעיון שהגאולה תלויה בקץ כלומר: כפי
שיטת רבי יהושע, בלעם וחביריו וכן נביאי ישראל מסכימים עם זה.
אולם על השאלה אימתי יהיה הקץ? אלו מקרבים ואלו מרחקים, כפי
יחוסם לישראל, ועוד יש ללמוד מכאן כי בזמנם של בעלי אגדה אלו
היו משתדלים למצוא תשובה על שאלה זו. וזה לא יפלא ממנו אם
אנחנו חוקרים ודורשים בפסיקתא רבתי. מיד בראש הספר אנו קוראים
כדברים אלו.[2] אמרו: אימתי אתה מחזירנו לאותו הכבוד? הרי כמה זמן
שחרב בית חיינו, הרי שבוע, הרי יובל, הרי שבע מאות וכו'. עוד
נראה כי הזמן נתוסף על ידי איזה מעתיק או מסדר מאוחר, אולם
השאלה עצמה עתיקה היא מאד. ובתפלה אומרת כנסת ישראל לפני
הקב״ה:[3] רבש״ע, עד אימתי יהיו בניך משועבדים? ואין אתה שומע

---

[1] פסיקתא רבתי ב' מא״ש, קע״ח ע״ב.

[2] שם, א' ע״ב.

[3] שם, ל״ג ע״א.

אותם שרצו לגלות את הקץ. טרם שנברר אלו התנועות והתנגדותם
בקרב המנהיגים והעם, נראה את ההשפעה של שיטת רבי יהושע.

מעניין שכבר במדרש התנאים דרשו את הברכה בברכת כהנים
"וישמרך", במובן: ישמור לך את הקץ.[1] זאת אומרת שהקב"ה
ישמור לישראל את הקץ ויביא את הגאולה בעתה, אף על פי שאין
ישראל ראוים להגאל, ועוד שהקב"ה שומר את הקץ להביא בזמן
הקצוב. בברייתא אחרת דרשו את הפסוק "ולא ימצאו דבר ה'"
על הקץ שיסתם מעיני החכמים כמו ההלכה והנבואה,[2] כלומר,
שיתאמצו לידע את דבר ה' ולא ימצאו אותו, או שעיניהם מיחלות
לקץ הישועה ואין מי שיגיד להם מתי תהיה הגאולה.

ועוד במקום שלישי במדרש התנאים נמנה הקץ עם אותם הדברים
שהם מכוסים מבני אדם ואין מי שיכול לעמוד עליהם.[3] לא רק חכמי
ישראל הקדמונים השתדלו להפליג את דעת העם מן הקץ שמכוסה
מבני אדם ולא ימצא על ידי אותות וחשבונות, אלא גם כותבי הכנסיה
הנוצרית העתיקה מזהירים: לא לכם לחשוב אותות וקצים כי הם
ידועים וגלוים רק להאב לבדו.[4] דבריהם מתאימים בעיקרם: יום
הנחמה מוגבל על ידי הקב"ה, הוא לבדו יודע אותו היום, וכל
התחבולות הם בלי תועלת לגלות מה שכסה בחכמתו ובטובו בפני
יריאיו. וכדי לאיים על העם שלא טוב הדבר הזה לדחוק את הקץ,
ציירו להם את מעשי שותלח בן אפרים שברח ממצרים קודם הקץ
ונהרג הוא וכל הנלוים אליו. ספור זה נמצא בכתבי הקודש ועליו בנו
התנאים את דבריהם. בשני מקומות במכילתא אנו קוראים את המעשה.
בראשונה על הפסוק אמר אלהים.[5] ז"א כי אמר אלהים מלחמת בני
אפרים שנאמר בני אפרים שותלח וכו' (דה"י א. ז' כ') וכתיב בני
אפרים נושקי וכו' (תהלים ע"ח ט' י) מפני מה? שלא שמרו ברית
אלהים ובתורתו מאנו ללכת, עברו על הקץ ועל השבועה. ושנית על
הפסוק "חיל אחז יושבי פלשת":[6] כיון ששמעו יושבי פלשת שישראל
נכנסין לארץ אמרו: עכשיו הן באין לעורר עירורן של בני אפרים
וכו'. ולפי דברי רב[7] מנו בני אפרים את הקץ וטעו, על כן נהרגו

[1] ספרי במדבר פיסקא מ'.
[2] תוספתא עדיות א. א, ד': שבת קל"ח ע"ב.
[3] מכילתא נ"ט ע"ב.
[4] מעשי השלוחים, א. ז.
[5] מכילתא כ"ד ע"א.
[6] שם מ"ג ע"א.
[7] סנהדרין צ"ז ע"ב, עיין גם שמות רבה כ', י"א.

כותב, כי הוא מאמין באמונה שלימה בגאולה אחרונה לעמנו, והגאולה
הזאת באה על ידי תשובה ועל ידי הקץ – הוא שאב דבריו ממדרשי
חז"ל וגם הכיר כמו שהכירו חכמי ישראל במאות הראשונות אחרי
החורבן, שאין שום תועלת בגאולה על ידי הקץ שאין בני ישראל
עושים תשובה וחוזרים אל אביהם שבשמים, כדי להכיר זאת נחוץ
להקדיש מאמר מיוחד לרעיון הקץ באגדת החכמים.

ג.

מכל הדברים שהזכרנו בפרקים הקודמים מוכח, כי אף על פי
ששתק רבי יהושע בויכוחו את רבי אליעזר, אם הגאולה תלויה בקץ
או בתשובה, מכל מקום גברה שיטתו של רבי אליעזר בבית המדרש,
וכמה תנאים ואמוראים החזיקו בדבריו. יש מהם קיימו וקבלו אותם
בכלל ובפרט, אם אין ישראל עושין תשובה אינן נגאלין או אם עושין
תשובה מיד הן נגאלין אפילו קודם הקץ. מובן מאליו, שאין הקץ
מקרב את הגאולה אם אינם עושין תשובה, כי מה תועלת בגאולה
בלא תשובה? אולם נמצאים גם רמזים כי השפעת שיטת רבי יהושע
לא זזה מפי החכמים והדורות והיתה קבועה בין כותלי בית המדרש
בדורות הבאים אחריו. לא רק במדרש אלא גם במעשה של כל יום
ויום לא פסקה האמונה שהקב"ה ישים קץ מוחלט לגלות ישראל
ולחורבן בית המקדש. מהאמונה הזאת נולדו כמה תנועות בעם,
שעליהן נדבר בזה הפרק. התנועה הראשונה הולידה את החשבונות
והחזיונות שעל ידיהן יש לקרב את הקץ או לגלות את הקץ או גם
לדחוק את הקץ. ההמון מחבב את התנועה הזאת, בפרט בשעת
השמדות והגזירות. חשבונות כאלו החזיקו את כחה של האומה לצפות
לרגלי של המשיח. כל התנועות המשיחיות שקמו בעמנו מיום שחרב
בית המקדש ועד היום הזה תלויות בחשבונות כאלו, פעמים גרמו
החשבונות לתנועה המשיחית, ופעמים ה,,משיח" הצדיק את עצמו
על-ידי חשבון כזה. יהיה זה איך שיהיה בהכרח כשהקץ הגיע והגאולה
טרם באה, או תקות המשיח נכזבה, יאוש מן הגאולה החליש את
האומה והביא לידי תקלה. החכמים היו עומדים ומזהירים את העם
נגד מחשבי קיצין. ונתנו להם דוגמאות ממפלתם של דוחקי קיצין,
ודרשו נגד אותם שרצו לעמוד על הקץ, והוכיחו בדברים קשים

דבריו נשנו גם באגדת רבי אחא.[1] אמוראים אחרים הרכיבו את דעות
רבי אליעזר ורבי יהושע יחד ומונים תשובה וגם קץ בתוך הדברים
המביאים את הגאולה.[2] איתא שם: חמשה דברים מביאים את הגאולה:
מתוך צרה אדם נגאל, מתוך הקץ באחרית הימים, מתוך תשובה,
מתוך רחמים, ומתוך זכות האבות.

והדרשן מוסיף לבסוף: והתשובה גורמת לרחמים ולזכות האבות, שכן
הוא אומר, ושבת עד ד' אלהיך וכו' ומיד כי אל רחום ה' אלהיך וכו'.

גם חכמים ודרשנים אחרים מחבבים לחבר את דעות התנאים
ולתת להם מקום בשיטתם. כמו רבי יצחק, שבאגדה שלו נתן מקום
לגאולה שהיא באה ע"י תשובה ומעשים טובים, ואם אין מעשים
טובים הקב"ה עושה למען שמו הגדול. בדרשה אחת על תהלים מ"ד
כו', אומר הקב"ה לאברהם: ושמתי את זרעך כעפר וכו' מה כתיב
בתריה? קומה עזרתה לנו. אם יש בנו מעשים טובים עשה עמנו
למען מעשים טובים שבנו, ואם לא, עשה עמנו למען שמך
בחסדך. אולם רבי ברכיה אחז לו שיטה אחרת, שאין הגאולה באה
אלא על ידי מעשים טובים, כי אין נותנים שכר אלא לעושה מצוה.[3]

כשם שחברו כאן את דעות רבי מתיא בן חרש עם דעת האומר
שישראל נגאלין למען שמו,[4] כן מצינו באגדה סתמית שהדורש משתמש
בשתי דעות של קץ ותשובה יחד. על הפסוק כי ימוך אחיך[5] מביא
דברי תהלים ק"ו מ"ג ומביא ראיה, מכאן שבימי השופטים כשעשו
תשובה מיד נגאלו ישראל, אולם מוסיף באותה נשימה: כשתבא שנת
הגאולה אני גואל אתכם, הרי שהגאולה תלויה בקץ כמו בתשובה.

הרי לפנינו כמה דרכים של גאולה. בראשונה תשובה וקץ, שנית
למען חסדו ואהבתו, שלישית למען שמו ורביעית בזכות הצדיקים
שבדור. ואל תתמה, שהגאון רבינו סעדיה במאמר הגאולה האחרונה

---

[1] עיין איכה רבתי א, יט.

[2] פסיקתא רבתי הוצ' רמא"ש קפ"ש רמא"ש קפ"ד ע"ב. עיין גם ירושלמי תענית א, א. במדרש
תהלים ק"ו. דברים רבה ה, ג, בשם ר' אלעזר והוא ר' אלעזר בן פדת, יש לדקדק
כי רחמים באיזה נוסחאות נתחלף בתפלה, ובאמת בקש רחמים אחד מלשונות
תפלה בדברי חז"ל. עיין גם דברי רבי יוסי ברבי חנינא „ברחמים עתיד להחזיר"
מדרש תהלים הוצ' רש"ב עמוד 324.

[3] מדרש תהלים עמוד 269.

[4] עיין לעיל.

[5] עיין תנחומא ויקרא הוצ' רש"ב עמוד 106.

בדבר. א) אחד מישראל גולה לברברייאה, ואחד מהם לסרמטיא,
דומה כמו שהגלה כולכם לארצות הללו. זאת אומרת: שכל יהודי
ויהודי שגלה לאומה אחת מן האומות מעלין עליהם כאלו גלו ישראל
לכל אומה ואומה ונשתעבדו שם. ב) אדום. מלכות הרשעה הזאת
מכתבת טרוניא מכל אומה ולשון הרי בין המשעבדים כל האומות,
ומעלה עליהם המקום כאלו נשתעבדו לכל ע' האומות שבעולם. וידוע
היום, כמו שידעו התנאים בזמנם שבמאה השניה היה חיל רומי מורכב
בעיקר מאומות שונות ורק מעטים היו ביניהם בני איטליה או רומי.
גם את זאת יש לאמת, כי היהודים באותו הזמן נתפשטו כמעט בכל
רחבי מלכות רומי כברברייאה, סרמטיא ודומיהם. אולי יש בידינו
למצוא אפשר דבר עוד אודות הנוסחאות בנוגע לשמות התנאים שלפנינו.
התשובה האחת מרבי אליעזר בן יעקב, והאחרת מרבי אליעזר בנו של
ר' יוסי הגלילי – וכדי לקצר הרכיבו אותם יחד. גם יש לשער כי
מתנגדי בר כוכבא, היה להם פתחון פה לומר שטרם הגיע הזמן להגאל
מפני שהשעבוד אינו גמור כמו שצריך להיות. באופן פורמלי האגדות
של ר' אליעזר ואותן של ר' יהודה וחבריו דומות וקרובות זו לזו.

אף על פי שלפי הברייתא התגברו ראיותיו של רבי יהושע על
רבי אליעזר ושיתקו, מכל מקום אנו רואים שבאגדת האמוראים נתנו
מקום יותר חשוב לדברי רבי אליעזר, שהגאולה באה על ידי תשובה
ואינה תלויה בקצים. נפן בראשונה לדברי רב ושמואל. רב אומר:
כלו כל הקצין. זאת אומרת: כל החשבונות שעשו בני אדם או
שעדיין עושים, אין בהם ממש. כוזבים ומוטעים ומטעים, ואין הדבר
תלוי אלא בתשובה ובמעשים טובים. שמואל משתמש בפתגם:
„דיו לאבל שיעמוד באבלו!" מה רצה שמואל לומר בפתגם
זה?[1] – האבלות היא הגלות והשביה ואין לתקוף את האבילות ביותר
מדי על ידי תוכחות. טוב לחכות לגאולה אפילו לא בא הקץ, אולם
יכולה היא לבוא גם כהרף עין. כרב כן גם רבי שמעון בן לקיש
קורא את העם לתשובה, באמרו, עשו תשובה והקב"ה גואל אתכם
מיד המלכיות.[2] גם במדרש בראשית רבה[3] משיב רבי שמעון בן לקיש
להשואלים אותו באיזה זכות יבא המשיח? והוא עונה: בזכות התשובה!

[1] עיין סנהדרין צב, א.
[2] פסיקתא רבתי הוצ' רמא"ש קנ"ב ע"ב.
[3] א. ב.

וישראל עונים: בדורות הראשונים היו ביניני צדיקים, כמו משה, יהושע,
שמואל ושאול, דוד ושלמה, אבל עכשיו כל שאנו הולכין דור ודור
והיא (ז. א. הצרה) מחשכת והולכת לנו בך ד' חסיתי (תהלים
לא, ב).[1] כלומר, אעפ״י שבדורנו אין לנו צדיקים וחסידים שבזכותם
ראוים אנו לגאולה, אנו חוסים ובוטחים בשמו שמביא גאולה למען
שמו באהבה.

רוח זו שולטת גם באגדה אחרת שבאותו מדרש. הדרשן אומר:
מכאן אתה למד שלא היה בידי ישראל כשיצאו ממצרים שיגאלו מהם,
לא מעשה אבות, ולא מעשה עצמם, שיקרע להם הים, אלא לעשות
לו שם.[2] למען שמו גאל המקום את ישראל, ולא במעשים או בזכויות
של אבותם או של עצמם. הדרוש הזה מתנגד להשיטות שזכרנו כבר.
הגאולה בידו של הקב״ה והוא יגאל את עמו לא במעשים ולא בזכות־
אבות או צדיקים אלא למען שמו, כלומר שידעו ישראל וגם האומות
שהקב״ה כל יכול וגואל את עמו מן השעבוד ויכירו ויראו שיש אלוה
בעולם.[3] כמו שהיה בגאולת מצרים. כן תהיה גם בגאולת מחר
העתידה לבוא.

כשם ששאלו אבותינו במצרים את משה רבינו כשבשר להם את
הגאולה, – לפי דברי רבי יהודה ורבי נחמיה ורבנן – היאך אנו נגאלים
הלא לא בא הקץ? הלא יש עבודה זרה בידינו? הלא אין בידינו
מעשים טובים? כמו כן שואלים בני הדור את המשיח: היאך אנו
נגאלים? מסדר אגדת שיר השירים לפסוק קול דודי הנה זה בא, מצא
קושיא זו באגדת רבי יודן בשם רבי יוסי הגלילי (אולי צריך לומר
רבי אליעזר בירבי יוסי הגלילי?) ובאגדת רב הונא בשם רבי אליעזר
בן יעקב. ואולי דבריהם לקוחים ממעשה שהיה בדורו של בר כוכבא.
האגדה אומרת שבשעה שמלך המשיח בא ומבשר לישראל שבחודש
הזה אתם נגאלין! הם אומרים לו: היאך אנו נגאלין? בעל האגדה
מקצר כאן במקום שהיה לו להאריך ולהוסיף הסבה או הטענה, אולם
המשיח חוזר על דבריהם ומדבריו אנו מכירים טענותיהם, הוא אומר
בתשובתו לבני דורו: מה אתם אומרים שהקב״ה נשבע שישעבד אתכם
בע' אומות ועדיין לא באתם לידי שעבודה? על זו יש שתי תשובות

---

[1] מדרש תהלים הוצ׳ מהרש״ב ע׳ 237.
[2] שם הוצ׳ מהרש״ב ע׳ 268.
[3] שם ע׳ 212.

ג) שלא שינו את שמם,

ד) שלא שינו את לשונם,

אם כן למה נתן להם מצוות פסח קודם צאתם ממצרים? מפני, –
ובזה מסכים הוא עם שיטת רבי נחמיה – שעבדו עבודה זרה, עבירה
שהיא שקולה ככל העבירות שבתורה. היה צריך לצוות עליהם להסיר
הגלולים מקרבם, כי מה תועלת בגאולי ד' שמחזיקים בטומאת עבודה
זרה בקרבם? בלי המשכת ידים מן העבירה, המקום אינו מדלג על
העוונות ומביא את הגאולה. קרבן פסח ודם המילה סימנים של טהרת
העם מגלולי מצרים שהיו בידם.

בעיקר הדבר, רבי יהודה בן בתירא, הדרשן השלישי במקור
שלנו, מסכים עם רבי נחמיה וגם עם ר' אלעזר הקפר, שבני ישראל
במצרים היו שטופים בעבודה זרה, אולם הוא מוסיף על עונם באמרו
שהיו כל כך אדוקים בע"ז שלהם ולא רצו להסירם מבתיהם. מסבה
זאת לא שמעו אל משה מקוצר רוח ומעבודה קשה. היש אדם
המבשרים אותו בשורה טובה של גאולה והוא אינו רוצה לשמוע
כזאת? אלא שהיו מחבבין כל כך את הגלולים שהיו צריכים להפריד
אותם בעל כרחם מהם. כדי להשיג זאת, צוה אותם המקום: משכו
את ידיכם מע"ז וקחו לכם לשחוט את תועבת מצרים. ובזה נצטוו
על מצות הפסח שהיא סימן וראיה של תשובה ליחודו של עולם.

ההבדל בין החכמים האחרונים ובין הראשונים שזכרנו הוא,
שהאחרונים רוצים לפרש את טעם מצות הפסח, אבל הראשונים
התעסקו בשאלה: היאך אנו נגאלים? סוף דבר יש שייכות ביניהם
ודבריהם קרובים זה לזה. ברור, שכולם הולכים, פחות או יותר
בשיטתו של רבי אליעזר שהתשובה מקרבת את הגאולה, ושאינה תלויה
בקץ, כדעת רבי יהושע.

השפעתם של השיטות האלו לא פסקה מבתי כנסיות ומבתי
מדרשות. בפרט יש לנו לשים לבנו לאגדות אחדות שמצד עצמם
מאירים על דרשות החכמים. הדעה השלישית שפגשנו כבר, כי הקב"ה
מביט בזכות הצדיקים וגואל את ישראל, נתבררה על ידי דרשן אחד,
שאומר: ישראל נכנסין לבתי כנסיות ובתי מדרשות ואומרים לפני
הקב"ה: גאל אותנו! והוא שואל אותם:

היש צדיקים ביניכם?

היש יראי שמים ביניכם?

ומוליד ספיקות בגואל ישראל. גם אל שיטת רבי אליעזר לא יכלו
להסכים ככתבה וכלשונה, כי יש כח בבורא עולמות למחוק עונות
אפילו כע״ג, או אם אין הדור כולו זכאי מכל מקום יש ביניהם
צדיקים שזכותם עומדת להם אפילו אין ביד האומה מעשים טובים.
בני הדור ששמעו את הדרשות הללו היו עדים של המלחמה הגדולה
של בר כוכבא וראו בעיניהם את חורבן ביתר וכל מה שבא אחרי
כן, והקושיא: היאך אנו נגאלים? וכו׳, היתה שגורה בפיהם, וחכמי
הדור מדמים את מצבם עם זמנו של משה ביציאת מצרים.

רוח חכמים הללו רוחפת גם על דרשות ג׳ חכמים אחרים שנזכרו
במדרש התנאים,[1] ואלו הם, רבי מתיא בן חרש, רבי אלעזר הקפר
בירבי, ורבי יהודה בן בתירא. נעבור בקיצור על דבריהם. רבי
מתיא בן חרש חשב – והאמת עמו – שאפילו ביאת הקץ אינה מספקת
לגאולה בלי מצוה. כי זהו הכלל: אין נותנים שכר אלא לעושה
מצוה. על כן צריכים ישראל למצוות או מעשים טובים שיהיו ראוים
לקבל שכר גדול כזה, כלומר גאולת העם, בידי יוצאי מצרים לא
היו מצוות ומעשים טובים על כן נתן להם דם פסח ודם מילה. רואים
אנו כי ר׳ מתיא השיב תשובה אחרת להשואלים: היאך אנו נגאלים
הלא אין בידינו מעשים טובים? על זה אמר, שהמקום נתן להם מצוות
כדי שיהיו ראוים להגאל. גם מתנגד הוא לדברי רבי יהושע, שהגאולה
תלויה בקץ. לא כן הדבר, כי הגיעה השבועה שנשבע הקב״ה לאברהם
שיגאל את בניו אפילו קודם הקץ. אולם מה תועלת בקץ בלי
מעשים טובים? ולמה יגאלו אם אינם כדאים לזה מצד מעשיהם? זוהי
באמת שיטת רבי אליעזר שקורא את העם לשוב בתשובה כדי שיהיו
נגאלין.

השני בחבורה הזאת הוא רבי אלעזר הקפר בירבי. דבריו דומים
קצת לדברי רבי נחמיה, אולם אינם שווים עמהם לגמרי, הוא מכחיש
את דעתו של רבי מתיא בן חרש שלא היו בידי אבותינו במצרים
מצוות כל עיקר, הדבר לא כן הוא, אלא אדרבה, היו בידיהם מצוות
יותר חשובות, ומונה אותם בזה הסדר:

א) שלא נחשדו על העריות,

ב) שהיו אוהבים זה את זה,

יכול לקצר את הקץ, אולם גם עם רבי אליעזר אינו מסכים בהדיא, כי לפי שיטתו הקב"ה גואל את ישראל לפי חסדו אפילו אם אין ישראל עושין תשובה. הוא בחר לו שיטה שלישית בענין זה, שהכל תלוי ברצונו של מקום.

נראה עתה את שיטתו של רבי נחמיה, שדורש את הפסוק באופן אחר. קול דודי וכו', זה משה שמכריז לישראל את הגאולה. והם משיבים לו: היאך אנו נגאלין וארץ מצרים מלאה גלולי ע"ז שלנו? זאת אומרת, שלא רק שלא היו בידיהם זכויות ומעשים טובים למהר את הגאולה, אלא אדרבא בהיפך: הם מאשימים את נפשותם בעבודה זרה שגורמת לעכב את הגאולה! גם רבי נחמיה מתנגד לשיטת רבי יהושע שהגאולה תלויה בקץ. הקץ אינו מעכב את הישועה, אולם האומה שהיא שקועה בעבודה זרה אינה ראויה להגאל. רבי נחמיה, כמו רבי יהודה, חשב שהדבר תלוי בחסדו של מקום והוא יכול לוותר אפילו על עברה כ"כ גדולה כעבודה זרה: מדלג על ההרים, אינו משגיח בקצים או בעבירות שבידם.

מלבד דברי רבי יהודה ורבי נחמיה נשארה גם שיטה שלישית פתוחה לפנינו באותו מקור עצמו, דברי רבנן. ולפי דבריהם, אמרו ישראל: הלא אין בידינו מעשים טובים היאך אנו נגאלים? המקום יכול לדלג על הקצים ומוחל אפילו על עבודה זרה, אולם אין בידינו זכויות ומעשים טובים והיאך תבא הגאולה? גם בדבר זה יש רעיון עמוק ונחמד. הגאולה אינה יכולה להיות שלימה או ממשית בלי מעשים טובים, זאת אומרת: כל האומה צריכה להשתנות לבריה חדשה. הגלות מגברת את העוונות והחטאים שגרמו אותה. על זה הדרשן משיב להם: בדור הזה יש בהם רשעים וצדיקים, המקום מדלג על הרשעים ומשגיח בזכות הצדיקים שהם מביאים את הגאולה.

מדרשות הללו יש ללמוד כמה דברים להתפתחות הרעיון של הגאולה בדור ההוא. בכלל אנו רואים שמרחיקים את שיטתו של רבי יהושע. המקום יכול להושיע את עמו אפילו טרם בא הקץ. באמת, בן דורם של הדרשנים האלו, רבי יוסי בר חלפתא, מתנגד ומחרף את האנשים שבלו ימיהם בחשבונות של הקץ,[1] מפני התקלה וההפסד שגורמים אם הקץ עבר והגאולה לא באה. עי"ז נולד יאוש בלב העם

---

[1] עיין לעיל.

קוראים את היהודים שומרי שבת ובית תפלתם בית שבת שלהם. על
כן היהודים בגלותם היו זהירים ביותר בשמירת מצוה זו כמו שידענו
ממעשה של הקברניט מאלכסנדריא במאה הרביעית.[1] אבל כדי שלא
לערבב את התחומין בין שמירת שבת קודש ובין שמירת שבת חול
הדגישו חכמינו שרק שמירת שבת כהלכתה יש לה כח לקרב או
למהר את הגאולה. כמה נאים ואמיתים דברי האגדה בזה! מי ששומר
את השבת לפי המסורת היהודית הוא מעמיק את תורת האל, הוא
מרחיב את רוחו ונפשו באמונת הבורא ובריאת העולם יש מאין ובכל
הפרטיות התלויות בשמירתה כהלכתה. על כן אמרו מי שמחזיק
בשמירת שבת כהלכתה אפילו עובד עבודה זרה כדור אנוש מוחלין
לו כל עוונותיו. והדגישו שלא נתן השבת לגויי הארצות, וקבעו מקום
לרעיון זה בתפלת שחרית של שבת. די להזכיר כי שמירת שבת כמו
העסק בתורה מסוגלות ביותר להביא את הגאולה, והם אופני התשובה.
אם רוצים אנו לצייר לפנינו את רוח הזמן ששלט בחיים ובבית המדרש
בתקופה הסמוכה לחורבן ביתר, יותר טוב לחקור ולדרוש בדרשות
חכמי הזמן על גאולת מצרים. המשא והמתן שביניהם על נושא זה
מראה כבאספקלריא המאירה את צורת הדור שלהם. באיזה זכות
נגאלו אבותינו ממצרים? – היתה הפרובלימה שלהם, אולם לא בתור
חקר בקדמוניות אלא כדי להראות לתלמידים את הדרך אשר בו יגיעו
לגאולת מחר. הם מדברים על העבר, אולם עיניהם צופות לעתיד,
ותמיד ההוה, המצב הרוחני והחומרי, מרחף לפניהם.

נרשום בראשונה את הדרשות של רבי יהודה ראש המדברים בכל
מקום, וחביריו רבי נחמיה ורבנן: רבי יהודה דרש על הפסוק בשיר
השירים: קול דודי הנה זה בא, זה משה. בשעה שאמר להם
בחודש זה אתם נגאלין, אמרו לו ישראל: היאך אנו נגאלין? הלא כבר
אמר הקב"ה ועבדום וכו' ארבע מאות שנה והרי אין בידינו אלא ר"י
שנה? אמר להם (משה): הואיל שהוא חפץ אתכם אינו מחשב חשבונות
אלא מדלג על ההרים וכו'.[2]

מדרשה זאת יש להכיר כי דברי רבי יהודה מתנגדים לשטת רבי
יהושע שהגאולה תלויה בקק. לא כן הדבר, כי אם הקב"ה רוצה הוא

---

[1] עיין ב„התור" שנה שמינית גליון י"א עמוד 7: שמירת שבת בגולה במאה
הרביעית.

[2] פסיקתא דר"כ מ"ג ע"א וע"ב.

למהר או לעכב את הישועה? מה חשבו ולמדו החכמים הקדמונים
והמאוחרים על זה? בלי ספק, הרעיון היה חביב בעיניהם בדרשותיהם.
רבי נתן, בסוף דורות התנאים אומר: כל העוסק בתורה ובגמילת
חסדים ומתפלל עם הצבור מעלה עליו הכתוב כאילו פדה את
הקב״ה ואת ישראל מבין אומות העולם.¹ הקב״ה משותף בגלותם של
ישראל ושניהם צריכים פדיון. הדבר היותר מסוגל לפדיון כזה הוא
תלמוד תורה, תכלית הלימוד להשלים את האדם עם בוראו וזוהי
התשובה היותר גמורה. שנית על ידי גמילת חסדים שמאחדת את
הלבבות בין אדם לחבירו, ושלישית התפלה בצבור. רבי נתן משתמש
כאן בשלש העמודים שעליהם העולם עומד א) תורה = עוסק בתורה,
ב) גמילת חסדים, ג) מתפלל עם הצבור = עבודה.

מצוה אחרת המסוגלת ביותר להביא את הגאולה ושקולה כנגד
כל התורה כולה היא מצות שבת, ואמרו אם ישראל משמרין שבת
כהלכתה מיד הן נגאלין.² החכמים הדגישו בצדק ובמשפט כי שמירת
שבת כמו לימוד התורה הם העמודים שעליהם הדת והאמונה הושתתו.
רעיון השבת כולל בעצמו את השקפות התורה, אמונת העם בבורא
עולם וטהרת החברה. במאמר אחר משתמשים במצוה זו באמרם: כל
מי שמשמר את השבת כהלכתה אפילו עובד עבודה זרה כדורו של
אנוש מוחלין לו עונותיו.³ בראשונה יש לדייק בלשון המאמר שרק מי
שמשמר את השבת כהלכתה או כראוי זוכה למחילת עונותיו וגם
אם ישראל בכלל משמרין את השבת בזה האופן נגאלין. ידוע כי
בדורות הראשונים אחרי ספירת הנוצרים וגם קודם לכן נתפשטה
שמירת שבת גם אצל העמים כמו שהוכיח לנו פרידלנדער על
פי ראיות מוכיחות.⁴ והמנהג של האומות עשה רושם גדול והשפיע על
חיי היהודים בחוץ לארץ שהיו מצוינים במצוה זאת, עד שהשכנים

---

¹ ברכות ב. א. ועיין גם דברי ר׳ אחא בר חנינא שם. יש להשוות גם דברי
רבי לוי בסנהדרין צט. ב.: העוסק בתורה לשמה מקרב את הגאולה, ולרעיון
שגמילת חסדים מביאה את הגאולה יש להשוות דברים רבה ח, ג.

² עיין שבת קיח, א. דברי רבי שמעון בן יוחאי, עיין גם שמות רבה ה׳ כ״ד, ועיין
גם דברי רבי לוי שם כה, טז.

³ גם כן שבת קיח, א.

⁴ עיין *Synagoge und Kirche in ihren Anfängen*. Berlin, 1908, pp. 14 ff.
עיין גם הרשימה עמוד 256.

דברי התנאים עצמם עוד צריכים באור! מה עלה על דעתם
באמרם שהגאולה תלויה בקץ או בתשובה? כי באמת רבו הדעות
ונתחלפו השיטות בדורות הבאים במהות התשובה או במדת הקץ. כאן
המקום לעיון ולהתבוננות יתירה במדת התשובה או הקץ בשייכות
לרעיון הגאולה בדור התנאים האלו ובדברי הבאים אחריהם, למלאות
את מקום הראשונים. במשך הדורות נעשו דברי הנביא דניאל לנהר
שלא פסקו מימיו לכל מחשבי קיצין כל כך, עד שרבי יוסי בירבי
חלפתא קם כנגדם בקללה נמרצה,[1] בכל זאת, בכל דור ודור מימיו
ועד עצם היום הזה, עמדו חכמים אמיתיים עם מתחכמים לדרוש את
הכתובים או לחשוב חשבונות כדי לפרט את זמן הקץ. צונץ[2] אסף
וקבץ חומר רב של חשבונות כאלו על שנת הגאולה, כפי שידו מגעת
בימיו. היום יכולים אנו לא רק לכפול, אלא אף לשלש את המספר
שנתן צונץ לפני הקוראים בימיו.[2]

יהודים וגם לא יהודים, חכמים ואי חכמים יחד התעסקו בחשבונות
כאלו. כולם היו מחפשים אחרי רמזים או אסמכתות במקראות למצוא
את זמן הקצים. כולם התאמצו למצוא תשובה לשאלה שנשאלה: אימתי
תהיה הגאולה? מצד אחד השתמשו בזאת ה,,חכמה'' כדי להחזיק את
העם באמונה שלא יתיאש מן הגאולה. בלי ספק כולם, המתיאשים מן
הגאולה והמתאוים לה היו צריכים חיזוק. אולם איזה התעוררות או
נחמה באה להם מן הקץ? – אין להכיר בראשונה, על כן אין להתפלא
שרוב הדרשנים החזיקו בדברי ר' אליעזר שהתשובה מביאה את
הגאולה. יוחנן הטובל קורא את אנשיו לתשובה כי מלכות שמים
קרובה להגלות,[3] לא כן רבי אליעזר האומר: עשו תשובה מיד אתם
נגאלין. אולי שניהם לדבר אחד נתכונו, כי מלכות שמים וגאולה
שוים הם בעניגם, והאמצעי שמביא אותן גם כן אחת היא, התשובה.
אולם יש הבדל קצת גם כן ביניהם, כי הטובל חשב שבא הקץ
והתשובה היא סגולה לכל איש ואיש שיבא מוכן ומזומן לסעודה, אבל
רבי אליעזר חשב שהתשובה ולא הקץ תביא את הגאולה לבני אדם.
נפן עתה אל פרטי הדברים להכיר באיזה אופן יכולה התשובה

---

[1] עיין צונץ *Gesammelte Schriften* III.
[2] עיין עוד לקמן פרק שלישי בנספחים, ששם נסדרו הידיעות שבאו לנו מיום
שנתן צונץ את רשימתו לפני החוקרים עד היום הזה.
[3] מתתיה ג. ב.

הכלל העולה לנו מן המקורות, שהראיות וההאסמכתות של הפסוקים
הן מעשה ידי האמוראים שסדרו או העתיקו את הברייתות ממקור
קדמון.[1] שנית אנו רואים שבסוף ר״א שתק וקבל דברי חבירו, ופלא
שרוב החכמים שנזכיר מיד הסכימו עם רבי אליעזר שהגאולה תלויה
בתשובה, או בתשובה יחד עם הקץ. אולם אין לקבל את הדעה
שהמחלוקת שבין התנאים תלויה ברכות לבו של רבי יהושע וקשיות
דעתו של רבי אליעזר,[2] אלא בפירוש הנבואות במקרא ובשטתם
הדתית. השיטות של שני התנאים היו ידועות גם לכותבי החזיונות,
כמו למחבר ספר עזרא הרביעי. החכם רוזנטל[3] חשב שהמחבר הזה
הלך בעקבות רבי אליעזר. אם נדקדק היטב בדברי החוזה,[4] נכיר
שעזרא אוחז בשתי שיטות יחד כמו שעשו גם חכמי האגדה בזמנים
מאוחרים. הוא אומר: הצדיק שואל את המלאך הנראה אליו – באותו
האופן ששאלו את הדרשנים בעלי הגדה, כמו שראינו לעיל – אימתי
תהיה הגאולה? עד מתי אנחנו מצפים להגאולה שקרובה לבוא? מתי
יאספו פירות הארץ לאוצר שלהם? על זה משיב המלאך: הגאולה
תהיה בזמן שיתמלא מספר האנשים הדומים לצדיקים כמוך: זאת
אומרת, שיש לפניו מספר קצוב של צדיקים העתיד לעמוד בעולם.
ובשעה שיתמלא מספרם אז – ולא קודם לכן – תצמח הגאולה! המלאך
מוסיף ומטעים את דבריו ואומר: כי במאזנים שקל את עולמו
ובמדתו מדד את העתים ,,ובמספר קצץ את הקצים״ ולא יאחר אותו.
כלומר את הקץ. ולפי תרגומו של מור: ולא ימוש ולא יהיה עד
שנתקיימה המדה הנזכרת. לפי דעתי, הכותב אינו מדבר כאן רק
מהתשובה, ז. א. מספר הצדיקים, אלא בהיפך הוא מאמין בקץ
וזוהי שטת רבי יהושע, ולא דעתו של רבי אליעזר. אולי ההבדל בין
רבי יהושע והכותב ספר עזרא הוא, שהראשון נוקט בקץ של ס׳
דניאל, והאחרון החזיק בקץ אחר שתלוי במספר הצדיקים העתידים
להבראות.[5]

[1] עיין הלשון בירושלמי ,,מה עביד ביה ר״א?״ וזהו סימן, שהחכמים הבאים
אחריהם הכניסו את הפסוקים בכוח שלהם.
[2] כמו שרצה ללמד ה׳ בן ציון באקנער Pharisaic Judaism in Transition
בחיבורו שנדפס בשנת 1935 ב־New York, עמוד 21.
[3] Vier apocryphe Bücher aus der Schule R. Akibas, Leipzig, p. 67 note 6.
[4] פרק ד׳ פסוק ל״ה והלאה.
[5] עיין מאמרי ,,מחשבי קיצין״ בהעברי שנה י׳ גליון מ״ד עמוד 12־13.

ארפא משובתיכם), ורבי יהושע מביא נגד זה ישעיה נב, ג׳ (חנם
נמכרתם ולא בכסף תגאלו, כלומר בתשובה, אלא על ידי דבר בלי
תשובה) כלומר, חנם נמכרתם בעבודה זרה, ולא בכסף – תשובה
ומעשים טובים – תגאלו (אולי הפירוש הוא הוספה מאוחרת?). על זה
הביא רבי אליעזר פסוק אחר ממלאכי ג, ז, (שובו אלי ואשובה אליכם).
רבי יהושע מתנגד לזה מירמיה ג, יד, (כי אנכי בעלתי בכם ולקחתי
אתכם). וע״ז אמר ר״א: הלא כבר נאמר בשובה ונחת תושעון (ישעיה
ל, טו), א״ל ר״י הלא כבר נאמר: ד׳ גואל ישראל קדשו לבזה נפש
(ישעיה מט, ז), א״ל ר״א הלא כבר נאמר: אם תשוב ישראל נאום
ד׳ אלי תשוב (ירמיה ד, א), א״ל ר״י והלא כבר נאמר: ואשמע את
האיש לבוש הבדים וכו׳ (דניאל יב, ז,). ושתק ר״א.

ג) בירושלמי הגירסא בדברי ר״א: אם אין ישראל עושין תשובה
אין נגאלין לעולם. אולם בירושלמי מרכיב את שתי הברייתות שבבבלי,
ומכיל הוספות גם ממקורות אחרים, כמו דברי רבי אחא בשם רבי
יהושע בן לוי, וגם סדר הפסוקים משונים שם, אולם מסיים גם כן
שבסוף ר״א שתק (אסתלק ר״א).[1]

ד) המקור הרביעי שפתוח לפנינו בתנחומא משלים את הברייתות
בבבלי ובירושלמי, שמביא לנו גם את דברי רבי יהושע שאמר: בין
עושין תשובה בין אין עושין תשובה כיון שהגיע הזמן מיד נגאלין.
בתנחומא מקצר את רשימת הפסוקים ומביא רק לסיוע של רבי
אליעזר ישעיה ל, טו, שנזכר בבבלי ובירושלמי, וישעיה ס, כב, לחזק
את דברי רבי יהושע, שהוא רק בירושלמי.

---

[1] סדר הפסוקים בבבלי ובירושלמי.

בבלי:		בירושלמי:	
א) ר״א ירמיה ג׳ כב,		א) ר״א ישעיה ל, טו,	
ב) ר״י ישעיה נב, ג,		ב) ר״י ירמיה ל, ז,	
ג) ר״א מלאכי ג, ז,		ג) ר״א ישעיה נב, ג,	
ד) ר״י ירמיה ג, יד,		ד) ר״א משלי ג, כ,	
ה) ר״א ישעיה ל, טו,		ה) ר״י ישעיה ס, כב,	
ו) ר״י ישעיה מט, ז,		ו) ר״א דברים י, יב,	
ז) ר״א ירמיה ד, א,		ז) ר״י דניאל יב, ז,	
ח) ר״י דניאל יב, ז,			

בגוף הדבר אין חילוק בין הנוסחאות אלא בסדור הפסוקים, שהם בודאי
הוספות מאוחרות שנתוספו בברייתות, יש פסוקים בבבלי שלא נמצאו בירושלמי,
ולהיפך בירושלמי שלא נזכרו בבבלי, הרי שהויכוח מיוסד על שינוי נוסחאות.

ב.

מהחומר שאספנו בפרק הראשון ניכר בלי ספק שתקות הגאולה
חיה באומה במשך הדורות מזמן החורבן עד סוף תקופת האמוראים.
בפרק זה רצוני להראות את הדרכים המביאים לידי גאולה בהשקפת
החכמים. נתחיל עם מאמרו של ר׳ אחא שחי כמעט בסוף דורות
האמוראים בא״י, והוא היה בן דורו של הקיסר יוליאנוס, וראה בעיניו
את התחלת הגאולה ובטולה, לפיכך עדותו חשובה ביותר, כי ממנה
יש ללמוד, שהשאלה לא היתה רק לימודית, אלא גם מעשית, שאלה
שהשעה צריכה לה. אולם גם בעצמה ראויה לתשומת עין, להתחיל
ממנה. אגדת רב אחא תופסת מקום מיוחד בקורות הרעיון הזה. לפי
שיטתו, הכח והאמצעי לקרב ולהביא את הגאולה שהוא מצפה לה,
היא התשובה. הקב״ה אומר לישראל: באלו דרכים הייתם עוברים
לפני, ומתוך כך הלכתם בגולה. עשו תשובה ואתם חוזרים! (מדרש
איכה רבתי א, יט).

שיטתו של ר׳ אחא אינה מקורית, כי כבר בדורות הראשונים,
עוד אחר חורבן הבית נתוכחו חכמי הדור אם הגאולה תלויה בתשובה,
בקץ או במעשים טובים. הדעות והאמונות בזה מיוסדות בפרט על
מחלוקת שבין ר׳ אליעזר בן הורקנוס ובין רבי יהושע בן חנניה.
לרגל מלאכתי אסדר כאן המקורות שמביאים ומבררים את השיטות
של שני חכמי הדור, דבריהם נשארו לפנינו בברייתות שונות:

א) רבי אליעזר אומר: אם ישראל עושים תשובה מיד הם נגאלים,
ואם לאו אינן נגאלין. א״ל ר׳ יהושע: אם אין עושים תשובה אין
נגאלין? אלא[1] הקב״ה מעמיד להם מלך שגזרותיו קשות כהמן וישראל
עושין תשובה ומחזירן למוטב.[2]

ב) בתניא אידך נמצאו דברים עם ראיות על דבריהם מן הפסוקים.
ר״א מביא בראשונה את הפסוק מירמיה ג, כ״ב (שובו בנים שובבים

---

[1] בודאי צ״ל: אמר לו במקום אלא. בכמה מקומות נתחלפו: אלא = וא״ל.
ועיין דברי רב״ז בכר בהגורן א 66 ודברי רבי׳ ירמיה לרבי זירא בב״מ כ״ח ע״ב
שצריך לגרום א״ל במקום אלא. ועוד יש כמה מקומות בתרמ״מ שצריכים
הגהה. ואכמ״ל.
[2] עיין סנהדרין ל״נ ב׳, ירושלמי תענית א. א., קלוזינר, הרעיון המשיחי עמוד
275. כפי הנראה הרכיב הירושלמי את שתי הברייתות שהובאו בבבלי, עיין עוד
תנחומא בחקותי הוצאת מהש״ב ע׳ 110 ועוד לקמן.

כל האגדות הללו הן ראיות ברורות שהשאלות היו שגורות בפיות
העם והתלמידים בכל דור ודור. איך השתדלו חכמי ישראל לענות
נברר בפרק הבא. נסיים כאן באגדה ממדרש שיר השירים זוטא (הוצאת
שכטר עמוד 24) אשר לפיה כבר בדורות הנביאים עמדו בני אדם
כדי לצערם בשאלה זו: אימת יגיע קצנו? והנביא משיב להם:
עוד אחת מעט! עד עכשיו יש להם עוד שתי מלכיות, כלומר יון
ואדום, שמשעבדים אותם. הדרשן מבלי להרחיב הדיבור פונה לשאלה
אחרת, כלומר באיזה זכות הגיעו המלכיות לגדולה? למה הם משעבדים
אחרים ולא אחרים אותם? ועל זה משיב: מפני שכבדו את אבותם.
בעיקר הדבר לא מצא הדרשן תשובה, אמנם מענין מאד שהחשב
שהשואלים מתכונים לצער את הנביא או העומדים במקומו, הדרשנים,
בדור המדרש!

עוד יש להכיר כי כמו ששאלו הדורות על הגאולה כן עמדו על
הקץ. הנה רבי שאול דנווה אומר ,,אם יאמר לך אדם מתי קץ
הגאולה? אמור לו: כי יום נקם בלבי'' (קהלת רבה י״ב, י). הוא
רבי שאול הוא רבי שילא שממנו שמענו המאמר בשם רבי שמעון,
כלומר בן לקיש. ובאמת בבבלי (סנהדרין צט. א) מובאים הדברים
בשמו שאמר: מאי יום נקם בלבי? ללבי גליתי, למלאכי השרת לא
גליתי, על כן אין שום תועלת לדרוש בדברים אלו, אף על פי שרבים
מבני הכנסיות שאלו שאלה כזאת. כי בכל מקום שמצינו הסגנון ,,אם
יאמר לך אדם'', מגיד שהעם או מינים ממינים שונים היו מתענינים
בשאלות כאלו.

עוד מצינו שגם רב אחא רב שידיו רב לו בתולדות הרעיון הלז
משיב בדרך חידה לעושי חשבונות כאלו. דבריו נמסרו לנו בשני
סגנונים, הם – אולי – משונים קצת מסגנונם העיקרי. בב״ר (ס׳׳ג יח)
הגירסא: כל מי שיודע לחשוב ימי הגלות ימצא שים אחד בלבד ישב
יעקב בשלוה בצלו של עשו. ובתנחומא (תולדות ד) גרסי׳: מי שיודע
לחשוב כראוי לא נטלו ישראל אלא אלף שנים, שיומו של הקב״ה
אלף שנים. בודאי לא נשארו דברי רבי אחא לפנינו באופן מתוקן,
כמו שנראה עוד בפרק שלישי לפנינו (עיין דברי רב׳׳ז בכר בהגורן
ח׳׳ב ע׳ 80 וצ׳׳ע). זאת ברור לנו לפחות כי גם בימיו היו בני הדור
מתעסקים בחשבון הקץ.

אליהו על ביאת המשיח. שאלתו: אמאי לא אתי מלך משיח היום?
שהוא יום הכפורים וכל העולם בנקיות ובטהרה מבלי חטא ועון (יומא
י"ט ע"ב).

ט) ובסנהדרין ל"ג ע"ב מגלה אליהו בפירוש את קץ המוגבל
וביאת המשיח, בודאי על השאלה אימתי יבוא משיח?

י) מענין הוא עוד הויכוח, שהיה בין רב נחמן ורב יצחק, בענין
שאנו עומדים בו. רב נחמן שואל את רב יצחק: מתי אתי בר
נפולי? רב יצחק אינו יודע מי הוא בר נפולי. זה מוכח בבירור
מתוך תשובתו: מי הוא בר נפולי? על כרחך שהוא לא ידע מי הוא
בר נפולי, ושבר נפולי הוא אחד משמותיו של המשיח, עד שאמר לו
רב נחמן שבר נפולי הוא המשיח! (סנהדרין צ"ו ע"ב) הדברים פשוטים
מצד עצמם שרב נחמן רצה לדעת זמן ביאת המשיח, אולם כמה דברים
באגדה, צריכין עוד ביאור, למשל, למה שאל זאת מרב יצחק? שנית,
למה מכנים את שמו בר נפולי? ואיזה יחס היה להחכמים הללו ולתורת
המשיח בזמנם?

יא) עוד יש להזכיר כאן ברייתא אחת שבה נמנו הדברים שהם
מכוסים מבני אדם ובתוכם גם שאלה של הקץ והגאולה; אולם שם
נקרא הקץ והגאולה בשם ,,יום נחמה" עם חזרת מלכות בית
דוד למקומה. התשובה על שאלות הללו הרי היא מכוסה מבני
אדם ואין איש אפילו חכמי הזמן והדורות אינם יכולים להגיד מתי
תהיה זאת? (פסחים נד, ב). אם אנו מסתכלים בדברים שנזכרו בברייתא
שמכוסים מבני אדם, יש להכיר כי בין הדברים שבני אדם התאמצו
לדעת אותם, כגון יום המיתה, ומה שעתיד להיות, ומה שבלבו של
חברו, רבו גם השואלים שחשקו לדעת מתי תהיה הנחמה, ואימתי
מלכות בית דוד חוזרת למקומה? שנית, שקמו בעם אנשים, ראוים או
שאינם ראוים לאותו איצטלא, שעושים את עצמם כאילו ידעו פשר
דבר בזה הענין בעמינו, כמו אצל שאר העמים בתקופה הזאת, עמדו
רואים או חוזים שהפיצו את האמונה בעד ממון או בצע שהם מסוגלים
להגיד עד מתי יחיה איש פלוני? ומה יהיה לעתיד, למחר, או מי הוא
אוהבו או שונאו של אדם זה. חכמינו ראו בכולם אחיזת עינים, כישוף
או דרכי אמורי, והזהירו את העם על זה, דברים אלו מכוסים הם
ממנו ואין אנו רשאים על ידי חשבונות או תחבולות או נבואות לעמוד
עליהם.

ד) כשהיו חכמי הדור אחרי חורבן ביתר יושבים ודורשים ביציאת
מצרים, היו מציירים את גאולת מצרים, ועל ידי ציור זה היו
מעוררים בלבב בני הדור את תקות הגאולה של מחר. בכל כחם
הדמיוני היו משימים בפיות בני דורו של משה את השאלות שהתעסקו
בהם בני ישראל בגולה כלומר: היאך אנו נגאלים? רבי יהודה בר
אילעאי ורבי נחמיה ורבנן נתוכחו בפרובלימה: איזה זכות עמד או
יעמוד לישראל להגאל משעבוד מלכיות? ועל שאלה זו משיב כל אחד
ואחד לפי שטתו, חכמתו ודעתו.

ה) השאלה נשארה במקומה, ולא זזה מלהיות הנקודה המרכזית
בחיי העם גם בתקופת האמוראים. רבי יהושע בן לוי שואל בעצמו
את אליהו הנביא – ודבריו רומזים על דברי החוזה בס׳ חנוך או עזרא
או ברוך בשאלתם את המלאך הדובר בם – מתי יבוא משיח? (סנהדרין
צ״ח ע״א).

ו) רבי זעירא היה מוצא את חבריו בבית המדרש שהיו עוסקים
בשאלה זו, והוא מבקש מהם שלא יתעסקו בדבר זה עוד, כי המשיח
יבוא בהיסח הדעת, אולם כשיוסיפו לחשוב את הקיצים או לסדר את
האותות והסימנים אז הם מעכבים אותו מלבוא (סנהדרין צ״ז ע״א).
הרי שלא רק המון העם אלא גם יושבי בית המדרש היו מתענינים
בענינים הללו. החברים הללו היו מ״דוחקי הקץ״ שנזכרו במקורות
מהתקופה הזאת.

ז) מצינו בזמן הזה מין אחד – שהיה בלי ספק ממאמיני ישו
הנוצרי – שואל את רבי אבהו מקיסרין: מתי יבוא משיח שלכם?
ורבי אבהו השיבו כהוגן (סנהדרין צ״ט ע״א).

ח) נשארו לנו רמזים שלא רק בארץ-ישראל, בטבריה או בקיסרין,
באושא או בלוד, היו שואלים שאלות כאלו, אלא גם בבבל. כמו רבי
יהושע בן לוי כן גם רב יהודה דרב סלא אחוה דרב סלא חסידא, שואל את

_____

מן הכים). ד) יאוש מן הגאולה. בגירסא אחרת מדלגים את הראשונים ונמנים
במקומם: א) עד שיהיו הכל הולכין בגולה. ב) עד שיהיה להם איש כמשה או
כדומה לו שיבקש רחמים עליהם. אף על פי שהסימנים האלו מובהקים ומדוייקים
הם, בפרט כשנחקור במקורות שלפנינו בספרות התלמודית והמדרשית עליהם,
מ״מ קשה להחליט בצמצום את זמן האגדה, וביותר שהדברים נשארו בכתובים
בנוסחאות שונות, ואין להכיר אם השינויים נולדו על ידי הוספות או שינויים במקור
יותר קדום שהיה לפניהם.

הוא בא?) לגאול את ישראל? הקב״ה משיב לו: לכשיגיע הקץ! ברור
שהדרשן אוחז בשטת רבי יהושע בן חנניה בעל מחלוקתו של רבי
אליעזר בן הורקנוס. רבי יהושע אמר שהגאולה תלויה בקץ ולא בדבר
אחר כמו תשובה ומעשים טובים. אולם הדרשן הלז מעשיר את
ידיעותינו באמרו שעם הקץ מחובר גם תנאי אחר לגאולת ישראל, וזהו
בנין ירושלים. עוד נראה כי חכמי הדורות לא היו שווים בדעותיהם
אם בנין ירושלים מעכב את הגאולה או לא. מדבריהם יש ללמוד כי
הקדמונים היו מיחסים חשיבות גדולה לסימן זה של בנין ירושלים.
נפן עתה אל החכמים הידועים לנו בשמותם שבאגדותיהם נשאלה
השאלה הזאת:

ג) תלמידיו של רבי יוסי בן קיסמא שאלו את רבם: אימתי בן
דוד בא? והוא מוכן להשיב להם על תנאי שלא יבקשו ממנו אות
(עיין סנהדרין צ״ח ע״א). כבר נתפשט בימיו הספרות של אותות
וסימנים שיקדימו את ביאת המשיח. ונתרבו ספרים וחיבורים ממין זה
מימים היותר קדומים בישראל. קטעים מספרות זו נשארו במשניות
ובברייתות שונות שמצאו להם מקום בתלמוד ובמדרש. אף על פי
שסימניהם שונים זה מזה, אולם כולם שווים במטרה אחת להשיב על
השאלה אימתי בן דוד בא? והתשובה על השאלה: בשבוע או בשעה
שבן דוד בא, אז נעשה או יעשה זאת וכזאת. לסוג זה של אגדות
שייכים דברי רבי נהוראי ודברי רבי נחמיה שמובאים בסוף מסכת
סוטה מ״ט ע״ב ובסנהדרין צ״ז ע״א שנשנו בדרך נבואה ומראים
בכל דבר לשונם של בעלי החזיונות (אפוקליפטיקס) באמרם מה
שיהיה ומה שלא יהיה כשבן דוד בא. כנגד זה מצינו בברייתא אחרת
סימנים אחרים שאין בן דוד בא עד שיהיה זאת וכזאת (עיין ספרי
דברים סי׳ שכ״ו, מדרש תנאים ע׳, סנהדרין צ״ז ע״א). בודאי יש
הפרש בין האגדה הסתמית בברייתא ובין דברי רבי נהוראי ורבי
נחמיה. ההבדל שביניהם נמשך גם על מהותם ותוכנם הפנימי, אולם
בזה אין הבדל והפרש ביניהם ששניהם משתדלים למצוא תשובה על
השאלה: אימתי יבוא בן דוד? זה משיב ,,בן דוד יבוא״, וזה ,,אין
בן דוד בא״ וכו׳, זה מדבר בלשון פוזיטיבי, וזה בדרך שלילה.[1]

---

[1] בספרי ובברייתא יש שינוים בין הגירסאות. לפי גירסא אחת יש לנו ד׳
סימנים: א) רבוי המסורות, ב) מיעוט התלמידים, ג) עניות (עד שתכלה פרוטה

את הצורה הקדומה בבגדים חדשים של זמנם ומקומם. על כן יש
למצוא באותו מאמר או בחזיון עצמו חומר עתיק אצל סימן חדש זה
בצד זה. החדש והישן שנתאחדו משמשים יחד כדי לתת כח להעשוקים
והנרדפים לעמוד בנסיון כנגד רודפיהם העזים.

הערבוב שבין המסורה הקדומה ובין קורות הזמן שמשמש בחזיונות
הללו טשטש את הגבולות שביניהם והביא את החוקרים במקצוע הזה
לידי השערות רחוקות. מסבה זאת אין להחליט בדיוק את הזמנים
והתקופות שבהן נכתבו או נסתדרו הספרים הללו. זה מעלה וזה מוריד
את הזמנים כל כך, שאין להעמיד אפילו בקרוב זמן את תקופתם של
הספרים הן העתיקים, כמו ספר עזרא הרביעי או ברוך וכדומה להם,
הן היותר מאוחרים כגון גילוי אליהו, זרובבל, אותות המשיח וכיוצא
בהם. לא כן הדבר באגדת התנאים האמוראים שם שם החכם או
הדורש ערב לדבר ולהגביל את הזמן וגם את המקום. ועל ידיהם יש
לאל ידינו גם כן לקבוע את זמנה של האגדה הסתמית בתור תניא
דמסייע ליה. גם יועיל לנו החומר לידע את היחוס בין האגדה ובין
ספרים גנוזים להראות את השפעת אלו על אלו. היום נשים עינינו רק
על השאלה עצמה בספרי האגדה.

השאלה מוזכרת הן באגדה סתמית הן באגדת החכמים, שזמנם
ומקום בית מדרשם ידועים לנו ממקורות שונים, שיש לסמוך עליהן.
ואלו הן:

א) במדרש תהלים מזמור מ''ה: אומרים ישראל לפני הקב''ה,
רבש''ע אימתי אתה גואלינו? [א''ל] כשתרדו לדיוטא התחתונה
באותה שעה אני גואל אתכם. כמה וכמה פעמים במאות הראשונות
אחרי חורבן הבית ירדו ישראל ל,,דיוטא התחתונה'', ובכל פעם ופעם
חיזקו הדרשנים במאמר זה את לב העם. עוד נראה לפנינו שהרעיון
הזה שגור גם בפי דרשנים ששמם וזמנם ידועים לנו.[1]

ב) במדרש תהלים, מזמור נ''א, הוצ' מהר''ש בובר ע' 221,
דרשן אחר מתרגם את גאולת העם באופן אחר. לפי דבריו דוד
המלך שואל מהקב''ה, רבש''ע: אימתי יבוא מלך המשיח (אימתי

---

[1] בויכוח אגדי בין כנסת ישראל ובין הקב''ה נמצאת גם כן השאלה של ישראל:
מתי אתה גואלנו? והוא משיב להם כמו כאן: כשתגיעו לדיוטא התחתונה. עיין
מדרש תהלים מזמור י''ט, ילקוט הושע 5.

רעיון הגאולה באגדת התנאים והאמוראים

א.

השאלה המרכזית שלא פסקה מפי העם והחכמים בכל הדורות מיום שחרבה ירושלים (ועוד קודם לכן) עד זמננו זה בכל המקומות (בפרט בארץ ישראל בתקופות התנאים והאמוראים), היתה: אימתי תבוא הגאולה? אימתי תהיה הישועה? אימתי יבוא המשיח או בן דוד? היאך אנו נגאלין? באיזה אופן מן האופנים יש לקרב את הגאולה ואת הישועה? או, איזה דבר מן הדברים מעכבים את הישועה? השאלות הללו הולידו כמה רעיונות שנמצאים בלשונם ובסגנונם העתיקים בתשובות שהשיבו הדרשנים והמורים בבתי כנסיות ובתי מדרשות וקבעו את מקומם בתלמודים ובמדרשים. ולא רק בדרשות ובלימודים נשארו רשמים הכי חשובים מתקות העם לגאולה ומחלומות וחזיונות שראו החוזים והנביאים, אלא גם הספרות העשירה של אותות המשיח, נסתרות ונבואות שיחסו לדניאל, אליהו, צפניה, זרובבל, ותלו באילן גדול כמו רבי עקיבא, ורבי ישמעאל ורבי שמעון בן יוחאי וזולתם, מעידים עדות גמורה שהתקוה לא פסקה מלב העם בכל הזמנים. ויותר מזה סדר התפלות של חול ושבתות וימים טובים ונוראים, גם הסליחות ותחנונים פזמונים ובקשות כולם יחד מדגישים ביתר שאת את בקשת העם שיגאל אותם הגואל משעבוד ויקבץ את נדחי עמו ויבנה ארצו וישרה שכינתו בהר קדשו. הדרוש והחזיון והתפלה נשתתפו יחד להחיות את תקות האומה, ולחזק את הלבבות האומללים בפרט בדורות השמד והרדיפות, בזמנים שהשונאים חשבו שהשיגו מה שזממו, לעקור ולאבד את זרע ישראל מן העולם. אמרתי ליתן לפני הקוראים פרקים אחדים מחקור זה.

אולם טרם אגש לסדר את החומר שאספתי ברעיון הגאולה בכלל, ובדורות התנאים והאמוראים בפרט, צריך אני להקדים ב' או ג' דברים על דרך החקירה עצמה. ברעיונות הללו נשארו רשמים עתיקים שחיו בלב העם מהקדמונים, שכבר בימי הנביאים הראשונים היו מסורות עתיקות ונשתלשלו מדור לדור, והבאים אחריהם הוסיפו והעשירו אותם. מלבד זה השתנו דבריהם בדורות האחרונים והיו מתאימים את הדברים עם קורות הזמן שחיו בו, זאת אומרת שהלבישו

2

בדרשה זו, בת ז' חלקים, מצייר הדרשן את ההווה והעתיד,
השעבוד והגאולה, ישראל ומלכויות והעולה על כולם היא האמונה,
שישראל אינם בטלים לעולם, שלהם העוה"ז וגם העוה"ב.

אסיים בדברי רבי אחא, שנאמרו בשמו על ידי רבי עזריהו. בא
סימן טוב. מה מלכות זו מכלה את העוברים ואת השבים, כך בניך
מכלים כל או"ה והן קיימים. מי שיודע את כל הקורות שעברו על
ישראל בימיו ורוח האגדה שמרחפת על פני תורתו, יכיר שרבי אחא
מראה באצבע המאורעות שאירעו בזמנו.

שקלל אחיה השילוני את ישראל מברכתו של בלעם הרשע את ישראל.
אחיה השילוני קללן בקנה: מה הקנה הזה עומד במקום מים גזעו
מחליף, שרשיו מרובין אפילו כל רוחות שבעולם באות ומנשבות אין
מזיזות אותו ממקומו, אלא הולך ובא עמהן, כיון שנשבה בו רוח
דרומית עוקרתו והופכתו על פניו (תענית כ, א). אחיה השילוני רצה
בקיומה ובעמידתה של האומה, לפיכך המשיל המשיל את ישראל לקנה.

בדרשה אחרת שהביא רבי שמואל בר נחמני, בשם רבי יונתן איש
הבירה מצינו טעם לרעיון של קיום עולמי של עם ישראל. הדרשן
משתמש ברעיון של ,,בריה חדשה'' ומלביש אותו בויכוח בין ישראל
ובין אומות העולם. אלה אומרים ומונים את ישראל, שאין להם תקומה
ונחמה בעולם. השמדות והצרות מעידות – לפי שיטתם – שהמקום עזב
את ישראל ואינו חוזר אליהם לעולם, ישראל משיבים לאומות העולם
ואומרים: אומר אני לכם במה אנו מתנחמים ולמה אנו יכולים לעמיד
בזעפו, מפני שמכה אותנו ומיד בורא אותנו בריה חדשה. וכן ישעיה
אומר: מי נתן למשיסה יעקב (מב, כד), הרי כלו הרי נמחו, אלא
חוזר מיד ובורא אותם בריה חדשה. ומה כתוב אחריו? ועתה כה
אמר ה' בוראך יעקב (שם מג, א). לפיכך אמרו ישראל בזה אנו
מתנחמין, שבורא אותנו מיד [בריה חדשה]. וזהו שאמר ירמיה: זאת
אשיב אל לבי (איכה ג, כא). למה? – חדשים לבקרים (שם כג), שהוא
מחדשנו מיד [בריה חדשה], שנאמר כה אמר ה' בוראך יעקב (אגדת
בראשית, הוצ' רש''ב, ע' 22). אף על פי שענן עב ושחור קשור על
מחנה ישראל והצרות מתגברות והולכות, בכל פעם ופעם בורא אותם
הקב''ה בריה חדשה ומקיים אותם בעולם.

נפן עתה אל דברי רבי אבון שמקדיש מקום חשוב לרעיון זה
בדרשה על השושנה, שמסוגלת לכלות את המדות של האומה. ישראל
כשושנה בין החוחים, באיזה אופן?

1) כל זמן שצלו של עשו קיים נראין ישראל כחוחין,
2) עבר צלו של עשו ישראל מרוטבין והולכין (כשושנה).
3) ישראל אינן בטלין אגב מצוות ומעשים טובים.
4) הצדיקים נבראו לגאולתן של ישראל.
5) ישראל הן הן לעוה''ז, הן הן לעוה''ב.
6) ישראל ניכרין בין או''ה.
7) ישראל מתוקנים לגאולה של מחר (שה''ש רבה ב, ב).

כן ישראל אינם בטלין לעולם, שנאמר כה אמר ה' נותן שמש לאור –
אם ימושו החקים ולא כשמים וארץ אלו, אלא כשמים וארץ העתידים
להבראות, שנאמר כאשר השמים החדשים וכו'.

ו) בויקרא רבה כט, ב, מסיים: או''ה שהן מכלין שדותיהן אעשה
כלה ואותך לא אעשה כלה, אבל ישראל שאין מכלים שדותיהם כד''א
לא תכלה פאת שדך – לא אעשה כלה, ויסרתיך במשפט. איסרך
ביסורין בעוה''ז כדי לנקותך מעונותיך לעתיד לבא. ואימתי בחדש
השביעי.

ז) בראשית רבה פ' א, הוצ' תיאודור ע' 395 והלאה:

1) מה עפר הארץ מסוף העולם ועד סופו, אף בניך מסוף
　　העולם ועד סופו.

2) מה עפר הארץ אינו מתברך אלא במים, אף בניך אין
　　מתברכין אלא בזכות תורה שמשולה במים.

3) מה עפר הארץ מבלה את כל מתכות והוא קיים לעולם
　　אף ישראל קיימים ואו''ה בטלים.

4) מה עפר הארץ עשוי דייש כך בניך עשויים דייש למלכויות.

ח) תנחומא דברים, הוצ' מהרש''ב, ע' 48, וא''ת מפני מה או''ה
מתחייבין כליה ואנן קיימין ועומדין? לפי כשבאין עליהם יסורין
מבעטין בהם ואתם מכירין (אולי צ''ל מברכין) שמו של הקב''ה,
שנאמר שפוך חמתך אל הגויים אשר לא ידעוך, אבל ישראל כשהיסורין
באין עליהם נכנעים, שנאמר צרה ויגון אמצא ובשם ה' אקרא, לפיכך
אמר הקב''ה: אע''פ שהקללות באות עליכם, הן הן מעמידות אתכם,
וכה''א למען ענותך ולמען נסותך להטיבך באחריתך, לכך אמר משה
לישראל: אע''פ שהיסורין באין עליכם אין לכם עמידה, לכך נאמר
אתם נצבים.

ו

מן האמוראים, שדבריהם עשירים בנושא שלנו אשים עיני בקדמונים
ורק שתים או שלש דוגמאות. נפן בראשונה אל דברי הדרשן היותר
מצוין, רבי שמואל בר נחמני. הוא מספר שיעקב אבינו ביקש מהקב''ה,
שבניו יהיו חיים וקיימים לעולם והמקום הבטיחו, שימלא את שאלתו
(מדרש תהלים, הוצ' מהרש''ב, ע' 29). בשם רבו רבי יונתן בן
אליעזר מוסר לנו אגדה זו באופן נחמד ומפואר באמרו: טובה קללה

ומקלסים שאין חלק יפה כחלקן ולא נחלה כנחלתן ולא גורל כגורלן
והם מודים ומשבחים על כך. וכן דוד הוא אומר: חבלים נפלו לי
בנעימים, אומר אברך ה׳ אשר יעצני, ישראל חלקם, נחלתם וגורלם
של המקום. זאת אומרת, שהם חיים וקיימים לעולם.

כבר נתפשט המנהג אצל הדרשנים לסיים את דרשותיהם בדבר
טוב או נחמה. חתימות הללו משמשות בבואה של הרעיונות היותר
חביבים בעם. בין רעיונות אלה נמצא גם האמונה בקיום העולמי של
ישראל. בזה אתן דוגמאות אחדות בצירוף פתגמים אחדים באגדת
הקדמונים.

א) תנחומא בא בסופו, הוצ׳ רש״ב, ע׳ נג. מסיים הדרשן את
דבריו באמרו: הקב״ה פורע לעתיד משר של כל מלכות ומלכות
ואחר כך פורע מכל אומה ואומה למשל מרומי מלכות הרשעה, או
מבבל, אבל ישראל כשם שאליהם חי וקיים לעולם ולע״ע, כך
ישראל חיים וקיימים לעולם ולע״ע. הרעיון, שהאלהים חי וקיים
לעולם, מיוסד על הפסוק וה׳ אלהים אמת הוא־אלהים חיים ומלך
עולם (ירמיה י, י), ובישראל כתוב ואתם הדבקים בה׳ וכו׳ (דברים
ד, ד). כמו שהאל חי לעולם כך עמו ישראל.

ב) שמות רבה מד, א. מיסד האמונה בזכות אבות. ישראל משולים
לגפן. מה הגפן כל זמן שעושה פירות נשען על עצים מתים, כך
ישראל נשענים על המתים, אלו האבות, שהם חיים וקיימים לעולם.

ג) תנחומא במדבר, הוצ׳ ר׳ שלמה באבער, ע׳ 25, מסיים: אבל
ישראל שהם עושין רצונו על אחת כמה וכמה שלא יכרתו ולא ישמד
שמם מלפני, אלא חיים וקיימים הם לעולם ולע״ע שנאמר: ואתם
הדבקים וכו׳.

ד) פסיקתא רבתי, פ׳ ויהי ביום כלות משה, מסיים עם ק״ו,
שמיוסד על האגדה שעגלות צב היו להן חיי עולם, מה אם העגלות
שנדבקו באהל מועד נותן להם תחייה שהן קיימות לעולם, ישראל שהן
דבוקין בהקב״ה עאכו״כ, שנאמר: ואתם הדבקים וכו׳.

ה) מדרש חסירות ויתרות, זאת לאמור. ויהי דבר ה׳ אל ירמיהו
לאמור – אם תפרו את בריתי, למה כשם ששמים וארץ אינם בטלים

וישראל עומדים לעולם, ז. א. המלכויות מצרים, בבל, מדי, יון ורומי נכנסות לגדולה ולשלטון וכשמגיעים לשיא הכבוד, נופלים, אבל ישראל אינו כן, אלא קיומם קיום עולם ונצחי (עיין גם במדרש תהלים מזמור לז, דף כ, ב).

מענין להשוות את דברי המדרש עם דברי הסיפרי עקב, פי׳ מג, ששם העתיקו את מאמרו של רשב״י בשם רבי יהושע בן קרחא. כלל הוא: בכל מקום שמעתיקים פתגם אחד בשם שני תנאים, או בשם שני אמוראים, הסופר או המסדר מדלג ממאמרו של זה למאמרו של חברו. אם נעיין היטב במדרש קהלת ניכר אמיתת הכלל הזה, כי במדרש קהלת מביא שני מאמרים, אחד מרשב״י ואחד מרבי יהושע בן קרחא. המעתיק דילג מגברא לגברא ומחליף את שמותם זה בזה.

כדי להשיג את הנוסח העיקרי שבסיפרי דברים עלינו להציג את הטכסטים זה לעומת זה ומשניהם יתברר הנוסח הנכון.

מדרש קהלת רבה	ספרי
אמר רבי יהושע בן קרחא צריך לקרא למימר אלא וכו׳. ארשב״י כתיב כימי העץ וכו׳. במדרש התנאים הובא רק המאמר הראשון (וגו׳ בכבודן של ישראל במקום צדיקים), כן ראה הוסיפו דברי רש״ב, ורי״ק ממקור אחר שהיה גם כן פתוח לפני מסדר מדרש קהלת.	ד״א למען ירבו ימיכם וכו׳, שיהיו חיים וקיימים לעולם ולעולמי עולמים כי כשאר השמים החדשים והארץ החדשה אשר אני עושה עומדים לפני נאום ה׳. והרי דברים קו״ח: מה שמים וארץ שלא נבראו אלא לכבודם של ישראל חיים וקיימים לעולם ולע״ע, ק״ו לצדיקים, שבשבילם נברא העולם.

ורבי יהושע בן קרחא אומר כימי העץ יהיו ימי עמי, אין עץ אלא תורה, שנאמר: עץ חיים וכו׳, והרי דברים קל וחומר: אם התורה שלא נבראה אלא לכבודו של ישראל הרי חיה וקיימת לעולם ולעולמי עולמים, קל וחומר לצדיקים, שבשבילם נברא העולם. רבי יהושע בן קרחא אמר דור הולך ודור בא והארץ לעולם עומדת.

אולם גם רבי יהושע בן קרחא לא היה מתנגד וחולק על האמונה בקיום הנצחי של עם ישראל! מי שמצייר את היחוס בין ישראל להקב״ה, כמו שהוא עשה בסיפרי ראה, פי׳ גג, לא היה יכול להכחיש רעיון זה. אחר שהביא משל נחמד הוא אומר: אף ישראל מודים

ישראל, לפיכך בא ודרש, שההטא של אדם הראשון שגרם מיתה עליו
ועל כל הדורות – הוסר על ידי מתן תורה. קבלת התורה בהר סיני
הביאה לחירות ישראל ממלאך המות, או בלשון אחר חיי עולם.

לא כן רבי נחמיה, שדרש הפסוקים כלפי האומות. ארשום הנקודות
של דרשתו, בקיצור, מן הספרי ומן המדרש הגדול.

א) בודאי (ולא בתמיה!) מגפן של סדום אתם (כלומר או"ה).
וממטעה של עמורה אתם.

תלמידיו של נחש הקדמוני אתם, שהטעה את אדם וחוה,

אשכולות וכו' שהגדולים שבהם מרתם פרוסה כנחש (כן הוא
בספרי)

ב) א"ל הקב"ה: ודאי מגפנם של סדום אתם וכו',
תלמידיו של נחש אתם, וכו'.

הגדולים שבכם מרירתן כנוסה בתוך מעיהן,
המתונים ויראי חטא שבכם חמתן קשה כתנין,
הראשים שבכם כפתן הזה אכזר (מדרש הגדול).

לפי זה יש לפרש את הד"א בספרי, שמעתיק או מסדר הרכיב
את דברי רבי נחמיה עם דברי רבי יהודה, אולם ברור שרבי נחמיה
שצייר לנו את הרדיפות והשמדות שעברו על ראשי העם תחת המלכויות,
בא ואמר, שעל ידי מתן תורה ניתן לישראל חירות מן המלכויות· הרי
שזה בזה תלוי.

ד

גם רבי שמעון בן יוחאי בן דורו של רבי יהודה ורבי נחמיה
משתדל לתקוע בלב שומעי דרשותיו האמונה הזאת. אדם גדול זה
ראה את שבט המושלים על שכם עמו לומד מקל וחומר את האמונה
שישראל חי וקיים לעולם. בישעיה סה, כב כתוב: כי כימי העץ ימי
עמי. העץ במקום ,,תורה''. שואל הדרשן: מי נברא בשביל מי?
התורה בשביל ישראל? או להיפך, ישראל בשביל התורה? בלי ספק
– התורה בשביל ישראל. אם התורה עומדת לעולם, שנבראה בשביל
ישראל וקיימת לעולם ועד, על אחת כמה וכמה, שבשבילה
נבראה התורה שיהיו חיים וקיימים לעולם ועד (מדרש קהלת רבה א,
ט על הפסוק והארץ לעולם עומדת). רבי יצחק מוסיף דבר משלו
ונותן טעם לשבח בדברי התנא ואומר: מלכות נכנסת ומלכות יוצאת

חמת תנינים יינם.

שההסידים והכשרים שבכם חמתן כתנינים.

וראש פתנים אכזר.

אלו הראשים שבכם כפתן אכזרים.

כבר לפני המסדר הנוכחי של ספרי דברים פי׳ שכג היתה דרשה
זו בשתי נוסחאות. ד״א חמת תנינים אכזר אלו המתונים ויראי חטא
שבכם שחמתם כתנינים.

וראש פתנים אכזר, אלו הראשים שבכם כפתן הזה.

במדרש הגדול מביא נוסח משונה בפרטים (עיין מדרש תנאים
לרד״צ הופמן ע׳ I). שם מובא הדרש שהקב״ה אומר לישראל: א)
וכי מגפנם של סדום אתם? וכי ממטעה של עמורה אתם? אין אתם
אלא זרע אמת שנאמר: ואנכי נטעתיך שורק (ירמיה ב, כא). ענבמו
ענבי רוש א״ל [הקב״ה], בניו של אדם הראשון אתם, שלא נצטווה
אלא על מצוה אחת בלא תעשה ועבר עליה. ראה כמה מיתות נקנסו
לו ולדורותיו ולדורות עד סוף כל הדורות [וכי איזה מדה מרובה
מדת הטוב או מדת הפורענות? הוי אומר מדת הטוב מרובה, מדת
הפורענות מעוטה], ראה כמה מיתות נקנסו עליו ועל דורותיו עד סוף
כל הדורות (ברור כי מעתיק אחד דילג מראה כמה מיתות וכי׳ עד
ראה כמה מיתות).

אשכלות מרורות למו. א״ל הקב״ה הגדולים שבכם מרירתן
כנוסה בתוך מעיהון כנחש, ומניין שאין אשכול אלא גדול, שנאמר:
אין אשכול לאכול (מיכה ז, א), [עיין למעלה הלשון מרתן פרוסה בהן
כנחש צ״ע].

חמת תנינים יינם. א״ל הכשרים ותלמידי חכמים שבכם שחמתם
קשה כתנין.

וראש פתנים אכזר. הראשונים שבכם כפתן הזה אכזר (גירסא
זו קרובה לזו שבספרי לעיל).

במדרש לקח טוב דברים, הוצ׳ רש״ב, דף נט, א, יש עוד
שינויים. למשל במקום ראשים גרס שונים. ובכלל מתאים עם גירסת
מדרש הגדול. בהזדמנות אחרת אשוב אל אחורי הפרגוד של המאמר.
כאן עלי לציין רק, שרבי יהודה האמין ברעיון של החטא העיקרי
כפי מה שנמצא גם בספרים הגנוזים ובאמונות ודעות של שאר חכמי

שאלות הללו, שהן רק דרך אגב! העיקר הוא, שכל האגדות מתעסקות
בשאלה יותר גדולה וחשובה מזאת. ז. א. מדוע האומות כלות וישראל
חיים וקיימים לעולם? הלשון ,,יורדין לגיהנם'' או להיפך ,,עולין לגן
עדן'' יש לה הבנה יותר רחבה ממה שמאמינים בו המון העם. הכלל
שאו''ה יורדין לגיהנם וישראל לגן עדן שגור בפי חכמי ישראל, ואין
כאן המקום לפרוט את המקומות. ארשום רק אחדים מהם: שמות
רבה יא, ז, רבי לוי; בראשית רבה כ, ב; ספרי דברים פי' שיא;
תנחומא דברים, הוצ' ר' שלמה באבער, לב, שם ע' כז; פסיקתא
רבתי מה, א, ועוד. האגדות עצמן מעידות, שהמשא ומתן היה באיזו
זכות זכו ישראל לחיי עולם. בכלל יש לומר, שבזכות התורה שקבלו
בהר סיני נטע בתוכם חיי עולם.

ג

כבר זכרנו פעם או שתים את המחלוקת שנולדה בין רבי יהודה
ובין רבי נחמיה, אם החרות שבאה לישראל עם קבלת התורה היא
חרות מן המות או חרות מן המלכויות. כאן יש מקום לצרף דברים
אלה עם מחלוקת אחרת שבין התנאים בפירוש הכתוב דברים לב,
לב: כי מגפן סדום גפנם. רבי יהודה דרש הכתובים כלפי מלאך
המות ורבי נחמיה כלפי אומות העולם או המלכויות. נפן בראשונה
לדרשת רבי יהודה. הוא מקדים דבריו בשאלה על הפסוק:

וכי מגפנה של סדום אתם?

או ממטעה של עמורה אתם?

והלא אין אתם אלא ממטע קודש?

שנאמר: ואנכי נטעתיך שורק כלה זרע אמת (ירמיה ב, כא).

ענבמו ענבי רוש

בניו של אדם הראשון אתם.

שקנס עליכם מיתה ועל כל תולדותיו הבאים אחריו.

עד סוף כל הדורות.

אשכלות מררות למו.

שהגדולים שבכם מרתן פרוסה בהן כנחש

ואין אשכול אלא גדול, שנאמר: אין אשכול לאכול בכורה
אותה נפשי (מיכה ז, א).

כל מה שהוא עושה אין ממחין על ידו, למה? שהוא קטן, כך כל מה
שישראל מתלכלכין כל ימות השנה בעבירות בא יום הכפורים ומכפר
עליהם, שנאמר כי ביום הזה יכפר וכו׳.

ה) נוסח חמישי נשאר בפסיקתא דר״כ, פיסקא אחרי מות הוצ׳
מהרש״ב קע״ו, א על הפסוק לדוד ה׳ אורי וישעי וכו׳ רבנן פתרין
קריא בר״ה ובה״כ: אורי בר״ה וישעי ביה״כ.

ממי אירא, עזי וזמרת יה,

בקמים עלי מרעים אלו שרי או״ה.

לאכול את בשרי לפי ששרי או״ה באין ומקטרגין על ישראל
לפני הקב״ה ואומרים לפניו אלו עע״ז ואלו עע״ז אלו מג״ע ואלו
מג״ע, אלו שופכי דמים ואלו שופכי דמים, מפני מה אנו יורדין
לגיהנם ואלו אין יורדין לגיהנם? צרי ואויבי לי. בימות החמה שס״ה
יום, והשטן גימטריא שס״ד, שכל ימות השנה מקטרג, וביה״כ אינו
מקטרג. אמרו ישראל לפני הקב״ה אם תחנה עלי מחנה של סמאל
לא ירא לבי, שכבר הבטחתני בזאת יבא אהרן אל הקודש.

ו) במעשיה אחד מן המעשיות שהוציא לאור הר״א יללינק, בבית
המדרש שלו, חלק ג׳, סח, מובאים הדברים בויכוח שבין סמאל
ומיכאל כפי מה שמספר אליהו הנביא לרבי יוסי בבית מדרשו. אעתיק
כאן רק מה שנוגע לענין שלנו. אומר (שרו של אדום) מפני מה מסרתני
בידו של מיכאל יבוא עמי וידון לפניך! מיד אמר הקב״ה למיכאל:
לך לדון עמו. עמד סמאל ואמר: אם הגוים עוברי עבירה (צ״ל עובדי
ע״ז) אף ישראל עוברי עברות (צ״ל עובדי עבודה זרה), אם אלו
מגלו עריות אף אלו מגלו עריות, אם אלו שופכי דמים אף אלו
שופכי דמים. מיד משתתק מיכאל. אמר לו הקב״ה למיכאל נשתתקת
ואני אלמד סניגוריה על בני וכל מעשיו של סמאל לא יועילו, לכך
נאמר אני מדבר בצדקה ואני מושיעם ביום דין. ממה שראינו למעלה
יש להחליט כי ,,בעל המעשה״ שאב דבריו מן המדרש.

מענין כי פיאניוס, שנהרג על אמונתו בישו בשנת ר״ן למספרם,
מוכיח את היהודים, שעומדים ושמחים על צליבתו ואומר להם: אתם
עובדי עבודה זרה, אתם מגלי עריות ואתם שופכי דמים כמו הגוים
(פ׳ ד, יא) ומביא ראיות מן הכתובים על כל אחת ואחת. בודאי
שאב דבריו וראיותיו מאבות הכנסיה שקדמו לו בזמן. על כן אין
לתמוה אם כבר רבי אלעזר המודעי נכנס בעובי הקורה להשיב על

שנאמר לא תירא לביתה משלג, ואעפ״כ אני אלך עמכם, שנאמר כי
כל העמים ילכו איש בשם אלהיו ואנחנו נלך בשם ה׳ אלהינו לעולם ועד.

ג) באותו מדרש, ע׳ 174, הוצ׳ מהרש״ב, הובאה האגדה עוד
בפנים אחרת, הדרשן מתחיל בפתגם כללי: יענך ה׳ ביום צרה ביום
שהכל מודים בו שהוא יום צרה לעליונים ולתחתונים, וכו׳. ומוסיף
והולך. והקב״ה אמר לאו״ה בואו ודונו עם בני בני ישראל! שנאמר
קרבו ריבכם יאמר ה׳ הגישו עצמותיכם יאמר מלך יעקב והן אומרים
רבש״ע מי יבא בדין עם ישראל? והוא אומר – אני כביכול. שנאמר
אל ישראל הוא נותן עוז ותעצומות לעם ואו״ה אומרים וכי משוא
פנים יש בדבר?

אלו מג״ע ואלו מג״ע.

אלו שופכי דמים ואלו שופכי דמים,

[אלו עע״ז ואלו עע״ז]

מפני מה הללו יורדין לגיהנם ואלו אין יורדין.

באותה שעה נמצא סנגורן של ישראל משתתק. שנאמר ובעת ההיא
יעמוד מיכאל השר הגדול העומד על בני עמך והיתה עת צרה אשר
לא נהיתה וגו׳. מהו העומד על בני עמך? שהוא עומד ללמד סניגוריא
על ישראל והוא שותק. ואין עמידה זו אלא שתיקה, שנאמר עמדו
ולא ענו עוד. וכיון שהוא נשתתק, אמר לו הקב״ה מיכאל נשתתקת
ואין אתה מלמד זכות וסנגוריא על בניי? שאני מדבר עליהם צדקה
ומושיעם, שנאמר אני מדבר בצדקה רב להושיע; באיזה צדקה, רבי
פנחס ורבי אלעזר ורבי יוחנן. חד אמר בצדקה שעשיתם עמי, שקבלתם
את התורה בסיני שאלמלא לא קבלתם את התורה בסיני הייתי מכלה
אתכם, וחד אמר בצדקה שעשיתם עמי שקבלתם את התורה שאם לא
קבלתם היכן מלכותי? וחד אמר בשכר שקבלתם את התורה, שאלמלא
לא קבלתם הייתי מחריב את כל העולם ומחזירו לתהו ובהו, שנאמר
אם לא בריתי יומם ולילה וכו׳.

ד) נוסח רביעי מן אגדה זו מובא בשיר השירים רבה, ח׳ ח׳ על
ידי רבי עזריהו בשם רבי יהודה בר סימן על הפסוק אחות לנו קטנה.
לעתיד לבוא עתידין כל שרי או״ה באין ומקטרגין על ישראל לפני
הקב״ה, ואומרין רבש״ע אלו עע״ז ואלו עע״ז, אלו מג״ע ואלו מג״ע,
אלו שופכי דמים ואלו שופכי דמים, אלו יורדין לגיהנם ואלו אין
יורדין לגיהנם. מפני מה? א״ל הקב״ה: אחות לנו קטנה, מה קטן זה

א) שיר השירים רבא ב א· עתידים שרי או״ה לע״ל שיבואו
לקטרג את ישראל לפני הקב״ה ואומרים רבש״ע:

אלו עבדו עכו״ם ואלו עבדו עכו״ם,

אלו גלו עריות ואלו גלו עריות,

אלו שפכו דמים ואלו שפכו דמים,

מפני מה אלו יורדין לגיהנם ואלו אין יורדין?

והקב״ה משיב להם ואומר:

אם כן הוא ירדו כל העמים עם אלהיהם לגיהנם.

הה״ד: כי כל העמים ילכו איש בשם אלהיו.

אולי כדי להוציא הזרות והגשמיות מתוך אגדה, מוסיף רבי ראובן
על האגדה ואומר: כי האמונה הזאת מיוסדת על הפסוק: כי באש ה׳
נשפט. ה׳ שופט אין כתיב כאן, אלא נשפט. אף על פי שאין ראיה,
מכל מקום יש אסמכתא, שהקב״ה יורד עם בניו לגיהנם. בודאי יש
לנו רשות ואמתלא להסתפק אם התנא הקדמון דרש אמונה זרה כזו
לפני קהל ועדה!

ב) במדרש תהלים א, כ הוצ׳ רש״ב, עמ׳ 21, נמצאת האגדה
בשלימות, ולא בקטעים. שם מביא מסדר המדרש דברי ר׳ אלעזר
המודעי לחזק את דברי החכמים המפרשים את הפתגם: אני הוא, אני
חביבה, ואומר: לע״ל באין כל שרי או״ה ומקטרגין על ישראל לפני
הקב״ה ואומרים לפניו רבש״ע....

אלו עובדי ע״ז ואלו עובדי ע״ז

אלו שופכי דמים ואלו שופכי דמים

אלו מג״ע ואלו מג״ע

הללו יורדין לגיהנם והללו אין יורדין

אמר להם הקב״ה, אם כן, תרד כל אומה ואומה ואלהיה עמה לגיהנם
ותבדוק את עצמה וגם ישראל ילכו ויבדקו את עצמם?

משיבים ישראל ואומרים לפני הקב״ה:

אתה הוא סיכויינו!

ואתה הוא סברנו!

אין לנו מובטח אלא אתה!

אם רצונך עבור אתה בראשינו!

ואומר להם הקב״ה, אל תיראו, שכולכם לובשי שני, זה ברית מילה,

הרעיון בטלית של שאלה ותשובה בין מלאך המות ובין הקב״ה.
בשיטתו של התנא המלאכים תופשים מקום קבוע. מה הביאו לידי כך,
למה התחזק וכנגד כל הקושיות שיש לשאול, באמונה זו בודאי היה
לו טעם הגון על זה. לפי הנראה יש לאמונה זו דו־פרצופין. מצד
אחד פנים של צרכי הדת ומצד שני פנים עממיים. זאת אומרת, שעל
ידי קבלת התורה ובחירת ישראל ודביקות האומה במצוות קנו להם
חיי עולם. דרישה זו היתה אקטואלית ביחוד במלחמת בר כוכבא
ואחר חורבן ביתר. הקיסרים יחלופו, הליגיונים היותר קלים נטרדו מן
העולם, אולם עם ישראל חי וקיים לעולם.

קול שני נשמע מתוך העלים של האגדות שקורא אלינו מן העבר
אל ההווה: לא תתיאשו מן הישועה, כי תקותכם לא תאבד. רבי
אלעזר המודעי, שהיה מתנגד לתנועה המשיחית של בר כוכבא מעיד לנו
עדות ברורה על זה. על הפסוק ,,מה תצעק אלי״ (שמות י״ד, טו)
דרש דרשה נפלאה, שיכולה להשתמש כאספקלריה המאירה להאיר
את כל אחורי הפרגוד של מצב הדור:

כך אמר הקב״ה למשה:

על בני אני צריך צווי?

על בני ועל פועל ידי תצווני? (ישעיה מה, יא).

הרי כבר מוכנים הם לפני מששת ימי בראשית!

שנאמר: אם ימושו החקים האלה מלפני נאום ד׳ גם זרע ישראל ישבתו
מהיות גוי לפני כל הימים (ירמיה לא, לה, עיין מכילתא דר״י יש ז
ע״א מכילתא דרשב״י ע׳ מח, ומביא שם עוד פסוק לו: כה אמר ד׳
אם ימדו שמים מלמעלה ויחקרו מוסדי ארץ למטה גם אני אמאס בכל
זרע ישראל). אין לדאוג – אמר המודעי – כי כבר הבטיח המקום,
שזרע בית ישראל לא ימוש מתוך העולם ויקיים לנצח. ביחוד כשהם
מוכנים לכך משש ימי בראשית ומי שמוכן לכך אין לו סוף ותכלית.
על כן, קורא המודעי לבני דורו: למה לכם כל התחבולות הללו?
מלחמות ולגיונות? ה׳ ילחם לכם ואתם תחרישון. ברור, כי גדולים
וחשובים מבני דורו, כמו רבי עקיבא וסייעתו, לא הסכימו לדעה זו
ואחזו בשיטה אחרת.

עוד יש לנו אגדה אחרת, המיוחסת לתנא שלנו, שמדברת בזו
האמונה אולם קודם שאכנס לעומק הדין צריך לברר את הנוסחאות
שלפנינו:

היום, טוב לברור רק אחת, מפני שהדברים עתיקים ונשמעים כמו
חדשים בימינו! מלבד שבכל דור ודור עומדים רשעים ארורים כמו
המן וסיעתו להשמיד ולהרוג את עם ישראל, קמו גם אחרים, מבני
עמנו להכרית תקות ישראל, ולבטל אמונתם בקיום העולמי ולהשריש
היאוש מן הישועה בקרבם. רוח המקום עומד כנגדם ומשיבם: וי שוטה
שבעולם, אני (המקום במעשה העגל) אמרתי להשמידם כביכול ולא
יכולתי! שנאמר ויאמר להשמידם לולי משה בחירו עמד בפרץ לפניו
להשיב חמתו מהשחית (תהלים קו. כג), ואתה אמרת להשמיד להרוג
ולאבד? חייך רישך מתורם חלף רישיהון דאינון לשיזבא ואת לצליבא
(מדרש אסתר רבה ב, ו, לפסוק ג, ו).

ד) בילקוט מכירי על תהלים נ, אמר רבי פנחס הכהן ב״ר חמא
על המחלוקת שבין רב יהודה לרבי נחמיה אם חרות מן מלאך המות
או מן המלכויות: אמר הקב״ה אם יבא מלאך המות ויאמר לי למה
נבראתי? אני אומר לו: קוסטינור נתתיך על אומות העולם ולא על
בני, ולמה? שעשיתי אותם אלהים שנאמר: אני אמרתי אלהים אתם.
לפיכך כשבא ליתן להם הדברות, אמר להם מה שאני אומר לכך:
שמעה עמי ואדברה.

ה) במקור חדש, מובא המאמר על ידי רבי יוחנן בשם ר״א בנו
של רבי יוסי הגלילי בזה הלשון. שיר השירים רבה ח, ג: בשעה
שעמדו ישראל לפני הר סיני ואמרו נעשה ונשמע, באותה שעה קרא
הקב״ה למלאך המות ואמר לו: אע״פ שמניתך קפוקליטור (צ״ל
ספקולטור, או קוסטינור, ז. א. רב החובל) וקוזמוקרוטור על בריותי
אין לך עסק באומה זו. הה״ד ויהי כשמעכם את הקול מתוך החשך.
וכי יש חושך למעלה והא כתיב ונהורא עמה שריא. מהו מתוך החושך?
זה מלאך המות שקרוי חושך, שנאמר: והלחות מעשה אלהים המה
והמכתב מכתב אלהים הוא חרות על הלוחות. אל תקרי חרות אלא
חירות. רבי יהודה ורבי נחמיה ורבנן. ר׳ יהודה אומר: חירות ממלאך
המות, ר׳ נחמיה אומר: חירות מן המלכיות. ורבנן אמרי חירות מן
היסורין.

ב

לכתחילה בא התנא להדגיש ביתר שאת את הרעיון, שאין למלאך
המות רשות על ישראל. וזאת מפני כמה סיבות שונות. הוא מעטף את

בטכסט שלנו ,,ליטול אחד ממנה'' אם הלשון הוא מקורי או גליון או
הוספת המעתיק, כי בודאי מוכח מכל הספרים שפתוחים לפנינו שדברי
התנא מוסבים רק על האומה בכלל ולא על כל יחיד ויחיד.

ג) שמות רבה ז, ב. כאן מביא מסדר המדרש את דברי ר''א
בנו של ריה''ג בסתם, בודאי ממקור אחר שמשתמש בו בפרשה מ''ח
(עיין לעיל). יש שינויים ביניהם שראוי לדקדק אחריהם. האגדה מיוסדת
על שמות כג, כ על הפסוק ,,הנה אנכי שולח מלאך'', הדרשן מרכיב
הפסוק לפי דרכי הדרוש על תהלים פב, ו. הה''ד אני אמרתי אלהים
אתם וכו. כשעמדו ישראל על הר סיני וקבלו את התורה, אמר הקב''ה
למה''מ, על כל או''ה יש לך רשות בהן, ועל אומה זו אין לך רשות
בה. שהם חלקי כשם שאני חי וקים לעולם, כך בני קיימים שנאמר
בהנחל עליון גויים, וכתוב כי יעקב חבל נחלתו (דברים לב, ח והלאה,
והראיה מכי חלק ה' עמו). הטעם לקיום הנצחי של ישראל הוא בחירת
ישראל, שהם חלקו של הקב''ה, אולם חוץ מן ההפרש הפורמלי, שכאן
המקום מעצמו אומר למה''מ שיש לו רשות רק על או''ה, ושם בתור
תשובה על שאלתו, יש עוד הפרש בטעם הרעיון, שם מובטחים ישראל
בקיום עולמי מצד קבלתם את התורה, וכאן מפני שהם חלקו של
הקב''ה, ובחר בהם, אולם זה רק לפי מראית העין, כי הא בהא
תליא, לא בחר הקב''ה בישראל, ולא נעשו חבל נחלתו אלא ע''י
קבלת התורה. מה שבולט מכל האגדות שזכרנו הוא הצד השוה
שביניהם שישראל חיים וקיימים לעולם. בודאי נתפשטה כבר האמונה
שעל ידי מתן תורה פסקה מיתה מישראל, על זה אמר הקב''ה אני
אמרתי אלהים אתם, אולם כשחבלו מעשיהם ובטלו את הדברות,
ואמרו אלה אלהיך ישראל, אמר אכן כאדם תמותון, ז. א. כמו שאדם
מת בחטאו ונקנסה מיתה על ידו, כן גם אתם חזרתם לרשותו של
מה''מ. וכן הבינו גם את סופו של פסוק כאחד השרים תפולו, ז. א.
כמו שאו''ה תחת ממשלה, כך ישראל פסקו מלהיות בני חורין משלטות
המות. מי שיכול לקרות בין השורות ומצייר לעצמו את אחורי הפרגוד
של הדרשה מכיר המשא והמתן של הדרשה בכחה ובעיקרה. מה
תועלת – שאלו בני הדור ובפרט אותם שעמדו תחת השפעת הכנסיה
החדשה – בהבטחת חיי עולם, אם ,,מעשה העגל'' בטל הכל? גם
הפיצו הדעה, שמעולם לא קבלה האומה את הברית מפני שחטאו
פשעו. מה השיבו חכמי ישראל על זה? מרוב התשובות שנשארו בידינו

ולתקוה, שכמו שאלהי ישראל אלהים חיים, כך עמו שקבל את עול
מלכותו, את עול תורתו, את עול המצוות, לא ישתנה ולא יכלה.
בעלי אגדה לא היו מתפלספים, אולם הרגישו בלבבם את כח האמונה
והחוק המשתף את האומה ואת הדת. העמודים שעליהם בנויים העבר,
ההווה והעתיד. אוה"ע יש להם שירים שמפארים ומעריצים את הגבורים
והחיילים, את המנהיגים והשרים, יש להם מוסדות של חכמה וגבורה
שמתפארים בהם ומגדלים את שמם, אולם לישראל אף־על־פי שאין
אנו עניים בכל אלו – לא נשארה רק האמונה הגדולה מכל ההיכלות
והארמונות, מכל כסף וזהב, כי – הם חיים וקיימים לעולם.

א

מאמרו של רבי אליעזר בירבי יוסי הגלילי נמסר לנו בנוסחאות
שונות. הטכסטים מצד עצמם צריכים תלמוד כדי להכיר מתוכם איך
נשתלשלו והתפתחו בו הרעיונות. גם יש לשים לב למה שמלמד הנסיון
שרבי אליעזר בחר לו באגדה שלו סגנון מיוחד. קודם כל יש לחקור
על המקורות שבהם נשארו דבריו.

א) שמות רבה מח, ט: אם יבוא מלאך המות לפני הקב"ה
ומהרהר אחרי מדותיו של המקום ואומר: בחנם בראתני בעולמך, הוא
משיב לו על כל אומה ולשון שבעולם נתתי לך שלטון, חוץ מן אומה
זו שאין לך רשות בה. ולמה? זוהי שקבלה את התורה ועל ידי כך
קבלה חרות מן מלאך המות (עיין עוד לפנינו). הרי שאומה זו חיה
וקיימת לעולם ולא ככל האומות שעומדות תחת רשותו של מלאך
המות.

ב) תנחומא, במדבר, הוצ' רש"ב, ע' 76 מביא דברי ר"א בנו
של ריה"ג בזה הלשון: אמר מה"מ לפני הקב"ה רבש"ע בחנם נבראתי
בעולם, א"ל הקב"ה בראתי אותך שתהא מושל באו"ה, חוץ מן אומה
זו שאין לך רשות... ליטול אחד ממנה... וזה עצה שיעץ עליהם
הקב"ה שיהיו חיים וקיימים לעולם שנאמר ואתם הדבקים בה' וכו'
(דברים ד, ד). אקדים לזה מסורה אחרת. באותה שעה מה עשה
הקב"ה? הביא מלאך המות ואמר לו, כל האומות ברשותך, חוץ מן
אומה זו שבחרתי לי. כאן קיום הנצחי של עם ישראל תלוי ברעיון
של בחירת ישראל מכל האומות. הרעיון הזה חשוב הוא מאוד באמונות
ודעות של בעלי האגדה וצריך חקירה מיוחדת ודרשה פנימית, אולם

האמונה בנצח ישראל בדרשות התנאים והאמוראים

הקדמה

אספתי ולקטתי כאן קצת מן החומר בו מדגישים חכמי ישראל את
הרעיון, שישראל חי וקיים לעולם. הם מביעים את דעתם בכמה
סגנונים. למשל, שאין למלאך המות שליטה על אומה זו, שאין ישראל
יורדין לגיהנם, שהם קבלו חרות מן המות, מובטח להם בכתובים שהם
חיים וקיימים לעולם, שהם אינם בטלים, וכשנגאלים בטלים מתחדשים
בריה חדשה. או"ה אובדות ונטרדות מן העולם, לא כן ישראל.
הרעיונות הללו אינם פשוטים כל כך, הם מסובכים עם נושאים אחרים,
שמחזיקים במדה מרובה את מחשבות הדרשנים והעם. למה הבטיחם
המקום והעלם למדרגה גבוהה כזאת? בודאי הרעיון הוא רק חלק
ומקצת מהאמונות ודעות, עליהן מיוסדות השקפות העומדות ברומו של
עולם ועקרים שיורדים לתהום רבה. כמו אהבת המקום לישראל,
בחירת האומה מכל האומות, מתן תורה, דבקות האדם בבוראו, עשיית
רצונו של מקום, החטא הקדמוני, חטא העגל, תורת בריה חדשה, יחוס
ישראל להאומות, ועוד דעות אחרות שפגשנו בחקירה זו. בכלל יש
להדגיש, כי החלק הגדול ביותר שייך לזכות התורה שנטעה חיי עולם
בקרב העם. אולם גם מצוות ומדות אחרות לא נעדרו מהרשימה
שמונה את הדברים שעל ידיהם זכו לחיי עולם, למשל זכות אבות,
דבקות בשכינה, זכות יום הכפורים, ועוד.

עלינו לשים לב על החכמים שמחבבים את אמונה הזאת, כמו
רבי אלעזר בנו של רבי יוסי הגלילי ורבי אלעזר המודעי, רבי יהודה
בר אילעאי, רבי שמעון בן יוחai מן התנאים, אחרים הם הדרשנים
שנכלללו בתוך האגדה הסתמית ששמותיהם לא נשארו בכתובים לפנינו,
רובם שייכים לדורות המאוחרים, לסוף תקופת האמוראים. אולם גם
גדולי האמוראים הקדומים נתנו מקום נכבד לרעיון זה באגדות שלהם,
כמו רבי יונתן בן אליעזר, רבי שמואל בר נחמני, רבי אבון, רבי
אחא. מלבד אלו התנאים והאמוראים ישנם אחרים שנשאו את קולם
לחזק ידי שומעיהם באמונה זו. כי בכל זמן וזמן כשערפל היאוש
כיסה את הלבבות על ידי המלחמות והגזירות, שמדות ורוחות, צמאו
הקהלות לשתות מבאר הנחמה. התורה והנביאים נעשו בסיס לישועה

1

תוכן העניינים

חלק ב׳ (עברית)

ספר זכרון

לכבוד

הרב ד"ר

אברהם מרמורשטיין זצ"ל

(מחקירותיו בחכמת ישראל)

נערך על ידי

יוסף ראבינאוויץ   מאיר לעוו

ספר זכרון

ספר זכרון